The Waite Group's®
UNIX® System V Primer

Second Edition

The Waite Group's®

UNIX® System V
Primer

Second Edition

Mitchell Waite
Stephen Prata
Donald Martin

A Division of Prentice Hall Computer Publishing

11711 North College, Carmel, Indiana 46032 USA

SECOND EDITION
FOURTH PRINTING — 1994

International Standard Book Number: 0-672-30194-6
Library of Congress Catalog Card Number: 92-70300

From The Waite Group, Inc.:
Development Editor: *Mitchell Waite*
Editorial Director: *Scott Calamar*
Managing Editor:*Joel Fugazzotto*
Technical Editor, Second Edition: *Harry Henderson*
Cartoons: *Bob Johnson*

From SAMS:
Publisher: *Richard K. Swadley*
Publishing Manager: *Joseph B. Wikert*
Managing Editor: *Neweleen A. Trebnik*
Editor: *Becky Freeman*
Cover Design: *Dan Armstrong*
Cover Illustration: *Ron Troxell*
Production Analyst: *Mary Beth Wakefield*
Production: *Paula Carroll, Michelle Cleary, Mark Enochs, Brook Farling, Audra Hershman, Carrie Keesling, Betty Kish, Michele Laseau, Juli Pavey, Caroline Roop, Sandra Shay, M. Louise Shinault, Lisa Wilson, Allan Wimmer, Phil Worthington*
Indexers: *Susan Vandewalle, Johnna VanHoose*
Technical Reviewer: *Ted Moore*

Composed in ITC Garamond and MCPdigital by Prentice Hall Computer Publishing
Printed in the United States of America

Overview

Contents

3   Electronic Mail and On-Line Help: *mail*, *write*, and *man*   49

4   Files and Directories: *ls*, *cat*, *pg*, and *pr*   71

7   Advanced Editing with *vi* and *ex*   163

8   The *emacs* Editor   185

9   Manipulating Files and Directories: *mv*, *cp*, and *mkdir*   209

10   Using Programming Languages: FORTRAN, Pascal, and C   241

11 The UNIX Shell: Command Lines, Redirection, and Shell Scripts 263

12 File Management Commands and Others: *wc*, *sort*, *lp*, and *chmod*   329

13   More Text Processing: *cut*, *paste*, *sed*, and *nroff*   361

14   Information Processing: *grep*, *find*, *sort*, *awk*, and *Shell Scripts*   399

15   UNIX Networking   435

About the Authors

Mitchell Waite is president of The Waite Group, a developer of computer books. He is an experienced programmer, fluent in a variety of computer languages, including C, Pascal, BASIC, Assembly, and HyperTalk. He wrote his first computer book in 1976, and is the coauthor of *New C Primer Plus, C: Step by Step, Microsoft QuickC Programming, UNIX Primer Plus,* Second Edition, and many other titles.

Stephen Prata is professor of physics and astronomy at the College of Marin in Kentfield, California, where he teaches UNIX and the C language. He received his B.S. from the California Institute of Technology and his Ph.D. from the University of California, Berkeley. His association with computers began with the computer modeling of star clusters. Dr. Prata is coauthor of *New C Primer Plus, C: Step by Step, UNIX Primer Plus,* Second Edition, and *UNIX System V Bible*, and is the author of *Advanced C Primer ++*.

Donald Martin received his A.B. from the University of California, Berkeley, and his M.A. from San Jose State University. He is currently the director of the Computer Science Center at the College of Marin in Kentfield, California. A long time interest in the problems that students have in developing their reasoning and critical thinking skills led him to the LOGO computer language. He now teaches LOGO using a UNIX-based system at the college. Mr. Martin is coauthor of *UNIX Primer Plus,* Second Edition, and *UNIX System V Bible*.

Acknowledgments

Any book attempting to teach the use of a computer operating system to beginners would surely be useless without copious amounts of human feedback and testing of the manuscript. This is especially true for the UNIX system because of its large number of built-in facilities and commands.

We first would like to thank the thousands of students over the last eight years who have offered invaluable criticisms and suggestions. Their success in using the book and in learning UNIX has been our driving force.

We also gratefully acknowledge the expertise and help of a succession of UNIX system administrators at the College of Marin: Jon Foreman, Dan Putterman, Michael Lindbeck, and Carlos Robinson. Their dedication to keeping the system, the students, and us "up and running" has often been heroic. We are particularly indebted to Brian Harvey, who made numerous technical contributions to our first edition. Thanks also to Michael Forte for his technical assistance with the emacs chapter.

The people at Howard W. Sams gave us the strong support necessary to make this book a reality, and we would like to give them our sincere regards. We also wish to thank our colleagues at the College of Marin for their help and support: Bob Petersen, Dick Rodgers, Bernd Enders, Fred Schmitt, and Nancy Zimfirescu.

We greatly appreciate the efforts of Peter Tostado and Rex Core of Microport who set equipment up to give us hands-on experience with Release 4.0.

We must also thank Phoebe Packer of Motorola and Ashley Crooker of AT&T who provided valuable assistance with earlier versions. Finally, thanks to Bob Johnson for his fantastic cartoons.

Even with this wonderful support, we may have allowed an error or two to creep into this book. For them, we are responsible.

Trademarks

All terms mentioned in this book that are known to be trademarks or service marks are listed below. In addition, terms suspected of being trademarks or service marks have been appropriately capitalized. Howard W. Sams & Company cannot attest to the accuracy of this information. Use of a term in this book should not be regarded as affecting the validity of any trademark or service mark.

Apple is a registered trademark of Apple Computer, Inc.

CP/M is a registered trademark of Digital Research, Inc.

Cray is a registered trademark of Cray Computer, Inc.

EtherNet is a trademark of Xerox Corporation.

Hewlett-Packard is a registered trademark of Hewlett-Packard.

IBM is a registered trademark of the International Business Machines Corporation.

Intel is a trademark of Intel Corporation.

Sun is a registered trademark of Sun Microsystems, Inc.

Unisys is a registered trademark of Unisys Corporation.

UNIX is a registered trademark of American Telephone and Telegraph Corporation.

Preface to the Second Edition

The two most important trends in computers to emerge from the 1980s were the demands for open systems and for the development of multivendor computer networks. These two demands were fueled primarily by the adoption of the UNIX operating system, first by the U.S. and European governments, and now by U.S. and European industry.

During the same period, two books, *UNIX Primer Plus* and *UNIX System V Primer*, became best sellers by setting the standard for introductory UNIX books. Both books are loaded with features that help orient the new UNIX user and get them up and running as quickly as possible. In these books, each chapter focuses on the most important topics. Commands are taught using hands-on examples. Each command is summarized and highlighted, both in the chapter and on a summary card at the end of the book. Figures and tables are spread generously throughout the text to clarify key points.

Whereas UNIX Primer Plus concentrates on Berkeley UNIX, this book focuses on UNIX System V. This book has been revised to bring it into line with Release 4.0 of UNIX System V. Where required, text in this new edition has been rewritten, figures have been improved and several new questions and exercises have been added to assist in review.

This second edition also contains two new chapters, Chapter 8 on the popular emacs editor, and Chapter 15 on the important subject of UNIX Networking. Both chapters reflect recent developments in the UNIX community. Two other major changes have been made. Chapter 14 on Advanced Electronic Mail has been merged into Chapter 3 on Electronic Mail and On-Line Help, and Chapter 13 on Advanced Editing with vi has been moved to Chapter 7 so that it comes after the standard UNIX editors.

With the issuance of Release 4.0, AT&T has incorporated many of the de facto standards of earlier versions of UNIX into what they believe will become the primary UNIX standard. This has resulted in over 100 new commands being added to Release 4.0. As we have done in the past, we have carefully selected and presented only the most useful and most important of these commands for the new UNIX user.

We think you will agree that this revision will continue to provide the easiest, quickest, and most enjoyable entry into the community of UNIX users.

How to Use This Book

Whether you are new to computers or an experienced programmer, this book will give you a good introduction to the UNIX operating system and to many of its important application programs. Here are a few suggestions on how you might use this book.

The first chapter contains a historical and conceptual overview, that will give you a good introduction to UNIX. Chapters 2, 3, 4 and one of the editor chapters 5, 6, 7, or 8 provide the basic UNIX commands needed for most new users. The choice of editors is very important, because people who learn one editor tend to stay with it, even in the face of newer or better editors. New users probably should use the same editor as their peers so that help will be available when needed. If all things are equal, the emacs editor, described in Chapter 8, is the easiest to learn and the most powerful of the editors described in this book. (Note that some systems may not support the emacs editor.) To a large degree, the presentation of the editors is independent from the rest of the book, so you can switch back and forth between studying an editor and reading the other chapters.

The best way to learn UNIX is to use it. When you start reading the book in earnest, sit down at a terminal and duplicate our examples and improvise your own examples. You may be surprised occasionally, but you will not hurt the system.

Try the Review and the Exercises at the end of each chapter. They should give you more confidence in your new skills and they may clarify a point or two for you.

The later chapters explore a variety of the more interesting and powerful UNIX commands and features. You may wish to just browse through them, picking up on those commands and usages that most interest you.

Use this book as a reference book. Our summaries document a large number of UNIX commands. You also can use this book as a lead-in to the official UNIX manual. The manual is rather terse and it is written for knowledgeable users; the summaries and examples that we provide can help you to understand the manual. Tear out the three reference cards. They provide a concise summary of the most important UNIX commands.

However you use this book, we hope that you will enjoy it as much as we have enjoyed writing it.

1

Introduction to UNIX

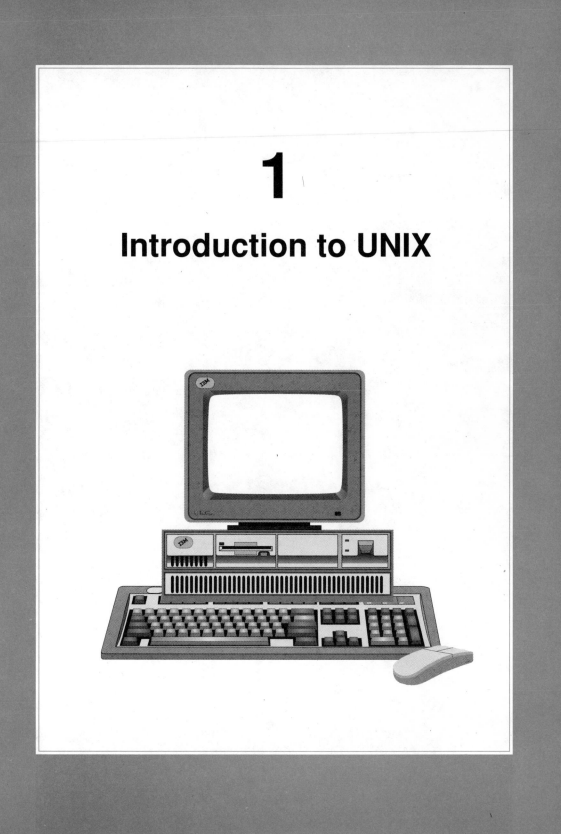

Chapter 1

Introduction to UNIX

Did you know that today more than 300,000 UNIX installations around the world are supporting over 1,000,000 users? The recent introduction of relatively inexpensive ($5,000—$25,000) computer systems capable of running UNIX means that in the next few years more and more people will become members of the UNIX Information Age.

This book will help you take that step toward membership. It is designed to introduce newcomers to the powerful magic of one of the world's most successful operating systems.

Who Should Read This Book?

The goal of this book is to introduce UNIX's powerful tools to both the beginning and the experienced computer user. The tools that we have chosen to present are those most needed for work in an electronic office and those needed to write and run simple programs in various computer languages, such as Pascal, FORTRAN, or C. Whether your interest in UNIX is at the professional or the hobbyist level, you will find the clear details and examples that you need to become a UNIX user. We hope you will enjoy learning UNIX as much as we have enjoyed writing this book.

An Overview of UNIX

A computer needs special programming called *software* to make it work. UNIX systems have two kinds of software: (1) the *operating system* software and (2) the *application* or *utility* software (Figure 1.1). The operating system software is what breathes life into the computer. It behaves somewhat like our subconscious, taking care of a myriad of every day housekeeping details. If the operating system is doing its job, you can do your tasks without ever needing to worry about the computer's inner workings.

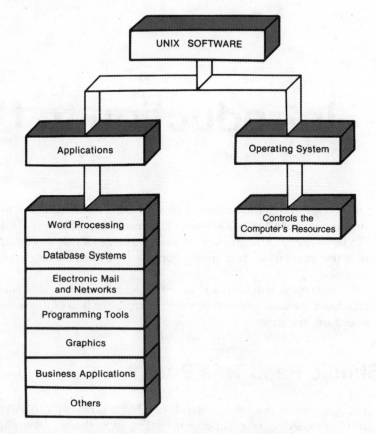

Figure 1.1.   An overview of UNIX.

The other kind of software, the utilities or application software, does *your* work. This software might include an *editor* (a program that lets you write, change, and store text and data), electronic mail programs, business applications, and languages for programming (such as Pascal).

UNIX consists of both kinds of software. The term *UNIX*, then, refers both to the operating system and to a host of useful application programs. In this book, we will only briefly describe the operating system part of UNIX. We will spend the majority of our time on how to use the powerful UNIX utilities.

What Is an Operating System?

Those of you who are new to computers and computing may find such terms as *operating system, utilities,* and *multiuser* to be confusing when you first encounter them. We will digress briefly here to explain these and other terms. We will discuss what an operating system is, why it is necessary, and what it does. If you are already familiar with operating systems, you may want to skip to the next section.

In a broad sense, an operating system is like a teacher in a classroom. The teacher gives out assignments, schedules use of equipment, and, in general, coordinates student activities. In a more restricted sense, the operating system coordinates the inner workings of the computer (Figure 1.2). The operating system relies on an internal clock within the computer to help make simple scheduling decisions, such as when to send information to the printer or when to load and execute user programs. Operating systems themselves are just programs created to reduce the amount of programming required of the user, especially the programming required to take care of routine, repeated tasks.

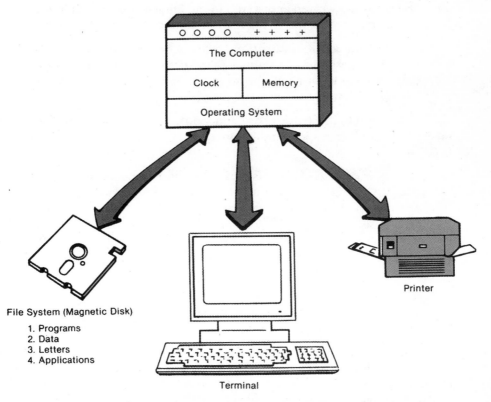

Figure 1.2.   The operating system.

An operating system can also be defined as the link between the computer and the computer user. Its purpose is to provide the user with a flexible and manageable means of control over the resources of the computer. All operating systems fulfill three primary functions:

- *They provide a filing system.* A *file* is a block of information stored in the computer. Files can hold letters, programs, budgets, schedules, and anything else that you can type on a typewriter. In UNIX, you can write new files, add to old files, copy files, rename them, or move them elsewhere, all by giving rather simple commands. The UNIX file management system keeps all unnecessary details "hidden" from the computer operator, making UNIX easy to use, unlike some other systems.

- *They provide for the loading and executing of user programs. Loading* a program consists of placing the program instructions into the proper locations. *Executing* a program means to run the program. In providing these services, the operating system lets you run programs that might be written in a high-level language, such as Pascal or C, as well as run programs already written and stored in the filing system. Again, the purpose of the operating system is to make these tasks as simple as possible.

- *They provide a communication link between the computer and its accessories.* The accessories, sometimes called *peripheral* devices or *input-output* devices, include terminals, printers, and information storage devices, such as magnetic tapes and magnetic disks.

In addition to these three basic functions, more elaborate features are found on the newer or larger operating systems such as UNIX. Some additional features in UNIX are

- *Multiuser time-sharing.* This means that several people at different terminals can use the computer at the same time. This process resembles the activities of the staff in a restaurant. The staff divides its time preparing and serving several customers simultaneously, sending out the soups, salads, main courses, and so on. An efficient staff will give each patron the feeling of being waited on as if he or she were the only customer. An efficient time-sharing computer will give you the same sensation.

- *Multitasking.* This feature allows one user to run several computing jobs simultaneously, such as printing one program while editing a second one. The user can assign different priorities to each of the jobs as appropriate.

Besides the five basic housekeeping operations just mentioned, UNIX has a library of application and utility software that has grown over the years to provide essential services to thousands of users. Before we discuss this software, let us look at how UNIX has evolved into what it is today.

The History of UNIX

During the early 1960s, computers were expensive and had small memories. For example, one middle-priced workhorse of that day, the IBM-1620, had only 24K of memory and was capable of storing about 40,000 numbers. The primary design criteria for all software—languages, programs, and operating systems—was to use memory efficiently and to make programs simple for the computer. This was usually at the cost of being unwieldy for the programmer and other users.

UNIX grew out of the frustrations that programmers faced when working with this early time-consuming software. UNIX was born in 1969 at Bell Laboratories, the prestigious research arm of the American Telephone and Telegraph Company. Surprisingly, it began when one man, Ken Thompson, decided to try to create a less expensive and more hospitable programming environment.

Ken Thompson was working on a program called *Space Travel* that simulated the motion of the planets in the solar system. The program was being run on a large computer made by General Electric, the GE645, that was using an operating system called *Multics*. Multics was developed at MIT and was one of the first operating systems designed to handle several users simultaneously. However, its use on the GE computer was expensive and awkward. Each run of the *Space Travel* program cost over $70.00. Thompson found a little-used smaller computer made by Digital Equipment Corporation called the PDP-7. He began the burden of transferring his *Space Travel* program to run on the smaller computer. In order to use the PDP-7 conveniently, Thompson created a new operating system that he christened UNIX, as an offshoot of Multics. Thompson was successful enough in this effort to attract the attention of Dennis Ritchie and others at Bell Labs, where they continued the process of creating a useful environment. UNIX became operational in the Bell Labs system in 1971.

During the early 1970s, UNIX ran primarily on computers that were manufactured by Digital Equipment, first on the PDP-7, then on the PDP-11/40 and /45, and, finally, blossoming on the PDP-11/70 where it achieved widespread acceptance throughout Bell Labs. During the same time, universities and colleges, many of whom were using the PDP-11/70 computers, were given license to run UNIX at minimal cost. This shrewd move by AT&T eventually led to UNIX being run at over 80 percent of all university computer science departments in the United States. Each year, thousands of computer science students graduate with some experience in running and modifying UNIX.

UNIX, like most operating systems, was originally written in what is called *assembly language*. This is a primitive set of instructions that controls the computer's internal actions. Since each computer model has its own particular set of internal instructions, moving UNIX to another computer would involve a significant programming effort. The solution to this problem, and perhaps the key to UNIX's popularity today, was Ken Thompson's decision to rewrite the operating system in a higher-level language—one less primitive than assembly language.

The language was called *B*. Soon it was modified extensively by Dennis Ritchie and, in 1973, was rechristened *C*. As a general-purpose language featuring modern commands, C is much easier to understand and use than assembly language. Although not as efficient as assembly language in terms of the speed with which the computer carries out its manipulations, C is much more convenient. This convenience has encouraged users to modify and improve UNIX. Thus a tremendous amount of additional UNIX software has been created, especially in the areas of word processing and programming support.

The use of C makes UNIX easily portable to other computer systems. Only a tiny fraction of UNIX is still written in assembly language. Today, UNIX can be run on many other computers, including computers made by HP, Unisys, Digital Equipment, NCR, IBM, Cray Research, Apple, and Sun.

Probably more important (for computer users) is the fact that C *compilers* (a compiler translates C into the host computer's internal language) are now available for every major 32-bit microprocessor on the market.

Microprocessors form the brains of microcomputers. One significant fact about microprocessors is that their sophisticated, complex, electronic circuits are all contained in a single small package called a *chip*. The first microprocessor was a 4-bit chip made by Intel in 1970. It was followed by the 8-bit chip, which launched the microcomputer revolution of the late 1970s. Today, 32-bit microprocessors promise even greater computing power at lower cost.

The net result of these advances in hardware is that UNIX can now run on newer, relatively inexpensive, microprocessor-based computer systems. For example, in the late 1970s, a PDP-11/70 time-sharing system with 15 terminals might have cost $150,000. In the 1980s, a microprocessor-based system with 15 terminals could have been installed for about $35,000. Single-user UNIX systems can cost as little as $5,000.

Like computer hardware, the UNIX operating system has gone through several iterations. In the early 1980s, UNIX and UNIX look-alikes multiplied like rabbits, with such names as Cromix, Idris, Ultrix, XENIX, Coherent, Version 7, BSD, and so on. However, by 1990, only two versions of UNIX dominated—Berkeley UNIX and System V UNIX (with its variations, XENIX, SunOS, and so on).

UNIX System V

In January of 1983, AT&T announced that for the first time it was licensing a new "standard" version of UNIX for the commercial OEM (Original Equipment Manufacturer) marketplace. This version, called UNIX System V, was based on the UNIX that AT&T was using internally. It contained many of the best features of the UNIX that was in use at most universities at that time (Berkeley UNIX, also called 4.1 bsd). AT&T also announced that it was becoming a software supplier and would offer full support for developers of UNIX. In addition, the licensing fee for UNIX System V became much more reasonable than previous versions.

At the same time that AT&T announced UNIX System V, it also announced that it was licensing the top three semiconductor manufacturers of 16/32-bit microprocessor chips to develop rigorous *standard* versions, or *ports*, of UNIX for these chips. Each *port* would consist of a 16/32-bit microprocessor, a ROM, and a set of disks containing the entire UNIX System V operating system.

The System V port was not a trivial undertaking—AT&T required manufacturers to reproduce 98% of all the known bugs in UNIX System V. The insistence by AT&T for a rigorous UNIX standard port means that, except for speed, UNIX System V software will run the same regardless of the computer it is running on. The net result of this standardization is that software developers are assured that their programs will work on the largest number of machines. To computer hardware manufacturers and designers, it means that they can focus energy on squeezing more speed and performance out of the computer without having to worry about software compatibility. Of course, the overall performance of a UNIX System V 16/32-bit microprocessor-based computer will still depend on the talents of the engineers that design the complete system. But regardless of performance, to the end user, a UNIX operation in one system will work exactly the same in any system.

UNIX System V, Releases 2.0 and 3.0

In January 1985, AT&T announced major revisions to System V as part of Release 2.0. In addition to running 5 to 10% faster than previous releases of UNIX, Release 2.0 provides better file handling, job control, security and several new commands, the most important being `mailx`. The `mailx` command is used to send and receive electronic mail in the Electronic Office.

In the later half of the 1980's, AT&T issued three major updates to System V— Release 3.0, Release 3.1 and Release 3.2. Release 3.0 concentrated on improving networking capabilities. Release 3.1 made System V more adaptable to international users by supporting 8-bit characters (instead of 7-bit characters). Release 3.2 added security enhancements and an alternative interface called FACE (see below).

UNIX System V, Release 4.0

In 1991, AT&T issued Release 4.0 of the operating system. The primary goal of Release 4.0 was to create a new standard version of UNIX by incorporating some of the most popular features of Berkeley UNIX, SunOS and XENIX. Major changes were made to the file system, networking protocol, command-line interpreters or shells (see Chapter 2), and command set. For example, Release 4.0 added or merged over 100 new commands into its command set, with the most useful ones discussed in this book.

Berkeley UNIX

For the past fifteen years, the University of California at Berkeley has been a focal point of UNIX development. The computer science department has been the major distributor of UNIX to several hundred colleges, universities, and organizations. As a research and development center, UC Berkeley has created a host of new UNIX features, such as the C shell with alias, history and job control, the vi editor, and improved file handling and communication programs.

The latest version of Berkeley UNIX is known as UNIX 4.3 BSD (which stands for *B*erkeley *S*tandard *D*istribution).

OSF versus UI

In 1988, AT&T shocked the UNIX community by purchasing a percentage of Sun Microsystems. Several major computer companies including IBM, Hewlett Packard, and Digital Equipment reacted quickly by forming a competing group called Open Software Foundation (OSF). They immediately raised over 90 million dollars to start development of a new UNIX standard.

Meanwhile, the AT&T-Sun group backed off slightly, and together with Unisys, Data General, and others founded UNIX International (UI). This open consortium of companies agreed to oversee the development of System V standards. As a result, today we have two major competing commercial standards for UNIX, System V, and OSF.

Part of the early competition between and within these groups has revolved around creating new user interfaces. An interface is what you see on the screen. It provides the environment for interacting with the computer.

UNIX Interfaces

Historically, the UNIX interface, called a command-line interface, has been considered cryptic and difficult to use. The major complaint against it is that commands are abbreviated and hard to remember. Here are two simple examples, the command to change your password is passwd, the command to copy a file is cp. Part of the problem stems from the enormous number of commands and options available. Experienced users consider this versatility and power a major feature rather than a problem. However, the UNIX community is responding to these concerns of new users by developing friendlier, more intuitive interfaces. Table 1.1 lists the five major types of interfaces and their availability.

Table 1.1.   The availability of five major types of interfaces.

Name	Commands given by	Status
Command-line	Typing	Standard
Menu-driven	Selecting	Available in Release 3.2
Graphical (GUI)	Clicking with a mouse	Available in Release 4.0
Pen-based	Selecting with a pen	Near future
Voice-based	Speaking	Near future

The standard UNIX interface is the command-line interface. The computer gives you a prompt and you type in commands. Even though newer interfaces are introduced, the command-line interface will always be available. It is the one described in this book.

In release 3.2, AT&T introduced a menu-driven interface called FACE, which stands for Framed Access Command Environment. FACE creates a world of windows or 'frames' that contain menus and forms. Commands are given by moving the cursor to select menu items. FACE can be considered a transition interface from the command-line interface to the Graphical User Interface or GUI (pronounced gooey).

In Release 4.0, AT&T defined a GUI standard called OPEN LOOK, which was jointly developed with Sun Microsystems. The purpose of OPEN LOOK (and other GUIs) is to provide a consistent interface, both in appearance and operation, for users on all kinds of UNIX computers and for all kinds of software. The goal is to create a consistent *look and feel* to applications as successfully pioneered by the Macintosh computer. However, OPEN LOOK has competition. The Open Software Foundation has created a popular GUI, called OSF/MOTIF. The Santa Cruz Operation (SCO) which currently has the most UNIX users, has used MOTIF to design their own interface, called Open Desktop.

There are several reasons why GUIs are considered better, friendlier interfaces. In a nutshell, these include:

- Icons provide visual reminders of what commands do. You do not have to remember and type commands, you select them.

- The graphics screen looks friendly and inviting. Scroll bars, pull-down menus, control buttons, and the mouse become tools that you use to manipulate your environment. You feel in control.

- Multiple windows can be opened with each one running a different job.

- You can easily do and see cut and paste operations of both text and graphics.

The net result is that for most people, a GUI dramatically reduces the time it takes to learn how to use both the operating system and new software programs. Not only do GUIs provide an easier environment for users, it also makes life simpler for developers, primarily because these GUIs are based on MIT's X-Windows.

X-Windows acts like a language translator, except that it includes a graphics language. If the computer wants to draw a square or menu on the screen, it does not have to send detailed instructions keyed to each type of terminal. It can send a generalized set of instructions to the X-Windows translator, called a server, residing at the terminal.

Another advantage of X-Windows is that a server can access any computer on a network, called a client, that produces X-Windows output. Thus client and server can reside on the same machine or they can be anywhere on a network.

For programmers, system administrators, institutions, and companies, other issues besides the GUI are important, too. Such issues include openness, flexibility, multi-processor use, development tools, file security, and networking. We will not discuss these here other than to say that in each of these areas, UNIX excels and provides many reasons why UNIX may well become the dominating operating system of the 1990s.

The UNIX Philosophy

The major design factors behind UNIX were to create an operating system and supporting software that were simple, elegant, and easy to use. Elegant, in this context, generally means good programming style and thrifty memory management. These design characteristics led to the following maxims among UNIX builders:

1. Make each program do one thing well. These simple programs often are called *tools.*

2. Expect the output of every program to become the input to another, yet unknown, program. This means that simple tools can be connected to do complex jobs.

3. Do not hesitate to build new programs to do a job. The library of tools keeps increasing.

The net result of these maxims is that UNIX systems are sometimes said to embody Schumacher's dictum that "small is beautiful." Each UNIX program is a compact, easily used tool that does its job well.

The verdict on UNIX software is already in. Thousands of students, teachers, engineers, programmers, secretaries, managers, and office workers have found that UNIX's friendly environment and quality software have become time-saving tools that improve their productivity and employ their creativity. The following drawing was created to give you a peek into the UNIX toolroom and to summarize some of the ideas presented here.

What Can UNIX Do for You?

Earlier we explained that UNIX has two kinds of software: the UNIX operating system, which manages the internal workings of the computer system, and built-in application or utility software, which provides a range of useful services. An easy way to get an overview of these UNIX services is to divide this software into two major categories. These software categories could be called the Electronic Office and the Programming Support areas. Most of the UNIX software that we will discuss here concerns services that can be categorized under the Electronic Office.

The Electronic Office

The concept of an electronic office is still new and changing. Most discussions of what it involves center around four interrelated functions:

- Word processing

- Electronic filing

- Electronic mail and networking

- Electronic databases

Word Processing

UNIX has dozens of tools to help you do word processing. These tools have such names as editors, text formatters, spellers, and syntax checkers (that check your sentence structure). With these tools, you can throw away the liquid correction fluid, correction tape, scissors, erasers, paper clips, scotch tape, and all the other paraphernalia you used for dealing with printed words on paper. You now manipulate words inside an electronic memory. They can be moved and changed easily, quickly, and efficiently, allowing you to type your words without thinking about the appearance of your finished product.

With a text formatting program, you can turn a ragged right margin into a beautiful, professional-looking typeset format just by using a few keystrokes. Or, suppose you want to add a new sentence in the middle of your ten-page document. No problem! Simply enter the editor's insert mode and start typing away. Because the editor has an electronic brain, it can instantly shift all the text in its memory to make room for new words and do it without losing its paragraph structure. Or, suppose you spelled the same word incorrectly in 157 places. Merely enter the search-and-replace command, and the computer will automatically change all occurrences of the misspelled word as you sit back and relax. With simple key operations, you can move paragraphs and blocks of text, boldface your text, underline, and make superscripts and subscripts.

These UNIX tools allow you to accomplish tasks that would require days of work using a standard typewriter. Examples of such tasks are: converting a long double-spaced document to a narrow column width, single-spacing a document so that it is suitable for publication, printing individually addressed copies of the same letter, sorting and merging mailing labels, proofreading large documents for spelling and syntax errors, and generating an index.

This kind of power will alter your writing experience drastically. The ability to change words quickly and easily gives them a new malleability. Words become like wet clay. You rework the same sentence over and over, deleting old words with hardly a care until the words say exactly what you mean. Because of the fluid nature of the work, you become braver. You are more creative because you are not concerned with how the typing looks. Neither are you hampered by the fear of putting an idea in the wrong place, for you can easily move the words around later. You create the words. Let the machine manage them.

Electronic Filing

Supporting the word processing function and providing even more services is the electronic filing system. To visualize the filing system, imagine that all the written information you now store in a filing cabinet or on shelves is placed in an electronic filing cabinet.

A file can contain anywhere from one to several thousand words or numbers. Anything you can type on a typewriter can be placed in a file. Each file has a name that you give it, and each file contains whatever information you put in it, as we discuss in Chapters 4 and 9.

Once you have a filing system set up and your information is stored there, here is what you can do. Using just simple commands, you can get a list of the titles of every document or file, or you can read any one file in its entirety. You can scan (search) the first ten lines (or the last ten lines) of a number of files looking for specific information. Better still, suppose you want to find a certain letter that was sent to you about a specific product. You can let "UNIX do the walking." One command will scan one or more files searching for the product name. Phone listings, product listings, bills, and bookkeeping can all be kept on file and scanned in the UNIX filing system. And the best part about the UNIX filing system is that the files can be organized in exactly the same way that you would arrange them in a cabinet.

You can build categories of files. For example, you might place all of your travel files in one drawer (called a directory in UNIX), insurance records in another drawer, clients' accounts in a third drawer, and so on. Files can be easily moved from one drawer to another, copies can be placed in several drawers, or files can be cross-referenced. Files can be combined, cut in two, or merged alphabetically. In fact, all of the word processing functions described earlier can be applied to any of your files, even though you may not have originated them.

Electronic Mail and Networking

Another related, necessary, and very useful function of the electronic office is electronic mail and networking (Figure 1.3). As you might suppose, electronic communication is the glue that holds together the Electronic Office. With electronic mail, you can turn paperwork shuffling into the more rewarding task of information processing. For example, in writing letters, you have all the advantages of word processing that were described earlier. And you can send copies instantly to anyone on the UNIX system.

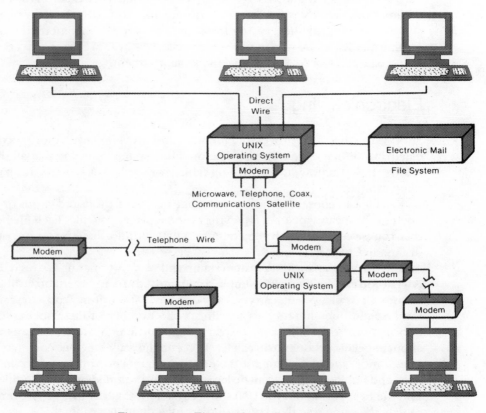

Figure 1.3.   Electronic mail and networking.

One valuable use of electronic mail occurs when two or more people collaborate on a letter, book, report, or other typewritten document while using the word processor/mail system. Each person can write his or her part of the document, mail it to someone else for changes or additions, and then receive a new copy back again.

No paper or postage is involved. These documents, as well as any UNIX file containing any kind of written information, can be mailed (transmitted) easily with just a few keystrokes.

Another useful and related feature of UNIX mail is the *reminder service.* If you keep a diary of your important dates in a file called "calendar," the UNIX operating system will send you mail each day, reminding you of your day's schedule.

In addition to sending *local mail* to people connected to your computer, the UNIX mail system can send mail to other UNIX computer systems anywhere in the country. This is done by having one UNIX computer automatically telephone other UNIX computers, using a device called a *modem* and then sending the "mail" over the phone. There are several such telephone networks that offer this service. Some, such as USENET, are devoted primarily to UNIX computer systems.

Sending electronic signals over telephone wires can be relatively slow (about one page of text per minute). Other types of networks, such as Ethernet, allow several UNIX computers to be connected together, sharing resources at very high speeds. Ethernet is a local network for use in one or more adjacent buildings. Meanwhile, over the horizon, there are various satellite networking systems.

However, no matter which network you use or what kind of computer you have, if your computer is running the UNIX operating system, you can communicate with other UNIX systems. And, in so doing, you will have available all the UNIX services just described—word processing, electronic filing system, and electronic mail.

Electronic Databases

An electronic database is essentially an extension of an electronic filing system. In fact, the UNIX filing system already has the features of a very simple database. For example, if you placed all the phone numbers you use (or even a whole telephone book full of numbers) into one or more UNIX files, you could search those files for a particular name and number with just a single command. Or you could pull out all the names beginning with "John" and place them in a new file.

An *electronic database* is a collection of information that you can add to or delete from, or can sort in various ways. It can be searched by using key words, and specific information can be copied and printed. The UNIX filing system can do all of this easily, as we will show you in later chapters.

There are more powerful database systems, such as INGRES, available for running under UNIX. These systems have more sophisticated searching and storing techniques. For example (using the telephone book again), you might want to find all the phone numbers listed under "John," living on "Beachside Avenue," but *not* all those starting with the numbers 454–. The beauty of a database system like INGRES is that you can pull out specific information and then create a new database from it fast and easily.

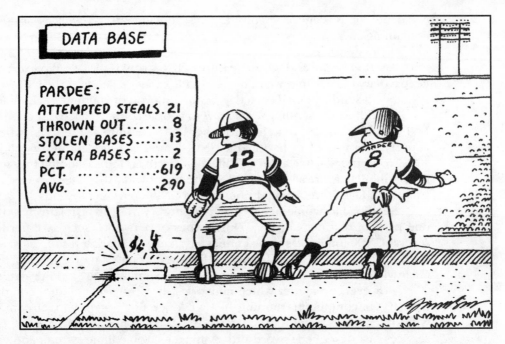

Electronic databases are becoming essential for many businesses. Payroll, sales, employee records, inventories, clients' records, and economic data can all be easily accessed within a database. However, for maximum use, databases must be tied into the electronic office. The services of word processing, electronic filing, and electronic mail give the database user additional powers. For example, as the inventory control manager, you could extract specific information about an inventory, add a few remarks, and mail the result to your staff.

The Sum Is Greater Than the Parts

In UNIX all four services of the electronic office are ready to go. These services combine synergistically so that the total is much greater than the sum of the parts. You could purchase computer systems and software that would do two or three of these functions or that would provide these services to just a few people. However, when all these services are provided to the majority of the office workers in a company, the nature of their work can change radically. Research shows that these services improve productivity and communications, save money, and improve people's attitudes towards work. That is why organizations large and small, local and national, have adopted UNIX as their software standard.

A key element in the widespread adoption of UNIX is its *user-friendliness*. How easy is it to use UNIX? Is it worthwhile to spend time learning to use UNIX's services? We believe the answer is an overwhelming "yes." Thousands of employees at Bell

Labs and AT&T, at colleges and universities, and in other businesses and industries would agree.

Besides the electronic office services offered by UNIX, another major service is to help programmers solve programming problems. This is the topic of the next section.

Programmer's Support Tools

UNIX was originally developed to make life easier for programmers. However, it turned out that programmers wanted the electronic office services just as much as everyone else. Thus, both types of UNIX software have evolved side by side and are widely used. The programmer's support tools can be classified into four major areas:

- *Programming languages and compilers.* All of the major languages (FOR-TRAN, BASIC, Pascal, COBOL, and so on) can be run under UNIX. This means that if UNIX has a standardized form of a language (for example, standard FORTRAN 77), then any FORTRAN 77 programs written anywhere in the country (and there are thousands) can be run on your system and vice versa. In addition to the most popular languages, dozens of other languages, such as LISP, APL, LOGO, RPG, and RP-1, have been placed on specific UNIX systems.

  Of course, since UNIX is written in C, that language is available and widely used to write programs. A *compiler* translates programs written in the high-level languages into the primitive instructions that the machine can under-stand. In Chapter 10, we show you how to write and run programs that are written in different languages.

- *Command-line interpreter* (called the *shell).* The shell is a program that forms the link between most users and the computer. The shell accepts commands that you type into the computer, and then it executes them. The shell contains over 100 built-in commands for your use. Actually, there is more than one version of the shell. The shell provided with the standard Bell Labs version of UNIX is called the *Bourne shell* after its developer. The other widely used current shell is the *C shell* developed at the University of California, Berkeley. Most of the features we discuss in this book are common to both shell versions, but some are exclusive to one version. A third shell, called the Korn shell after its developer, is now becoming widely available. In this book, we will explain over 60 shell commands and what they can do for you.

  The shell can be used as a programming language that has many features of C. The programmability of the shell—a feature that few other systems offer—plus the large number of built-in commands that the shell already knows, gives programmers exceptional flexibility and power. This power is enhanced by the *pipe*, a UNIX concept that has since been widely copied. Pipes, as you will learn later, allow programs or commands to be coupled together. The output of one program becomes the input to another, and so on.

- *Programmer debugging tools.* The first time a program is written it rarely runs correctly. Usually the program has errors or "bugs" that need fixing. UNIX, like most systems, has built-in programs that help locate these errors. However, we will not be discussing these programming aids in this book.

- *The Programmer's Workbench.* This package of UNIX tools is especially valuable for team-oriented programming projects. These software tools maintain a complete record of all changes made to a program as it is written. They also allow programs to be tested in part as they are developed, and they simplify the task of transferring programs to other computer systems. We will not discuss the Programmer's Workbench in this book.

The electronic office, together with the programmer's support tools, new applications, and the adaptability of the UNIX software in general, are the main reasons that UNIX is gaining such wide popularity today.

2

Getting Started: *login*, *passwd*, and *who*

Chapter 2

Getting Started: *login*, *passwd*, and *who*

Frederick Porteous Ramshead III answered the door. Outside stood a small, white-haired woman with rosy cheeks, a merry grin, and an avaricious glint in her eyes.

"Freddie Pet, let me in!"

Frederick made way, noting the small suitcase in her hand.

"Grandma! You haven't left Grandpa again! And my name is Frederick, not Freddie Pet."

"Of course I haven't, and of course it is, deary. Now offer your dear Granny a seat and a pitcher of lemonade."

"Yes, yes, please make yourself comfortable. But why . . ., I mean, to what do I owe the honor of this visit?"

"Freddie, I am here to make you a wonderful offer, one that will change your life for the better, and you certainly can use that!"

"That's wonderful, Grandma," beamed Frederick, while inwardly groaning. He recalled the twenty newspaper subscriptions she sold him last year so she could win that trip to Disneyland.

"You have a computer terminal, right?"

"Right, Grandma." She had sold him one last Christmas.

"Well, I'm going to give you access to a UNIX system."

"A UNIX system?"

"You're sure quick on the uptake, Pet. Yes, a UNIX system." Grandma spilled open the suitcase, liberating a mass of documents, brochures, and contracts. She fixed Frederick with a steely gaze. "Now pay attention to what I am going to tell you."

An hour later, a triumphant Grandma left with a signed check, and a dazed Frederick Porteous Ramshead III sat down at his terminal, wondering what he had gotten into this time. He attached the modem and dialed the number Grandma had given him. Soon the following display appeared on his screen:

```
Grandma's Old-Fashioned UNIX
Login:
```

He typed the *login name* Grandma had given him: freddie (someone already had taken "frederick"). The terminal responded with

```
password:
```

He typed the *password* Grandma had given him: pet. The system responded with

```
WELCOME TO GRANDMA'S OLD-FASHIONED UNIX, WHERE
VALUE AND QUALITY ARE NEVER COMPROMISED.
$
```

What did that $ mean? Did it indicate that Grandma was getting part of his computer payment? Oh, now I remember, he thought. It was the signal that UNIX was ready for his next command. Grandma called it the UNIX *prompt*. The first thing he wanted to do was change the password Grandma had given him. He typed the passwd command and changed his password to hotshot. Ah, that was better.

What next? He tried date, and the system displayed today's date and time. Frederick set his calendar watch by it. Next, he typed cal 11 1912 to find out on which day of the week Grandma was born. The UNIX system showed the month of November for 1912. Ah yes, she was born on a Tuesday. Then he typed who to find out who else was logged in. Hmmm, was pierre his brother? He looked at the nice book that Grandma had left him and found the command finger, which gives more detail on users. He typed finger pierre and found that pierre was, in fact, his brother, Pierre Robustus Ramshead. Yes, Grandma had hit him up, too. Well, he'd better learn more about UNIX.

An hour later, much more knowledgeable about the UNIX file system, he sat back, pressed Ctrl-d, and gave a sigh of relief. *This* time, Grandma really had done him a favor. UNIX *was* going to improve the quality of his life.

Getting Started

How do you get involved with UNIX (aside from the obvious method of being hustled into it by your grandmother)? For many, it is a matter of circumstances. UNIX is one of the leading computer operating systems used on college and university campuses. Now, college graduates, in increasing numbers are entering business and industry and are demanding access to UNIX and UNIX-like systems. Computer manufacturers are responding to this demand by offering a wide range of microcomputer and minicomputer systems. Businesses, too, are turning to UNIX because it is an open system supported by hundreds of vendors.

We will suppose that by choice or fate you now are involved with UNIX, so let us begin our study of the nitty-gritty of UNIX. First, we will show you how to get started on a UNIX system, and we will describe the major characteristics of a typical terminal that you might use to communicate with UNIX. Then, we will discuss the *login* and *password* process in detail. Finally, we will look at the first of many simple, yet powerful, commands in the UNIX shell.

Establishing Contact with the Shell

Lured on by the wonders of UNIX, you want to unleash its powers. But how do you get in touch with the system? The precise details will vary from system to system, but the following general features are necessary:

1. You will need a means of communicating with the system. Normally, the means will be a keyboard and a screen display, and that is what we will assume you have.

2. You will have to tell the system who you are by *logging in*. (Computers that handle multiple users are usually selective about whom they deal with.)

3. You may have to give the system a password. (Computers are not too good at recognizing faces, so they may need a password to reassure them that you are who you say you are.)

4. When you are done, you will need to *logout* to tell the UNIX system you are finished. Otherwise, the system will just sit there, waiting for your next instructions.

Now we will explain how these features are implemented.

The Keyboard

If you have seen a typewriter, you should find the typical computer terminal keyboard at least vaguely familiar. It will have keys bearing letters of the English alphabet such as *D* and *U*. Other keys have symbols on them, such as #, *, ~, @, and ^. Some of these symbols (or *characters,* as they are called) are not usually found on a typewriter. Then there are keys bearing words or abreviations of words—keys such as Return (Enter or C/R on some keyboards), Ctrl (for control), Break, Shift, and Esc (for escape). Many of these keys are special keys, not found on the standard typewriter, that have been added to the keyboard to make life easier for computer users. We will discuss some of these special keys and their meaning to UNIX later in this chapter. Figure 2.1 shows a typical keyboard.

Figure 2.1.   Standard keys on a typical keyboard.

Some Keyboard Conventions

In this book we capitalize the name of a key, for example the Return key or the Backspace key. When a key name is used in a program, it will be enclosed in greater-than and less-than signs like this <Return>, to distinguish it from the user input. In other words, when you see <Return> at the end of a program line, you should press the Return key, not type "<Return>."

In addition, we use lowercase letters to refer to an alphabet key—for example, the *a* key—even though many keyboards use capital letters on the face of the key. Our reason for doing this is simple. When you press the *a* key (or any other alphabet key), the screen will show the lowercase version, not the uppercase. Of course, if you want an uppercase letter, you must hold down the Shift key while you type the letter, or use the Caps Lock key, which we will explain soon.

You may have noticed that we use a special typeface to simulate what you see on the display screen. In case you have missed it, it looks like this:

```
Grandma's Old-Fashioned UNIX
Login:
```

Whenever you are to type something on the keyboard, such as a command or other information, we use this same typeface. For example, the text might read: "To find out the current date and time, type date and press Return." You then type the letters *d a t e.*

Sometimes we use an italic version of this typeface. The italic font means that you must substitute an actual value, filename, command, or other appropriate information for the italicized word. For example, the text might say, "The format for using the calendar command is `cal` *year*." This means that to use the calendar command, you must type `cal` and then type an actual year, say 1942, for *year*. Your command would be

```
cal 1942
```

The ASCII Character Set

It would be nice if there were a standard keyboard layout, but not all keyboards are identical. Fortunately, there is a standard *character set* that most keyboards carry. It is called the *ASCII* (pronounced askee) character set. *ASCII* stands for *A*merican *S*tandard *C*ode for *I*nformation *I*nterchange. You can find a copy of this set of characters in Appendix B. Although terminal manufacturers agree on where to place the alphabet and the numbers, they go their separate ways when it comes to the placement of the other characters of the ASCII set. Thus, if you learn the placement of keys on one terminal, be aware that many terminals have special keys not found in the ASCII character set, such as keys with special editing or graphics uses.

Using the Keyboard

Using the keyboard is a straightforward procedure. You depress a key to send the symbol on it to the computer. For example, to send a 6, press the *6* key. Here are a few additional facts you should know about keyboards:

1. Some keys have two symbols on the face of the key. Ordinarily, the lower of these two characters is sent when the key is pressed. To send the upper characters, press one of the Shift keys at the same time you press the character key. Some examples are

Key(s) Pressed	Result
5	Sends the number *5*
Shift-4	Sends the percent sign, *$*
a	Sends a lowercase *a*
Shift-a	Sends an uppercase *A*

2. Pressing the Caps Lock key is like permanently holding down a Shift key. However, Caps Lock affects only the letters. Some terminals have a small light on the Caps Lock key to show you that it is engaged. Other terminals will lock down the Caps Lock key when it is engaged. Some examples are

Key Pressed	Result
Caps Lock	Turns on capital letters
a	Sends an uppercase *A*
5	Still sends a *5*
Caps Lock	Turns off capital letters

Note that the actual keys on the terminal are usually labeled with uppercase letters, but since they normally transmit lowercase letters, we will use lowercase letters like *a* rather than *A* to stand for the key.

3. Additional characters are produced by pressing the Ctrl (or Control) key and then pressing a regular key. Such characters are known as *control characters*. Some examples are

Keys Pressed	Procedure
Ctrl-d	Hold down the Ctrl key and then press *d* once
Ctrl-c	Hold down the Ctrl key and then press *c* once

Control characters are not always displayed on the screen, but when they are they usually appear as ^d, for example. The ^d is truly one character, although it takes two symbols to represent it on the screen. Such control characters are often used for special purposes in computer systems.

4. The keyboard has special keys to correct typing errors. Because all terminals are not the same, here are several possibilities:

Key(s) Pressed	Result
Backspace	Backs up and erases the last character you typed
Left Arrow	If not part of arrow set, works the same as Backspace
Rub	Usually works the same as Backspace
Ctrl-h	An older version of Backspace
Del (or Delete)	Deletes the character under the cursor
Ctrl-x	Deletes the entire line

These commands are described in more detail later in the chapter.

5. On many typewriters, the lowercase letter *l* and the numeral *1* are interchangeable. This is not true on a computer keyboard. If, in your typing, you have used the letter *l* for the number *1*, you must break the habit. The same situation holds true for the uppercase letter *O* and the digit *0* (zero). They are *not* interchangeable.

6. Develop a good touch. Many keyboards will repeat a letter if you hold down a key too long. You may find yourself typing lines like "Myy ssincreest apoloogiees.." if your terminal is sensitive and your fingers are not.

The Return Key

The Return key is also known as the C/R (for carriage return) or Enter key. On an electric typewriter, pressing this key advances the paper a line and returns the typewriter to the left-hand margin of the page. The Return key performs a similar function on a computer terminal. More important, pressing the Return key tells the system that you have finished that line. For example, suppose that you are on the system and you wish to enter the UNIX command who. If you merely type the letters *w h o* and nothing else, nothing will happen. Is who a useless command? No, the problem is that UNIX does not know you are finished. You could be a slow typist working on whoami or whoa there, black thunder, i think i see trouble ahead. After entering your command, you must press the Return key! Pressing Return tells the system, "Okay, I'm done; take it from here." Thus, the correct way to use the who command is to type

> who <Return>   ← *type* who, ***then press the Return key***

where <Return> stands for the Return key. It does not mean to type the word "return." At first, we will remind you to press the Return key after each new command line, but later we won't bother—we have confidence that you will soon be pressing Return automatically.

Logging In

The first step in using a UNIX system is to log in. The word *log* comes from the old shipping era when the captain filled out the daily log with a record of activities. In this context, you are signing into the "log" of the UNIX system. We will assume that the screen display on your computer is turned on and that you are raring to go. The first key you should press is the Return key. UNIX should respond with something like this:

> Welcome to UNIX VERSION 7.3. Enjoy Your Computing
> Login:□   ← *cursor*

Immediately after the colon in the word login:, you should see a rectangle of light, or else an underscore mark (blinking on some terminals), called the *cursor*. The cursor is your guiding light—it shows you where your next letter will be placed on the screen. Now type your login name. Your *login* name is the name by which you are known to the UNIX system, and it usually is assigned to you by the folks running the system. Let's assume your login name is sneezy. Each time you type a letter, it appears on the screen and the cursor moves over a space. *Don't* put in a space before or after your name. A space is a character, just like *a* or 7. Thus, adding a space would make your login name different. Login names normally are in lowercase letters only, so type sneezy, not Sneezy or SNEEZY. Finish with a Return as follows:

```
Login: sneezy <Return>          ← type sneezy, then press Return
```

The Prompt Character

If your account has been set up without a password, and if the system recognizes sneezy as a valid name, there will be a pause while the system sets up things for you. It may give you some messages, and then it will display a *prompt*, a special symbol at the left of the screen telling you that UNIX is in operation and waiting for your next command. Each time you give UNIX an instruction, it will give you a new prompt symbol when it has finished and is ready for the next instruction. The standard prompt is usually % or $. We will assume the prompt is $ (see Figure 2.2). The Return key and the $ serve the same purpose as "over" in CB talk. Return tells UNIX that you are done and that it is UNIX's turn, and $ tells you that UNIX is done and it is your turn.

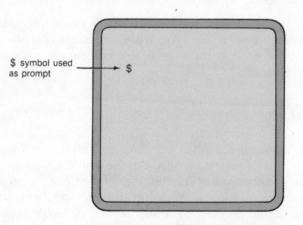

Figure 2.2.   The UNIX prompt.

The Password

What happens if you have a password or if the system does not recognize sneezy as a login name? In either case, the system responds to the previous line with

```
password:
```

You then type your password. The letters you type *will not* appear on the screen as you type them. (After all, what good is a password if someone can look over your shoulder and read it off the screen!) Again, follow with Return. (Your account may be set up so that you neither have nor need a password to use the system.) If you have no password and still get this message asking for one, then you do need a password. The system does not recognize you, but, being a bit cagey, it asks you for a password anyway. The login procedure will not continue unless you give some password (anything) at this point, so fake one. The fake password will not get you on the system, but it will cause the system to ask for your login name again. At this point, you may notice that you mistyped your login name. For example, suppose in answer to password, you (sneezy) typed

```
snowwhite
```

for your password. UNIX then compares the password you typed with its record of sneezy's password. If the two agree, you are welcomed to the system and presented with the system prompt. If you typed either your login name or the password incorrectly, the system responds with

```
Login incorrect
Login:
```

and you get to try again. You can repeat this as many times as necessary unless the powers-that-be are worried about CPU thieves and have installed a trap to catch repeated attempts to log in.

Setting Up and Changing Passwords

It is a simple matter to give yourself a password if you lack one. Once you are logged in and have the UNIX prompt, type the command

```
$ passwd <Return>
```

Notice that the command passwd is in lowercase letters. Also note that the command is passwd, not password. (This dubious shortcut saves you time in typing a command that you may use once a season, if that often. (For some people, these UNIX abbreviations are a minor system foible, since the abbreviations are harder to remember than the full word!) After you type passwd, UNIX responds with

```
changing password for sneezy
New password:
```

You then type in your choice of password. It will not appear on the screen. Press Return and UNIX responds with

```
Re-enter new password:
```

This is a check to see that both you and UNIX have the same word in mind. Since you do not see what you type, this check is valuable. If the two words you typed disagree, UNIX responds with

```
They don't match; try again
$
```

The return of the $ prompt means that UNIX is finished with the passwd command. If you want to continue, you have to start over again by typing passwd and pressing Return. You should get use to the fact that when UNIX does something successfully, it does not say "good" or "correct." It just gives you the old prompt.

If the words you typed did agree, UNIX will accept the new password and you will have to use it the next time you log in. It is a good practice to write down your password and keep it somewhere handy.

To change your password, you go through the same procedure, except there is one extra step. After you type passwd and press Return, UNIX asks

```
old password:
```

You type it, press Return, and the procedure continues as described previously. This step is a precaution to keep your friends from jokingly changing your password when you get called away from the terminal for a moment.

What sort of passwords can you use? Generally, a password should contain at least one nonnumeric character and should be at least 6 characters long if you use only uppercase or only lowercase characters. Thus, some unacceptable passwords are 007007, pip, and doog. Some acceptable examples are cowboy, hog666, TOADLIFE, 747F22, and rPg@2. Oh yes, make sure you remember your password. If you forget it, you will have to get help from the system administrator.

Logging Out

The process of signing off when you are done is called *logging out*. To log out, the UNIX prompt must be showing. Thus, you can't log out in the middle of the passwd process. If the prompt is showing, just press

```
<Ctrl-d>
```

(This means hold down the Ctrl key while pressing the *d* key once.) You will now be logged out, and the screen should show your system's standard welcome message:

```
Welcome to UNIX VERSION 7.3 Enjoy Your Computing
Login:
```

You can walk away knowing that you have said goodbye properly to UNIX and that the terminal is ready for the next user.

There are things you can do that will cause the system to not log you out right away after you press Ctrl-d. We assume that you do not know how to do these things yet. Later, we will give some examples (such as background jobs running) and tell you what to do.

Correcting Typing Errors

Even the most talented fingers sometimes stumble as they sweep across the keyboard, and even the most brilliant minds sometimes have second thoughts about commands they have typed. One of the major advantages of an interactive system such as UNIX is that it gives you the opportunity to see and correct errors immediately.

The mechanics of making corrections depend on the terminal you use and on how your particular system has been set up. Therefore, the methods we describe here are just possible examples. You will have to check out what works on your system.

Erasing Characters

The key most commonly used to *erase* a character (usually moving the cursor back one space and removing the offending character) is the Backspace key. For example, if you mistakenly type

```
passqr
```

and then press the Backspace key twice, the cursor will back up (move left) over the last two letters, erasing them and leaving the word

```
pass
```

You can then correctly complete the command by typing w and d to produce

```
passwd
```

Another common way to erase characters is to use Ctrl-h. (Depress the Ctrl key and press the *h* key once.) Yet another way, widely used on "hard-copy" terminals, is to use the Pound or Number Sign (#) key. This choice works somewhat differently from the other two, since a hard-copy terminal cannot erase parts of text on a screen. In this case, using the # key erases the character from the computer's memory but not from the screen. Thus, the correction for the last example would appear this way on the screen:

```
passqr##wd
```

The first # cancels the r, and the second # cancels the q. When you press Return, passwd is transmitted to the computer.

Unfortunately, even with all these correction techniques, you still can't erase a letter in the middle of a word without also erasing all the letters after the erroneous one. For example, to correct

```
pusswd
```

you would type, using the # key,

```
pusswd#####asswd
```

Here you had to erase (from right to left) the d, w, s, and s to reach the u. You then had to retype the letters s, s, w, and d after replacing the u with an a. Other keys less commonly used to erase characters are the Del key and the Rub key. (These last two keys are sometimes used to *interrupt* a process. See the next section.)

Canceling Lines and Interrupting a Command

A character that cancels an entire line instead of just one letter is called a *kill* character. For example, on our system, the kill character is Ctrl-x. (Note that Ctrl-x is considered a single character even though it involves pressing two keys—Ctrl and *x*—simultaneously.) Thus, the sequence

```
$ passwd <Ctrl-x>        ← pressing <Ctrl-x> kills the line
```

produces a blank line—passwd is deleted.

Some systems use @ as a kill character. In this case, the line is usually not erased from the screen, just from what is transmitted. For example, the following sequence will transmit passwd:

```
osddef@passwd
```

Another special character is the *interrupt* character, which usually is generated by a Ctrl-c or by the Del (Delete) key. This causes the system to "interrupt" what it is doing. The interrupt character will not only erase lines, but will halt many procedures after they have started running. This is the common way to stop the computer from doing something and returning to the shell ($).

The Break key will sometimes do the same thing—*interrupt* a process. However, on some systems, pressing Break will lock up a terminal, interrupting not only UNIX, but also the user. We suggest that you *do not* use Break.

Some Simple Shell Commands

Suppose you have logged on successfully by answering the login: and password: prompts correctly. The UNIX prompt appears on the screen, telling you that UNIX is ready to obey your every command. After your first flush of joy and power, you may wonder "What do I tell it to do?" There are literally thousands of legitimate possible answers to that question and, in this section, we will look at four of the simplest: the commands date, cal, who, and finger. These are examples of *shell commands*, which are standard commands recognized by the shell program. We chose these four commands because they are useful and easy to understand.

The Bourne Shell and C Shell

The *shell* is the part of the UNIX operating system that acts as an intermediary between you and the computer. It relays your commands to the computer and returns its responses to you. As we write this book, there are two main varieties of shells in widespread use (plus two newer shells mentioned below). The first is the Bourne shell, named after the man who developed it. It is the shell that comes with the standard Bell Labs release. (It may vary slightly from older to newer releases.) The second is the C shell, developed at the University of California at Berkeley, and included as part of Berkeley Software Distribution (BSD) packages. Most of what we say in this book applies equally to both shells, but there are differences. This book is written for the Bourne shell. For the C shell, see the book *UNIX Primer Plus*, Second Edition, by Waite, Prata, and Martin, published by Howard W. Sams.

How can you tell which shell you have? You can ask. You can try using a C-shell-only feature and see if it works. Usually you can tell by the prompt. The Bourne shell normally uses a $ as the main prompt, and the C shell normally uses the % as the main prompt.

Actually, Unix System V, Release 4.0 supports four shells. In addition to the Bourne shell and the C-shell, it offers the Korn shell, and a job-control shell. These shells are accessed through the commands, sh, csh, ksh, and jsh, respectively, and are described in Chapter 11.

We have talked about the shell as being the liaison between you and the computer. Let's see how that works in the context of shell commands. First, after you log in, the shell provides you with a prompt (a $ we are assuming). It is now ready for your move. You type a command, such as date, and press Return. The shell then identifies this command as something it knows and causes the command to be executed, usually giving you an output on the screen. Whether it gives you an output or not, you will know when it is finished since the shell sends another prompt to the screen to let you know it is your turn again. If you type in a command it does not recognize—getlost, for example—the shell lets you know with a response such as

```
$ getlost              ← you type this command
getlost: not found     ← UNIX responds
```

Now let's try out one of the commands that does work—the date command.

The *date* Command

The date command displays the current date and time on the screen. To use it, type date after the prompt. The line will appear as follows:

```
$ date
```

UNIX provides the $—you provide the word date. (Don't forget that you have to press Return. In a way, the Return key is *your* prompt to UNIX and $ is its prompt to you.) This line of instruction is known technically as the *command line*. The result of giving this command is that UNIX prints the date. It will look something like this:

```
Tue Jun 2 14:49:10 PST 1992
```

Note that UNIX uses a 24-hour clock and gives the time to the second. The full sequence of command and response would look like this:

```
$ date
Tue Jun 2 14:49:19 PST 1992
$
```

You can now give another command after the last prompt.

Throughout this book, after each new command has been presented, you will find a summary of that command. Here is the summary for date:

date Displays Date and Time		
Name	**Options**	**Arguments**
date	**None**	**None**
Description:	When you type date, UNIX displays the date and time of day to you.	

In the preceding summary of the date command, notice the two categories "Options" and "Arguments." Although these categories are empty for date, we will explain their meaning here. Some commands perform operations such as printing or listing information. These types of commands often need something to operate on. The name of the thing operated on is called the *argument*. Many commands are not complete without an argument, and some commands can have more than one argument. For example, to print two files one after the other, you would use a print command and the names of the two files. These two filenames would be two arguments. The cal command, described next, is an example of a command requiring an argument.

Options generally are variations on the command. For example, a printing command may have an option to double-space the output. In Figure 2.3, you can see commands, arguments, and options being displayed on the screen.

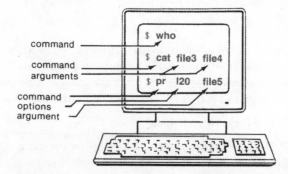

Figure 2.3.   Commands, arguments, and options.

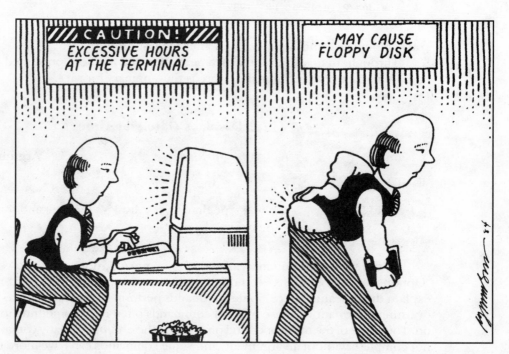

The *cal* Command

You might want to use the cal command next. It does not give information about California, but it will print a calendar. This command is more sophisticated than the date command because it requires an argument. This argument does not mean to give UNIX any backtalk—it means to provide additional information needed by the command. In this particular case, the `cal` command needs to know the year for which you want the calendar. Thus, to produce a calendar for the year 1776, enter the following command line

```
$ cal 1776
```

Here, the command is `cal` and the argument is 1776. When you press Return, the display shows

	1776	
Jan	*Feb*	*Mar*

S	M	Tu	W	Th	F	S		S	M	Tu	W	Th	F	S		S	M	Tu	W	Th	F	S
	1	2	3	4	5	6						1	2	3							1	2
7	8	9	10	11	12	13		4	5	6	7	8	9	10		3	4	5	6	7	8	9
14	15	16	17	18	19	20		11	12	13	14	15	16	17		10	11	12	13	14	15	16
21	22	23	24	25	26	27		18	19	20	21	22	23	24		17	18	19	20	21	22	23
28	29	30	31					25	26	27	28	29				24	25	26	27	28	29	30
																31						

To save space, the preceding display shows only the first three months. However, you will see all twelve months on your screen. If the full calendar does not fit on your screen, press Ctrl-s to stop the display before January rolls off the screen and then press any key to restart it. (Some systems may use different keys, such as Ctrl-q, for this.)

You can display the calendar for a single month by typing the number of the month before the year. You can use either a one-digit or a two-digit number for the month. Thus, May is 05, or 5. The following is the command line to get the calendar for July 1872:

```
cal 7 1872
```

The month is an *optional argument*, meaning it can be omitted. The year is not optional, so you must give it. The format for this command is

```
cal [month] year
```

The brackets around *month* signify that *month* is an optional argument. You do not actually type the brackets when you use the command. The italic typeface indicates that you do not literally type the word; rather you type a value in place of the word.

You can use `cal` for future calendars (up to the year 9999) as well as for the present and the past.

cal Provides a Calendar		
Name	**Options**	**Arguments**
cal	**None**	[month] year
Description:	The cal command provides a calendar for whatever year you type in after the word cal. There must be at least one space between the command and the year. The year should be in the range of 0—9999 AD. You can get the calendar for just one month by preceding the year with the number of the month, numbered from 1 to 12.	
Example:	To see the calendar for May 1942, type cal 5 1942.	

The *who* Command

UNIX is a time-sharing system which means several people can use the system at the same time. In recognition of the inquisitiveness of human nature, UNIX has a who command. When you give this command, UNIX responds with the list of people logged into the system at that moment. The command and its result might look something like this:

```
$ who
bob           tty04        Aug 23          8:27
nerkie        tty07        Aug 23          8:16
catfish       tty11        Aug 23          8:38
sneezy        tty15        Aug 23          8:52
granny        tty21        Aug 22         23:13
boss1776      tty24        Aug 23          9:01
$
```

The first column gives the login name of the user. The second column identifies the terminal being used. The label tty is a throwback to the days when most terminals were Teletype machines that printed on paper rather than on a screen. The tty number can provide a clue to the person's location if you know in which room specific terminals are placed. The remaining columns give the date and the time that each user logged in, using the 24-hour clock. From the display, it looks like granny has been on the system all night, or maybe she forgot to log out again. But who is catfish? Your system may have some commands that tell you more about your comrades in computing. An example is the finger command (standard in Release 4.0), that we will discuss next.

who Who's on the System		
Name	**Options**	**Arguments**
who	**Several**	**[am I]**
Description:	The who command, when typed without an argument, tells you who is currently on the system. It gives you the user's login name, the terminal name, and the time that the user logged on. If you ask who am I, it gives you this information about yourself, and it may also tell you which UNIX system you are on. The options for the who command are not important here. If you would like more information about them, you can check the on-line manual, as described in Chapter 3.	
Example:	To find out who's on the system, type who.	

The *finger* Command

The finger command can be used with or without an argument. Without an argument, it works like who but it also gives the full name, idle time, and office number of users. The *idle time* is the time, in minutes, since the user last gave UNIX a command. The finger command might give the following display:

```
$ finger
Login          Name          TTY   Idle   When       Office
bob       Robert Sniggle     04           Tue 9:27    SC256
nerkie    Nercules Pigrow    07     7     Tue 10:16   BH019
catfish   Kitty Trout        11           Tue 9:38    WD40
sneezy    U. R. R. Reader    15           Tue 10:52   WD38
granny    Henrietta Goose    22     15    Mon 23:13   ZX280
boss1776  V.I. Parsons       26           Tue 11:59   Penthouse
$
```

Aha! The mystery is explained; catfish is the new person in the next office. To learn more about her, use finger with an argument. In this case, the argument is her name: login or first or last. For example, use the login name:

```
$ finger catfish
Login name: catfish              In Real Life: Kitty
                                     Trout
Directory: /home/catfish         Shell: /usr/bin/csh
Last Login: Tue Aug 23 9:38 on
```

```
       tty11
Plan: To utterly master Pascal
$
```

Here you learn her home directory (more about home directories in the next chapter), and you learn that she uses the C shell (/bin/csh is the C shell and /bin/sh is the original Bell Labs shell). You also learn her current intentions in using UNIX. This full printout of information is called the *long form*. Yes, there is also a *short form*; it is the one-line-per-user form that you saw in the first example.

If you had used finger Kitty as a command, you would have obtained a similar listing for all persons named Kitty who have accounts on the system, whether or not they are currently logged in. The command finger Kitty Trout would provide information about all persons named Kitty or named Trout.

The finger command is useful if you need to know someone's login name (to send mail, for example) but you know only the person's real name. The finger command also has what are known as *flag options*, or *options*, for short. Such options come after the command and before the argument and usually are in the form of a hyphen followed by a letter. Here is an example:

```
finger -s catfish
```

The -s option stands for "short form." Note that there is no space between the hyphen and the s but that there are spaces on either side of the option. The result of giving this command would be

```
catfish  Kitty Trout       11        Tue 9:38  WD40
```

You can use more than one flag option in a command. An example would be finger -m -s catfish. Some commands allow options to be strung together in any order. For example, the following commands would all give the same results:

```
finger -m-s John
finger -ms John
finger -sm John
```

Note that rearranging option flags is usually, but not always, possible.

In the following command summary and in future summaries, we will include descriptions of the most important options available.

Although your system may not have finger, the information that finger uses will be stored somewhere in the system. Much of the information is kept in a file named /etc/passwd, and we will discuss this file in Chapter 14.

In Chapter 3, you will learn how to communicate with your fellow computer users by using electronic mail.

finger Provides Information about Users

Name	Options	Arguments
finger	[-m, -l, -s]	[*name*...]

Description: When used without an argument, the finger command provides a list of all the users on the system, giving the login name, the real name, the terminal, the idle time, the login time, and the office, if known, for each user. (This list of information constitutes the *short form*.)

When used with one or more names, finger provides the previous information plus information about the home directory and the shell of the named users. (This argument list of information constitutes the *long form*.) The finger program will search for all users whose login name *or* real name matches the given name.

Options: -m   Causes finger to search only the *login* names that match the argument name(s). Thus, finger -m john will give information only about a person whose login name is john and will ignore people named john who have a different login name.

-l   Forces finger to display the long form.

-s   Forces finger to display the short form.

Examples: To find out the login names of every user named "john," and to print just the one-line summary, type

```
finger -s john
```

This result might look like this

```
Login     Name           TTY  Idle       When      Office
jonny     John Grock     5                12:13     ACH000
buny0234  John Bunyon    17   <Jul  4     14:14>
daffy     John Duck      18   <Aug  2     06:02>    CB122
suzie     Susan John     19   <Aug 22     15:23>
john      Johannes Brahms 22  <Aug 17     09:42>    MU244
```

Notice that finger finds all users named john, whether that is the first, last, or login name of the user. The < and > indicate that the user is not currently logged in.

In searching for names, `finger` ignores capitalization. It will find both `john` and `John`. The command

```
finger -s -m john
```

would produce just the last line of this listing since the `-m` option restricts the `finger` command to searching only login names.

Review Questions

Here are some exercises to help you review the important points in this chapter.

A. Matching Commands

Match the command in the left column to the corresponding description in the right column.

1. `who`   a. Gives the date and time

2. `passwd`   b. Tells who's logged in

3. `date`   c. Produces a calendar

4. `cal`   d. Lets you choose a password

5. `finger`   e. Gives information about users

B. Questions

1. Which of the following commands include arguments. Identify the arguments, if any.

   a. `cal 1984`

   b. `cal 09 2025`

   c. `who`

   d. `finger don`

2. What is the difference between `passwd` and `password`?

3. Which of the following is the basic purpose of the UNIX prompt ($)?

     a. To demonstrate UNIX's ability to produce unusual symbols

     b. To tell you that UNIX is ready to accept a command

     c. To tell UNIX that you are finished

4. What happens when you fail to press Return?

5. What does the phrase "press Ctrl-s" mean?

6. How do you correct a typing error on the same line as the cursor?

7. Which keystroke combination interrupts the current job and returns the prompt?

8. What happens if you hold down a key?

9. How do you stop the screen from scrolling? How do you restart it?

10. What is a kill character?

Answers

A.   1—b, 2—d, 3—a, 4—c, 5—e

B.   1. a. 1984 b. 09 and 2025 c. no argument d. don. 2. password is a prompt from UNIX asking you to type your password; passwd is a UNIX command that initiates the process of changing your password. 3. b, of course. 4. Nothing happens; UNIX just sits patiently, waiting to be told that you are done and that it is its turn to do something. 5. It means that you hold down the Ctrl key while pressing the *s* key once sharply. 6. It depends on the terminal you use. Generally, terminals use either the Backspace key, the Rub key, the Ctrl-h combination, or the # key. 7. Ctrl-c. 8. The key repeats, sending the same character to the computer. 9. Use Ctrl-s to stop screen scroll. Use Ctrl-q to restart it. 10. A character that cancels a whole line instead of a single letter.

Exercises at the Terminal

The best way to learn UNIX is to use it. We hope you have been trying out the commands as you read about them. Here are some additional activities that you can try.

1. Log in to your UNIX system.

2. Type whp and correct it to who.

3. Type fenger and correct it to finger.

4. If you do not have a password, give yourself one now. If you do have one, change it to a new one.

5. Find out how many people are logged in and who has been logged in the longest.

6. Find the time of day.

7. Find out on which day of the week you were born.

8. Find out which day of the week is January 1, 1991.

9. Type a command and then use Ctrl-x to kill the whole line.

3

Electronic Mail and On-Line Help: *mail*, *write*, and *man*

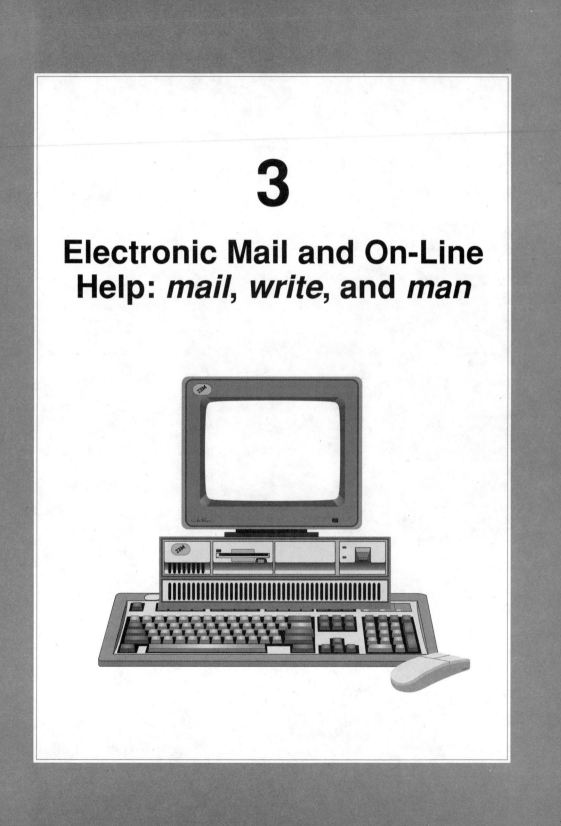

Chapter 3

Electronic Mail and On-Line Help: *mail*, *write*, and *man*

The term *electronic mail* refers to a mail delivery system that replaces conventional mail delivery with an electronic computer-based service. Electronic mail can also replace some types of telephone calls and interoffice memos. The form of electronic mail used with UNIX is sometimes called a *mailbox* system. Each user with a login account has a mailbox file to which other users can send mail.

An electronic mail system has several major benefits:

- Correspondence can be conveniently created on a keyboard or terminal, and word-processing capabilities make entry and corrections easy.

- You can print paper copies and even have them typeset.

- The mailing process is much faster than postal letters—a message reaches its destination almost instantaneously.

- You can mail identical copies to several users simultaneously.

- Electronic mail doesn't interrupt the recipient the way a phone call does; you can read your messages at your leisure.

- Electronic mail can be electronically filed with all the inherent advantages of that process.

- Electronic mail may be mailed locally, such as in a local UNIX time-share system, or it may be routed through one of several worldwide distributing networks, such as USENET.

- No paper, envelopes, or stamps are required, and no trips to the post office are needed.

The major disadvantage of this type of electronic mail is that the recipient must log into his or her account to notice whether mail has been sent. Other forms of electronic mail can overcome this disadvantage. For example, mail can be printed on paper at the receiving end and then be hand-delivered like an office memo or telegram.

The UNIX Mail System

UNIX uses the command mail (Mail or mailx, on some systems) to initiate both the sending and the receiving of mail. The mail system actually contains several options for preparing, delivering, reading, and disposing of mail. These options are briefly described later in this chapter. However, most new users can get along very nicely with the command sequence we will describe next.

Sending Mail to Yourself and Others

The UNIX mail system provides a handy way to send mail to yourself. Suppose that your login name is `fred` and that you want to send yourself a memo about an upcoming meeting. When the shell prompt appears on the screen, type `mail fred` and press the Return key. You may see the prompt, `Subject:`. Enter a subject and begin typing your memo. Press the Return key whenever you wish to start a new line, just as you would press the carriage return on a typewriter. When your memo is complete, type Ctrl-d at the beginning of a new line. Your memo might look like this:

```
$ mail fred <Return>                        ← send mail to yourself
Subject: Meeting with Susan <Return>     ← enter subject; then press Return
Just a reminder of our meeting <Return>   ← now start typing
with Susan at the Admin Bldg. <Return>
Fred <Return>
<Ctrl-d>                                    ← press Ctrl-d to send mail
$                                           ← UNIX shell prompt
```

The next time you log in, or a few minutes later if you stay logged in, the screen greeting will include the happy announcement "you have mail" (see Figure 3.1).

Note that the `mail` program can be customized to ask you to enter a subject (as shown here) or to skip the subject. Entering a subject is a good idea because it helps you identify and organize responses to incoming messages. (We will assume your system administrator has set up your account with the Subject feature turned on.)

Reading Your Mail

To read electronic mail, give the single command `mail` from the shell. The system responds by displaying a summary of the messages received. We will assume that you have received several letters. Here is the sequence:

```
$ mail <Return>      ← to read incoming mail
mail version 2.14 08/01/89 Type ? for help.
"/usr/spool/mail/fred": 4 messages 4 unread
>N  4  fred     Wed Oct 29 15:24   5/56      Meeting with Susan
 U  3  stephen  Thu Nov  6 14:52  32/1332    Hockey game
 U  2  stephen  Thu Nov  6 14:52  27/1315    Hockey game
 U  1  susan    Tue Nov  4 12:00  12/388     Conference room
?                    ← command mode prompt
? p4 <Return>        ← type p4 to print message number 4
```

```
From fred Wed Oct 29 15:24 PST 1992    ← mail responds
To: fred
Subject: Meeting with Susan
Status: R
Just a reminder of our meeting
with Susan at the Admin Bld.
Fred
?                                       ← command mode prompt
? q <Return>                            ← quit mail
$                                       ← UNIX shell prompt
```

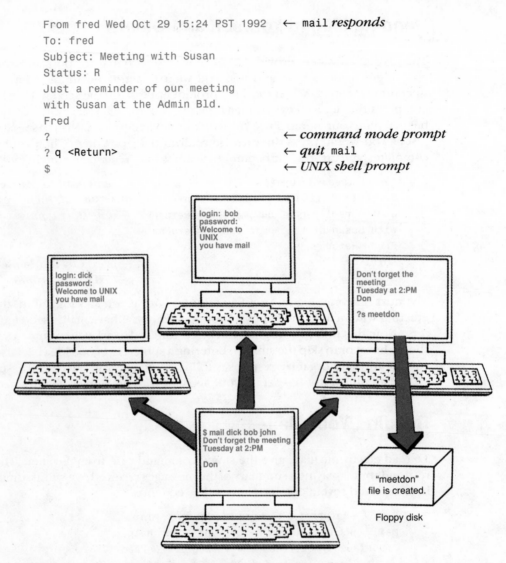

Figure 3.1.   Sending mail to others.

This example shows how helpful it is to enter a subject when sending mail. Subjects appear as part of the incoming mail *header* listing the messages to be read.

Besides giving the subjects, the header tells whether the letter is new (N) or unread (U), the date and time the letter was sent, and the length of the letter in terms of lines and characters. The ? is the `mail` prompt, similar to the UNIX prompt $.

What happens after you have read a letter? Once letters are read they are automatically placed in a file called `mbox` located in your home directory. (Your UNIX system administrator may set up `mail` so that the already read letters remain in your system mailbox where you will see all of them each time you read mail. This is a clever way of encouraging you to get rid of old letters.)

Ideally, you will take matters into your own hands and make use of `mail`'s many tools for handling letters. The simplest choices for disposing of mail are:

1. Delete the letter from your mail file (d).

2. Save the letter to any new or old file (s).

3. Reply to the author (R).

4. Leave the letter in the `mbox` file.

To select a choice, give the appropriate command (d, s, or R) right after reading the letter, or give the command followed by the number of the letter (d4, s3, R1, and so on). For example, after reading the first letter, you can type the d command to delete the letter:

> ? d   ← *delete the letter just displayed*

If you want to save letter number 2 in a file called `bobstuff`, just give the command

> ? s2 bobstuff   ← *save to a file called* `bobstuff`

Since the disposition of each letter takes place immediately after reading the letter, an easy way is needed to return to (and dispose of) previously read mail. There is such a way. You can use the - command (a minus sign) to display the previous letter:

> ? -   ← *display previous letter*

To continue back through other letters, just type another minus sign. To step forward through each letter, type a plus sign command (+) or, easier yet, just press the Return key.

When you are reading mail, `mail` is in the *command mode*. The question mark prompt (?) means that `mail` is waiting for you to give it a command. There are more than thirty commands available for reading mail. If you are a beginning user, the - and + commands are all that you need to start using `mail`. However, if you like to explore or play with new gadgets, there is a quick way to see what `mail` has to offer— ask for help.

Getting Help in *mail*

When sending or receiving messages, you can get a partial listing of the mail commands by using the help command. Type ~? (a tilde and a question mark) at the beginning of a new line while sending mail or type ? at the ? prompt while receiving mail. These commands will display *help screens* (see Tables 3.1 and 3.2).

For Advanced Users: Sending Mail

Some of the features referred to in this discussion assume that you have advanced UNIX experience. If you are unfamiliar with these features, you can read about them in later chapters. The vi screen editor, for example, is described in Chapter 5. Other advanced features are connected with the filing system, described in Chapters 4 and 9.

When you enter mail to send a letter, mail is placed in a *compose mode* (as opposed to the command mode) that starts up the primitive mail editor. Here, the keyboard acts like a typewriter, and the only word processing feature is the Backspace key used to erase and back up the cursor.

While you are in the compose mode, a number of commands are available, the most important being the command ~v, which invokes a UNIX editor. This command must be given at the beginning of a new line. The default editor is vi, but that can be changed in a start-up file called .mailrc which is located in your home directory.

When you finish editing and leave an editor like vi in the normal fashion, you are returned to the compose mode of mail. This means that you have the primitive editor back to add anything else or to give the command to send your letter (Ctrl-d).

If you change your mind in the middle of an outgoing letter and want to quit sending mail, press the Interrupt key twice (usually Ctrl-c). This will kill the letter, and the mail program, and put you back in the shell.

To see a screen display of other commands available in the send-mail (compose) mode, use the help command, ~?. This command, like all tilde commands, must be given at the start of a new line. Table 3.1 shows the commands for sending mail that you would see on a typical help screen.

The commands in Table 3.1 give you full control of the message headers, provide advanced editing capabilities, offer interaction with the UNIX file system and allow commands to be run in the UNIX shell. For example, to start the "good" editor, type the command

> ~v <Return>   ← *starts an advanced editor like* vi

Here are three more examples:

> ~c name <Return>   ← *adds* name *to carbon copy list*
> ~w filename   ← *places a copy of the letter in the file* filename
> ~m 3   ← *reads message number* 3 *into your letter*

Table 3.1.   Commands for sending mail in the compose mode.

Tilde Command	Result
~~	Quotes a single tilde
~b *users*	Adds users to blind Cc list
~c *users*	Adds users to cc list
~d	Inserts dead.letter
~e	Edits the message buffer
~h	Prompts for the To list, Subject, and Cc list
~r *file*	Reads a file into the message buffer
~p	Prints the message buffer
~m *messages**	Inserts messages, right-shifted by a tab
~s *subject*	Sets the Subject
~t *users*	Adds users to the To list
~v	Invokes display editor on message
~w *file*	Writes message to file
~?	Prints this message
~! *command*	Invokes the shell
~¦ *command*	Pipes the message through the command

* This command can be given only when replying to incoming mail.

Note: In the first column, the italic font indicates that you must substitute an actual filename, message number, and so on, for the word in the italic font. For example, in the ~r command, *file* must be replaced by an actual filename, for example, ~r bobstuff.

The last feature (~m) is often used when responding to an incoming letter. It reminds the other person of the message he or she sent to you. The inserted message is offset by a tab space to make it clear that it is not your writing but the sender's. However, the ~m command can be given only when responding to incoming mail as described next.

For Advanced Users: Reading Mail

When you give the command mail at the UNIX prompt, you are placed in the command mode of mail (rather than the compose mode). The mail command displays a summary of incoming letters and a command mode prompt, ?.

A host of commands is available for reading or disposing of mail. The most important of these are listed in the help screen. To see the help screen, just type a question mark at the ? prompt. Table 3.2 shows the commands for reading mail that you would see on a typical help screen.

Table 3.2.   Commands for reading mail in the command mode.

Command	Result
t *<message list>*	Types messages
n	Go to and type next message
e *<message list>*	Edits messages
f *<message list>*	Gives headlines of messages
d *<message list>*	Deletes messages
s *<message list>* file	Appends messages to the named file
u *<message list>*	Undeletes messages
R *<message list>*	Replies to message senders
r *<message list>*	Replies to message senders and all recipients
pre *<message list>*	Returns messages to /usr/spool/mail
m *<user list>*	Sends mail to specific users
q	Quits, saving unresolved messages in mbox
x	Quits, does not remove system mailbox
h	Prints active message headers
!	Shell escape
cd [*directory*]	Changes to named directory or to home directory if none given

A *<message list>* consists of integers, ranges of same, or user names separated by spaces. If omitted, mail uses the last message typed.

A *<user list>* consists of user names or aliases separated by spaces. Aliases are defined in .mailrc located in your home directory.

In the last command, the brackets in [*directory*] indicate that the inclusion of a directory is optional.

The format for using `mail` commands is

`[command] [message list] [arguments]`

The brackets indicate that each part of the command line is optional. The italic font indicates that you must replace the italicized word with an actual command name, a message number, and so on. Here are some sample command lines and what they do:

`t1-3`	← *type message numbers* 1 *through* 3
`s 1 2 file1`	← *save message numbers* 1 *and* 2 *in* `file1`
`3`	← *read message number* 3; *no command given*
`r3`	← *reply to message number* 3
`d3`	← *delete message number* 3
`u3`	← *undelete message number* 3

Notice how `mail` accepts variations on numbering. You can give either the command `s 1 2 file1` or the command `s1-2 file1` to save messages in `file1`. Note, however, that the commands `s1 2` and `s 1 2` both save message number 1 to a file called 2.

Here are a few more examples:

`d 1-3`	← *delete messages numbered* 1 *through* 3
`d fred`	← *delete all messages from* `fred`
`d /Meeting`	← *delete all messages with* `Meeting` *in the subject*
`u *`	← *undelete all messages*
`R3`	← *reply to the senders of message* 3

You can see how helpful `mail` tries to be in the examples using the `delete` command, `d`. The `d` command will work with message numbers or names or even parts of the Subject.

The last command shown is the most useful one of all. The `R` command lets you reply to incoming messages simply and conveniently. Actually, there are two versions of the `reply` command, `reply` and `Reply`. The difference between the two is worth noting:

- To respond to everyone who received a copy of the letter, use `reply` or `r`.

- To respond to the author(s) only, use `Reply` or `R`.

Be careful with the `r` command. If someone sends you a letter and sends carbon copies to a half dozen others, the `r` command will send your reply to everyone. To avoid polluting mailboxes, use the `R` command whenever possible. (*Note:* Some systems may reverse the roles of `r` and `R`.)

For Advanced Users: Adjusting the *mail* Environment

The `mail` program has over 40 options, called *environmental variables*, that can be set to change its behavior. Options include such features as creating an abbreviation or autograph for your signature, changing the escape character (~), or creating a special *folder* for saving incoming messages.

Options can be set temporarily by using the `set` command while receiving mail. Or, options can be created semipermanently by placing them in the `.mailrc` file in your home directory. If you want to see which options are currently set, type

    `? set`   ← *displays options you have set*

In addition to options, certain other commands are helpful for customizing the `mail` environment. One of the most important of these is the `alias` command. It can be used to create an alias for login names as shown in the last line of the next example.

A typical `.mailrc` file might look like this:

```
ask                              ← asks for a Subject when sending mail
hold                             ← keeps mail here rather than in mbox file
set folder=/home/fred/Mail       ← creates a folder for storing mail
set crt=21                       ← sets the number of lines displayed by More
set dot                          ← allows a dot to substitute for Ctrl-d
alias staff bob don fred susan   ← creates an alias called staff
```

Notice that the third line in the preceding `.mailrc` file creates a folder for storing incoming mail. The mail can be stored in several ways: by a person's name, by subject matter, or by job title. However, in order for the folder to work, you must first set up a directory, here called `Mail`, for storing mail. Then, as you read mail, you can use a new version of the `save` (s) command like this:

    `? s4 +susan`   ←*stores or appends letter 4 in the file* susan
                          located in the Mail *subdirectory*

To see a description of all the `mail` options, check your on-line manual or the `mail` reference manual. Another handy reference is *UNIX System V Bible* (Prata, Martin, and The Waite Group, published by Howard W. Sams).

Local Network Mail

Network mail lets you send mail to fellow UNIX users who have login accounts on other UNIX computers. Just as the `mail` command lets you send mail to people on your own UNIX computer, network mail lets you send mail to people on other UNIX computers. For example, you might be working for a large company or university with several UNIX computers tied together electronically. Network mail lets you be the "postperson." You can route mail directly to its destination. Network mail is routed by giving the name of the computer and the login name of the person receiving the mail. Each computer has previously been given a name, for example, daisy, lilac, or petunia. An exclamation point is used to separate all names. Here are two typical addresses:

```
$ mail daisy!beth
$ mail lilac!dick
```

In the preceding example, the mail command sends your mail from your UNIX computer to the computer named daisy or lilac for delivery to beth or dick. If for some reason your UNIX computer is not communicating directly with lilac, but you know that daisy is talking to lilac, you can route the mail through daisy with the following command:

```
$ mail daisy!lilac!dick
```

Here, the mail goes to the daisy computer, which sends it to the lilac computer for delivery to someone with the login name dick. Of course, this type of network mail works only if the computers are electronically connected by wire, phone lines, satellite, or other means.

Worldwide Network Mail

Suppose that you have a friend halfway across the country who uses UNIX. Is it possible to send electronic mail to your friend? Yes, indeed. You can send mail anywhere in the country, either directly from one computer to another using modems (via *uucp*, which we will describe soon), and telephone lines or more commonly by routing mail through a large network like USENET. With USENET, you can route electronic mail to any other UNIX user in the network. Right now, over 8,000 UNIX computers are on the USENET system, serving thousands of users. However, in order to route mail through a large network like this, you need a *network map*.

In a simplified view of a large network, one UNIX computer might communicate with other UNIX computers once every hour or once every six hours by telephone or other means. Not every computer in the network calls every other computer. In order to limit phone calls and distribute costs, a network map is created, with some UNIX computers serving as *nodes*, or relay stations, and other UNIX computers being at the end of the line. Part of a typical map is shown in Figure 3.2.

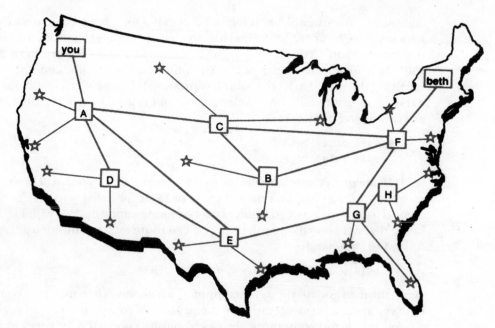

Figure 3.2.   A hypothetical UNIX network.

Looking at the figure, if you wanted to send mail to beth, then the mail could be routed by either of the following commands (other routes are also possible), where the names of the computers are A, B, C, D, E, and F for simplicity:

```
$ mail A!E!G!F!beth
$ mail A!C!B!F!beth
```

If network node E was not working because of a severe winter storm or similar calamity, then the mail would not get through. If E was down for some time, it is possible that A would give up trying to contact E and remove the letter from its files and you might never know that the mail did not get through. For that reason, it is always helpful to acknowledge mail received, both with network mail and regular mail.

Network mail is part of a larger communications system called *uucp*, *UNIX to UNIX Communications Package*. The *uucp* system has commands that allow file transfer between remote UNIX computers. It also allows the remote execution of commands. That is, from one UNIX computer you can send a package of commands to be run on another UNIX computer. With *uucp* you can use your computer's modem to dial, or call, another UNIX computer in order to transfer files or run commands. If you are interested in these services, see Chapter 15 for more details.

Electronic Chit-Chat: *write*

UNIX systems have a second form of electronic communication, one that lets you hold a conversation with another user (see Figure 3.3). This method can work only if the person you want to talk to is logged in and wants to talk back. The first step is to see who is on the system. The who command will tell you this. Suppose you spot your old friend Hortense Grigelsby and that her login name is hortense. Then you would give the command

```
write hortense
```

She would see this message on her screen:

```
Message from abner on tty 14 at 09:56 ...
```

(We are assuming that your login name is abner.)

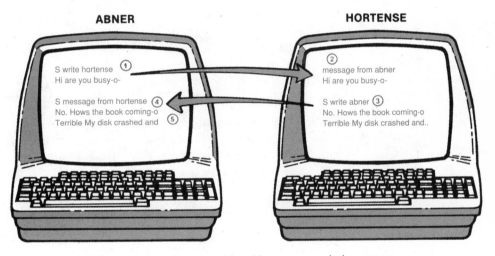

Figure 3.3.   Abner writing Hortense and vice versa.

Meanwhile, on your screen, the cursor will advance to a line with no prompt. Now each line you type on your terminal will be transmitted to Hortense's terminal when you press the Return key. (The line also shows on your screen as you type it.) When you have finished you say, hit <Ctrl-d>. This will restore your regular prompt to you and will send the message EOT (for "end of transmission") to Hortense's terminal, so that she will know you are done.

To get a two-way exchange, once she learns that you are writing to her, she can enter

```
write abner
```

Then she can send you messages while you send her messages. On most systems, what she types can appear in the middle of your typing and vice versa. It is best to adopt a sensible code of behavior. A simple one to use, that is similar to CB radio, is to type

```
-o-
```

for "over" when you have completed a thought, and to type

```
-oo-
```

for "over-and-out" when you intend to quit. These are not commands, they are just ways to help you coordinate communication with your partner.

In Chapter 12, we will show you how to block write messages by using the mesg command if you wish to work undisturbed. (A more advanced version of terminal to terminal communications, called *talk*, is available on some systems. However, it only works on machines with the same architectures.)

write Write to Another User		
Name	**Options**	**Arguments**
write	**None**	[*user loginname*]
Description:	The write command, transmits lines from your terminal to the other user's terminal. Transmission occurs when you press the Return key. Transmission is terminated by pressing Ctrl-d; this sends EOT to the other user. *Note*: To block incoming messages from interrupting your work, use the mesg command described in Chapter 12.	

Mail Etiquette

Whenever you use the communications capabilities of UNIX, whether it is *electronic mail*, *netnews* or write, good etiquette is important. Here are a few basic suggestions:

- Be brief.

- Choose your recipients carefully. Avoid sending carbon copies whenever possible. Nobody likes junk mail.

- Get into the habit of using a good editor, and not the mail editor, so you can revise your mail easily.

- Exercise restraint and good taste. Do not send mail you may regret later. Do not use profanity or be rude.

- Some users save a copy of all outgoing mail so they have a record of what they have said.

- When you state an opinion outside your company or institution, you should include a disclaimer, such as, "This opinion is my own and does not represent my company in any way." This disclaimer is often stored as an *autograph* and can be given with an ~a in some mail programs.

- If you are sending mail to someone you do not know well, identify yourself briefly. Some people get dozens of letters daily and may not associate incoming mail with you.

- Read your mail often and give timely responses when required. Remember that when someone sends you mail, they do not know if you have read it until you respond.

- Avoid personal criticisms whenever possible, both of people you write to, or write about. If you disagree and have to respond, criticize ideas, not people.

These guidelines for good manners are plain common sense, but sometimes they get overlooked in the convenience and exhilaration of electronic communications.

Getting More Information with *help* and *man*

There are two commands that may or may not be installed on your UNIX system. These commands are help and man. The help command varies greatly from one UNIX vendor to another. The command is used by typing help from the shell:

```
$ help
```

UNIX then provides a series of menus or questions that lead to a description of the most commonly used commands.

In addition to the help command, there is a very large document called the *UNIX System V User's Manual*. It is available in bound printed form; part of the manual may also be stored in a file on disk memory. This second version is called the *on-line* manual. All the UNIX commands and utilities are documented in this manual, and if it is available you can easily summon this information to your terminal screen. Sound great? It is, except for one point. The manual is written for experienced UNIX programmers, not for beginners. (That's one reason we wrote this book!) This may not be a problem if the command you wish to study is a simple one like date. But other commands may require a lot of trial-and-error work to see how to apply the information to your needs. But, then, that's a great way to learn!

How do you tap into this fount of knowledge? Simply type man followed by the name of the command you wish to study. For example, to learn all there is to know about date, type

```
man date
```

(Don't forget the space between man and date and remember to press Return.)
To learn more about the man command itself, type

```
man man
```

(Don't forget the Return key.) Be prepared to wait a bit; sometimes the system takes a while to find the desired entry. Here is an excerpt from one version of the UNIX on-line manual as it might appear if you had typed man who:

```
WHO(1)        UNIX User's Manual    WHO(1)
NAME
 who - who is on the system
SYNOPSIS
 who [ - uTlpdbrtas] [ file ]
 who am I
DESCRIPTION
 Who lists the user's name, terminal line, login time,
 elapsed time since activity occurred on the line, and the
 process-ID of the command interpreter (shell) for each
 current system user. It examines the /etc/utmp file to
 obtain its information. If file is given, that file is
 examined. Usually, file is /etc/wtmp, which contains a
 history of all the logins since the file was last created.

 Who with the am i option identifies the invoking user.

 Except for the default -s option, the general format for
 output entries is:

   name [ state ] line time activity pid [ comment ]
   [ exit ]

With options, who lists logins, logoffs, reboots, and
changes to the system clock, as well as other processes
spawned by the init process. These options are:

-u List information about those users who are currently
   logged in. The name is the user's login name. The line
   is the name of the line as found in the directory /dev.
 The time is the time that the user logged in. The
```

```
activity is the number of hours and minutes since

. . . . . more information follows, but is not
shown here . . .
```

```
FILES
    /etc/utmp
    /etc/wtmp
    /etc/inittab
SEE ALSO
    init(1M) in the SYSTEM V/68 Administrator's Manual.
    date(1), login(1), mesg(1), su(1), wait(2), inittab(4),
    utmp(4).
```

This example follows the typical format of the UNIX Manual entries.

First, under the heading of NAME, there is the name and a brief description of the command. Next, there is a SYNOPSIS that shows how the command is used:

```
who   [- uTlpdbrtas] [file]
```

This form indicates that the who command has several optional arguments, indicated by the presence of brackets.

Then comes DESCRIPTION. As you can see, the DESCRIPTION presupposes knowledge about the system (such as what /etc/wtmp is), but you can just filter out the parts that don't yet concern you.

Next comes FILES. It contains a list of files used by UNIX to run this particular command.

The SEE ALSO section lists some related commands and utilities. The numbers in parentheses tell which section of the manual contains the description. Thus, who(1) is in the first section and utmp(4) is in the fourth section.

For most UNIX systems, the first section of the User's Manual describes general-purpose commands. It is also the manual that is available on-line. Sections 2 through 5 of the manual usually describe programmers and administrator commands. AT&T documentation uses two terms to distinguish between the manual material and any other material. Any document entitled *Manual* contains manual pages consisting of UNIX commands, and any entitled *Guide* contains text describing some aspect of the UNIX environment.

Other specialized reference manuals are available describing graphics commands and other utilities. Generally, each topic having its own reference manual will also have a guide.

Another good source of information, clearly written with lots of examples, is the *UNIX Bible,* written by Waite, Prata, and Martin, and published by Howard W. Sams & Company in 1987.

man Find Manual Information by Keywords		
Name	**Options**	**Arguments**
man	**Several**	[*section*]

Description:	When used with no argument, the man command searches the entire on-line manual for the section containing the keyword. It then prints a description of the command similar to the printed version of the manual.
Example:	man cat
	This command will display on the screen the on-line manual explanation of the command cat.
	Note: man is usually quite slow in carrying out its service, have patience.
	Note: To keep the screen from scrolling too much information, try using Ctrl-s.

Review Questions

Here are some questions to help you review the important points in this chapter.

1. What are the two modes of mail and when are they used?

2. Which command is used to send a letter?

3. Give a command that will save letter number 2 to a file called jobs.

4. If you see the question mark prompt (?), are you in the command mode or the compose mode of mail?

5. When you have finished reading your mail, how do you leave the program?

6. When you are sending mail, which command calls the vi editor? How do you leave the editor? When you leave the editor, what happens?

7. Why is it important to enter a Subject when you are prompted by mail?

8. How do you send mail to more than one person at a time?

9. What is the help command for the compose mode? for the command mode?

10. When reading mail, why is Reply (R) often preferred to reply (r)?

Answers

1. The command mode and the compose mode. The command mode is used to read mail, and the compose mode is used to send mail. 2. `mail` `loginname`. 3. `s2 jobs`. 4. Command mode to read your mail. 5. `q`. 6. Use `~v` to call the editor. Use Esc `:wq` to leave the editor. You are then back in `mail` compose mode. 7. `mail` can list or search Subject lines. 8. Just add login names after the command `mail`: `mail` `loginname1` `loginname2`. 9. Use `~?` in compose mode and `?` in the command mode. 10. `R` sends responses only to authors, not to carbon holders. It reduces the number of messages sent.

Exercises at the Terminal

1. Send yourself mail, perhaps some reminders of things to do today. When the message that you have mail arrives at your terminal, read the mail and save it in a file called `today`.

2. Try the command `who` to see who is on the system. Choose someone from the list of login names and send that person electronic mail.

3. Send yourself three separate letters. (Each letter could be a short sentence about someone you know.) When the mail arrives at your terminal (maybe ten minutes), use the `s` command to save each letter as a file. (You will use these files in the next chapter.)

4. Send mail to someone you know (or perhaps would like to know).

5. Try the command `who` to see if anyone you know is using a terminal right now. If so, use the `write` command to ask him or her if you can practice sending some mail.

6. Try out the on-line manual. Select a command you already know about. Then experiment using the manual; you can't hurt it. (*Note:* Some systems may not have the `man` command.)

4

Files and Directories:
ls, *cat*, *pg*, and *pr*

Chapter 4

Files and Directories:
ls, *cat*, *pg*, and *pr*

The UNIX file and directory system is wonderfully simple yet versatile. The best way to learn its features is to use them, so we strongly urge you to experiment with the commands we will present, even if you do not need them yet.

You need to know three things to use the file and directory system with ease and understanding. First, you need to know the structure of the system. That will be the first topic of the chapter. Second, you need a way of finding out what files you have; the ls command will help you there. Third, the commands cat and pg will handle the next necessity—seeing what is in the files. These three commands form the core of your relationship with your files.

Of course, it would be nice to have a way to create files, and that will be the subject of Chapters 5 through 8. However, this chapter will give you a head start by showing you a quick and easy way to produce files. (Actually, you already have learned one way—sending mail to yourself!)

That is what is coming up, so let's begin by seeing how UNIX organizes files.

Files and the UNIX Directory System

Files are the heart of the UNIX system. The programs you create, the text you write and edit, the data you acquire, and all the UNIX programs are stored in files. Anything you want the computer to remember for you, you must save in a file. One very important skill to acquire, then, is the ability to create files. But unless you can keep track of your files, it does not do much good to create them. The UNIX directory system is designed to help you with this extremely important task.

Just as a telephone directory contains a list of subscribers, a UNIX directory contains a list of files and subdirectories, each of which can contain lists of more files and subdirectories. Let's look at the most basic example of a directory—the *home directory*.

When you are given an account on the system, you are assigned a home directory. When you log in, you can think of yourself as being "in" your home directory. (Later you will learn to change directories but, for now, let's keep you confined to your home directory.) Now, suppose you create a file. You will have to give it a name. (See the upcoming box on file and directory names.) Suppose you call it ogre. This name will then be added to the list of files in your home directory and, in future instructions, you can refer to the file as ogre. After you have created a few files, you can visualize your home directory as looking like the sketch in Figure 4.1. (We will explain the "branches" and "leaves" in a minute.) Also, you can think of your directory as being your personal filing cabinet and of the files as being labeled file folders.

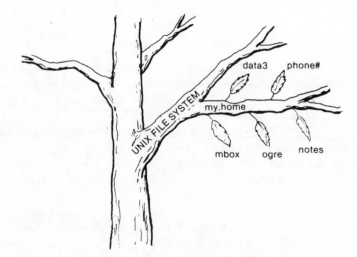

Figure 4.1.   A *home* directory.

Of course, every other user has a home directory, too. Thus UNIX needs a way to tell home directories apart. UNIX accomplishes this by giving your home directory a name, usually your login name. Next, UNIX needs a way of keeping track of all these home directories. It does this with a new directory—a directory of directories. Typically, this directory is called home, and the user home directories are termed subdirectories of home. (Older systems may use the directory name of usr instead of home.) The diagram in Figure 4.2 will help you visualize this. Notice that the home directory in this example contains some files (leaves) as well as directories (branches). In general, any directory can contain both files and subdirectories.

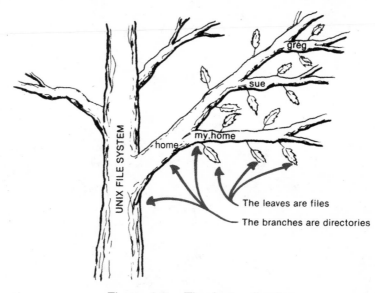

Figure 4.2.   The *home* directory.

Is home the ultimate directory? No, that distinction goes to a directory known informally as root. (Computers are usually not that informal—they insist on /. However, root is easier to say, so we will use that name.) All other directories stem directly or indirectly from root which, of course, is why it is called root. The sketch in Figure 4.3 represents a complete directory system.

The sketch looks a lot like a tree—the directories are the trunk and the branches, and the files are the leaves. For this reason, the UNIX directory system is often described as having a tree structure. (Here the metaphors become a bit confusing, for the root directory is actually the trunk of the tree.)

A different analogy, shown in Figure 4.4, portrays the system as a hierarchy. At the top is the root directory. Serving under root is the next rank of directories: mnt, etc, home, and so on. Each of these, in turn, commands a group of lower-ranking directories, and so on. Figure 4.4 represents the hierarchial view.

The directory system, then, provides structure for the organization of files. It also provides a clear way of specifying the location of a file, and we will explore that in Chapter 9.

What can you do in the UNIX directory system? You can expand it by adding subdirectories (branches) to your home directory and subdirectories to those subdirectories. You can change directories (move to another limb), moving to, say, one of your subdirectories. And, you can place files (leaves) in any directory or subdirectory that you control.

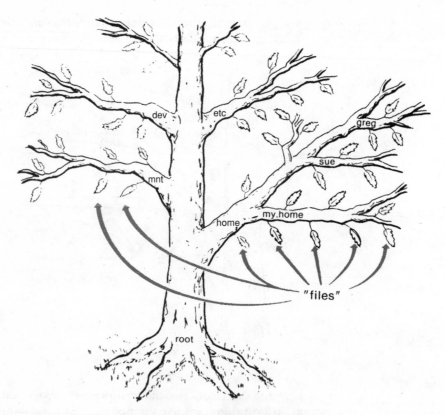

Figure 4.3.   The directory system.

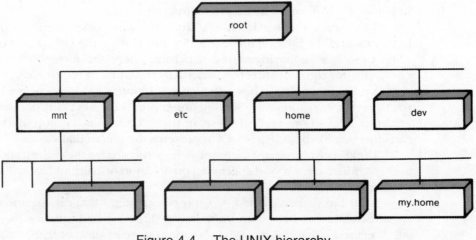

Figure 4.4.   The UNIX hierarchy.

The words file and directory are sometimes used with two different meanings and can create confusion at first. We often talk about the "file system" or the "directory system," where both terms refer to the entire system of files and directories. On the other hand, we say that a file can contain only information; it cannot have directories coming from it. In reality, UNIX has three types of files. There are data files for storing information, directory files for storing the names of data files and other directory files (subdirectories), and device files for storing information about devices such as, printers and terminals. The analogy of the files being like leaves and the directories being like branches of a tree keeps the proper relationship.

Listing Directories: *ls*

The list command (ls) is used to list the contents of a directory. Let's take a hypothetical example and see how this command is used. Sammy Spade is a new student enrolled in a burgeoning computer science course (called cs1) at a very large university. His UNIX login name is sammy, and his instructor has identified his account in the UNIX hierarchy as shown in Figure 4.5. (In this case, a directory other than /home is being used to house the student accounts.)

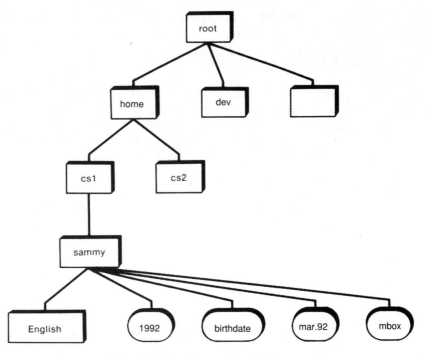

Figure 4.5.   Sammy's directory.

We assume that Sammy is properly logged on and has established contact with the shell as indicated by the $ prompt. At this point, the shell is ready to execute his every command. If Sammy types

```
ls
```

the system will respond with

```
1992  English  birthdate  mar.92  mbox
```

We will list the file and directory names horizontally. Your system might list them vertically.

These are the names of the four files and one subdirectory in Sammy's account. The directory is English, and it is listed along with the files. How can you tell that it is a directory? You can't tell just by looking at this list. Either you have to remember from Figure 4.5 that it is a subdirectory, or else you have to use the -P option (described later). Or, you create directory names beginning with a capital letter.

Well, that first command was pretty simple, and you probably won't need to know more than this at first. But there is more to ls than what you have just seen. For example, you can list the contents of almost any directory, not just your own. And, in the words of one version of the on-line manual, "There is an unbelievable number of options." We will look at some of these options now. If you want to skip ahead, that's okay, but remember to come back to these pages when you need them.

Listing Other Directories

If you type ls with no options, you will get a listing of your *current working directory*. Right now, that would be your login directory but, later, when you learn how to change directories, it will be whatever directory you are currently working in (just like the name says!). To get a listing of files and directories in some other directory, just follow ls with the name of the directory you want to see. For instance, the command

```
ls English
```

would show what is in the directory English. Note that there has to be a space between ls and the directory name. Some directory names are more involved than this example, and you will learn all about that when you get to the section on *pathnames* in Chapter 9.

Some *ls* Options

Option flags are a way of telling UNIX which options you want. (Remember the option flags described for who in Chapter 2?) Use spaces to separate the flag from the command name and from any following arguments. Suppose, for example, that Sammy types

```
ls -s
```

File and Directory Names

UNIX gives you a lot of freedom in naming your files and directories. The name can be over 200 characters long, and you can use almost any character you want. However, you should avoid using characters that have a special meaning to UNIX. In particular, avoid using the characters / \ " ' * ; - ? [ ] ( ) ~ ! $ { } < >. (It is not impossible to use these characters, just inconvenient.) You can use digits as part of a filename with no difficulty. In fact, you can have names like 22 if you wish. However, you should try to make the names as descriptive as possible.

UNIX uses spaces to tell where one command or filename ends and another begins, so you should avoid spaces in names. The usual convention is to use a period or underline mark where you normally would use a space. For example, if you wanted to give the name read me to a file, you could call it read.me or read_me.

Uppercase letters are distinguished from lowercase letters. Thus, fort, Fort, forT, and FORT would be considered four distinct names.

UNIX makes no distinction between names that can be assigned to files and those that can be assigned to directories. Thus, it is possible to have a file and a directory with the same name. The snort directory could contain a file called snort. This doesn't confuse UNIX, but it might confuse you. Some users adopt the convention of beginning directory names with an uppercase letter and beginning filenames with a lowercase letter.

The -s option is a *size* option—it gives the size of the file in blocks. (In our example, the blocks have a size of 1024 bytes.) The UNIX response would look like this:

```
total 17     1 English      1 mar.92
1 1992       13 birthdate    1 mbox
```

Thus, the file birthdate contains 13 blocks, or 13 x 1024 = 13,312 bytes.

The bulkiest and most informative option is the -l, or *long*, option. For Sammy, this option would produce the following listing:

```
total 17
-rw-r--r-- 1 sammy     231 Aug 18 12:34 1992
drwxr-xr-x 2 sammy     112 Aug 29 10:15 English
-rw-r--r-- 1 sammy   13312 Jul 22 16:05 birthdate
-rw-r--r-- 1 sammy      52 Aug 01 17:45 mar.92
-rw-r--r-- 1 sammy     315 Aug 28 09:24 mbox
```

On the first line, total shows the number of blocks used. After that there is one line for each file or directory. The first character in each line indicates whether the entry is a file (shown by -) or a directory (shown by d). Following the file or directory character are several letters and hyphens. These describe *permissions* to read and use files; you'll learn about these when we discuss chmod in Chapter 12. Then comes a numeral that gives the number of *links*; you will find out about links when we examine the ln command in Chapter 9. Next is Sammy's login name. This column tells who "owns" the file. The fourth column gives the actual length of the file in bytes. Then come the date and time that the file was last changed. Finally, there is the filename.

You can use more than one option with the ls command by stringing together the option letters. For example, the following command produces a long listing of all the files revealed by the -a option:

```
ls -la
```

ls	**List Contents of Directory**	
Name	**Options**	**Arguments**
ls	[-a,c,l,p,r,s,R + others]	[*directory...*]

Description:	The ls command lists the contents of each directory named in the argument. The output, which can be a list of both files and subdirectories, is alphabetical. When no argument is given, the current directory is listed.
Options:	-a Lists all entries, including dot entries.
	-c Lists by time of last file change.
	-l Lists in long format, giving links, owner, size in bytes, and time of last file change.
	-p Marks directories with a /.
	-r Reverses the order of the listing.
	-s Gives the size in blocks of 1024 (may vary) bytes.
	-R Also list each subdirectory found.
Example:	ls -c
	This command lists the contents of the current directory in the order that they were created.
Comments:	Remember that directories contain only the names of files and subdirectories. To read information contained in a file, use cat. Note that the option letters for ls may vary from system to system. This is true for many UNIX command options.

Reading Files: *cat*

The cat command is used to *concatenate* and display files. Concatenate means to link together. Some people prefer to think of cat as meaning catalog. It can be used to display the contents of one or more files on the terminal screen. To display the mar.92 file in Sammy's account, you would type

```
cat mar.92
```

The system would then print the contents of the file mar.92. We assume that it looks like the following:

```
      March 1992
  S   M Tu  W Th  F   S
                      1
  2   3  4  5  6  7   8
  9  10 11 12 13 14  15
 16  17 18 19 20 21  22
 23  24 25 26 27 28  29
 30  31
```

As you can see, this file contains a calendar for the month of March. Apparently, Sammy has mastered the cal command (Chapter 2) and has learned how to save the output. (See the discussion of *redirection* later in this chapter.)

AT THE COMPUTER MAGAZINE STAND...

To read the `mbox` file, you would type

```
cat mbox
```

If you make a mistake and type

```
cat box
```

UNIX will respond

```
cat: No such file or directory.
```

cat **Concatenate and Print**		
Name	**Options**	**Arguments**
`cat`	`Several`	`[file...]`
Description:	The `cat` command reads each file in sequence and writes it on the standard output (terminal).	
	If no filename is given or if - (a hyphen) is given as the filename, `cat` reads the standard input (the keyboard). A Ctrl-d will terminate keyboard input.	
	If the file is too large for a single screen, use Ctrl-s to control the file information appearing on the screen, or use the `pg` command described next.	
Options:	Several	
Example:	`cat file2`	
	This will print `file2`.	
Comments:	If no input file is given, `cat` takes its input from the terminal keyboard. Later in this chapter, we show that `cat` and redirection together are very useful. Note that the redirection operator uses the symbol >. You can use `cat > file5` to create a new file called `file5`, and you can enter text into that file. You can use `cat file2 file3 > > file4` to append `file2` and `file3` to the end of `file4`.	

Reading Files with *pg*

The major problem with `cat` is that it won't wait for you. For example, if we assume that the file `1992` is a full twelve-month calendar, there will not be enough room to fit it on the screen. The cat command does not care. It will fill the screen full and then continue adding more information at the bottom of the screen, scrolling the screen upward. The first few months go by too fast to read, let alone reminisce.

There are two ways to handle the problem of screen scrolling. If you have too much information for one screen, you can use Ctrl-s to stop the scrolling and any key to restart it. The second way to handle large amounts of information is to use the pg command.

The pg command is designed to make it easier to look through long files. With it, you can look through a file one screen at a time. If you like, you also can back up and review material that you read earlier. To use pg to read a file, follow the command name with a space and the filename. For instance,

```
pg mbox
```

lets you scan the mbox file. When you give this command, you will see the beginning of the mbox file on the screen. The pg command places a *command line* at the bottom of the screen. This is a line beginning with a colon (:) prompt. When you type a command to pg, your command appears on this line.

Yes, pg has its own repertoire of commands. The most important command is generated just by pressing the Return key. This causes pg to show the next screen of text. By pressing Return repeatedly, you can scan through the entire text of the file. When you reach the end of the file, EOF will display on the command line. Press Return one more times to exit the file.

To scroll back a page, type

```
-1
```

(You do have to press the Return key to complete the command.) As you might guess from this example, -3 takes you back three screens, and +2 takes you ahead two screens.

What happens if you type a number without a sign? Then pg takes you to that particular screen. For example, typing a 6 takes you to the sixth screen of the file.

You can move back and forth a given number of lines or to a certain line number by appending an ell (1) to these commands. For example, +31 advances the screen three lines, and 801 displays the eightieth line at the top of the screen.

If you wish to quit without looking through the entire file, type q on the command line.

The pg command has additional features, but these basic features will take you through the file of your choice.

pg Display a File One Screen at a Time

Name	Options	Arguments
pg	[-, c, s + others]	[*filename(s)*]

Description:	The pg command displays the named file one screen at a time. Commands can be typed on a command line at the bottom of the screen to control what part of the file is displayed. Here is a partial list of commands:
Options:	Return Advance one screen.
	+n Advance n screens (n should be an integer).
	-n Back up n screens (n should be an integer).
	n Go to screen n (n should be an integer).
	+nl Advance n lines (n should be an integer).
	-nl Back up n lines (n should be an integer).
	q Quit.
	The pg command displays EOF on the command line when it reaches the end of the file. Pressing Return at this point causes pg to leave the file.
Options:	-c Home the cursor (place it in the upper left-hand corner) and clear the screen. (May not work with some recalcitrant terminals.)
	-s Print messages and prompts in standout mode (typically reverse video).
Example:	pg myths
	This command lists the contents of the myths file as described previously.

Reading Files with *more*

One of the commands added to Unix System V, Release 4.0 was the BSD command more, a very powerful utility for reading files. To use the more command on the file mbox, type

```
more mbox
```

The mbox file will be displayed and at the bottom of the screen, the words more...44% will be displayed. This means that the screen holds 44% of the file. To display more, try some of these commands:

Key Pressed	Result
Return	Advance the screen one line
d	Advance the screen 11 lines
Spacebar	Advance one full screen (usually 22 lines)
b	Scroll back one full screen
h	Help screen
q	Quit more at any time

All of these commands act instantaneously. They do not require a Return to complete.

Formatting and Printing Files: *pr* and *lp*

The next two commands can be used to format and print files. The commands are pr for print (or format) and lp for line printer. There is a possibility for confusion here because the pr command stands for "print" when it really is a formatting command; while the lp command sends a file to the printer for producing a paper copy. Let's look at the lp command first.

Suppose that you want to print a copy of a file on a printer. It can be any kind of printer—dot-matrix, laser, line, or whatever is connected to your UNIX computer. The format for the lp command is

```
$ lp filename
```

where *filename* is the name of a file in your directory. Usually, the printer must be turned on before you give the command. The lp command has options for selecting different printers, checking printer status, making multiple copies, and so on, and these options are described in Chapter 12.

If you are printing a file that is longer than a single page, the printing will continue right off the bottom of the first page onto the second page and so on (assuming that you are using continuous form paper). For long files, you can improve the appearance of the printed output by formatting it before printing it.

The pr command was created primarily to prepare file information for printing with a line printer. When used without options, the pr command formats text to fit on a page 66 lines long. At the top of the page, it puts a five-line heading consisting of two blank lines, an identifying line, and two more blank lines. At the bottom of the page, it puts five blank lines. For instance, the command

```
pr mbox
```

would produce the following output

← two blank lines

```
Jul 27 19:34 1992 mbox Page 1
```

← two blank lines

```
Hi Beth,
How about...
```

← 56 lines of text, then 5 blank lines

The problem with pr is that it formats a file and displays the file on the screen, not the printer. Here is an example. Suppose that you have a long file called mbox and you use the following commands:

```
$ pr mbox          ← formats mbox, but the output is on the screen

$ lp mbox          ← prints mbox on paper, but not in formatted form
```

How can you get formatted files to the line printer? The solution is to use a UNIX feature called a *pipe*. Pipes are used to direct the output of one command to the input of a second command. The pipe command is a vertical line, either a solid line (|) or a dashed line (¦). You can use the pipe command to direct the output of pr to lp:

```
$ pr mbox ¦ lp     ← format mbox file and pipe it to the printer
```

Note that you must use a space after pr, but you need not use a space before or after the pipe command. Pipes are discussed in more detail in Chapter 11.

pr **Prints Partially Formatted File onto Standard Output**		
Name	**Options**	**Arguments**
pr	**[d,l,p,t,w + others]**	**[*filename(s)*]**
Description:	The pr command prints the named file or files onto the standard output. It divides the text into 66-line pages, placing five blank lines at the bottom of the page and a five-line heading at the top. The heading consists of two blank lines; a line bearing the date, filename, and page number; and two more blank lines.	

Options:	-d	Double-space lines.
	-l*k*	Set page length to *k* lines.
	-p	Pause until Return is pressed before displaying a page.
	-t	Suppress the five-line head and tail.
	-w	Set line width to *k* positions.
Examples:	`pr myths`	

This command prints the file `myths` as just described; the heading would include a line such as

```
May 1 12:29 1992 myths Page 1
```

```
pr -pl20 myths
```

Printing pauses until you press Return, then prints 20 lines and pauses. (*Note:* Release 1.0 of System V did not include the `pg` command. This example provides an alternate way of displaying one screen at a time.)

```
pr myths ¦ lp
```

The file myths is formatted and the output piped to the printer rather than displayed on the terminal.

Creating Files with *cat* and Redirection

Now that you can list files and display the contents of text files, you undoubtedly are eager to create files of your own. After all, that is where the action is! The best way to create files is to use one of the UNIX editors that we discuss in Chapters 5 through 8. However, using the UNIX editors will require some practice. Luckily, you know an easy way to create files without using an editor. You can use cat (a versatile animal) to produce your files.

Suppose you wish to create a file called poem to contain an original composition. Type the following:

```
cat > poem
A bunch of officers
Sat in their tunics
Hoping to learn
more about UNIX
<Ctrl-d>
```

When you type Ctrl-d, your words are funneled into the file poem. To make sure that the procedure worked, type cat poem. Your glorious work will shine again on the screen.

You now can create files, so please go ahead and create some; then you can try out this chapter's commands as you read along. Right now, however, we are going to take a brief side excursion to explain why this last procedure works. If you are eager to move ahead, you can skim through the explanation, but do pay attention to the parts on redirection.

How does this command work? There are two tricks involved. The first trick is that if you don't tell cat which file to look at (that is, if you type cat and press Return without providing a filename), it will look at whatever you type in next on the terminal (see Figure 4.6). Indeed, it considers *your input* to be a file. You can have as many lines and Returns in your file as you like before pressing Ctrl-d. Pressing Ctrl-d tells UNIX that you are done pretending to be a file. The second trick uses the magic of redirection, a UNIX capability that we will discuss fully in Chapter 11. The > is a redirection operator. It takes information that ordinarily would be sent to the screen and channels it to the following file instead. You can remember this easily by seeing that the > character looks like a funnel!

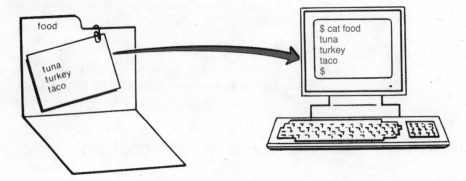

Figure 4.6.   Using *cat* to read a file.

Any command that normally sends output to the screen can be followed by the operator > and a filename. This will cause the output to be sent to a file instead of to the screen. For instance, the following command will place into a file called turkeys all the users who are logged onto the system:

```
who > turkeys
```

Where does this file come from? It is created on the spot! As soon as UNIX sees the redirection operator, it looks at the name following the operator and creates a file by that name.

What if you already have a file by that name? It is *wiped out* and replaced by the new version. As you can see, this is an area in which you should be very careful. A careless command like the preceding example could wipe out your previously existing turkeys file of famous turkeys from history! Note that Chapter 12 outlines ways to protect your files.

Look back at our earlier example of the poem. Notice how the command line (cat > poem) contains all the necessary instructions—where to get the material (the keyboard), what to do with it (cat it), and where to put the results (into the file poem). Of course, this method of creating files does not allow you to make corrections to the file. To gain that ability, you really do need to learn about editors.

Input and Output

Creating files by using the cat command and the redirection operator involves the concepts of input and output. Let's look briefly at what these concepts mean. UNIX deals with at least three different levels of input and output. First, there are input and output *devices* like terminals, printers, and disk storage units. Second, there is the information transmitted through these devices. Depending on its destination, the information is termed either "input" or "output." An interactive system such as UNIX normally accepts input from the keyboard (the characters you type) and sends its output (the characters it produces) to the screen. The keyboard and the screen are termed the *standard input and output devices*.

Third, a command can also have an input and output. For example, cat takes its input from the filename following it, and, normally, it sends its output to the output device, the screen. On the other hand, you don't have to supply date with an input, but it does give you an output. The redirection operators deal with the input to, and the output from, commands.

More on Redirection

Figure 4.7 shows yet another example of redirection. The > operator is a very useful redirection tool. It can be used with any command or program that normally sends output to the screen. For example, the following command first creates the file mar.92 and then executes the cal command:

```
cal 03 1992 > mar.92
```

The output of cal, which is the calendar for March 1992, is placed in the mar.92 file.

Note that > redirects output from a command to a file, not to other commands or programs. For example,

```
poem > cat
```

does not work because poem is not a command.

The command pr poem > lp would not redirect poem to the line printer. It would create a file called lp and put a formatted version of poem there. Notice that you can use pr, redirection, and the line printer as follows:

```
$ pr mbox > mbox.pr     ← formats the mbox file and stores in mbox.pr
$ lp mbox.pr            ← sends a copy of the mbox.pr file to the printer
```

The advantage of redirecting the formatted file before printing is that you can proofread the formatted file first.

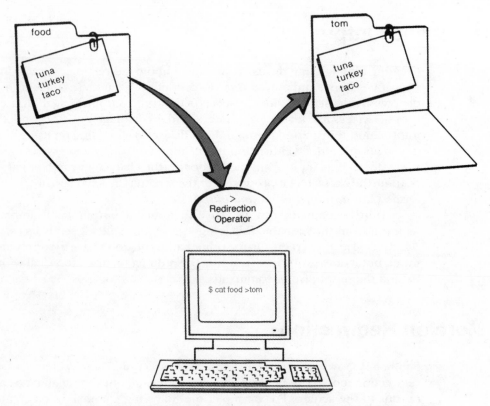

Figure 4.7.   Using *cat* to read a file but redirecting the output into a file named *tom*.

Let's look at one more example of cat and redirection. Assume that you have files called bigbucks and morebucks. What will the following command do?

```
cat bigbucks morebucks > laundry
```

Let's answer the question step by step.

1. What's the input? The files `bigbucks` and `morebucks`.

2. What's the operation? `cat`, or concatenate.

3. What's the output of the operation? The input files printed in succession.

4. What's the output destination? The file `laundry`.

5. What's the final result? The file `laundry` contains combined copies of the files `bigbucks` and `morebucks`.

   Now for one more word of *Caution*: Do not try a command of the form

```
cat bigbucks morebucks > bigbucks
```

You might think this would result in adding the contents of `morebucks` to what was in `bigbucks`. However, the right-hand side of the command begins by erasing `bigbucks` before any concatenating is done. When UNIX gets to the `cat` part, `bigbucks` is already empty!

All in all, `cat` is a pretty useful command. You can use it to see the contents of a file, to create new files, and to make copies of one or more files. And, unlike the domestic variety, the UNIX `cat` obeys instructions! You will learn more about redirecting input and output later in Chapter 11.

Redirection and Electronic Mail

Redirection does not always have to point to the right (>). There are some cases where left-pointing redirection (<) is not only possible, but very desireable. Electronic mail is a good example.

Normally, to send `mail`, you give the command, `mail` *loginname*, and enter the `mail` editor to draft the letter. But suppose that you want to mail an existing file. Do you have to retype it? No. Use redirection. Here is an example:

```
mail michael < schedule
```

This command says send `mail` to `michael`, just as described in Chapter 3, but take the input from the file `schedule`.

UNIX provides two kinds of redirection, one dealing with output > and the other dealing with input <. Let's compare these two operations.

```
who > turkeys
```

says, funnel the output of `who` to the file `turkeys`. Most commands send information to the standard output, the screen. The greater-than symbol, >, redirects this output, usually to a file. The command

```
mail michael < schedule
```

says, funnel the file `schedule` into the `mail` command. Some commands take information from the standard input, the keyboard. The less-than symbol, <, redirects the source of input, usually from a file.

Removing Files with *rm*

In creating files with redirection, you may have created files that you do not want to keep. How do you remove files? Use the *remove* (`rm`) command as follows:

```
$ rm laundry
$ rm poem mbox.pr
```

Caution! The remove command is irreversible. Be sure you know what is in the file before removing it. The `rm` command is described in more detail along with other file-handling commands in Chapter 9.

Review Questions

The basic commands of this chapter will become second nature as you begin to depend on the UNIX file system to help you handle information. Here are some review exercises to give you confidence in using the system and in matching commands to functions.

Match the command in the left column to the corresponding description in the right column.

1. `cat dearsue`

    a.   Prints the contents of a file, one page at a time

2. `pg butter`

    b.   Lists the contents of the present directory

3. `cat story.1 story.2`

    c.   Prints the contents of `story.1` and `story.2` on the screen

4. `ls`

    d.   Displays the contents of the file `dearsue`

5. `who > userlist`

    e.   Places into the file `userlist` a copy of the users presently logged into the system

6. `lpr dearsue`

    f.   Formats a file and sends it to the printer

7. `pr userlist ¦ lp`

    g.   Produces a printed copy of the file `dearsue`

Answers

1—d, 2—a, 3—c, 4—b, 5—e, 6—g, 7—f

Exercises at the Terminal

Even if you have been following the chapter while sitting at a terminal, you might like to try these exercises to illustrate the major commands and to practice their use.

1. List the contents of your home directory.

2. Use both `cat` and `pg` on each file (assuming you have only three or four files to look at).

3. After using a command that works as you expect, try the command again but with an error in it to see what happens. For example, try `lss` or `cat date` or `dates`.

4. Use `cat` and redirection to place a copy of all your files into a new file. Hint: Try `cat a b c d > e`

5. Try to read the file(s) you created in Exercise 4, using `cat` and `pg`.

6. Send mail to yourself using the method shown in Chapter 3.

7. Read your mail and then save any letters in a new file, perhaps calling it `letters1`.

8. Create a file using `cat` and call it `today`. Put in a list of some of the things you have to do today.

9. Make a printed copy of one of your files.

10. Use the `pr` command to format a file and pipe it to the printer.

11. Get a printed list of all the people currently logged into your system.

5

The *vi* Screen Editor

The *vi* Screen Editor

The UNIX editors are the key to creative use of the computer. These editors allow you to create and alter text files that might contain love letters, form letters, sales data, interactive programs, programs in FORTRAN or BASIC, and much more. This chapter and the next chapter introduce the major features of the ex family of editors. The ex family of editors consists of three different editors called ex, edit, and vi. In addition, an old cousin, the ed editor, is available on most UNIX systems. The ex family of editors consists of

ex   A sophisticated line editor (replaces ed)

edit   A slimmed down version of ex, useful for beginners

vi   A visual editor, great for everyday editing

ed   The original standard line editor

A *visual* editor displays a screenful of text and has a cursor that can be moved anywhere in the text. It is much easier to start using than a line editor. A *line* editor does not have a movable cursor. Thus, changes to text must be made by specifying lines and text, as described in Chapter 6.

Many other editors are available on UNIX besides the ex editors. Chapter 8 discusses another editor, the emacs editor.

Introduction to Editing

In the UNIX operating system, everything is stored in files, even the UNIX operating system itself. In Chapters 3 and 4, you learned to place text, data, or programs into files by using either `mail` or redirection (>). The chief problem with those two methods is that the only way to make changes or corrections to a file is to erase the entire file and start over.

The UNIX editors overcome this problem. They let you alter files efficiently and easily, providing you with the basic support you need for most UNIX tasks. This chapter will give an overview of how editors and editor buffers work, and will describe the major features of `vi`. Chapter 6 will take up the `ex` editor.

The Memory Buffer

Files are stored in the system's memory. When you use an editor to work on a file, it leaves the original file undisturbed. The editor creates a copy of the file for you to work with. This copy is kept in a temporary workspace called the *buffer*. The changes you make are made in this copy, not in the original file. If you want to keep the changes you have made, you must replace the original file with your altered copy. This is simple to do. Just give the `w` (*write*) command, and the original file will be replaced by the updated version.

This *buffered* approach has a big advantage. If you really botch your editing job (accidentally deleting a page, for example), you haven't damaged the original file. Just quit the editor using the `q` (quit) command (without using the `w` command). All evidence and effects of your error(s) will disappear, leaving the original file unchanged.

There is, we confess, a disadvantage to this method of operation. Your changes are not saved automatically. *You must remember to write your changes* with the `w` command! If you quit without doing so, your changes are discarded. Most versions of UNIX editors try to jog your memory if you try to quit without writing your changes, but some don't. The failure to save editing changes has led to many an anguished cry and slapped forehead across this great nation. It may even happen to you, but you have been forewarned.

Next, we look at how the editing process works.

Two Modes of Editor Operation

The `ex` and `vi` editors have two basic modes of operation: the *Text Input Mode* and the *Command* (or editing) *Mode*. Figure 5.1 shows an overview of these two modes.

When you first enter an editor, you are placed in the Command Mode. This means that any keyboard entry is interpreted to be a command. In this mode, you can delete a word or a line or change a spelling error. To enter the Text Input Mode, use the `a` (append) command. Now any key entry will be interpreted as text to be stored in the buffer, not as a command. You can enter text representing FORTRAN programs, sales data, chapters in a book, and so on. For each editor there is only one way to leave (exit) the Text Input Mode. Use the Esc key to leave `vi`, or use a period (.) as the first and only character on a line by itself to leave `ex`, as shown in Figure 5.1.

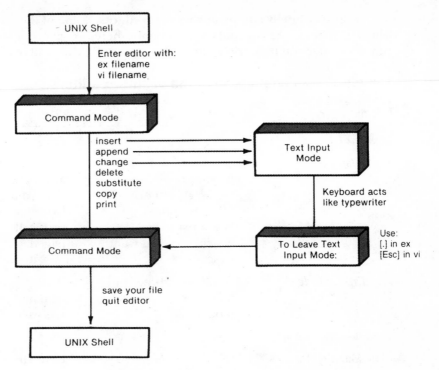

Figure 5.1. Two modes of operation.

If you like what you have written in the Text Input Mode, or what you have modified in the Command Mode, you can save it in memory by using the w (write) command. The w command is quite versatile. You can save the entire buffer or a portion of the buffer by using line numbers. You can also save or write to the existing file (created when you first went into the editor), or you can write to a new file (creating the new file in the process). These saving techniques are almost identical in both UNIX editors. They will be discussed in detail later in the specific sections devoted to each editor.

You might be wondering which editor you should use. The next discussion presents an overview of these two editors and how to use them.

Comparing the Line Editor and the Screen Editor

All UNIX systems running Berkeley UNIX (BSD) or UNIX System V support the ex family of editors. Some UNIX systems support other editors like emacs or ined. Which editor should you use? We recommend that you start with the screen editor, vi, if you generally use a CRT (cathode ray tube) terminal.

Table 5.1 briefly compares these two editors. Some of the terms used in the table might be new to you and the comments, therefore, may not mean much now. However, after you have tried some editing yourself, they will make more sense.

Table 5.1.   A comparison of the *vi* and *ex* editors.

Function	ex	vi
Terminal	tty, crt.	crt.
Text Display	Fair. Instead of displaying a page of a file, in ex you display only lines. You must tell ex which lines you want to see.	Good. In vi you always have a full page of text before you. Text can be scrolled or paged.
Text Input Mode	Good. Has three commands to enter this mode.	Better. Has eleven commands to enter this mode.
Command Mode		
1. Making changes within lines	Cumbersome, since you must type the words you want to replace.	Easy, since you can type over the words you replace.
2. Handling large text files	Somewhat cumbersome.	Easy, since you can scroll and page.
3. Deleting lines	Easy.	Easy.
4. Moving lines around	Easy.	Easy.
5. Global searching and replacing	Easy.	Easy.
6. Saving text	Easy.	Easy.

Note: The last three text editing features use almost identical commands. In fact, from vi you can access all commands in ex simply by prefacing those commands with a colon (:).

The *vi* Editor

The vi editor is an interactive text editor designed to be used with a CRT terminal. It provides a *window* into the file you are editing. This window lets you see about

20 lines of the file at a time, and you can move the window up and down through the file. You can move to any part of any line on the screen and can make changes there. The additions and changes you make to the file are reflected in what you see on the screen. The vi stands for *visual*, and experienced users refer to it as "vee-eye." The vi editor has approximately 100 commands. Because a complete description of so many commands would overwhelm the beginning vi user, our presentation of vi commands is divided into three parts. Each part represents a different level of expertise:

I. Basic Commands to Start Using vi

- Commands to position the cursor: h, j, k, l, and Return
- Commands to enter the Text Input Mode: a, i, o, O
- Commands to leave the Text Input Mode: Esc
- Commands that delete or replace: x, dd, r
- Commands that undo changes: u, U
- Commands to save and quit the editor: ZZ, :w, :q!, :wq
- Commands from the shell for erasing: Del or Ctrl-h or # or Rub, depending on your terminal

II. Additional vi *Commands to Enhance Your Skill*

- Commands to position the cursor including scrolling, paging, and searching: Ctrl-d, Ctrl-f, Ctrl-b, Ctrl-u, e, b, G, *n*G, Ctrl-g, /*pattern*, $, 0
- Commands that will operate on words, sentences, lines, or paragraphs: c, d, y
- Abbreviations for words, sentences, lines, or paragraphs: w, b, e, <, >, 0, $, {, }
- Commands to print storage buffers: p, P
- Joining lines: J

III. Advanced Editing Techniques

- Chapter 7 explains 60 or so additional commands that do more of the same kinds of editing as that described previously. Chapter 7 also explains how to use special features of vi, such as mapping, editing multiple files, and customizing vi.

Starting *vi*

Although vi is a very sophisticated editor with an enormous number of commands, its basic structure is simple. There are two modes of operation: the Command Mode and the Text Input Mode, as shown in Figure 5.2 and on the vi *Start-up Card*.

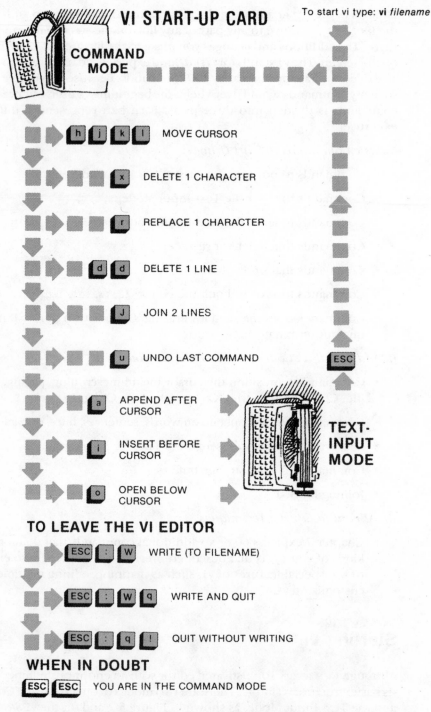

Figure 5.2.   Starting and exiting the *vi* editor.

This section will cover only the minimum number of commands that you need to start using `vi`. Even though these commands are only a few of the many commands available in `vi`, they can handle most of the major editing tasks:

Starting the editor: `vi` *filename*

Cursor positioning: `h`, `j`, `k`, `l`, and Return

Text insertion: `a`, `i`, `o`, `O`

Deletions and changes: `x`, `dd`, `r`

Permanent storage of information: `:wq<Return>`

Note: For most commands in `vi`, you do not have to press the Return key to complete the command. The major exceptions to this rule are commands beginning with a colon (`:`), a slash (`/`), or a question mark (`?`).

The first example shows you how to get into and out of the `vi` editor. You must be in the UNIX shell, as indicated by the shell prompt (`$`). Give the command

$ `vi` *filename* `<Return>` ← *start the editor*

where *filename* is the name of the file that you want to edit. The *filename* may be a file already in your directory; in which case, the file contents are copied into a temporary buffer for editing. If you do *not* have a file by that name, then a new file is created. When you call the `vi` editor, it responds by displaying on the screen the contents of the file, followed by a series of tildes (`~`)—only if the file is less than a screen in length—and, at the bottom of the screen, the name of the file. The editor is now in the Command Mode and the cursor is positioned in the upper left-hand corner of the screen.

To leave `vi`, press the Esc (Escape) key and enter the command

`:wq <Return>` ← *leave the editor*

Remember that `:wq` stands for write and quit. Note that the colon is actually a prompt and will show up at the bottom of the screen.

In using the `vi` editor, any changes, deletions, or additions must be made with reference to the cursor position. So the next question is, "How do you move the cursor?"

Moving the Cursor

The `vi` editor has more than 40 commands to help you position the cursor in the buffer file. In this section we will show you how to get anywhere on the screen (and, therefore, in a text file) by using the five basic keys shown in Figure 5.3. In a later section, "Cursor-Positioning Commands," we will demonstrate many more cursor commands.

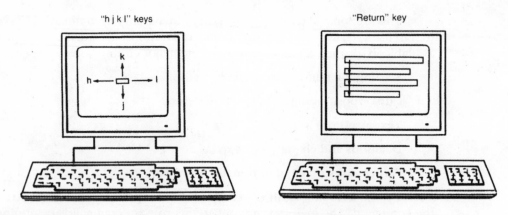

Figure 5.3.   Basic cursor-positioning keys.

Most terminals have arrow keys to move the cursor. However, most experienced typists prefer the *h, j, k,* and *l* keys since they are easier to reach. The Return key is similar to the *j* key in that it moves the cursor down one line. However, the Return key always positions the cursor at the *beginning* of the next line down, whereas, the *j* key moves the cursor straight down from its present position, which could be in the middle of a line.

If you have never tried moving the cursor, you should try it now. It's fun and easy to do. Make sure that you practice moving the cursor on an existing file, since the cursor cannot be moved in a new file that doesn't contain any text. That is, these keys will move the cursor only over lines or characters of text that already exist in a file. Figure 5.4 shows this situation.

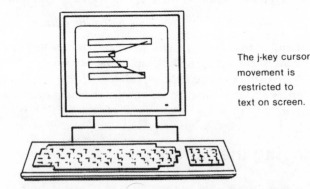

The j-key cursor movement is restricted to text on screen.

Figure 5.4.   Positioning the cursor.

Here is an exercise to give you practice in moving the cursor. You will begin by listing the contents of your directory in order to find a file to practice on. Let's assume that you are logged in and showing the prompt. Here is what you will see:

```
$ ls <Return>          ← list the files in your directory
mbox notes today       ← typical listing
$ vi mbox <Return>     ← you will edit this file
```

The screen now fills up with the contents of the mbox file and/or with tildes (~). Try the following suggestions for moving the cursor:

Use the *j* and *k* keys several times to move the cursor up and down the file.

Now use the *h* and *l* (ell) keys to go left and right on the same line.

Use all four keys to move the cursor to the first ten *e*'s that appear in the text.

Experiment as long as you wish. When you are finished practicing with the cursor, press Esc and enter this next command:

```
<Esc> :q <Return>      ← to quit the editor
```

Note that you used :q to quit (not :wq) to make sure that you did not write any unwanted changes. (If changes were made to the buffer, then the editor will not quit without warning you. Use :q! to force the editor to quit without writing.)

The Text Input Mode

How do you turn the keyboard into a typewriter? Any one of the following four commands will do that:

```
a              for append

i              for insert

o and O        for open
```

The usual way to start a new file is to type vi and follow it with a space and the filename that you want to use. When the editor is ready, type i. Then start typing away as if you were using an electric typewriter. Press the Return key to start a new line. If you make a typing error, you can use Backspace or your regular erase key to back up and correct your error. On some terminals, the erased letters don't disappear from the screen until you type over them, but they are erased from the buffer regardless.

Line Lengths and Wraparound

There is an interesting point about line lengths that may not be obvious to you: The length of a line on the screen may not correspond to its actual length in the editor. The reason is that when you type in text, on most systems the screen will start a new line when you exceed 80 characters or press the Return key (whichever comes first), but the editor will start a new line in your file only when you press Return. Thus, you could type a line of, say, 150 characters before pressing Return. This line would be "wrapped around" on the screen and would look like two lines. However, the editor would count it as just one line. Not only would this throw you off if you were counting lines, but it could produce surprising results when you sent the file to a line printer.

There are three solutions to the problem of lines being too long. The simplest solution is to use the Return key as it is used on a typewriter. As you near the end of a line on the screen, press Return to start a new line.

The second approach to setting line lengths is to ignore them until you finish using `vi`. Then use a text formatter like `pr` or `nroff` to set the line lengths.

The most common solution is to use the `wrapmargin` command to let the editor insert Returns automatically. Suppose you want the right margin to be set 15 spaces from the end of the screen. While in the Command Mode, give the command

```
:set wrapmargin=15
```

or

```
:set wm=15
```

Do not insert any spaces in the command `wm=15`. Now enter the Text Input Mode and try typing some text. When you reach column 65 (that's 80 <MIN> 15), the editor will start a new line, just as if you had pressed the Return key. Actually, the editor is even cleverer than that. If you are in the middle of a word that would take you past column 65, `vi` will move the whole word to the next line. This means that your right margin may not be even, but your lines won`t end with broken-off words.

The `wrapmargin` command will stay in effect until you quit the editor. This command can also be set semipermanently by placing it in a file called `.exrc` as described in Chapter 7.

In this next example, we begin a new file and use the i (insert) command to insert text in it:

```
$ vi ohio <Return>                        ← invoking the editor
i        ← to get into insert mode (this command doesn't show on screen)
What is the capital of Ohio? <Return> ← you type this
Columbus.
<Esc>                                     ← to leave the Text Input Mode
<Esc> :wq <Return>                        ← to leave the editor
```

Now that you have a file called ohio, let's look at ways to add text to it. The following example assumes that you have gone into vi and have moved the cursor to the position shown on the first line:

```
What is the capital ▋f Ohio?
Columbus
```

The cursor is on the letter o in the word of. What happens when you use the four text input commands, a, i, o, and O?

Each command puts you in the Text Input Mode for entering text. You can enter one letter or dozens of lines of text. The major difference between the commands is *where* the new text is entered. For example,

a   Enters whatever you type *after* the cursor, pushing the rest of the line to the right. (On many terminals, you don't see the words pushed over until after you press the Esc key to leave the Text mode. The new text will appear to obliterate the old text while you type, but the old text reappears when you press Esc. See the upcoming box, "Dumb Terminals and Smart Terminals.")

i   Enters whatever you type *before* the cursor, again pushing the rest of the line to the right.

o   Opens up a line *below* the cursor, places the cursor at the beginning of the new line, and enters whatever you type.

O   Like o, except that it opens a line *above* the present cursor position.

Suppose that you try each of the commands just described and enter 33333 from the keyboard. Here is what each command would do to the text:

Example: Using the append command, a

```
What is the capital ▋f Ohio?          ← cursor is on letter o
Columbus
a        ← enter append mode (this command doesn't show on-screen)
```

```
33333                                                 ← type this
<Esc>                                                 ← leave Text Input Mode
What is the capital o33333f Ohio?                     ← here is the result
Columbus
```

Example: Using the insert command, i

```
What is the capital ▋f Ohio?                          ← start with cursor on o
Columbus
i                    ← enter insert mode (this command doesn't show on-screen)
33333                                                 ← type this
<Esc>                                                 ← leave Text Input Mode
What is the capital 33333of Ohio?                     ← here is the result
Columbus
```

Example: Using the open command, o

```
What is the capital ▋f Ohio?                          ← start with cursor on o
Columbus
o                    ← enter open mode (this command doesn't show on-screen)
33333                                                 ← type this
<Esc>                                                 ← leave Text Input Mode
What is the capital of Ohio?                          ← here is the final result
33333
Columbus
```

If you had used the O (Open) command instead of the o (open) command, then the 33333 would have appeared before the first sentence.

Now that you have a changed version of ohio, how can you "clean" it up? To *clean up* is a commonly used expression in a computer environment. It means to make the text or program right; to remove all unnecessary garbage. Unfortunately, there always seems to be a lot of cleaning up to do. This leads to our next set of commands for deleting and changing words and lines.

Deleting and Changing Text

You will find that the next three commands are handy for making small changes to the contents of a file. These commands are: the x command for erasing one character, the r command for replacing one character, and the dd command for deleting one line. All three commands are made from the Command Mode, and all three leave you in the Command Mode after using them. Of course, all three commands use the cursor on the screen as the reference point for making changes.

Dumb Terminals and Smart Terminals

A *dumb terminal* consists of only a keyboard and a monitor. It has no computing power of its own and allows you only to type information into the main computer and to display information presented by the computer. If you are using a dumb terminal to append and insert text in the middle of a line, the new text may appear to write over the old text. However, when you finish inserting or appending with the Esc command, the old text reappears in the right place.

A *smart terminal*—one with its own computing power—does not have this problem. As text is inserted or appended in the middle of a line, the screen shows the correct location of each character at all times.

The `vi` editor can make a dumb terminal appear somewhat smarter by setting the `redraw` option. To set this option, go into Command Mode and give the command

```
:set redraw
```

The `redraw` option, like other options, can be set semipermanently as described in Chapter 7.

The following example uses the old `ohio` file to illustrate these commands. Begin by typing

```
vi ohio
```

The `vi` editor responds by displaying

```
What is the capital o33333f Ohio?
33333
Columbus
~
~          ← the left column is filled with tildes ~ ~ ~
~
~
~
~
~
"ohio" 3 lines, 49 characters
```

The cursor is in the upper left-hand corner on the letter W. Let's eliminate the 3's in o33333f. First use the *l* (ell) key to move the cursor to the first number 3. Then type

    x   *← deletes one character under cursor*

This deletes the first 3 and very conveniently moves the rest of the line to the left. Repeat the process four more times. That is, type

    xxxx   *← repeating the x-deletion four times*

or

    4x   *← another way to repeat the deletion command*

to delete the remaining 3's. The screen should look like this:

```
What is the capital of Ohio?
33333
Columbus
```

The cursor is on the letter f in of. Now, to get rid of the remaining 3's, move the cursor down one line. There are two ways to do this. You can use either the *j* or the Return key. The *j* key moves the cursor straight down. However, since there is no text below the f, the closest point is the last number 3 in the next line.

The Return key would position the cursor at the beginning of the line, on the first 3. Actually, when you want to delete a line, it doesn't matter where in the line the cursor is located. Just type

    dd   *← delete one line*

and the line is deleted. On some terminals, the editor places an @ symbol on the deleted line and moves the cursor down to the next line. It looks like

```
What is the capital of Ohio?
@
Columbus
```

The @ symbol means that the line does not exist in the buffer even though you still see the space it left behind on the screen. Some terminals are "smart" enough to actually remove the line on the screen right after you delete it. The screen is redrawn with the remaining text moved up line by line to replace the deleted line.

Suppose that you wanted to make one last change—you wanted to capitalize each letter in Ohio. First, move the cursor up to the letter h by pushing the *k* key to move up one line and then the *l* key to move to the right. Once you are on the letter h, type the following sequence:

    rH   *← replace character under the cursor with H*

The first letter you typed was r, the replace command. This replaced whatever was under the cursor with the next keystroke, in this case a capital *H*. The cursor remains on H.

In order to replace i with I, move the cursor one letter to the right using the *l* key and type

    rI   ← *replace character under the cursor with* I

Repeat the process and type

    rO   ← *replace character under the cursor with* O

You may think that there ought to be a better way to make these changes. There is. In fact, there are two slightly easier ways, but in order to keep this introduction to vi simple, we have postponed discussion of these until later in the chapter.

Undoing Changes: *u* and *U*

Sometime you will make a change and suddenly wish that you had not made it. When that time comes, you will bless the "undo" commands. As the name implies, these commands undo what you have just done. The u command, which can be given only in the Command Mode, negates the preceding command. If you delete a line with a dd, then typing u will restore it. For example, if you use the i command to insert the word *mush* in a line, then u will remove it. (You must return to the Command Mode to undo.)

The U command is more general. It will undo *all* the changes you have made on the current line. For instance, consider the earlier example in which you used the r command to change Ohio to OHIO. Pressing the u key would undo the last command (which was replacing o with O), restoring OHIO to OHIo. But the U key would undo all the changes, restoring OHIO to Ohio.

The undo command is nice to have around. With it you can practice changing a line and then restore the line to its original pristine condition.

How to Leave the *vi* Editor

Probably the single most frustrating experience you can have with a computer is to lose several hours worth of work. When you are leaving an editor, a single careless command can wipe out your work. Before you leave the editor, ask yourself this question: "Do I want to save the changes made during this editing session?" There are three possible answers: Yes, No, and Maybe.

There are several ways to save information and leave the vi editor. Here is a summary:

Command	What It Does
ZZ	Writes contents of temporary buffer onto disk for permanent storage. Uses the filename that you used to enter vi. Puts you in the shell. *Caution:* ZZ stands for capital *Z*'s. You must type Shift-z (press Shift and type *z*) twice. However, if you accidentally type Ctrl-z, the editing process will probably stop and you will be returned to the UNIX shell. To restart the editor where you left off, type fg.
:wq <Return>	The normal way to leave the editor, writing and saving buffer contents; w stands for write, q stands for quit.
:w <Return>, :q <Return>	Writes the buffer contents to memory and then quits the editor. A two-step version of :wq.
:q! <Return>	Quits the editor and abandons the temporary buffer contents. No changes are made.

All of these commands must be made from the Command Mode. Each will return you to the shell as indicated by the prompt ($). Remember to press Return after entering your command.

To leave the vi editor and save any changes made, it is best to use :wq while in the Command Mode. You could also leave the editor by entering either ZZ or :w Return :q Return.

To leave the editor *without* saving changes, use the :q! command. Normally, you might use this command if you started to edit a file and did not like the way the changes were shaping up. The :q! leaves the original file unchanged and lets you abandon the editor's temporary buffer.

If you are not sure about saving changes, the best step is to save both versions of the file, the original and the changed version. To do this, use the write command with a new filename, for example:

    :w ohio.new

or

    :w ohio2

Thus, if you are editing ohio and make some changes, this command creates a new file under the new name. Here are two common ways to create similar names: add either .new or 2 to the existing name. After creating your new file, the vi editor will provide confirmation:

    "ohio.new" [New file] 2 lines, 39 characters

You can now safely leave the editor with :q or with :q!. The difference between the commands :q! and :q is that :q will leave the editor only if there have been no changes since the last w command. Thus, it provides some protection against accidentally quitting the editor. The command :q! leaves the editor in one step.

Actually, when you are involved in long editing sessions, it is advisable to use the write command every 15 to 20 minutes to update your permanent file copy. Some users use cp to make a copy of a file before editing. This allows them to update their copy every 15 to 20 minutes and still retain the original version. All of these comments about saving text apply equally to all types of files, whether they are programs, data, or text files.

If you have been trying out these commands, you now have the basic skills needed to edit a file. You can create a file with the vi command and insert text with the a, i, o, and O commands. You can delete letters and lines with x and dd and replace letters with r. Rash changes can be undone with u and U. When you are finished, you can save your results and exit the editor. With these basic commands, you are equipped to edit or create short files. Try to practice them, if at all possible, before beginning the next section on additional commands. For your convenience, a tearout reference card at the back of the book summarizes the structure of vi and lists the vi commands.

Additional *vi* Commands

If you need to edit or create short text files once or twice a week, the basic vi command list, discussed in the previous section, will probably be satisfactory for most of your work. However, if you must edit long texts, you may wish for greater editing power, and vi has plenty of power. In this section, we will further explore the magic of the vi editor.

Since cursor positioning in the text buffer is so important, especially in medium-size and long files, we will show you how to place the cursor anywhere in the file with just a few keystrokes. Then we will explore three commands known as *operators* that can make changes to words, lines, sentences, or paragraphs. Two of these operators actually provide you with temporary storage buffers that make relocating lines and paragraphs within a text file very easy to do.

Cursor-Positioning Commands

You have already used five basic keys to position the cursor—the *h, j, k, l*, and Return keys. Now we will add nine more keys and a searching function that will position the cursor easily over any size text file. We will start by considering four keys (*b, e, $, 0*) that are useful in short text files. Then we add four keystrokes (Ctrl-d, Ctrl-u, Ctrl-f, Ctrl-b) that are handy for medium (2 to 10 screen pages) text files. At this point, we will also explain scrolling and paging. Then, we will complete our cursor-positioning repertoire by looking at two commands used to position the cursor in large (10 to 100 or more screen pages) text files. These are the *n*G and */pattern* commands.

The *b, e, $,* and *0* keys have a certain symmetry in their operation. Let's look at them:

b Moves the cursor to the beginning of a word. Each time you push the *b* key, the cursor moves left or *back* to the first letter of the preceding word.

e Moves the cursor to the *end* of a word. Each time you press the *e* key, the cursor moves *right* to the last letter of the next word.

Both the *b* and *e* keys will move to the next line, unlike the *h* and *l* keys, which can move the cursor back and forth only to the end of the line. Figure 5.5 shows the *b* and *e* key operations.

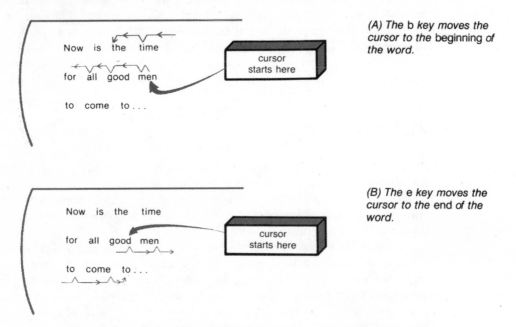

(A) The b key moves the cursor to the beginning of the word.

(B) The e key moves the cursor to the end of the word.

Figure 5.5.   Using the *b* and *e* keys to move the cursor.

The *0* (zero) and *$* keys move the cursor to the beginning and end of a *line* (rather than a word) as follows:

0 (Zero) Moves the cursor to the *beginning* of the line.

$ Moves the cursor to the *end* of the line.

These two keys can be used only on the line containing the cursor. The cursor does not jump to the next line as it does with the *b* and *e* key commands. Recall that the Return key will jump lines and is similar to the sequence *j, 0*. Figure 5.6 shows the *0* and *$* operations.

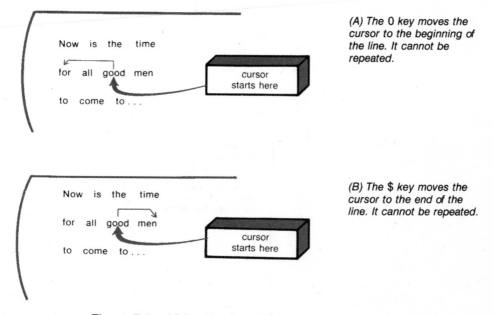

(A) The 0 key moves the cursor to the beginning of the line. It cannot be repeated.

(B) The $ key moves the cursor to the end of the line. It cannot be repeated.

Figure 5.6.   Using the *0* and *$* keys to move the cursor.

Screen Scrolling and Paging

Sometimes there is more text in the buffer than can fit on the screen at one time. When this happens, you may have noticed that you can bring more text into view by trying to move the cursor past the bottom (or top) of the screen. The cursor stays put, but a new line moves up (or down) into view. This is called *scrolling*. Until now you have accomplished scrolling by using five cursor-positioning keys: *b, e, j, k*, and Return. These keys scroll the screen only one line at a time. Soon we will introduce four new keys that scroll multiple lines.

To visualize scrolling, imagine that the text is arranged on one long continuous page (like a scroll) and that only a portion of it appears on the screen at any particular time. Your CRT screen, then, is like a window into the text, usually showing 24 text lines with 80 characters per line (see Figure 5.7). Imagine that the window moves while the text remains fixed.

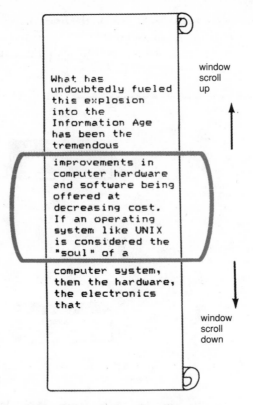

Figure 5.7.   Scrolling.

The direction of scrolling usually refers to the direction that the window moves past the text. For example, when you give the command to scroll down, the window moves downward and the text below the original window comes into view. When you scroll up, you "push" the window up, revealing portions of the text that precede the text in the original window location.

Different terminals will behave differently, even though the same vi commands are used. Some terminals can scroll down but not up. If a terminal cannot scroll up, then it must page up. *Paging* means that the screen is completely erased and redrawn in a new position. Paging has the same end effect as scrolling 24 lines, but the process is different.

The cursor-positioning keys *b, e, j, k*, and Return will generally page or scroll the screen one line at a time. However, since a screen usually contains 24 lines, moving the text one line at a time in a large text file is unnecessary and time consuming. The vi editor has four handy scrolling (or paging) commands that solve this problem. They are the commands Ctrl-u, Ctrl-f, Ctrl-b, and Ctrl-d. Recall that to get a Ctrl-d, you hold down the Ctrl key and press the *d* key once.

Here is a summary of these four cursor-positioning keys:

Ctrl-d   Scrolls or pages the cursor *down*, usually 12 lines at a time.

Ctrl-f   Scrolls or pages the cursor *forward*, usually 24 lines at a time.

Ctrl-u   Scrolls or pages the cursor *up*, usually 12 lines at a time.

Ctrl-b   Scrolls or pages the cursor *back*, usually 24 lines at a time.

Most users generally prefer scrolling to paging, since it is easier to follow the positioning of the cursor in the text file as the file moves up or down. Recall that paging erases the screen and redraws it, so you cannot follow the cursor to its final position.

If you have really long text files, even several Ctrl-f keyings can take too long. For example, this chapter contains about 1400 lines of text. You would have to press Ctrl-f over 50 times to reach the end of the file. Fortunately, there is an easier way. The command

```
nG
```

where *n* is an integer number that will place the cursor on the line number *n*. Thus, to move to line 1400, type

```
1400G
```

A similar command is the G command (capital *G*), which moves the cursor to the end of the file. Thus, if you type

```
G
```

while in Command Mode, the cursor is positioned at the end of the file. To get to the beginning of the file, tell the editor that you want the first line; that is, type

```
1G
```

One very useful command related to the *n*G command is the Ctrl-g command, which tells you the line number that the cursor is currently on. This is valuable in two ways. First, if you remember the number or write it down, you can come back to the spot later. Second, if you want to copy a portion of a file, Ctrl-g can be used to get the beginning and ending line numbers of the section. You can then save the section by using the write command with line numbers. The write command would look like this:

```
:120,230w chapter4.2b <Return>
```

This command copies lines 120 to 230 and places them in a newly created file called chapter4.2b. If a file already exists with that name, the w command either destroys the file or does not work, depending on your particular version of vi.

Pattern Searches

Another way to position the cursor in the file is to give the editor a word or string of characters to search for. If you are in the vi command mode, you can type the character /, followed by a string of characters that are terminated by a Return. The editor will position the cursor at the first occurrence of this string after the cursor. For example, if you want to find the words *happy day*, just give the command

```
/happy day <Return>
```

If the first occurrence of happy day was not the one you wanted, you can move to the next occurrence by typing n for next. These searches will wrap around the end of the file and return to the beginning, continuing the process as long as you type n.

If you prefer to search backward through the file instead of forward, use the ? command. Thus, the following command will start from the current cursor location and search backward through your file for the word *malodorous*:

```
?malodorous <Return>
```

Again, the ? command will continue the search for the next preceding example. The search will wrap around to the end of the file when you reach the top. To repeat backward searches, use the n command.

Once you have the cursor where you want it, you are ready to make changes, move text around, or add new text to the file. We will look at these activities next.

Operators That Delete, Duplicate, Change, and Rearrange Text

In the discussion of basic vi commands, you learned how to delete a line using the command dd. This delete command is actually made up of two parts: the delete operator (d) and the operator's scope (the line to be deleted is symbolized by another d). The command dw uses the delete operator d, but has as its scope a word as defined by the cursor and symbolized by w. We can represent these types of commands as follows:

Operator + Scope = Command

In this section we will discuss three operators and nine scopes. The operators are the *delete, change*, and *yank* operators. They can operate with the following scopes: words, lines, sentences, and paragraphs. We will then use the commands formed by these operators to delete, duplicate, change, and rearrange text. Sometimes, these kinds of changes are referred to as "cut and paste," describing the old-fashioned changes made with scissors and glue. This electronic version of cut and paste is more powerful, however, since you can "cut" more precisely and can make multiple copies for pasting.

Tables 5.2 and 5.3 summarize the three operators and their scopes. (The *put* command is included because it teams up with the yank and the delete commands.)

Table 5.2. The *vi* operators.

Command	Operator
d	*Delete* operator. Deletes text but stores a copy in a temporary memory buffer. The copy can be recovered by using the *put* command, p.
y	*Yank* operator. Places a copy of text (word, sentence, line, and paragraph) into a temporary memory storage buffer for positioning elsewhere. The original text is left unchanged. The copy is "pasted" relative to the cursor position using the *put* command, p.
p	*Put* command. Works with the yank and delete commands. Puts whatever was last deleted or yanked in place after or below the cursor.
c	*Change* operator. Equivalent to a delete operation and an insert command. Deletes a word, sentence, etc., and enters the Text Input Mode to allow changes to be typed in. You must end the command with an Esc.

Table 5.3. Scopes of the *vi* operators.

Scope	Operation
e	The scope is from the cursor to the *end* of the current word. For example, if the cursor is on the *u* in *current* and you type *de*, then *urrent* is deleted.
w	The scope is from the cursor to the beginning of the next *word*, including the space.
b	The scope is from the letter before the cursor backward or to the *beginning* of the word.
$	The scope is from the cursor to the end of the line.
0	The scope is from just before the cursor to the beginning of the line.
)	The scope is from the cursor to the beginning of the next sentence. A sentence is ended by ., !, or ? followed by either an "end of line" (provided by the Return key) or two spaces.
(	The scope is from just before the cursor back to the beginning of the sentence containing the cursor.
}	The scope is from the cursor to the end of a paragraph. A paragraph begins after an empty line.
{	The scope is from just before the cursor back to the beginning of a paragraph.

In Table 5.2 you might have noticed that there is no symbol for a whole line. The creators of vi decided that since an operation on a whole line is done so often, the easiest way to do it would be to press the operator key twice. Thus, dd, cc, and yy are commands affecting the whole line.

Of course, to appreciate the commands formed by these operators and their scopes, you need to practice them. The next three sections give you practice in using the delete, change, and yank operators and the put command.

The Delete Operator, *d*

The delete operator is easiest to visualize, since it is a one-step process. Consider the short line:

```
The sky opened up. Morning awoke.
```

Assume that the cursor is on n in opened. Using various scopes, practice the following deletions, as shown.

```
The sky opened up. Morning awoke.     ← de deletes to end of word
The sky opened up. Morning awoke.     ← dw deletes to next word
The sky opened up. Morning awoke.     ← 2dw deletes two words (a period
                                          is a word)
The sky opened up. Morning awoke.     ← db deletes to beginning of word
The sky opened up. Morning awoke.     ← d0 deletes to beginning of the line
The sky opened up. Morning awoke.     ← d) deletes to beginning of next
                                          sentence
```

To delete the entire line, type

```
dd
```

The line will disappear.

A fun way to practice these deletions is to use the undo command, u. Since the u command *undoes* the last command, you can easily try one of the deletions just described and then use the u command to return to the starting point. Here is an example. Assume you have the text

```
123 456 789. ABC.
```

The cursor is on 5. Type dw to delete 56 and the following space. Then type u to get back the original text. It would look like this:

```
123 456 789. ABC.
123 4789. ABC.                        ← type dw to get this
123 456 789. ABC.                     ← type u to get this
```

For fun, you can type u again, and undo your undo!

All of the delete operations and the undo commands are used in the Command Mode and they keep you in that mode. Now, let's consider the change operator.

The Change Operator, *c*

The change operator, c, can use the same scopes as the delete operator, d. In fact, the change operator deletes the same characters as the delete operator. The difference between the two operators is that the change operator places you in the Text Input Mode. You then can use the keyboard as a typewriter and can enter as much text as you like. Existing text moves to the right and wraps around as necessary to make room for your text insertion. You leave the Text Input Mode just as always by using the Esc key. Some versions of vi include a marker with the change operation. It marks the last character to be deleted using the $ symbol. Here is an example of a small change being made. Suppose you are in the vi command mode and have the following text on the screen with the cursor on 6:

```
1234. 5678. 90.
```

You now type

```
cw
```

and the editor deletes to the end of the *word* leaving the result:

```
1234. 567$. 90.
```

Notice that the final character scheduled for replacement (8), is replaced by $. The cursor is still on the 6, the first character scheduled for replacement. Now, if you type

```
Helloooo! <Esc>
```

you will get

```
1234. 5Helloooo!. 90.
```

The cw command lets you change everything from the cursor to the end of the word. The other change commands, c), c}, and so on, operate similarly, but with different scopes. If you do not want to change or delete text but just want to make a copy elsewhere, then the yank operator and the put command are what you need.

Using the Yank and Delete Operators with the Put Command

You can use *delete* (d) and *put* (p) commands to move text around in a file. Both the *yank* (y) and put commands, on the other hand, are ideal for *copying* and moving text. The nine scopes allow you to precisely mark various parts of words, lines, sentences, and paragraphs. The yank and delete commands store these pieces of text in a temporary buffer that can be copied onto the screen with a put command. As usual, the commands are made with respect to the position of the cursor. As far as the put command is concerned, yank and delete work identically. The difference to you is that yank leaves the original text unchanged, while delete removes it.

Here is an example using y. Assume that you are in the vi Command Mode with the following text on the screen and the cursor on 6:

```
1234. 56789.
```

If you type

    y$ ← *yank (a copy) to end of line*

you will have stored a copy of 6789. in the temporary buffer. You can now move the cursor to another position (for example, at the end of the line) and type

    p   ← *print last yank or delete*

This *puts* a copy of the buffer contents immediately after the cursor as in an append command. The result would look like this:

```
1234. 56789. 6789.
```

You might be wondering if the p command empties the buffer or if the buffer contents can be reused. You can, in fact, use the buffer contents repeatedly to *put* down as many copies as you like. The only way to change the buffer's contents is to yank or to delete something else. The new text then replaces the old yank contents.

The fact that the delete command and the yank command have to share the same buffer seems to be a problem. Also, suppose that you wanted to save some text for longer periods of time in an editing session. How could you do it? You might think that there should be more buffers for temporary storage! In fact, there are, and this is the subject of the next section.

Deleting, Duplicating, and Rearranging Text Using Temporary Buffers

As we explained earlier in the chapter, when you wish to edit an existing file, a copy of that file is brought from memory to the editor buffer. The use of memory buffers is so convenient that the vi editor actually has over 30 such temporary memory areas that are used for duplicating, rearranging, and temporarily storing text. In addition, if you accidentally delete lines of text, you can recover not only the last deletion made but the eight previous ones as well. These deletions are stored in a set of temporary buffers numbered 1 to 9. You can get the nth previous block of deleted text back into your file by using the command `"np`. (The double quotes alert the editor that you are about to give the name of a buffer.) This command will place text after the cursor. A similar put command is `P`, which places the buffer contents before the cursor. Thus, the command

    "1p

recovers the last deletion made and puts it *after* the cursor, and the command

    "1P

places the last deletion *before* the cursor.

The *undo* (`u`) command is especially helpful if you want to search any of deletion buffers 1 through 9. For example, you can display the contents of buffer number 4 by commanding

    "4p

If you do not want to keep the buffer contents, type

    u

You could repeat this procedure to take a quick look at several buffers.

Using buffers 1 through 9 to save, duplicate, and rearrange text has a drawback. The drawback is that buffer 1 always has the last deletion made. Thus, if you move some text and then make a deletion, the contents of the buffers change. If you plan to move or copy text, it is better to use a set of buffers that are unchanged by the ordinary delete operations. There is such a set, and the members are named with alphabetic letters from *a* to *z*. To use these buffers, you precede the delete operation with the name of the buffer in which the text is to be stored. Again, you need to use double quotes (`"`) to inform the editor that you are using a buffer name. For example, the command

    "c5dd

will delete five lines and store them in buffer `c`. These lines can be put back in their same place or in several places in the file by using the put commands, `p` and `P`, as follows:

    "cp

This command will put the contents of buffer `c` after the cursor. You can move the cursor and repeat the command to place additional copies of buffer `c` anywhere in the file.

These alphabetically labeled buffers will also store your yank contents if you wish to just copy and store information. The commands are used identically. Consider the next example. Assume that you have the following text on the screen and that the cursor is on the line Bountiful Beauties:

```
Ancient Adages
Bountiful Beauties
Credulous Cretins
Diabolic Dingos
```

Now type

```
"fdd
```

The editor deletes the line containing the cursor and stores the contents in a buffer labeled f, leaving on the screen

```
Ancient Adages
Credulous Cretins
Diabolic Dingos
```

If you then move the cursor to the bottom line and type

```
"fp
```

you will see on your screen the contents that are stored in buffer f:

```
Ancient Adages
Credulous Cretins
Diabolic Dingos
Bountiful Beauties
```

Now, if you were to start with the same original text, but substitute yy for dd, the screen would display

```
Ancient Adages
Bountiful Beauties
Credulous Cretins
Diabolic Dingos
Bountiful Beauties
```

As you can see, the yank command leaves the original text (the second line) in its place, while letting you place a copy elsewhere.

Just as before, the delete and yank commands share storage buffers for saving deleted or copied text. The text stored in buffer f ("f) will remain in the buffer until new text is placed there or until you leave the vi editor. Thus, these buffers are extremely helpful for rearranging text.

These delete and yank commands may be repeated by using commands like

```
"g7yy
```

which copies seven lines of text and stores them in buffer g.

Moving Larger Blocks

You can extend the range of these operator-scope combinations by prefixing the command with a number. The number specifies the *number* of lines, words, sentences, and paragraphs that you wish affected. For example,

    20dd

would delete twenty lines, and the command

    5cw

would let you change five words. If you use this last command, a $ will appear in place of the last character of the fifth word, so that you can see which words would be replaced. You are free, of course, to replace the five words with one, two, seven, or any number of words.

If you want to move large blocks of material, you probably will find it more convenient to use the co and the m commands of the ex editor. You don't have to change editors to do this because these commands are available from vi. We will show you how to get to ex commands shortly.

Joining and Breaking Lines

All of these cutting and pasting operations can leave the text on the screen somewhat messy looking. How can you clean it up? (That is, how can you even out the line lengths?) There are three major ways to join sentences together. The slowest way is to retype the lines leaving out the blanks. A much easier way is to use the J command in vi. The J command joins the next line down to the current line. For example, if you are in vi and have four short sentences, each on a separate line, you can place the cursor on the top line and type

    J   ← *join the next line down to the current line*

three times. This would join the sentences on the same line and wrap them around the screen, as shown in Figure 5.8. However, the computer now sees this as one line.

If you wind up with lines that are too long, just insert a Return where you wish to break the line. You can do this most easily by placing the cursor on the space where you wish to make the break and then using the r command to replace the space with a Return. You can reshape your line lengths to suit yourself by using this and the J command.

The third way to clean up text is to use one of the text-formatting utilities discussed briefly at the end of Chapter 6 and more fully in Chapter 13. We will conclude this long chapter by mentioning some additional commands that are available in vi and by providing a vi summary.

Start	Finish
The tall man strolls away.	The tall man strolls away. An alarm
An alarm sounds.	sounds. RUN! A dead end.
RUN!	*Sentences joined and wrapped around.*
A dead end.	
Four short sentences.	

Figure 5.8.   Joining sentences.

Additional Commands and Features of *vi*

The commands you have learned so far will probably meet most of your editing needs. However, vi has some additional commands, as well as some special features, that we will touch on here. (For detailed information on using these commands and features, see Chapter 7.)

With vi's special features, you can

• Specify your terminal type.

• Adjust the screen size.

• Adjust indentation, tabs, and wrap margin settings.

• Use macros and abbreviations to simplify a complex operation or a long keystroke entry.

• Edit two or more files at the same time.

• Use ex-like commands.

The last feature deserves further mention, especially since we have already used it several times without telling you. To use an ex command, enter the Command Mode and then press the : key. You will see the prompt : at the bottom of the screen. Now you can give any of the commands listed for ex in Chapter 6. Note that ex commands require a Return key. As soon as the command is executed, you are returned to the standard vi Command Mode.

If you prefer a longer stay in the ex line editor, you can give the Q command while in the vi Command Mode. This, too, will give you a : prompt at the bottom of your screen, but you will stay in the ex mode until you type vi to return.

The examples that we have used so far have involved the write commands (such as `:w` and `:120,230w chapter4.2b`) and the quit commands (`:q`, `:wq`, and `:q!`). Of the other `ex` commands available, the most useful are those that let you deal with large blocks of material. Two important examples are the copy command, `co`, and the move command, `m`. These perform the same tasks as delete-and-put and yank-and-put, respectively, but they work only on entire lines. For example, the command

```
:20,300m500
```

will move lines 20 through 300 to just after line 500. The command

```
:20,300co500
```

places a copy of lines 20 through 300 just after line 500, but leaves original lines 20 through 300 in place.

Another very useful `ex` command is the global search-and-replace command. For example, the command

```
:g/e/s//#/g
```

will find every `e` in the file and replace it with a `#`. (See Chapter 7 for a complete description of global search and replace commands.) Try it; it is visually stimulating. Just remember that you can undo this change with the `u` command. For more details on the preceding commands, see Chapter 6 on `ex`.

The `vi` editor also has a read-only option that is called up by typing `view` instead of `vi`. This is useful if you want to use the cursor-positioning keys to read text without worrying about accidentally adding or changing the file. Of course, you can do the same thing by leaving `vi` with the `:q!` command. This command quits `vi` without writing any changes made.

A Summary of the *vi* Screen Editor

The `vi` screen editor has an abundant set of commands rivaling the best word processing software in terms of flexibility and power. However, you don't have to be an expert at word processing to use `vi`. It can also be used by the beginning user who limits his or her commands to a few basic commands. It is very important to remember that `vi` has two modes of operation—the Command Mode and the Text Input Mode (see Figure 5.9). A point to remember about the Command Mode is that most of the commands are used to position the cursor or to find text. The rest of the commands either delete something or place you in the Text Input Mode. The upcoming box summarizes the various keys, commands, operators, and scopes used in `vi`.

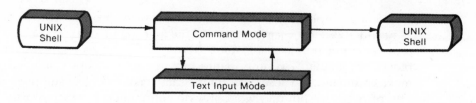

Figure 5.9. The *vi* modes of operation.

vi Screen-Oriented Text Editor

Cursor-Positioning Keys in the Command Mode

b   Moves cursor one character to the left.

j   Moves cursor down one line anywhere in text.

k   Moves cursor up one line anywhere in text.

l   Moves cursor one character to the right.

Return   Moves cursor down to beginning of next line.

Commands to Enter the Text Input Mode

Note: End this mode with Esc.

a   Appends text after the cursor. You can type as many lines and Returns as you wish.

i   Inserts text before the cursor. You can insert as many lines of text and Returns as you wish.

o   Opens a new line below the cursor, ready for your text input.

O   Opens a new line above the cursor, ready for your text input.

R   Replaces characters on the screen, starting at the cursor, with any characters you type.

Commands from the Command Mode

Note: After execution, these commands return you to the command mode.

r   Replaces a single character under the cursor with a single character that you type.

/happy   Search sequence. Looks for next occurrence of pattern following /; in this case, the word happy.

?Lark	Search sequence. Like /, but searches backward from the cursor.
n	Used after / or ? to advance to the next occurrence in the buffer of the pattern.
u	Undoes the last command.
U	Undoes all the changes on the current line.
x	Deletes character under the cursor.
Del or # or Ctrl-h or Rub	This backspace feature of the shell also works in the editor. These commands move the cursor character by character leftward within a line, erasing each character from the buffer.
Ctrl-f Ctrl-b	Scrolls or pages the screen forward or back, one page at a time.
Ctrl-d Ctrl-u	Scrolls or pages the screen down or up, one-half page at a time.
*n*G	Positions the cursor at line *n* in the files.
Ctrl-g	Identifies the line where the cursor is located by giving the line number.

Operators in the Command Mode

d	Deletes indicated text starting at the cursor. For example, use dw to delete a word and dd to delete a line; 3dd deletes three lines. Deleted text is stored temporarily in a buffer whose contents can be printed with the p command. Also, d can be used with named buffers in the manner described for y.
c	Deletes indicated text starting at the cursor and enters the Text Input Mode. Thus, cw deletes from the cursor to the *end* of the word, allowing you to add text between those positions.
y	Copies indicated text, starting at the cursor, and stores it in a buffer. There are 9 unnamed buffers (1–9) that store the last nine delete or yank operations and 26 named buffers (*a–z*) that can be used for storage. A double quote (") is used to tell the editor the name of the buffer. Thus, "cy$ will store text from the cursor to the end of the line in a buffer named c.

p	The put command. Used to put down delete-and-yank buffer contents after the cursor or on the next line. Command p puts the last item yanked or deleted back into the file just after the cursor, and "cp will put the contents of buffer c after the cursor.
P	The put command. Identical to p, except that it places the buffer contents before the cursor.

Scopes for Use with Operators

e	The scope from the cursor to the *end* of the current word. For example, if the cursor is on the *u* in *current*, and you type *de*, then *urrent* is deleted.
w	The scope is from the cursor to the beginning of the next *word*, including the space.
b	The scope is from the letter before the cursor, backward, to the *beginning* of the word.
$	The scope is from the cursor to the end of the line.
0	The scope is from just before the cursor to the beginning of the line.
)	The scope is from the cursor to the beginning of the next sentence. A sentence is ended by ., !, or ? and followed by an "end of line" (provided by the Return key) or by two spaces.
(	The scope is from just before the cursor backward to the beginning of the sentence containing the cursor.
}	The scope is from the cursor to the end of a paragraph. A paragraph begins after an empty line.
{	The scope is from just before the cursor backward to the beginning of a paragraph.

Leaving the *vi* Editor

:w	Writes the contents of the buffer into the current file of the same name. Can be given a new filename to write to. Also, can send partial buffer contents using line numbers, such as :3,10w popcorn.
:q	Quits buffer after the command :w.
:wq	Writes and quits, placing buffer contents in file.
:q!	Quits buffer without making changes in file. Dangerous.
ZZ	Writes and quits, placing buffer contents in file.

Using the *ex* Editor While in *vi*	
:	Gives a colon (:) prompt at the bottom of the screen and lets you make one ex command. Requires a Return key. You are returned to the vi mode when the command finishes execution.
Q	Quits vi and places you in the ex editor, giving you a Command Mode prompt—the colon (:)—at the bottom of the screen. You can return to vi by typing the command vi while in the Command Mode.
When in Doubt	
Esc	Puts you in the Command Mode.

Review Questions

A. Matching Commands

Match the commands shown on the left to the functions shown on the right. Assume that all the commands are given in the Command Mode only; none are given from the Text Input Mode.

1. 35G	a.	Scrolls screen down one-half page
2. 3yw	b.	Moves cursor down one line
3. r2	c.	Stores four lines in buffer c
4. /fun	d.	Prints line number of the current line
5. Ctrl-g	e.	Moves cursor to left one character
6. 2dd	f.	Replaces character under cursor with number 2
7. j	g.	Yanks three words
8. "c4dd	h.	Deletes two lines
9. Ctrl-d	i.	Puts cursor on line 35
10. h	j.	Finds the word fun

B. Questions

1. When you invoke the editor with a file, that is, when you type `vi file3`, how can you tell whether it is a new file?

2. What four commands put you into the Text Input Mode?

3. When you first enter the editor with an existing file and type `a` (the append command to add text), where is that text placed?

4. Which command is used to save the editor buffer contents?

5. Where does the insert command `i` place new text?

6. What is the command that will save the first three lines only of an editor buffer containing seven lines of text? Write the command.

7. How do you exit the Text Input Mode?

8. What is the command(s) needed to correct the following misspelled word, sometome? Write the command(s).

9. What is the command(s) needed to delete the last five lines in ten lines of text? Write the command.

Answers

A. 1—i, 2—g, 3—f, 4—j, 5—d, 6—h, 7—b, 8—c, 9—a, 10—e
B. 1. The left column of the screen fills with tildes (~). 2. The commands a, i, o, O.
3. After the cursor. 4. `:w` to write and `:wq` to write and quit. 5. Before the cursor. 6.
`:1,3w` *filename*. 7. Use Esc. 8. Position the cursor over o and type `ri`. 9. Position the
cursor on the first line to be deleted and type `5dd`.

Exercises at the Terminal

Here are some exercises to practice your editing techniques. You can use either the vi or the ex editor.

1. Enter the following text into a new file called `letterrec1`.

```
Dear Sir:

This is a letter of recommendation for john doe.
john doe is a good worker.
john doe has a find character.
john doe is a-ok.

sincerely
jane doe
```

2. Now, do the following:

    a. Save the letter with the `:w` command.

    b. Correct all spelling errors.

    c. Capitalize `jane`, `john`, and `doe`.

    d. Delete the last sentence containing `a-ok`.

    e. Save the corrected letter as `letterrec2`. (Use the `w` command.)

    f. Leave the editor with the `:q` command.

    g. Use `cat` to print both copies on the screen at the same time.

3. Go into the shell; list your files with `ls` and make a copy of one of your files, for example, `mbox`, calling it `mbox2` or something similar.

4. Invoke the editor with the copy of the file you made in Exercise 3 and do the following:

    a. Insert somewhere the line `This is a test.`.

    b. Move three lines using the buffer method.

    c. Find all occurrences of the word `the`, using the search operator (`/`).

    d. Copy two lines and place them in the beginning of the file.

    e. Use the command `cw` to change `the` to `thy`.

    f. Use the command `4dw` to delete four words.

6

The *ex* Line Editor

The *ex* Line Editor

The ex line editor is the standard UNIX editor. Even if you plan to do all of your editing in vi, which most people do, it is a good idea to learn the basic operation of ex. The vi editor is a subset of ex, and much of its power is derived from ex.

The ex editor is called a *line editor* because most operations are referenced to lines (vi uses the cursor as a reference point). The line-referencing system makes ex good for moving or copying large blocks of text and for making global search and replace operations. A third editor, called edit, is also a line editor and is a subset of the ex editor.

All of the commands in this chapter apply equally well to the two line editors, ex and edit. The major difference between these editors is that edit lacks some of the features of ex.

We will be using ex throughout this chapter. However, if you have a knack for getting into strange places, feel free to substitute edit for ex. The two principal advantages of ex over edit are that you can move from ex to vi and back again, and that ex has more abbreviations that can be used for text searches.

We will begin this section by describing how you get into and out of the editor. Then the format for issuing commands in ex will be discussed. After that, we present examples of how to input and edit text. This chapter concludes with an ex command summary.

Calling the *ex* Editor

Different expressions are used for starting up an editor. You can "call" the editor or "invoke" the editor or "get into" the editor. No matter how you say it, the command issued from the UNIX shell is just

```
ex filename
```

The `filename` can be a file already in your directory. If the `filename` is in your directory, the file contents are placed in the ex temporary buffer for you to edit. If you have no file by that name, then a new file is created. When you call up ex with an existing file, the editor responds on the screen with the number of characters stored in the file. If the file is new, then ex responds with the comment [new file] and the filename. If you want to edit an existing file but you have mistyped its name, this convention will alert you that ex is starting a new file. (The exact responses may vary slightly from version to version.) Let's look at two examples. If you invoke ex with the command

```
ex poem
```

then the editor will respond with

```
"poem" [new file]          ← a new file is created and named poem
:                          ← the colon is the editor prompt
```

or

```
"poem" 26 lines, 462 characters   ← existing file has 462 characters
:                                 ← the colon is the editor prompt
```

The ex editor gives you the number of lines and characters that are in the file, but it does not print the file on the screen unless you give it the appropriate print command.

The editor is now in the Command Mode, ready to accept such commands as append, move, delete, write, quit, print, and so on. The commands that you give must follow a set format, which is described next.

The *ex* Command Format

A complete ex command, in general, has three parts: an address, a command, and a parameter. The *address* tells the editor which line or lines are affected. The *command* tells the editor what must be done. Examples of commands are p (for print a line onto the screen), d (for delete a line), and s (for make a substitution). The *parameter* provides additional information, such as what substitution will take place. Often, however, a complete command will have just one or two of these parts. All ex commands require a Return to complete them. Table 6.1 shows a few examples of the command format.

Table 6.1.   The *ex* command format.

Sample Command	Address Range	Command	Parameter
1,2p	1,2	p	
3d	3	d	
3s/The/the/	3	s	/The/the/
p	None given. Thus, print the current line.	p	
.,$d	Current line to end of file.	d	

Soon we will explain all these commands and more. But if you are impatient, here is a brief rundown of what the commands in Table 6.1 do. The first command prints lines 1 and 2. The second command deletes line 3. The third command substitutes the word *The* for *the* in line 3. The fourth command prints the current line. The fifth command deletes everything from the current line to the end of the file.

Locating Lines

Half of the difficulty in using editors is telling the editor *where* in the text file you wish to insert text or make changes. The ex line editor approaches this task by using *line numbers*. The reason is that text in the ex editor's temporary buffer is organized into numbered lines. A line is considered to be everything typed up to a carriage return, i.e., everything up to a Return. Each line in the buffer is numbered consecutively and renumbered whenever a new line is inserted, deleted, or moved. In addition to maintaining this list of text lines, the editor always knows which is the *current line*. You might imagine the current line as a line pointed to by an invisible cursor, as shown in Figure 6.1.

Which line in the buffer is the current line? When you first invoke the editor with an existing file, the current line becomes the *last* line in the editor buffer. If you were now to type a command like print or append or insert, this command would be carried out with respect to the current line. For example, if you use the print command by typing

   p

the current line is printed on the screen. On the other hand, if you type

   3p

then line 3 is printed. In this latter case, we gave the editor a specific line to work on. Now line 3 becomes the current line. In general, when you issue a command, the last line affected by that command is considered to be the new current line.

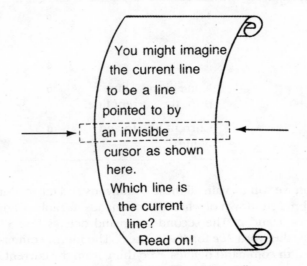

You might imagine
the current line
to be a line
pointed to by
an invisible
cursor as shown
here.
Which line is
the current
line?
Read on!

Figure 6.1. The current line.

An abbreviation for the current line is the dot character (.). The current line is also called *line dot*. Thus, we can speak of line 3 or line 4 or line dot. Do not let the multiple use of the dot in ex confuse you. Recall from Chapter 5 that you can leave the Text Input Mode with a single dot placed alone on a line. However, in the Command Mode, a dot is an address abbreviation for the current line. Thus, you can type

.p

to print the current line, or you can type

.d

to delete the current line.

Another useful abbreviation is $ for the last line of a file. For instance,

$p

prints the last line of the file.

You also can give relative addresses by using the + and - signs followed by a number. They work like this:

.+3   ← *3 lines after the current line*
$-2   ← *2 lines before the final line of the file*

You can specify a range of lines by giving two line numbers separated by a comma. For example,

```
3,8d
```

deletes lines 3 through 8, while

```
1,$p
```

prints all the lines in your file onto the screen, and

```
.-9,.+9p
```

prints 19 lines altogether, with the current line in the middle.

So now you have several ways of giving line addresses. You can give a line number or a range of line numbers, you can use the special symbols . and $ for the current line and for the final line, respectively, and you can use plus signs and minus signs to locate lines relative to the current line or the last line. But how do you find out what the line numbers are?

If the file is short, you can use 1,$nu to show the whole file on the screen. The second thing you can do is find the line number of the current line (line dot); you do this by typing an equal sign after the dot as follows:

```
.=
```

The ex editor will respond by telling you the line number of the current line. (Remember that ex commands, like UNIX commands, should be followed by Return.) This command is particularly handy after you have moved around a bit using the + and - commands described previously or when you are using the pattern searching described next.

Pattern Searching

The ex editor offers an interesting and useful alternative for finding lines. Instead of specifying the line number, you can give ex a pattern to look for. You do this by enclosing the pattern in slashes. For example, if you give the command

```
/bratwurst/
```

the ex editor will search your file for bratwurst and then print the line that contains the first example it finds. After that, it stops searching. The search starts after the current line and proceeds forward through the file. If ex doesn't find the pattern by the time it reaches the file end, it goes to the file beginning and proceeds to the original line. If it hasn't found the pattern yet, it will let you know by printing a question mark.

The ex editor interprets the pattern as a character string rather than as a word. A *character string*, or *string* for short, is just a series, or string, of characters. If you were to set ex looking for the string

```
/man/
```

it doesn't care whether that string is a separate word (man, in this case) or part of a longer word (the *man* in the word *manual* or the word *command*, for example). It will just find the first occurrence (either on the current line or after it) of the consecutive letters m a n.

Note that a space is a character—the space character—and it can be used as part of the search string. So the command

```
/man /
```

will find *man* and *woman*, but not *command*, since there is no space after the *n* in *command*.

Stepping Through Text

Here is another technique that is useful for finding lines of text. If you type

```
<Return>
```

alone without any other command, ex will interpret that to mean

```
.+1p
```

That is, ex will advance one line and print it on the screen. So if you want to go slowly through your buffer looking for changes to make, the following sequence is easy to use:

```
1p
<Return>
<Return>
<Return>
```

and so forth. When you find a line you want to change, you have two choices. You can address the current line by line number, or you can use the default address, which is a line dot. That is, if you type

```
p
```

by itself, the address is the current line by default.

Here is an example of how you might read through a file called energy one line at a time:

```
ex energy
"energy" 4 lines, 320 characters
:1p
Energy consumption during the last six months
<Return>
```

```
has been brought down 17%, thus saving our
<Return>
company over $6,000,000. Everyone is to be
<Return>
congratulated.
<Return>
: At end-of-file
```

The `end-of-file` means that there are no more lines of text in the buffer.

You also can step backward a line at a time by typing a minus sign:

```
-
```

followed by a Return. This is short for

```
.-1p
```

Thus, there are four approaches to locating text in the buffer. The first approach is to use specific line numbers, such as 1, 4, $, and so forth. The second method is to use the *current* line as a reference point and move relative to this *line dot* by using the + and - keys. Third, you can let `ex` search for particular words or patterns. Finally, you can use the Return key to step through the file line by line.

The `ex` editor also has a convenient way to print a screen full of text at one time. To do this, use the z command. The z command fills the screen from the current line to the bottom of the screen with text. The z command can also take a line number for positioning, so that a good way to view a file would be to give the following commands:

```
:          ← Command Mode prompt
1z         ← print text on screen starting at line 1
z          ← print additional text as required
```

Now that you can locate lines, we can turn our attention to creating and altering files.

The *ex* Text Input Mode

There are three commands in `ex` that will turn your keyboard into a typewriter for entering text (or data or programs) into the editor's buffer. These commands are a for append, i for insert, and c for change. If no address is given, these commands affect the current line. Otherwise, a and i must be given a single line address, and c can be given an address of one or more lines. The a command will place text after the addressed line, and the i command will place text before the addressed line. The lines addressed using c are all deleted to make way for any new text you type in. Using the a command to enter the Text Input Mode is illustrated in the next section.

The Append, Write, and Quit Commands: *a*, *w*, and *q*

Jack Armstrong has just received a terrific job offer and wants to draft a letter accepting the position. His first step is to invoke the editor using

```
ex jobletter
```

This creates a new empty file called `jobletter`, placing Jack in the Command Mode and printing

```
"jobletter" [new file]
```

(or something similar, depending on which UNIX system is being used). Since Jack wants to use the keyboard as a typewriter, he now enters the Text Input Mode by typing

```
:i
```
        ← use insert to enter Text Input Mode

for insert. Be sure to press Return after giving an `ex` command.

Note that there is no prompt to indicate the Text Input Mode. Jack now begins typing his letter:

```
Dear Sir:
I am delighted to accept your offer as chief
troubleshooter for the Eon Corp. for $250,000 a year.


Sincerely,
Jack Armstrong
```

Recall that once `ex` is in the Text Input Mode, the keyboard acts like a typewriter. The Return key is used as a carriage return to end each line. To indent lines, Jack can use either the Spacebar or the Tab key.

Satisfied with his work, Jack now leaves the Text Input Mode by typing a lone period at the beginning of a new line:

```
.
```
        ← leave Text Input Mode
```
:
```
        ← Command Mode prompt

Using a period like this may seem strange at first, but remember, when you use the keyboard as a typewriter, every key you press will place characters on the screen. The designers of the `ex` editor had to find some rare keystroke that would never be needed in the typewriter mode so that Jack and you could use it to leave that mode. While a period is not a rare keystroke, it is rare to begin a line with a period.

After leaving the Text Input Mode and reentering the Command Mode, Jack can save his text using the `w` (write) command as follows:

```
:w
```
                                            ← write contents to file
```
"jobletter" 9 lines, 171 characters
```
                    ← editor responds

(Don't forget to follow commands with the Return key!) If the command is successful, the editor will respond with the name of the file and the number of lines and characters saved. Jack now leaves the editor with the q (quit) command by typing

    `:q`   ← *quit the editor*

This places him back in the UNIX shell and gives him back the shell prompt ($). He can now read the `jobletter` file and verify that his letter was properly saved with the write command by typing

    `cat jobletter`

While rereading his letter, Jack has a new thought. He wants to add a postscript to the letter. So he invokes the editor with his new file by typing

    `ex jobletter`

The editor responds with the number of lines and characters in the file as shown:

    `"jobletter" 9 lines, 171 characters`

Jack uses the append command and types

    `:a`   ← *enter Text Input Mode*

He adds his new message by typing

```
PS. Could you advance me $25,000? Thanks.
.
:w "jobletter" 9 lines, 171 characters
:q
```

The a command at the beginning of an editing session appends the text at the end of the file. Every time you first invoke ex, the imaginary cursor is at the very end of the file. (Later, we show how the append command can add text elsewhere within the buffer file, rather than just at the end of the file.)

Summary of Examples

Here's a summary of these first two examples:

    $ ex jobletter   ← *Jack invokes* ex
    `"jobletter" [new file]`   ← ex *prints this*
    `:i`   ← *insert command*
    Dear Sir: ← *Jack starts typing*

```
I am delighted to accept your offer as chief
troubleshooter for the Eon Corp. for $250,000 a year.
```

```
          Sincerely,                                  ← Jack ends text entry
          Jack Armstrong

          .                                           ← writes to memory
          :w                                          ← UNIX confirms save
          "jobletter" 9 lines, 176 characters         ← Jack quits ex
          :q                                          ← shell prompt returns
          $                                           ← Jack invokes editor
          $ ex jobletter                              ← editor responds
          "jobletter" 9 lines, 176 characters         ← append after last line in file
          :a                                          ← Jack types this
          PS.Could you advance me $25,000? Thanks.    ← Jack ends text entry
          .                                           ← writes contents to memory
          :w                                          ← editor responds
          "jobletter" 11 lines, 212 characters        ← Jack quits editor
          :q                                          ← shell prompt
          $
```

These examples illustrate the major features of the Text Input Mode using the a and i commands. Later in this chapter, we will give examples of creating text using the change command (c).

Meanwhile, a day has passed, and Jack wants to make some changes to his text. To do this, he needs the often-used substitute command, s.

The Substitute Command: *s*

If you want to change the spelling of a word or add new words to a line, you must use the substitute command, s. Since ex is a line-oriented editor, our imaginary cursor can distinguish only lines. It *cannot* move within a line; this is the major drawback of a line editor. Thus, to tell the editor which word you want to change, you have to literally spell out the word as shown in the following entry:

```
3s/old word(s)/new word(s)/
```

Recall that the number is an address. If you omit the number, then the substitution is made to the current line.

You can also add a print (p) parameter (a parameter is like a command) to the end of the substitute command. This will cause the editor to print the line *after* making the substitution. It would look like this:

```
3s/old word(s)/new word(s)/p
```

The substitution patterns are strings, just like the search patterns, so you must exercise some care when using them. For example, suppose line 3 reads

```
He commanded the next man to paint the cows blue.
```

What would be the effect of this next command?

```
3s/man/woman/p
```

Since the first occurrence of the string man is in command, the result would be

```
He comwomanded the next man to paint the cows blue.
```

For this example, a better command would have been

```
3s/man /woman /p
```

The editor will move to the first occurrence of man followed by a space.

Now, let's go back to our previous example and see what changes Jack wants to make and how he does it. Jack begins by typing

```
ex jobletter
```

The first change that Jack wants to make is to replace the word delighted with *happy*. "It's best not to sound overeager," he thought. He could find the line he wants by typing p and stepping through the letter using the Return key. It's easier, though, to use the search mode; in which case, the process would look like

```
:/delighted/          ← search for pattern delighted
I am delighted to accept your offer as chief
:s/delighted/happy/p    ← substitute command
I am happy to accept your offer as chief
```

He could have combined his two commands into one:

```
:/delighted/s/delighted/happy/p
```

The first /delighted/ identifies the line; the second /delighted/ identifies the word to be changed. If this is too much typing for you, this command can be shortened to

```
:/delighted/s//happy/p   ← the most common form of search and replace
```

If you have a search pattern followed by a substitution command, as we just did, and the search word is the one you want to replace (again, as we just did), you can use the form just shown. The *ex* editor, upon seeing the two slashes in a row (no spaces) after the s, will understand that it should use the preceding pattern (delighted, in this case) for the word to be replaced.

In any case, after Jack makes the change, the affected line is the current line. He makes one more substitution as follows:

```
:s/chief/Chief/p
I am happy to accept your offer as Chief
```

Since no new address was given, this change took place on the same line.

Finally, he wants to make a change on the next line. In order to read the next line, Jack again presses the Return key to get

```
troubleshooter for the Eon Corp. for $250,000
```

Jack wants to delete the word the in this line, so he uses the command

```
:s/the //p
```

This command means: Take the current line and substitute for the string the the blank space that is between the slashes (that is, nothing) and print the results. This gives

```
troubleshooter for Eon Corp. for $250,000
```

Notice the space after the in the substitution command. In the sentence, there is a space on each side of the. If Jack just typed

```
:s/the//p
```

two spaces would remain between for and Eon. The command he used eliminated one of the spaces, thus keeping the word spacing regular. Jack can now record these changes using the write (w) command and then leave the editor with the quit (q) command.

Although the commands you have used so far (append, insert, print, substitute, write, and quit) are enough to get you started, there are a few more commands that can augment your editing prowess considerably.

Additional Editing Commands in *ex*

We hope you have tried out the previous editing commands on a terminal and are ready to add additional editing power to your repertoire. Here is a brief summary of the new editing commands that we will cover next.

- *Commands that operate on lines:*

  The move command, m

  The delete command, d

  The copy command, co

- *Commands that enter the Text Input Mode:*

  The insert command, i

  The change command, c

- *Special commands:*

  The global parameter, g

  The undo command, u

We will now illustrate these commands by considering the efforts of Paul the Poet, who is trying mightily to create a short poem. So far, Paul has produced a file called `April.Rain`. He cannot use the filename `April Rain` with a space between the names because UNIX interprets this as two files. Paul now wants to edit what he has, so he types

```
ex April.Rain
"April.Rain" 4 lines, 113 characters
```

and then

```
:1z
```

to print the entire file as follows:

```
It's not raining rain on me,
  It's raining whippoorwills
In every dimpled drop I see
  Streaming flowing hills
```

Paul wants to make some changes. Specifically, he wants to delete the last line and put in a new line. He can do this in either of two ways. First, he could delete line 4 with

```
:4d                              ← delete line 4
```

Then, he could add the new line with the append command, typing

```
:3a                              ← append after line 3
```

The second way to make this change is to use, not the delete command, but the change (c) command, which deletes and replaces in one step. Paul does this by typing

```
:4c                              ← change the 4th line
 Wildflowers on the hill         ← new 4th line
.                                ← leave Text Input Mode
```

Now, Paul wants to start a second stanza with the same lines that started the first. That is, he wants to copy the first two lines and place them at the end of the buffer file. He does this by using the co command:

```
:1,2co$                          ← copy lines 1 and 2; place at end of buffer
```

He can check his results by printing the current line (line dot) as follows:

```
:p                               ← print current line
```

which gives the last line copied:

```
It's raining whippoorwills
```

To see if the preceding line was copied, Paul types the minus character, or - command, as follows:

```
:-                                   ← print previous line
```

and the editor responds with

```
It's not raining rain on me,
```

Now Paul thinks of some new lines to add at the end of the poem. He types

```
:$a                                  ← append new text at end of buffer
Where clever busy bumblebees
 Will find their board and room.
 .                                   ← leave Text Input Mode
```

Remember that the $ symbol stands for the last line, so $a means append after the last line.

"Aha," thinks Paul, "let's change whippoorwill to daffodil!" He can do this with the substitute command, as follows:

```
:1,$s/whippoorwills/daffodils/p      ← substitute on all lines
```

Here the command s is the substitute command applied from line 1 to the end of the file ($). The last p prints any lines containing the substitution. Paul now wants to step through the poem from beginning to end using the Return key. Here is how it looks on the screen:

```
:1p
It's not raining rain on me
<Return>
 It's raining daffodils
<Return>
In every dimpled drop I see
<Return>
 Wildflowers on the hill
<Return>
<Return>
It's not raining rain on me
<Return>
 It's raining daffodils
<Return>
Where clever busy bumblebees
<Return>
 Will find their board and room
<Return>
:
```

In a flush of growing excitement, Paul decides to change the seventh line before continuing. To double-check that he has the right line, he types

```
:.p
```
← *print current line*

and gets

```
It's raining daffodils
```

He replaces that line by typing

```
:.c
  But fields of clover bloom
```
← *change current line*

```
.
```
← *leave Text Input Mode*

"Aha," says Paul, "this is it!" He prints the entire poem using

```
:1z
```

The editor responds with

```
It's not raining rain on me
  It's raining daffodils
In every dimpled drop I see
  Wildflowers on the hill

It's not raining rain on me
  But fields of clover bloom
Where clever busy bumblebees
  Will find their board and room
```

(*Note:* This poem is an adaptation of "April Rain" by Robert Loveman.)

Gleefully, Paul saves his work and quits the editor using

```
:wq
```
← *write and quit*

```
"April.Rain" 10 lines, 233 characters
```

Making Searches and Substitutions Global: *g*

The search command and the substitution command share the property that each looks for the *first* occurrence of the pattern. A search ends as soon as it finds a line containing the search pattern, and a substitution acts only on the first occurrence in the line of the pattern. Suppose, for instance, that you are editing a file whose text is as follows:

```
It was a hot, blustery day. Most folks stayed indoors. Not me.
A dog came ambling down the street. He wasn't a big dog,
and he wasn't a small dog; he was just an in-between dog.
```

Suppose for this and for the following examples that the first line is the current line. Then, the command

```
:/dog/s//tiger/p
```

would produce the following result:

```
A tiger came ambling down the street. He wasn't a big dog,
```

That is, ex found the first line containing dog and replaced the first occurrence of dog with tiger. You can make the command more universal or *global* by using the g parameter and command. There are two ways to use it in this example. First, you can put a g command in front of the search pattern. This will cause ex to find *all* lines containing dog. The interchange would look like this:

```
:g/dog/s//tiger/p
A tiger came ambling down the street. He wasn't a big dog,
and he wasn't a small tiger; he was just an in-between dog.
```

Still, however, only the first dog on each line is changed to tiger. The second way to use the g command remedies this. By putting a g parameter after the substitution command, you make ex replace *every* occurrence of dog on a given line. By using a g command in both places, you get a truly global substitution that affects all dog entries on all lines:

```
:g/dog/s//tiger/gp
A tiger came ambling down the street. He wasn't a big tiger,
and he wasn't a small tiger; he was just an in-between tiger.
```

The Undo Command: *u*

One of the truly great innovations in electronic editing is the invention of the undo command, u. This command, given in the Command Mode, undoes the last change made to the buffer. Here are two daring demonstrations of its use on the file April.Rain:

```
$ex April.Rain
"April.Rain" 10 lines, 233 characters
:1,$d                        ← delete all lines
10 lines                     ← the editor confirms deletion
:1z                          ← let's try to display buffer
No Lines                     ← the editor responds
:u                           ← THIS HAD BETTER WORK
10 more lines                ← the editor responds
:1z                          ← print a screen from buffer
```

```
It's not raining rain on me,
 It's raining daffodils
In every dimpled drop I see
 Wildflowers on the hills


It's not raining rain on me,
 But fields of clover bloom
Where clever busy bumblebees
 Will find their board and room
```

Whew!! The lines came back. Fortunately, the undo command works on the last change made in the buffer and not just the last *command* given, which, in this case, was the command 1z.

Another demonstration of the undo command can be shown after making a rather interesting global substitution. Let's substitute two *e*'s for every one *e* that now exists in the poem and print the result:

```
:g/e/s//ee/gp
It's not raining rain on mee,
 It's raining daffodils
In eeveery dimpleed drop I seeee
 Wildfloweers on thee hills


It's not raining rain on mee,
 But fieelds of cloveer bloom
Wheeree cleeveer busy bumbleebeeees
 Will find theeir board and room
:u
```

You can have lots of fun playing with letter and word substitutions like this, just as long as you remember to give the undo command immediately after each substitution.

If you like this version of the poem and want to keep a copy, it is possible to keep both versions of the poem using the w command with a new filename, as described in the next section.

On the other hand, if you make a mistake and forget to use the undo command at the right time, there is an undo command of last resort called the q! command.

The command q! allows you to quit the editor without writing any changes to the buffer. If you feel that your current editing changes are not worth keeping, then this form of the quit command is what you want.

Reading, Writing, and Moving: *r*, *w*, and *m*

One of the handiest features of electronic editing is the ability to move, duplicate, or insert large blocks of text—an electronic version of cut and paste. You've already seen how to use the co command to copy from one part of a file to another part of the same file. Now, we'll look at three additional editing commands: read (r), write (w), and move (m).

Suppose you want to insert an entire file into the text presently being edited. You can use the r command to do this. For example, the command

    `:5r Mayclouds`   ← *read the* `Mayclouds` *file into the buffer*

would paste a copy of the contents of the file `Mayclouds` after line 5 of your present file.

The w command can be used to copy excerpts from a text file for use in another file. This can be done from the editor by using a command like

    `:3,7w April.Rain2`   ← *write lines 3-7 to the file* `April.Rain2`

This command would place lines 3 through 7 in the file called `April.Rain2`, creating the file in the process.

Our last text-rearranging command is the m command. For example, suppose that you have a file containing the lines

```
Apolexy
Bongo
Doobidoo
Cackle
```

You want to make this list alphabetical. Suppose that `Cackle` is on line 4. You can have it moved to just after line 2 by commanding

```
4m2
```

which will move line 4 to a position after line 2, and all is well.

Is this word processing? Or is there more to word processing than just using the editor? Yes and yes.

Word processing involves two major functions. First, you must beg, borrow, or create words or text and put them into a file. Second, you must *format* the text for displaying on the screen or printing on paper. You can use the editor for both tasks, just as we have shown in the examples in this chapter.

However, UNIX offers other ways to format text by using special utilities such as `nroff`. The power of formatting utilities is that you can experiment with different formats in order to choose the style you want. For example, you can adjust margins, line lengths, and paragraph indentation, or you can center, justify, number pages, create tables, and much more. Instructions for formatting text are called *control lines* and are entered into a file as separate lines. Usually, these lines begin with a period to distinguish them from normal text.

Here is a very simple example where we place two control lines into the file `April.Rain`:

```
$ex April.Rain
April.Rain 10 lines, 233 characters
```

```
:2a                                       ← append after line 2
.pl10                                     ← set page length to 10 lines
.ce10                                     ← center justify 10 lines
.                                         ← leave Text Input Mode
:w                                        ← write changes
"April.Rain" 12 lines, 245 characters     ← editor responds
:q
```

It is simple to use the `nroff` formatter. Just give the command and the name of the file to be formatted. The output appears on the screen as follows:

```
$nroff April.Rain
It's not raining rain on me,
 It's raining daffodils
               In every dimpled drop I see
                Wildflowers on the hill


              It's not raining rain on me,
                But fields of clover bloom
              Where clever busy bumblebees
                Will find their board and room
```

Notice that the two control lines take effect after line 2, since that is where they were inserted. If you would like to see more `nroff` magic or read about other word processing utilities, take a look at Chapter 13.

We have just introduced the major features of the ex editor (see Figure 6.2). There are some aspects of ex that we have left out, mainly in the use of metacharacters and regular expressions. These topics are described in detail in Chapter 7, "Advanced Editing Techniques." We will conclude our discussion with a summary of ex.

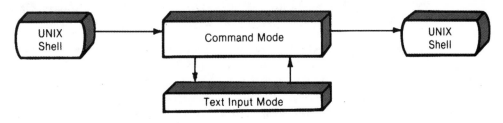

Figure 6.2.   Two modes of the *ex* line editor.

ex Line-Oriented Text Editor

Text Input Mode

a	Append lines after line dot unless line number is specified. For example, 3a adds new text after line 3.
i	Insert lines before line dot unless line number is specified. For example, 3i adds new text before line 3.
c	Change line dot or lines specified in address. For example, 2,4c deletes lines 2 through 4 and adds new text that you type in.
.	Leave Text Input Mode, enter Command Mode

Command Mode

p	Print on the screen the specified lines. If no lines are specified, print the current line. For example, 2,4p prints lines 2, 3, and 4.
d	Delete specified lines. If none specified, delete line dot. For example, 5,8d deletes lines 5 through 8.
m	Move specified lines to line named after m. For example, 1,2m5 moves lines 1 and 2, placing them after line 5.
co	Copy specified lines to line named after co. For example, 2,4co$ copies lines 2 through 4, placing them at end of buffer.
r *filename*	Read in the contents of *filename* at current line or at line specified.
s/one/two/	Substitute the word two for the word one for the first occurrence of one in the specified lines.
/nice/	Search for the next line to contain the word(s) between the slashes; in this case, the string nice.
g	Global search or substitute generally used with s or s/. For example, /pat1/pat2/g substitutes pat2 for pat1 for all occurrences of pat1 in the specified lines.
nu	Number the lines and print them on the screen. For example, 1,$nu numbers and prints all the lines in a file.
u	Undo command. Undo the last change made in the buffer.
z	Print lines on the screen. For example, 3z prints the file on screen starting with line 3.

	Leaving the Editor
w	Write the specified lines that are addressed to a named file. For example, `2,5w popcorn` writes lines 2 through 5 into file `popcorn`.
q	Quit.
q!	Quit without writing changes to file.

	Addressing Lines
.	This character addresses the current line, called *line dot*. The current line is the last line affected by a command. Thus, `.p` prints the current line.
.=	Prints the line number of the current line. For example, editor responds with the number 5.
$	This character addresses the last line in the buffer. For example, `$d` deletes the last line.
n	A decimal number *n* addresses the *n* th line. For example, `3p` prints line number 3.
+ and -	Used in conjunction with a reference line, which may be specified with *n* or $ or line dot, if unspecified. For example, `$-5,$p` prints the last six lines of the buffer.
Return	When used with no command, pressing Return is equivalent to `.+1,`, that is, the next line. Return is very useful for stepping through the buffer.
	Note: If you accidentally type o or vi while in ex, you can get back to ex by pressing Esc and then typing q.

Review Questions

Here are some questions to give you practice in applying the commands of this chapter.

A. Matching Commands

Match the commands shown on the left to the functions shown on the right. Assume that all the commands are given in the Command Mode only; none are given from the Text Input Mode. The functions can be used more than once.

1. `$p`

2. `2,4d`

3. `3s/fun/funny/`

4. `5,6m$`

5. `5,6co$`

a. Deletes lines 2 to 4.

b. Prints the number of the current line.

c. Copies lines 5 and 6, placing them at the end of the file.

d. Moves lines 5 and 6 to end of file.

e. Substitutes `funny` for `fun`.

6. `2,4/s/no/yes/g`   f.   Substitutes yes for no in all
                                      occurrences in lines 2 to 4.

7. `/fun/`   g.   Prints the next line containing
                                      the string `fun`.

8. `.=`   h.   Enters Text Input Mode after line 6.

9. `6a`   i.   Prints current line number.

                                 j.   Prints final line.

B. Questions

1. When you invoke the editor with a file, for example, using `ex file3`, how can you tell if it is a new file?

2. Which three commands put you in the Text Input Mode?

3. When you first enter the editor with an existing file and type a, the append command to add text, where is that text placed?

4. Which command is used to save the editor buffer contents?

5. Where does the insert command (i) place new text?

6. Write out the command that will save the first three lines only of an editor buffer containing seven lines of text.

7. How do you leave the Text Input Mode?

8. Write out the command(s) needed to correct the following misspelled word, *sometome*.

9. Write out the command(s) to delete the last five lines in ten lines of text.

Answers

A. 1—j, 2—a, 3—e, 4—d, 5—c, 6—f, 7—g, 8—i, 9—h.
B. 1. ex responds with the number of characters. 2. a (append), i (insert), and c (change). 3. At the end of the file. 4. w. 5. Before the addressed line. 6. `1,3w newfile`.
7. Use a lone dot (.) at the beginning of a new line. 8. `s/sometome/sometime/p` will also print the line. 9. `6,10d`.

Exercises at the Terminal

Here are some exercises to practice your editing techniques. These exercises are similar to Chapter 5 exercises so you can compare editing features of the two editors.

1. Enter the following text into a new file called `letterrec1`.

```
Dear Sir:
This is a letter of recommendation for john doe.
john doe is a good worker.
john doe has a fine character.
john doe is a-ok.

sincerely
jane doe
```

2. Now, do the following:

   a. Save the letter.

   b. Correct all spelling errors.

   c. Capitalize `jane`, `john`, and `doe`.

   d. Delete the last sentence containing `a-ok`.

   e. Save the corrected letter as `letterrec2`.

   f. Leave the editor.

   g. Use `cat` to print both copies on the screen at the same time.

3. Go into the shell and list your files with `ls`.

4. Make a copy of one of your files, for example, `mbox`, calling it `mbox2` or something similar. Then invoke the editor with this copy of a file and do the following:

   a. Insert the line `This is a test` somewhere in the text.

   b. Move three lines.

   c. Replace all occurrences of the word `the` with `thee`.

   d. Copy two lines and place them in the beginning of the file.

   e. Delete the last four lines.

   f. Substitute `ai` for all a's and then undo the substitution.

5. Start at the shell, list your files with ls, and do the following:

   a. Make a copy of one of your files, for example, mbox, calling it mbox3 or something similar.

   b. Now start up the editor on this copy and

      1. Write lines 2 to 6 to a new file called mbox.test.

      2. Leave the editor using q or ql if necessary.

   c. List your files with ls, then check the contents of the mbox.test file with either cat or more.

   d. Remove the files mbox3 and mbox.test.

6. Start at the shell, list your files with ls, and do the following:

   a. Make a copy of one of your files, for example, mbox, calling it mbox5 or something similar.

   b. Now start up the editor on this copy and

      1. Read in (insert) a file after line 4 using the command, 4r filename, where you select a file from your directory.

      2. Leave the editor using wq.

   c. List your files with ls then check the contents of the mbox5 file with either cat or more.

   d. Remove the file mbox5.

7

Advanced Editing
with *vi* and *ex*

Chapter 7

Advanced Editing with *vi* and *ex*

Once you become comfortable with the vi editor, you may want to add more editing power to your repertoire. In this chapter we will assume that you are doing your editing in vi. Here are some of the advanced features that vi has to offer:

- Repeat or undo the last command.

- Use abbreviations for faster typing.

- Create command macros for repetitive changes.

- Edit multiple files.

- Run shell commands while in the editor.

- Use advanced search and replacement commands.

- Customize vi to fit your needs and your jobs.

Most of these features come from the ex editor. Because vi is part of ex, vi has access to all ex commands. To use an ex command while in vi, just press the colon (:) key while in the vi Command Mode. The colon prompt (:) will appear at the bottom of the screen. If you prefer a longer stay in ex, you can give the Q command while in the vi Command Mode. This, too, will give you a colon prompt at the screen bottom, but you will stay in the ex mode until you type vi to return.

We have described some ex commands already: the :w, :wq, and :q! commands used to leave the vi editor. Most ex commands (except those just mentioned) that are given while you are in vi return you to the vi editor Command Mode after being run.

The Last Command

One handy vi feature is the ability to repeat or undo the last command given. We've already described the undo command (u) in Chapter 5. Just as the undo command will undo the last text change, the dot command (.) will repeat the last text change. The dot command can be used to repeat insertions, deletions, and changes.

Here is an example showing the undo and dot commands in use on an editor buffer. We won't show the file itself, only the sequence of commands. The dot command is used to repeat a deletion; then we undo the dot command.

j	← *move the cursor down to a specific line*
3dd	← *delete three lines*
j	← *move the cursor down to another line*
.	← *repeat last text change, deleting three lines*
u	← *undo last text change; restore three lines*

Our next example demonstrates a much more powerful use of the dot command in conjunction with the search operator (/). The search operator is used to find the word country; then we change the word to County. The n operator repeats the search (as described in Chapter 5), and the dot command repeats the correction.

/country	← *find the next occurrence of* country
country	← *cursor on the* c *in* country
cwCounty <Esc>	← *type* cw *to change word; then retype word correctly and press Esc*
n	← *find next* country
.	← *repeat last text change—make* country County
n	← *find next* country
.	← *repeat text change*

These shortcuts for repeating the last command are great for making identical changes to a file. It is not necessary to use the dot command after each n operator. If there is a country that you want to leave unchanged, just type n to continue searching.

Using Abbreviations for Faster Typing

In this section, we use the word *abbreviation* several times. We have simplified our typing requirements by creating an abbreviation for the word *abbreviation*. Here are some examples given from the Command Mode:

```
:ab abb abbreviation
:ab mse math, science, and engineering
:ab lo longing for you
:ab word rhs          ← general form of the abbreviation command
```

The last example shows the general form of the command. After giving the command :ab, enter the abbreviation or word and what it stands for on the right-hand side. Abbreviations are used in the Text Input Mode of vi. As you type along, just enter the abbreviation, lo or mse or abb, then a space. The vi editor expands lo to longing for you, and so forth. If you type lo as part of a word, say, "long, low, and sleek," no substitution is made because there is no space after lo.

To remove an abbreviation or to see which abbreviations have been created, use these two commands:

```
:una word          ← to unabbreviate word
:ab                ← to see which abbreviations are set
```

Abbreviations given while in vi are temporary—they disappear when you leave vi. Abbreviations can be made permanent by placing them either in the .exrc file in your HOME directory or in a local directory as described later.

Using the *map* Command to Create Macros

When you start up the vi editor, you enter the Command Mode. The vi editor has dozens of commands available—commands like h, k, and so on. These commands let you move around a file, making changes and insertions. The map command, :map, can be used to save command sequences for repeated use. Just as abbreviations give you a shorthand in the Input Mode, map macros give you a shorthand in the Command Mode. The map command has a format similar to the abbreviation command:

```
:map lhs rhs
```

One difference between the two commands is that the lhs of the map command is limited to specific single characters. The following lhs characters can be used by map as macros:

K	V
q	^
v	Ctrl-a
Ctrl-d	Ctrl-x
Ctrl-e	Ctrl-y

The reason there are so few characters available as map symbols is that `vi` uses most of the letters, symbols, and control characters on the keyboard for commands. On some terminals, the `lhs` can be set to a function key with the sequence #*n*, where *n* refers to the function key number. You can use any key if you are willing to forfeit its normal Command Mode use.

The right-hand side of a `map` macro contains Command Mode commands. These commands can include cursor positioning, insertions, changes, and deletions. To include an Esc or a Return key in the macro, type Ctrl-v. The Ctrl-v combination is called an *escape* sequence that turns off the special meaning of the character that follows.

Here are some examples of `map` commands. (Note that all colon commands must be completed with a Return key.) From the Command Mode of `vi` type:

```
:map q  rG
```

Replace the character under the cursor with the letter G.

```
:map v /hairy<Ctrl-v><Return>cwhoary<Ctrl-v><Esc>
```

Find the word `hairy` and change to `hoary`. Note that you must precede Return and Esc with Ctrl-v if they are part of the `map` sequence.

```
:map = })i <Ctrl-v><Esc>
```

Find the next paragraph and then find the beginning of the first sentence and insert three blank spaces. The } and) characters are `vi` scopes described in Chapter 5.

```
:map ^ 067lwi<Ctrl-v><Return><Ctrl-v><Esc>
```

This complicated `map` macro does simple text formatting by inserting a Return before the first word following the 67*th* character on a line. The initial zero (0) sets the cursor to the beginning of the line. The 67l uses the l (ell) key to move the cursor 67 spaces to the right. The w key moves to the beginning of the next word, and then we insert an i, a Return, and an Esc.

The best way to create a `map` macro is to do the editing once manually, write down the keystroke sequence, and then enter the `map` macro. Remember, you can always undo or repeat the last command given, which includes `map` macros.

Maps created while in `vi` are temporary—they disappear when you leave `vi`. Maps can be made permanent by placing them either in the `.exrc` file in your HOME directory or in a local directory as described later.

Editing Multiple Files

The vi editor lets you edit more than one file during an editing session. There are three major advantages to editing multiple files. One advantage is speed. It is much faster to start the vi editor once rather than several times. A second advantage is that abbreviations and map macros created temporarily while in vi can be used for several files. A third advantage is that you can *yank* and store lines from one file for insertion into a second or a third file.

Multiple files to be edited are called sequentially; the editor works on one file at a time. Before going to the next file, changes should be saved with the :w command.

There are two ways to edit multiple files. One method is to start vi on one file and then call in a second file with the :e command or the :r command. The second method is to list all the files to be edited when starting vi—we will describe this first. To edit multiple files at the beginning of an editing job, give the command

```
$ vi file1 file2 file3    ← edit these three files
```

or

```
$ vi ch*                  ← edit all files beginning with ch
```

The vi editor responds by telling you how many files are to be edited, and then it displays the first file for editing. After you have made your changes, type :w to write the changes and then type :n to display the next file as shown here:

```
$ vi file1 file2 file3    ← edit these three files
3 files to edit           ← vi responds

"file1" 12 lines, 456 characters

cw, etc                   ← enter changes in the first file
:w                        ← save changes by writing

"file1" [Modified] 13 lines 512 characters

:n                        ← go to the next file

"file2" 45 lines, 2014 characters

cw, etc                   ← enter changes in the second file
:w                        ← save changes by writing

"file2" [Modified] 43 lines, 1977 characters

:n                        ← go to the next file

"file3" 6 lines, 289 characters
```

```
:wq                    ← write and quit the editor

"file3" [Modified] 6 lines, 289 characters

$                      ← the shell prompt
```

Another way to edit multiple files is to call in a new file using the :e command while still in vi. Here is an example in which you call in a second file, yank eight lines, and put them into the first file. We will assume that you are editing a file called chapter4:

```
:w                     ← write changes to the first file

"chapter4" [Modified] 987 lines, 23078 characters

:e appendix            ← call in new file

"appendix" 98 lines, 4555 characters

j, etc                 ← move the cursor down to specific lines
"a8yy                  ← yank 8 lines and store in buffer a
:e chapter4            ← return to first file
j, etc                 ← move cursor to specific line
"ap                    ← put contents of buffer a below cursor
:wq                    ← write and quit

"chapter4" [Modified] 995 lines, 23478 characters
```

When using the :e command, you can give the abbreviation :e# to switch back to the other file. Remember to *save before you switch*. You must save the file with :w before switching to another file, unless you have made no changes.

In addition to editing a second or third file, the vi editor lets you read a file into the current editor by using the :r command. The command, given while in the Command Mode of vi, looks like this:

```
:r filename            ← read in a file
```

The :r command places the named file into the editor at the location of the cursor. Using the :r command like this is not really editing two files; the :r command involves placing a copy of the second file into the editor buffer where it can be edited as part of the first file. (No change is made to the original of the second file.)

Running Shell Commands

The shell command-line interpreter is a powerful programming language. The vi editor provides four ways to make use of the shell while in the editor. You can

- Run a shell command.

- Temporarily escape to the shell.

- Read in the results of shell commands.

- Filter text through a shell command.

Most of these "escapes" to the shell start with a colon and an exclamation mark as shown here:

```
:!ls            ← runs the command ls to list files
:!who           ← runs the command who
```

After the command is run, you are returned to the `vi` editor. If you want to run more than one command, you can create a shell with the command

```
:sh             ← create a shell
$               ← shell prompt
<Ctrl-d>        ← leave the shell and return to the editor
```

If you want to read in the results of a shell command, then use the command combination `:r` and `!` like this:

```
:r !who         ← read in a who listing into the buffer
:r !cal 1 1992  ← read the month of January 1992 into the buffer
:w              ← write buffer to the file before spelling check
:r !spell filename  ← list all misspelled words in file
```

The last two lines show how to write the `vi` buffer contents to a file and then run the file through a spelling checker. (The *spell* command is optional on UNIX, so this example will work only if you have it on your system.) All misspelled words are listed in the file for handy reference. After correcting misspelled words, you would delete this listing.

In addition to reading the results of a shell command into the current editing buffer, you can write parts of the editing buffer to a shell command, for example,

```
:w !sort        ← run the command sort with the current editing
                  buffer as input. Output of the command goes to the
                  terminal, not to a file.
```

Note that the current editing buffer remains as it was before the command. (If you wish to replace the current editing buffer with the results of the shell command, read on.)

Writing the editing buffer to a shell command is useful for getting information about the file you are editing (with your modifications) without having to save the buffer first. For example,

```
:w !wc -lw        ← run the command wc to find out how many lines and
                    words are in the current editor buffer you are working
                    on
:.w !spell        ← run the spelling checker on the current line (line dot).
                    This is useful for quickly checking the spelling of one or
                    more words on the current line.
```

You also can filter lines of text in the vi buffer through a shell command. The most common commands used for filtering are sort and nroff, both described later in the book. Here are three examples of their use:

```
:.,+7!sort        ← sort the next 7 lines
:5,10!nroff       ← format lines 5 to 10 with nroff
!5)nroff -ms      ← format the next five sentences with the ms option of
                    nroff
```

The first two examples use the line-addressing format of ex. The last example uses the scope-addressing format of vi. In all cases, the lines addressed are replaced by the filtered output of the shell command. Remember, if things do not look right, you can always undo the last command (but only the last command).

If a file gets messed up beyond the last command, there are two forceful ways of undoing changes that involve returning to the original file: either give the command q! to quit the editor without writing or give the command e! to reenter the original file into the buffer, eliminating all changes made since the last write (:w).

Using Advanced Search and Replace Commands

One of the earmarks of a powerful editor is the ability to conduct both large-scale and detailed search and replace operations. There are two general approaches to searching with the vi editor. One approach is to use the vi search operators, / and ?, to find patterns. The other approach is to use the ex search format, :n,m /pattern /, to find lines and patterns on lines. We will begin this section by describing the ex search format. However, we will assume that you are working from the vi editor and that you will run ex search commands by prefacing them with a colon.

The key to the search ability for the ex editor lies in the address part of the command format as shown here:

```
:address /command /parameter
```

The address can have two parts—lines and patterns—as shown in the following examples:

```
:1,7/man /s//person /
```

For lines 1 to 7, find the first occurrence of man and substitute for that word (s//) the word person. Note that the space following man is used to avoid matching up *man* within words such as in *mandate*.

Often, we are interested in searching all lines and finding all occurrences:

```
:g/man /s//person /g
```

The first global (g) searches all lines, while the last global means to apply the substitution to all occurrences on a line.

Precaution

Global replacements occur throughout the text. If unwanted changes are made, they can be undone with the undo command. However, it can easily happen that unwanted changes are not discovered soon enough to undo them. To protect yourself, write the buffer contents to disk with the command :w before making any global changes. If problems are discovered later on, you can return to the last written version of the file by using the command :e!. One way to double-check global substitutions is to use the *confirm* parameter, c (see Example 7 in the upcoming list).

What makes ex search operation very powerful is the use of special characters called *metacharacters* that can be used to form search patterns called *regular expressions*. Here is an example:

```
:g/ occ[a-z]*ces /s// occurrences /g
```

The metacharacter combination [a-z]* stands for any letters. This command will correct various spellings of the word occurrences. Table 7.1 shows some of the metacharacters used by vi and ex.

The best way to understand these special characters is to see them in action in the following examples:

1. *Delete all blank lines:*

   ```
   :g/^$/d
   ```

   Find all lines (g) that have a beginning (^) and an end ($) with no characters in between and delete (d) them.

2. *Change* county *or* County *to* COUNTY:

   ```
   :g/[cC]ounty/s//COUNTY/g
   ```

   Find all lines with county or County and substitute for this pattern (s//) the word COUNTY. The last character (g) means to replace all patterns, not just the first one on each line.

3. *Double-space all lines:*

   ```
   :g/$/s//<Ctrl-v><Return>/g
   ```

Find the end of each line ($) and substitute for it (s//) a Return. The Ctrl-v is required to enter a Return. If you want to double-space all lines of text only, delete all blank lines and then double-space all lines.

4. *Shift the beginning of each line three spaces to the right:*

```
:g/^/s//      /
```

Find the beginning of each line (^) and substitute for it (s//) three spaces. *Note*: You can also use the shift operator in vi (>L) to do the same thing, assuming shiftwidth=3.

5. *Remove the leading blanks on each line:*

```
:g/^   *\(.*\)/s//\1/g
```

Find the first blank at the beginning of each line (^) and any other blanks (*), followed by any character string \(.*\) and retain the character string (\1). This will not remove tabs. This command demonstrates use of the escaped parenthesis to define a regular expression. A simpler way to remove leading blanks is to give the command

```
:g/^   */s///g
```

6. *Remove all tab stops:* If the keyboard does not have a Tab key, you can use Ctrl-i.

```
:g/<Tab>/s///g
```

or

```
:g/<Ctrl-i>/s///g
```

Find the Tab key or the Ctrl-i key and substitute for it the empty space. What should you do if you do not want to remove all tab stops, but just some of them? Use the "confirm" parameter.

7. *Remove all tab stops but confirm each occurrence before removing:*

```
:g/<Tab>/s///gc
```

or

```
:g/<Ctrl-i>/s///gc
```

The confirm parameter, c, will cause the editor to display each line and mark each substitution requiring a change. You are prompted for a yes or a no, y or n. This is not as convenient as it sounds because the line displayed is taken out of context. Another way to do the same thing is to use the dot command (.) and the search operator (/) as described under search and replace with vi.

8. *Replace one or more spaces following a period with one space for lines 20 through 33:*

```
:20,33/\.  */s//\. /g
```

The search is now restricted to lines 20 to 33. Find a period followed by a space (\.), followed by zero or more spaces (*), and replace with a period and one space (\.).

Table 7.1. Metacharacters used by *ex* for pattern matching.

Character	Function
\	Turns off the special meaning of the following character; the \ character is called an *escape* character.
^	Matches the beginning of a line.
$	Matches the end of a line.
.	Matches any single character.
*	Matches the preceding character (or expression) any number of times, including zero.
[string]	Matches any one of the enclosed characters. A dash (-) between characters specifies a range. Thus, [a-d] is the same as [abcd].
[^string]	Matches any character not enclosed. Thus, [^a-d] is the same as all other characters, *e—z, A—Z, 1—9*, and so on.
&	Used in a substitute command to stand for the text in a search, for example, /giant/s//&s/ replaces giant with giants.
\(pat\)	These escaped parentheses can be used to define a regular expression or pattern for substitution.
\n	The number *n* is used to refer to previous patterns defined by parentheses.
Ctrl-v	Used to escape an Esc or Return in the replacement part of the command.

Search and Replace with *vi*

All of the previous search and replace expressions are formed by using ex editor commands. The other way to search for patterns is to use the vi editor search operators, / and ?. The search command

> /pattern

searches for *pattern* forward from the cursor, while the ? operator searches backward from the cursor. In both cases, the key n is used to repeat the search. The vi editor can make use of regular expressions to conduct searches. Here are a few examples:

1. *Find the beginning of each line:*

   /^   ← *find the beginning of the next line*
   n   ← *continue the search*

2. *Find the word* county *or* County *and change to* COUNTY:

   /[Cc]ounty   ← *find* County *or* county
   cwCOUNTY   ← *change to* COUNTY
   n   ← *repeat the search*
   .   ← *repeat the change*

3. *Find the misspelled word* occurance *and correct:*

   ?occ[a-z]*nce   ← *find the word beginning with* occ *and ending with* nce
   cwoccurrence   ← *change to* occurrence
   n   ← *repeat the search*
   .   ← *repeat the change*

4. *Find the word* Section *and remove:*

   /Section   ← *find the word* Section
   dw   ← *delete the word*
   n   ← *repeat the search*
   .   ← *repeat the deletion*

You can see that the search operators are used to find the patterns but not replace them. Then the change (cw), or delete (dw), or other operators are used to make changes. The advantage to using the vi search and replace method is that patterns are displayed in context and can be selectively replaced.

Customizing the *ex* and *vi* Editors

The ex editor and its offshoot, vi, have a number of options that can be set to change their behavior. You have already seen two of those options in Chapter 5—the `wrapmargin` and `redraw` options. Altogether, there are more than 30 options available and, fortunately, all of them have default or preset values. Thus, you can work in the default environment, or you can create a custom environment to fit your special needs.

The `set` command is used to change `ex` and `vi` options and customize `vi`. Options can be set temporarily by using the `set` command while in the editor. Or, options can be created semipermanently by placing them in files, such as the `.exrc` file in the HOME directory or in a `.exrc` file in a subdirectory. Options placed in a subdirectory let you customize the editor for particular jobs. For example, when you use the editor to write programs in FORTRAN or C, you can create a subdirectory for those programs and then set the `autoindent` option to simplify program indention.

In all of the following examples, we will assume that you are working in the `vi` editor and in the Command Mode. Options are set from the `ex` editor, which you call with a colon (:). The `vi` editor responds by displaying the colon prompt on the bottom line and waits for you to enter the option. After giving the option and pressing Return, you are returned to the Command Mode of `vi`.

There are three types of options available: *numeric options, toggle options*, and *string options*. Numeric options have the format

```
:set option = value     ← general format of numeric option
:set wrapmargin=15       ← example
```

Toggle options have the format

```
:set option             ← general format of toggle option
:set redraw             ← example
```

To turn off a toggle option, use the format

```
:set nooption           ← general format for turning off toggle option
:set noredraw           ← example
```

String options are similar to numeric options. They have the format

```
:set option = string    ← general format of string option
```

If you want to see which options you have set, type

```
:set                    ← displays options you have set
```

If you want to see all the editor options, including those set by you and default options set by the editor, type

```
:set all                ← displays all options
```

Here is a list of the `set all` options. There may be some variations in these options from one computer to another, but the ones described here are the most common.

noautoindent	mesg	noshowmatch
autoprint	nonumber	noslowopen
noautowrite	nooptimize	tabstop=8
nobeautify	paragraphs=IPLPPPQPP LIpplpipbp	taglength=0
directory=/tmp	prompt	tags=tags /usr/lib/tags
noedcompatible	noreadonly	terse
noerrorbells	redraw	window=23
hardtabs=8	remap	wrapscan
noignorecase	report=5	wrapmargin=10
nolisp	scroll=11	nowriteany
nolist	sections=NHSHH HUnhsh	
magic	shiftwidth=8	

This is an impressive list of options. Experimenters and tinkerers will have a field day exploring combinations of options. For those who are more discriminating, here are the more useful options:

Option	Abbreviation	Default
autoindent	ai	noai

Indents the new line to align with the previous line. Use Ctrl-d one or more times to backspace one or more indents (see shiftwidth). Useful for writing structured program text in FORTRAN, C, Pascal, and other languages. Also useful for indenting tables and text like this copy.

| ignorecase | ic | noic |

Ignores letter case in searching and in regular-expression matching. Most useful for finding and rearranging text, but not to correct spelling.

| magic | | magic |

Creates the magic characters ., *, [, and ~ for use as wild cards or metacharacters in searching and in regular expressions. If nomagic is set, only ^, $, and \ have special meaning.

| number | nu | nonu |

Each line in the editor buffer is numbered. This option displays line numbers on the left side of the screen and is useful with the move and copy commands.

| redraw | | noredraw |

This option makes the editor simulate an intelligent terminal by displaying each character in its proper location at all times. The noredraw option is useful for terminals operating at slow speeds like 300 and 1200 baud.

Option	Abbreviation	Default
shiftwidth	sw	sw=8

Sets the number of spaces used by Ctrl-d in autoindent and by the shift operators < and >.

showmatch	sm	nosm

In vi, when a) or } is typed, the cursor is moved to the matching { or (for 1 second—it is useful for programming, especially in LISP and C.

slowopen	slow	**Varies**

In vi, it prevents update of the screen during input and is essential for terminals operating at slow speeds. The default value depends on line speed and terminal type.

tabstop	ts	ts=8

Sets the number of spaces that a Tab or Ctrl-i uses to expand tab stops for a file.

terse		noterse

When set, terse error messages are shorter. It is useful for fast typists and slow terminals.

window	w	**Varies**

Sets the number of lines of text in the vi editor, which generally ranges from 8 lines for slow terminals to 16 to 24 lines for faster terminals.

wrapscan	ws	ws

When set, it allows searches using a / or ? to proceed from the cursor around the end of the file and back to the cursor.

wrapmargin	wm	wm=0

Defines a right margin for automatic wrapping of text (by inserting Returns). A typical value of wm=15 would create text lines having 80–15, or 65, or fewer characters in length.

Remember that options set while in the editor are lost when you leave the editor. The .exrc file is normally used to create semipermanent options.

The *.exrc* File

The .exrc file is used to create customized editing environments. When the ex or vi editor starts up, it looks at the .exrc file for instructions, which may be set options, abbreviations, or maps. You can enter these instructions into the .exrc file just like any other file by using the vi editor. Give the command

```
vi .exrc
```

in the HOME or other directory. A typical .exrc file might look like this:

```
set wm=15
set redraw
set ai
ab nyc New York City
ab abb abbreviation
map ^ 067wi<Ctrl-v><Return><Ctrl-v><Esc>
```

The last line, map, helps do simple formatting as described in a previous section. You can copy the .exrc file in your HOME directory to put in any subdirectory and then modify it to fit the editing jobs of that subdirectory. If you want to have more than one custom editor file in a directory, vi lets you read in an editor file of instructions by using the source command. Just give the command

```
:source filename
```

where *filename* contains the appropriate options, abbreviations, and maps. The advantage of the .exrc file is that vi "sources" that file automatically.

Once you have mastered this chapter, along with Chapters 5 and 6, you are well on your way to becoming a vi expert. There are a few odds and ends we have left out for brevity—more options, more scopes, more commands, and so on. These can be added to your editing routine by consulting the *UNIX System V Bible* (Prata, Martin, and The Waite Group, published by Howard W. Sams) when you feel ready for them.

Review Questions

1. Will the dot command repeat cursor movement? How about the undo command?

2. Will the dot and undo commands repeat only the last command or can they be used to sequentially repeat and undo commands?

3. Why are two- and three-letter word abbreviations better than single-letter word abbreviations?

4. What is the major difference between an abbreviation and a `map` macro?

5. Can a macro do the same thing as a substitute command?

6. Why do the Return and Esc keys need to be escaped in a `map` macro?

7. What key is used to escape a Return in a `map` macro? What key is used to escape metacharacters in a regular expression?

8. In creating regular expressions for `ex` search and replacement, what does `.*` mean? Why would the following command *not* be a good way to correct the spelling of `receive`:

   `:g/rec.*ve/s//receive/g`

9. What is the difference between `.` and `\.` in a regular expression?

10. What does the confirm parameter, `c`, do in a search expression?

11. Why is the `.exrc` file a good place to put abbreviations and maps and option settings?

12. If you set the option `ai` and indent several lines of text in a row, how can you start a new line, not indented, without leaving the Text Input Mode?

Answers

1. No. 2. Only the last command. 3. Because you might want to run an `ex` command that uses the same single letter, for example, `:r`, `:a`, `:w`, and so on. The abbreviation would expand these single letters. 4. An abbreviation works in the Text Input Mode, and a `map` macro works in the Command Mode. 5. Yes, by placing a `cw` operation in the macro. 6. Pressing Return or Esc while in the `map` macro leaves the `map` command. To insert these keystrokes in the `map` macro, they must be escaped with Ctrl-v. 7. Use Ctrl-v in `map` macros and the `\` character in regular expressions. 8. The `.*` stands for any number of any characters. It is very broad. The example not only would replace `receive` but also would replace the words `recalled the damage done by the river`. 9. An unmarked dot is a metacharacter standing for any single character. An escaped dot (`\.`) stands for a period or dot. 10. It lets you respond with a yes or no before carrying out each substitution. 11. The `.exrc` file is sourced on starting the `vi` editor. 12. Use Ctrl-d.

Exercises at the Terminal

There are lots of examples in this chapter to try. We suggest that you make a copy of a file with about 20 lines of text in it to use as a practice file.

1. In your practice file, do each of the following:

    a. Delete 3 lines of text. Move the cursor and use the dot command to repeat the deletion.

    b. Find the word the and change it to th#, using the cw operator. Now use the search repeat key, n, and the command repeat key, dot, to change all the's to th#.

    c. To return the file to its original state, type :e!.

2. Create an abbreviation for a friend of yours and type a short letter of recommendation for him or her.

3. Create a map macro that changes the spelling of the word the to thee. Use the search operator, /, along with n, to find and change every the to thee.

4. In your practice file, use Shift-j to join several lines of text. Now create the map macro, ^, defined in this chapter, to format long lines.

5. In your practice file:

    a. Use the shell command, date, to put the date and time at the top of the file.

    b. Escape to the shell to list your files.

    c. Read in a short file using the command :r *filename* into the middle of your practice file.

    d. Now filter the editor buffer through the sort utility.

    e. Now filter the buffer through nroff.

    f. Use :e! to return your practice file to its original state.

6. In your practice file, do each of the following:

    a. Delete all blank lines. If you had a blank line consisting of a single tab, was it deleted? Why or why not? Try it.

    b. Double-space all lines.

    c. Shift all lines three spaces to the right.

    d. Undo the shift and then tab all lines to the right.

    e. Try some of the other substitute examples in this chapter.

7. Try the autoindent and number options.

8. In your practice file, do each of the following:

    a. Escape to the shell.

    b. Edit your `.exrc` file. (If you do not have one, then create one.)

    c. Enter one or more abbreviations and `map` macros.

    d. Write and quit the `.exrc` file and return to the editor with Ctrl-d.

    e. Now give the command `:source .exrc` and try out the abbreviations and maps.

    f. Try the commands `:ab`, `:map`, `:set`, and `:set all`.

8

The *emacs* Editor

Chapter 8

The *emacs* Editor

Editors are the workhorses of the UNIX world. In UNIX, all data, programs, and information are stored in files that are created or changed by editors.

The emacs editor (also known as *GNU Emacs* or *gnuemacs*) is a public-domain editor created by Richard Stallman, formerly of the MIT Laboratory for Computer Science, and now president of the Free Software Foundation. Several editors go by the name emacs. All are similar in general, but they may differ in details. This chapter is based on GNU Emacs version 18.

If you are new to UNIX and looking for a good editor, we recommend emacs rather than the standard UNIX editors, vi and ex. The emacs editor is a modern, powerful, easy-to-use display editor. Here are some of the features that emacs offers.

For the beginning user:

- On-line help facility

- Special on-line tutorial

- Easy text entry—to enter text, just start typing

- Text display as you type

- An echo area providing timely prompts

- Cut and paste or search and replace using simple commands

- Automatic justification

For the advanced user:

- The creation of multiple screens

- Customized command definitions

- The ability to run and capture UNIX shells in a window
- The creation of key command macros
- Special modes for C and Lisp programming
- Programs for sending and reading electronic mail
- Formatting and outlining modes

If you are interested in the advanced features, you can check either the on-line manuals or the well-written 285-page paper manual, available from the Free Software Foundation, 675 Massachusetts Ave., Cambridge, MA 02139. In this chapter, we will cover all of the beginning features and briefly describe the first three advanced features.

Writing Your First Letter with *emacs*

The two most important questions concerning any UNIX program are, "How do I start it?" and "How do I stop it?" These questions can be answered with the following simple example.

Start the emacs editor from the UNIX shell by giving the command emacs *filename*, where you choose the filename, in this case mom:

```
$ emacs mom                    ← start the editor
```

Now enter the following text. Press Return at the end of each line. Remember that control combinations are entered by holding down the Ctrl key while typing the letter key.

```
Hi mom <Return>                        ← just start typing
This is my first letter using the emacs editor. <Return>
I am fine. <Return>
I hope you are well. <Return>
Love, Jan <Return>
<Ctrl-x><Ctrl-s>                       ← save buffer contents to file
<Ctrl-x><Ctrl-c>                       ← quit the editor
$                                      ← UNIX prompt
```

This example demonstrates the basics of entering and leaving emacs. However, there are some further points that you should know about. We will begin with a comment about the Return key. In the example, you pressed the Return key to start a new line. Later in the chapter, we will show you how Returns can be entered automatically by emacs.

When you start emacs, it opens up a temporary workspace called a *buffer*. When you quit emacs, this workspace is cleared. Therefore, you have to save or write the buffer contents to a permanent file before quitting.

There are several commands that can be used to save your work. The emacs manual suggests using the command sequence Ctrl-x Ctrl-s to save the buffer contents. However, on some UNIX systems, Ctrl-s can temporarily FREEZE YOUR TERMINAL. If this happens, either on purpose or accidentally, press Ctrl-q to resume screen display. Then see your system administrator to have this problem fixed (or check the emacs manual).

The command Ctrl-x Ctrl-c is the standard way to exit emacs. It can be given at any time. If there are changes in the buffer that have not been saved, then emacs will remind you and ask you if you want to quit anyway. You can answer yes or no. Note that the easiest way to give the command to save and quit is to hold down the Ctrl key and press the four keys, *x, s, x, c* one after the other.

When you try this example, you will see two lines of information at the bottom of your screen. These two lines are called the *echo area* (or *message line*) and the *mode line*. We will discuss them next.

The Echo Area

The echo area is the bottom line of the emacs screen. It is used to display certain commands to emacs or to prompt you for input to a command. For example, if you type Ctrl-x and pause for one second or more, the symbol C-x will appear in the echo area. The reason is that emacs always expects another command to follow Ctrl-x; thus, it displays C-x and puts the cursor after it to remind you to complete the command.

If you give the command Ctrl-x and follow it quickly with any command, say Ctrl-c, within one second, emacs will carry out the command without displaying it.

When the cursor is in the echo area, you can use any emacs editing tools that work on one line to change what you have typed. For example, you can use the Rub or the Del key.

To abort a command started on the echo area, type

<Ctrl-g>   *← aborts the current command on the echo area*

The cursor then returns to the text part of the screen, where you can enter text or start another command to emacs.

The Mode Line

The beginning user can easily ignore the mode line when doing simple text editing on single files. The information displayed is not necessary for editing.

For those of you who want to know what is happening, here is a brief explanation. The mode line sits at the bottom of the screen just above the echo area and may be displayed in inverse video. It shows status information about the emacs editor using the following format:

```
**CH-Emacs: BUFFER-NAME    (MAJOR    MINOR)----POSITION----
```

CH contains two asterisks (**) if the text in the buffer has been edited or modified and not yet saved. CH contains two hyphens (- -) if the buffer has not been changed. If CH is two percent signs (%%), then the file is read-only.

BUFFER-NAME is the name of the chosen buffer, the window that the cursor is in, and the buffer where editing takes place. POSITION describes where the cursor is located in the buffer. It can read All, Top, or Bottom, or can give a percentage.

MAJOR is the name of the *major mode* for the buffer. The four possible major modes are Fundamental, Text, Lisp, and C. The default mode for normal editor use is the Text mode. The C and Lisp modes change the behavior of the editor slightly to simplify indention and parenthesis location. The Fundamental mode is the least-specialized mode for editing files.

MINOR is a list of several minor modes that can be turned on or off. These modes let you use abbreviations (Abbrev), automatic filling of text (Fill), overwriting of text (Ovwrt), and restriction of editing of text (Narrow). The emacs editor may also display other information on the mode line. See your manual for a complete description.

Basic Cursor Moves

Now let's answer the third most important question concerning a new editor, "How do you move the cursor?"

The cursor is usually a white line above or below a character or a white block superimposed on top of a character or space. In emacs, the cursor position is called *point*. Point should be thought of as lying just to the left of the cursor symbol between characters. Point will become more important later when we talk about marking blocks of text.

For now, think of the cursor as the place where new characters are added when you type. The four basic cursor-moving commands, shown in Figure 8.1, are

Command	Action	Mnemonic Help
Ctrl-p	Up	Previous line
Ctrl-n	Down	Next line
Ctrl-b	Left	Backward
Ctrl-f	Right	Forward

Note that on many terminals these same moves can be accomplished with the arrow keys.

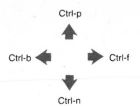

Figure 8.1.   The basic cursor-moving commands.

There are dozens of commands that can be used to move the cursor. However, these four basic commands plus one modifier and two additional cursor-positioning commands may be all that you need. Here are the two additional commands:

Command	Action
Ctrl-a	Beginning of line
Ctrl-e	End of line

Most cursor-positioning commands in emacs can be given a numerical argument that causes them to be repeated. To do this, precede the numerical argument with an Esc. Here are some examples:

Command	Action
Esc 4 Ctrl-p	Move up 4 lines
Esc 5 Ctrl-f	Move forward 4 characters
Esc 8 Ctrl-n	Move down 8 lines

Note that you must press and release the Esc key first, then press the numeric key, and then press the normal cursor command. (Do NOT hold down the Esc key while striking the following key, and do NOT press the Spacebar between commands.) If you wait more than one second after pressing the Esc key, you will see an ESC on the echo area, prompting you for the rest of the command input.

Simple Editing: Adding and Removing Text

Once you have learned to move the cursor, you can easily change a file by adding or removing text. Adding text is the simplest; just move the cursor to the correct position and start typing. In emacs, the keyboard always acts like a typewriter, inserting text into the buffer as you type.

Because the keyboard acts like a typewriter, emacs requires special keystroke combinations to remove text. The most important remove commands are shown here:

Command	Action
Ctrl-d	Delete character after the cursor
Del	Delete character before the cursor
Rub	Delete character before the cursor (may not work on some systems)
Esc Del	Kill the word before the cursor
Esc d	Kill the word after the cursor
Ctrl-k	Kill from cursor to end of line
Ctrl-y	Yank back a previous kill

The words *delete* and *kill* have different meanings in emacs. Characters that are deleted are not meant to be used again. Words or lines that are killed are temporarily stored in a *ring buffer* and up to thirty previous kills (depending on the system) can be restored. A ring buffer is a buffer that has no end. However, once a ring buffer is filled, adding a new kill causes the oldest kill to be dropped. You can cycle through the ring buffer indefinitely. After reaching the 30*th* killed text in the buffer, one more Ctrl-y retrieves the first killed text stored in the buffer.

Kill and yank may not sound friendly, but it is the normal way to "cut and paste" in emacs. You can do several kills in a row and one yank will bring them all back. For example, the best way to move five lines of text would be to kill one line at a time (do this one line at a time to make sure you get just the lines you want) and then yank back the series of kills with one Ctrl-y.

If you happen to move the cursor between kills, Ctrl-y restores only the last kill. If you want to restore a previous kill, you can cycle back through the ring buffer by pressing Esc y several times. Thirty Esc y combinations will bring you back to the last kill made. Here are some examples.

Command	Action
Esc d	Kill the word after the cursor
Ctrl-n	Move the cursor
Ctrl-k	Kill one line
Ctrl-y	Yank back the killed line
Esc y	Replace yanked-back line with killed word
Esc y	Replace killed word with previous kill
Esc y	Replace previous kill with next previous kill

You must press Ctrl-y to start this process before you can use Esc y. Remember that Esc y means to press and release the Esc key and then press the *y* key. Ctrl-y means to hold down the Ctrl key while you press the *y* key once.

If you make a mistake and want to undo it, give the command Ctrl-x u. If you decide to scrap all the changes made to the buffer since you started editing, you can leave emacs without saving your work by pressing Ctrl-x Ctrl-c. Or you can restore the buffer to its original contents with Esc x. Here are the undo commands:

Command	Action
Ctrl-x u	Undo last change
Ctrl-x Ctrl-c	Leave without saving your work
Esc x	Restore buffer to original contents

Saving CPU Time When Adding Text

If you are using emacs on a multiuser system that is heavily loaded, you can save CPU time when adding text by opening up new lines. When you insert new text into the middle of existing text, emacs has to make room for each character by moving all of the remaining characters to the right (and down). This redrawing of the screen takes considerable CPU (central processing unit) time and can be avoided by opening up two or more blank lines.

To open up two lines, type Ctrl-o and Return. Later on, extra blank lines can be killed with Ctrl-k.

Line Lengths in *emacs*

A line in the emacs editor is limited only by the amount of memory available to the editor. In practical terms, lines may be longer than is reasonable for human beings to handle. How does emacs display long lines?

Suppose that you have an existing line 100 characters long. On most screens, emacs displays 79 characters and a backslash (\) at the end of the line. The \ means that the next line is not really a different line but a continuation of a line too long to fit on the screen. Instead of "continuation," long lines may also be displayed by *truncation*—characters too long to fit on the screen are not displayed at all. The remaining line stays in the buffer, temporarily invisible. The dollar sign ($) is used to indicate that the line is truncated.

Avoiding the Line-Length Problem

There are two ways to avoid long lines. One method is for you yourself to press Return at the end of each line, making sure that no line is longer than 80 characters. However, the best way to limit line lengths is to use the auto-fill mode of emacs and limit line lengths. Here are some examples:

Command	Action
Esc x auto-fill-mode	Toggle auto-fill on or off
Esc 64 Esc x set fill-column	Set line length to 64 characters
Esc 64 Ctrl-x f	Alternative method of setting line length

Unfortunately, these commands apply only to your current editing session. When you leave emacs, the line-length setting no longer exists. You can make these commands semipermanent by placing them in a file called .emacs (described later in this chapter).

Ideally, new users will have both commands set in a .emacs file by the system administrator. If you want to check the current setting of the right margin, give the help command:

```
<Ctrl-h>v fill-column
```

If the fill-column is on, the word fill will be seen in the MINOR mode position.

The *emacs* Commands

The emacs editor has over 400 commands available, ranging from abbrev-mode to lowercase-region to yank-pop. All emacs commands have such long names. However, some common emacs commands have an abbreviated form like Ctrl-n for next-line or Ctrl-k for kill-to-end-of-line.

A keyboard abbreviation like Ctrl-n is "bound" to a command through a table called the *command dispatch table*. Experienced emacs users can easily change this table and redefine keys in a file called .emacs. Our discussion will concentrate on the unmodified emacs editor.

Running an *emacs* Command Using Its Long Name

Each of the over 400 emacs commands can be run by using its long name. Just type the sequence Esc x and then type the command name. Here are some examples of long forms of commands:

Command	Action
Esc x `next-line`	Move cursor down, same as Ctrl-n
Esc x `fill-column`	Automatically insert a Return at the right margin
Esc 64 Esc x `set fill-column`	Set the right margin at 64 characters

Because long forms of commands are tedious, emacs speeds up the process in two ways. First, it provides keystroke abbreviations like Ctrl-n. Second, it assists you with the typing. For example, if you type

```
<Esc>x next-l <Spacebar>
```

the emacs editor completes the line by typing

```
next-line
```

However, if you just type

```
<Esc>x next
```

emacs gets confused because there are three similar commands, `next-line`, `next-page`, and `next-window`. In this case, emacs will supply you with a list of possible completions to choose from.

The Spacebar key can be used twice in a line. For example, if you type nex and press the Spacebar, emacs will add the t - and wait for you. Then you add a p and press the Spacebar, and emacs adds the age to get `next-page`.

If you are slow giving an Esc x command, emacs prompts you by displaying `<Esc>x` (actually `M-x`) in the echo area.

Getting Help

There are numerous sources of help for using emacs, both on-line and off-line. These include

- A 285-page written manual

- A reference card that comes with the manual

- An on-line tutorial

- An extensive on-line help system documenting all commands

The help system is invoked by the Ctrl-h command, which is used only for help commands. The characters you type after Ctrl-h are called *help options*. One help option is Ctrl-h itself, which gives information on how to use the help system.

Pressing Ctrl-h Ctrl-h prints a list of possible help options and then asks you to type the option. The help system prompts you with a string:

```
A, B, C, F, I, K, L, M, N, S, T, V, W, C-c, C-n, C-w
or C-h for more help:
```

You should now type one of those characters (you can enter lowercase letters).

Note that the manual uses the convention C-n to stand for Ctrl-n, and M-x to stand for Esc x. (Although the conventions C-n and M-x have the same form, they have different keystroke operations.)

Pressing a third Ctrl-h displays a description of what the options mean. However, the help system still waits for you to enter an option. To cancel any command, press Ctrl-g.

Here are examples of some of the options. You may enter them in lowercase, as shown.

Option	Action
Ctrl-h t	Run the emacs tutorial
Ctrl-h a *word*	Display a list of all commands whose names contain *word*
Ctrl-h b	Display a table of all key bindings in effect
Ctrl-h k *key*	Display name and information about the command *key*
Ctrl-h l	List the last 100 characters typed
Ctrl-h i	Run info, the program for browsing files, which includes the complete emacs manual

These commands are enough to get you started. Then you can use the help system itself to discover more, both about the help system and about emacs.

Searching for Text

The emacs editor has two commands that search for text strings:

Command	Action
Ctrl-s *(string)*	Incremental search forward for string
Ctrl-r *(string)*	Incremental search backward for string

Both commands prompt you for a string on the echo area, and both commands search only from the cursor (point) to one end of the buffer, either forward to the end of the buffer (or backward to the beginning of the buffer).

Both commands start the search as soon as you begin typing the search string. For example, if you are searching for the string Indian Ocean and you type I, the command will find the first character I in the text. Then when you type n it will find In, and so on.

If you type something incorrectly, just use the Del key. To end the search string, type Esc. Typing Ctrl-s while in incremental search will move the cursor to the next occurrence of whatever you have already typed.

Caution: On some systems, the command Ctrl-s will FREEZE THE TERMINAL. If your screen appears stuck, press Ctrl-q to restart it. If Ctrl-s freezes your terminal, then you have four choices in searching for text. You can stick with Ctrl-r. You can use the long form of the command, Esc x isearch-forward. You can redefine the keystroke abbreviation from Ctrl-s to something else. Or you and/or your system administrator can disable the Ctrl-s and Ctrl-q commands in the .emacs file. This latter solution should be your first choice.

The editor remembers the last search string used, so you can repeat a forward search by typing Ctrl-s Ctrl-s. A good way to search a whole file, forward and backward, is to give the command

```
<Ctrl-s>(search string)<Esc>        ← search forward for string
<Ctrl-r><Esc>                       ← search backward for same string
```

In addition to the searching techniques already described, emacs can search for patterns using *regular expressions* (described in the emacs manual and in Chapter 7 of this book).

Search and Replacement of Text

There are several commands to search for and replace text strings, with the query-replace command (Esc %) being the most common. For example, to replace the word book with the word epic, type the following:

```
<Esc><                              ← go to beginning of buffer
<Esc>% book <Return> epic <Return>  ← replace, depending on next key
```

Here are some of the options available:

Option	Action
Spacebar	Make the change and advance to the next occurrence
Del	Skip this change and advance to the next occurrence
Esc	Exit query-replace
!	Replace all remaining occurrences
^	Back up to previous occurrence
Ctrl-h	Display a help screen

If you type any other character, the query-replace command is exited and the character is executed as a command. To restart query-replace, type Ctrl-x Esc. To return to where you were before the query-replace command, type Ctrl-x Ctrl-x.

Defining Regions with Point and Mark

In emacs it is possible to select a portion of the text in the editor buffer by using the cursor to define two positions, one called *point* and the other called *mark*. The cursor itself is at point. Mark is set by using the command Ctrl-@ or Ctrl-space. The text between point and mark is called a *region*.

To specify a region, move the cursor to the beginning (or end) and press Ctrl-@. Then move the cursor to the other end. Now you have the region.

Because emacs shows you only the cursor and not the mark, you have to remember where you put it. The emacs editor helps you with this by providing a command to interchange the point and the mark—the command Ctrl-x Ctrl-x. Here is the procedure for selecting a region:

1. Move the cursor to the beginning of a region.

2. Press Ctrl-@.

3. Move the cursor to the end of the region.

4. Press Ctrl-x Ctrl-x to double-check the location of mark.

5. Do something to the region.

What can you do to a region? Here is a list of commands that operate on a region. The commands are shown in their long form with key bindings where they exist.

Command	Action
upcase-region or Ctrl-x Ctrl-u	Capitalize all text
downcase-region or Ctrl-x Ctrl-l	Lowercase all text
append-to-file *(filename)*	Append region to a file
write-region *(filename)*	Write region to a file
kill-region or Ctrl-w	Kill the region
copy-region-as-kill or Esc w	Copy region (to kill buffer)
fill-region or Esc g	Justify region

As you can see, regions are useful. You might be wondering if changes to a region are reversible. The answer is yes; emacs does have a global *undo* command: Ctrl-x u.

Formatting Text

UNIX provides several ways to format text. In the UNIX shell, there are simple formatting commands like pr and complex formatting programs like nroff. And, of course, you can always format text yourself by using an editor. The emacs editor has several commands to help you. These are

Command	Action
auto-fill-mode	Word wrap at right margin setting
fill-region	Justify region
Esc q	Justify paragraph at right margin setting
Esc *n* Ctrl-x	Set right margin *n* characters

Here is an example showing how to change the right margin and justify the text throughout an entire buffer:

```
<Esc><                   ← go to beginning of buffer
<Ctrl-@>                 ← set mark
<Esc>>                   ← go to end of buffer (define region)
<Esc>44<Ctrl-x>          ← set right margin at 44 characters
<Esc>x fill-region       ← justify text
```

To obtain paragraphs with different right margins, set the right margin at the value you want, move the cursor into the paragraph, and press Esc q. Then reset the right margin to a new value, move the cursor into the next paragraph, and press Esc q again.

Creating Multiple Windows

One of the advantages of emacs is its ability to split the screen into two or more windows. Windows can be used to display two parts of the same file or to display two different files.

The window containing the cursor is called the *current* window, and it is the only window active. (However, you can page or scroll the inactive window.)

Here are some of the window commands available:

Command	Action
Ctrl-x 2	Divide current window into two windows, one above the other
Ctrl-x 5	Divide current window into two windows, side by side
Ctrl-x 1	Delete all windows but the current one
Ctrl-x 0	Delete current window and redistribute space
Ctrl-o	Switch to other window (cycle through all)
Esc Ctrl-v	Page other window
Ctrl-x ^	Grow current window one line, vertically
Ctrl-x }	Grow current window horizontally

When you create a second window, the same buffer contents appear in both windows. That is, you now have two windows on the same buffer. This is handy for cutting and pasting, for example, moving a paragraph from one part of the buffer to another. Or you can use a second window as a reference, referring to previous text entered into the buffer. Of course, any changes made in one window are made to the buffer contents and will be seen in both windows when they display the same text.

How do you view different files in each window? The answer to that question is to put a different buffer in each window. Before we do that, let's take a look at how to create multiple buffers.

Creating Multiple Buffers

If you want to work on two different files at a time, then each file needs its own buffer. Here are some of the commands used to work with buffers:

Command	Action
Ctrl-x b daisy	Create a new buffer called daisy or switch to the buffer daisy
Ctrl-x k daisy	Kill the buffer called daisy
Ctrl-x Ctrl-f lilac	Find the file lilac, put it in a buffer, and switch to the new buffer
Ctrl-x Ctrl-b	List all buffers in separate window

As you can see from these commands, it is possible to create several buffers, each with different contents. However, only one buffer is displayed on the screen unless you create a second window.

Multiple Buffers and Multiple Windows

The most convenient way to get emacs to display two buffers, each in its own window, is to start emacs on a file, which creates the first buffer; then use the command Ctrl-x 4f *(filename)* to display a second file in its own window. The command Ctrl-x 4 may be followed with either b, f, or . as shown in the following examples:

Command	Action
Ctrl-x 4b *(buffer name)*	Open buffer in new window
Ctrl-x 4f *(filename)*	Open file in new window
Ctrl-x 4. *(tag name)*	Open a tag file in new window

(*Note:* In Berkeley UNIX, tags are used under a program called ctags. They are not discussed here.)

The Ctrl-x 4b command is equivalent to Ctrl-x 2 Ctrl-x b, and the Ctrl-x 4f command is equivalent to Ctrl-x 2 Ctrl-x f.

Working with Files

Any information stored in UNIX is stored in files. When the emacs editor is started on an existing file, a copy of that file is brought into an emacs buffer. Any changes made to the buffer are not permanent, unless they are written to a file.

The following examples show some of the most commonly used emacs commands for dealing with files.

Starting emacs:

emacs *(filename)*   ← *starts the editor on* filename

Saving changes:

<Ctrl-x><Ctrl-s>   ← *save changes to file*

Other ways to save buffer contents:

<Esc>x write-file *(filename)*   ← *usually used to change filename*
<Esc>x append-region-to-file *(filename)*   ← *region must be marked*

Inserting a file into the buffer:

<Ctrl-x>i *(filename)*   ← *insert* filename *at the cursor*

Reading a file:

<Ctrl-x><Ctrl-r> *(filename)*   ← *visit a file, no editing*

Visiting a file:

```
<Ctrl-x><Ctrl-v> file
```
← *visits* `file`, *replacing original file*

Caution: If you are editing a file and visit another file, the new file replaces the original file in the buffer. The emacs editor will offer to save the old file, but it does so only if you respond yes. You should be careful not to type ahead after giving the Ctrl-x Ctrl-v command because emacs may interpret your typing as new commands.

For Experienced Users: Customizing *emacs*

The .emacs file is used to create customized editing environments. When the emacs editor starts up, it looks at the .emacs file for instructions, which may be key bindings, mode setups, or variable settings. You can enter these instructions into the .emacs file just like any other file by using the emacs editor. Give the command

```
emacs .emacs
```

in your *home* directory. A typical .emacs file, with comments indicated by one or more initial semicolons, might look like this:

```
;;;set the text mode as the default mode.
(setq default-major-mode 'text-mode)

;;;turn on justification for the text mode
(setq text-mode-hook 'turn-on-auto-fill)

;;;set the right margin at 64
(setq fill-column 64)

;;;define a new key binding
(global-set-key "\<Ctrl-g>" 'enlarge-window)

;;;define a new key binding
(global-set-key "\<Ctrl-x> u" 'upcase-region)
```

There are two things to notice about these commands. First, the format is in the form used by the Lisp programming language because the editor itself is written largely in Lisp. Second, you must precede a Ctrl key with a backslash (\).

These examples are just a few of the many possibilities available for personalizing your own editor. The best way to see what you might want to change is to get a copy of the written emacs manual and check the list of long commands and their key bindings.

emacs Public-Domain Editor

Entering and Exiting *emacs*

emacs *filename*	Starts editor.
Ctrl-x Ctrl-s	Saves text. *Caution:* On some systems, Ctrl-s may suspend, or freeze, the terminal display. Ctrl-q will unfreeze the display.
Ctrl-x Ctrl-c	Quits editor.

Adding or Inserting Text

Just start typing.

Moving the Cursor

Ctrl-f	Moves forward a character.
Ctrl-b	Moves backward a character.
Ctrl-n	Moves to next line.
Ctrl-p	Moves to previous line.
Ctrl-a	Moves to beginning of line.
Ctrl-e	Moves to end of line.
Esc f	Moves forward a word.
Esc b	Moves backward a word.
Esc]	Moves forward a paragraph.
Esc [	Moves backward a paragraph.
Esc <	Moves to beginning of buffer.
Esc >	Moves to end of buffer.

Repeating a Command

Esc *n* *(command)*	Repeats command *n* times.

Quitting a Command

Ctrl-g	Aborts command.

Redrawing the Screen with Cursor on Middle Line	
Ctrl-l	Redraws screen with cursor in center.
Avoiding the Redrawing of the Screen	
Esc *n* Ctrl-o	Opens *n* blank lines for text.
Killing and Deleting Text	
Del	Deletes the character just before the cursor.
Rub	Deletes the character just before the cursor.
Ctrl-d	Deletes the next character after the cursor.
Esc Del	Kills the word before the cursor.
Esc Rub	Kills the word before the cursor.
Esc d	Kills the word after the cursor.
Ctrl-k	Kills from cursor position to end of line.
Esc k	Kills to the end of the current sentence.
Ctrl-w	Kills region.
Restoring a Previous Kill	
Ctrl-y	Yanks back the text. *Note:* If you type Ctrl-k several times consecutively, one Ctrl-y will yank back all of the lines.
Esc y	Yanks back next previous kill from ring buffer. Can be used only after a Ctrl-y.
Undoing the Last Change	
Ctrl-x u	Undoes last change.
Getting Help	
Ctrl-h Ctrl-h	Gets help about the help program.
Ctrl-h t	Starts the tutorial.
Ctrl-h l	Lists the last 100 characters typed.
Ctrl-h i	Runs info, a program for browsing that includes the emacs manual.

Ctrl-h a *(descriptor)*	Lists commands containing descriptor.
Ctrl-h b	Lists key bindings.
Ctrl-h k *(key)*	Lists the command (key) runs.
	Note: Many other options are available.

Searching and Replacing

Ctrl-s *(string)* Esc	Incremental search forward for string. *Caution:* May freeze display. Ctrl-q will unfreeze display.
Ctrl-r *(string)* Esc	Incremental search backward for string.
Esc % *(string1)*	Searches and replaces, depending on next key:
Return *(string2)*	
Return	

Key	Action
Spacebar	Makes the change and advances to next occurrence.
Del	Skips this change and advances to next occurrence.
Esc	Exits query-replace.
!	Replaces all remaining occurrences.
^	Backs up to previous occurrence.
Ctrl-h	Displays a help screen.

Defining a Region

Ctrl-@	Sets *mark* at beginning of region.
(Cursor on screen)	Sets *point* at end of region.
Ctrl-x Ctrl-x	Interchanges *mark* and *point*.

Changing the Case of Text

upcase-region	Capitalizes all text.
downcase-region	Lowercases all text.

Esc l	Converts following word to lowercase.
Esc u	Converts following word to uppercase.

File-Handling Commands—Input and Output

Ctrl-x Ctrl-s	Saves text.
Ctrl-x Ctrl-c	Quits editor.
append-region-to-file *(filename)*	Appends region to a file.
write-region *(filename)*	Writes region to a file.
Ctrl-x Ctrl-v *(filename)*	Visits *filename*, replacing old file.
Ctrl-x Ctrl-r *(filename)*	Reads a file; no editing.
write-file *(filename)*	To change *filename*.
Ctrl-x i *(filename)*	Inserts *filename* at the cursor.
Esc ! *(UNIX command)*	Captures *UNIX command* in buffer.
shell-command-on-region *(UNIX command)*	Filters region through UNIX.

Buffer Commands

Ctrl-x b *(file)*	Creates a new buffer called *file* or switches to the buffer *file*.
Ctrl-x b	Switches to another buffer.
Ctrl-x k *(file)*	Kills the buffer called *file*.
Ctrl-x Ctrl-f *(file)*	Finds *file* and puts it in a buffer.
Ctrl-x Ctrl-b	Lists all buffers.

Window Commands

Ctrl-x 2	Divides the current window vertically into two windows.
Ctrl-x 5	Divides current window horizontally into two windows.

Ctrl-x 1	Deletes all windows but the current one.
Ctrl-x 0	Deletes current window.
Ctrl-o	Switches to other window.
Esc Ctrl-v	Pages other window.
Ctrl-x ^	Grows current window one line.
Ctrl-x }	Grows current window wider.
Ctrl-x 4b *(buffer name)*	Opens buffer in new window.
Ctrl-x 4f *(filename)*	Opens file in new window.
Ctrl-x 4. *(tag name)*	Opens a tag file in new window.
Formatting Text	
auto-fill-mode	Wraps word at right margin setting.
fill-region	Justifies region.
Esc q	Justifies paragraph at right margin setting.
Esc *n* Ctrl-x f	Sets right margin *n* characters.

Review Questions

1. How do you save buffer contents to a file?

2. What command will unfreeze a terminal display if Ctrl-s freezes it?

3. What command aborts an emacs command?

4. What command is used to kill a line of text?

5. What is the normal way to do "cut and paste" in emacs?

6. With what sequence do all the long forms of commands begin?

7. What does the command Ctrl-h Ctrl-h do?

8. Give the command to search an entire buffer and replace county with County.

9. What is a region? How is it defined?

10. What command is used to justify text in a region?

11. How are margins set? Give an example.

Answers

1. Ctrl-x Ctrl-s. 2. Ctrl-q. 3. Ctrl-g. 4. Use Ctrl-a to move to the beginning of the line; then press Ctrl-k. 5. Press Ctrl-k one or more times to kill lines; then press Ctrl-y. 6. Esc x. 7. It is a help command. 8. Esc % county Return County Return. 9. A *region* is any text between *point* (the cursor) and *mark*. Mark is defined by typing Ctrl-@. 10. Esc x fill-region. 11. Set the right margin with Esc 65 Ctrl-x f, where 65 is the setting. Then to justify the current paragraph, enter Esc q.

Exercises at the Terminal

1. Create a practice file by writing a short letter to a friend or relative. Save the buffer contents without leaving the editor. Do each of the following:

   a. Make a global substitution. Find the word the and change it to th## using this command:

      <Esc>% the <Return> th## <Return>

   b. Now practice using the cursor-moving keys to move to each occurrence of ## and change it back to e.

   c. Do some cutting and pasting. Move the second line to the end of the buffer.

   d. Now leave the editor without saving your changes.

   e. Reenter the editor and see if it contains your original letter to a friend.

   f. Repeat the global substitution. Change all a's to 3's. Again, practice the cursor-moving commands.

2. Start the editor on a file and practice using the search commands and then the search and replace commands.

3. Start the editor on a file and practice using regions. Define a region and capitalize all text. Then try to set the right margin to 30 characters and justify the region. Leave the editor without saving any changes made.

4. Start the editor on a practice file and try using the help commands.

5. Try using the emacs tutorial by giving the command Ctrl-h t.

6. Start the editor on a file. In the middle of the file, insert another UNIX file.

7. Start the editor on a file. Give the command Ctrl-x 2 to create two windows. Switch between windows and then try to cut and paste from one window to the other.

9

Manipulating Files and Directories: *mv*, *cp*, and *mkdir*

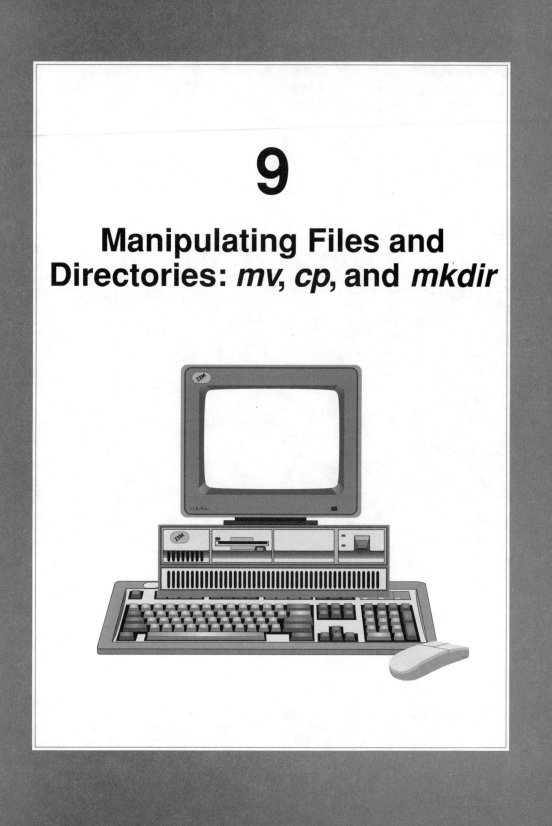

Manipulating Files and Directories: *mv*, *cp*, and *mkdir*

Now that you know the basic commands for reading files (see Chapter 4), you can get into the real fun of directory and file manipulation. However, before you do that, let's take a brief look at how UNIX names its files so that they do not get mixed up. We will conclude this chapter by showing some typing shortcuts that you can use with metacharacters (abbreviations).

Filenames, Pathnames, Heads, and Tails

What happens if Bob, Lola, and Nerkie (each of whom has his or her own UNIX account on the same system) all decide to create a file called whiz? Does UNIX become confused about the multiple whiz files? Does Lola find Bob's work in her file? Of course not! UNIX is much too clever for that. To understand what happens, you first should review the tree structure of the UNIX directory system. The full name of Lola's whiz file includes the name of the directory it is in. The full names of the three whiz files would be

```
/home/bob/whiz
/home/lola/whiz
/home/nerkie/whiz
```

These are called the *pathnames* of the files because they give the path through the directory system to the file (see Figure 9.1). The very last part of the pathname (the part after the last /) is called the *tail*, or basename, and the rest of the pathname is called the *head*.

pathname

/home/ **nerkie** / **whiz**

head   tail

Figure 9.1. A pathname, a head, and a tail.

The head of the first file tells us that the bob directory branches off the home directory and that the home directory branches off the / directory (our old friend root). For this example, all three pathnames have the same tail, that is, whiz. On the other hand, they all have different heads (/home/bob/, /home/lola/, and /home/nerkie/), so UNIX has no problem distinguishing between them. Figure 9.2 shows a directory tree for the three whiz files.

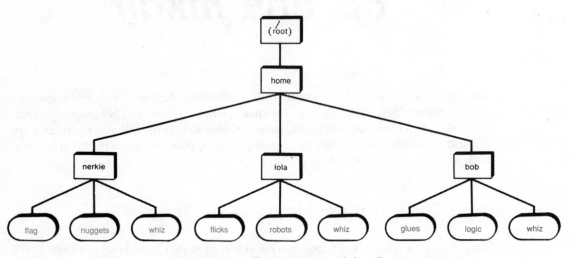

Figure 9.2. Pathnames and the directory tree.

The slash (/) takes on two roles in a pathname. The slash at the very beginning stands for the root directory. The other slashes serve to separate the name of a directory from the name of the following directory or file.

When a file is in your working directory, you can be casual and call it by its tail name. When the file is in a different directory, however, you need to tell UNIX which directory the file is in. One foolproof method is to use the pathname. For example, if Nerkie wishes to read Bob's whiz file, he can enter the command

```
cat /home/bob/whiz
```

There are other ways to identify files—namely, by using abbreviations and conventions—but, if you are in doubt, use the pathname!

Let's look at one more example. Lola has created a directory called `Bigstuff`, and in it she has placed the file `walrus`. The pathname of this file is

```
/home/lola/Bigstuff/walrus
```

The tail name is

```
walrus
```

The head is

```
/home/lola/Bigstuff/
```

If Lola is in the directory `/home/lola/Bigstuff` and wants to read the files, she can simply call the file `walrus`. However, if she is in her home directory (`/home/lola`), she can refer to the file as `/home/lola/Bigstuff/walrus` or, more simply, as `Bigstuff/walrus`.

This illustrates an important special case, shown in Figure 9.3. If a file is in a subdirectory of the one you are in, the only part of the pathname you need to use is the subdirectory name and the tail. A partial pathname such as `Bigstuff/walrus` is called a *relative* pathname because it gives the path relative to your current directory.

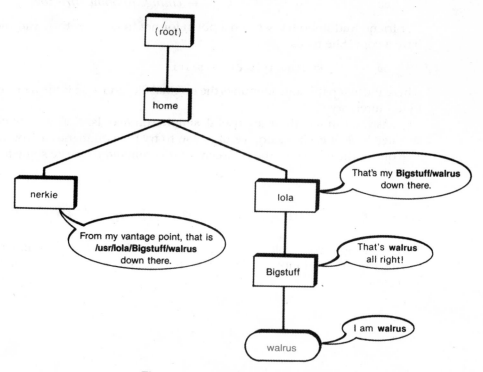

Figure 9.3.   What to call a walrus.

Basic File and Directory Manipulation Commands

As a walrus once said, "The time has come to talk of many things." We now will look at the commands `rm`, `cp`, `mv`, `ln`, `mkdir`, `rmdir`, `cd`, and `pwd`. These commands will let you manipulate your files and directories with ease and versatility. Their basic use is rather simple, but many of them can be used in more than one way. We will show you all you need to know soon enough, but first let's run through a sample session to highlight some of the most common uses.

Mimi has some files called `roses` and `daisies`. She would like to create a new directory called `Flowers` and move those files into it. So she types

```
mkdir Flowers          ← makes the new directory
mv roses daisies Flowers   ← moves files to the directory
```

Next, she wants to change to the `Flowers` directory so that she can do some work there. She types

```
cd Flowers             ← changes to new directory
vi violets             ← works on a new file there
```

The `violets` file joins the other files in that directory. When she finishes, she wants to return to her home directory, so she types a simple

```
cd                     ← change to home directory
```

Her friend Rudolpho has written a poem for her in his directory, and she wants to have a copy. She types

```
cp /home/Rudolpho/iris Flowers/iris
```

where the first pathname identifies the original file, and `iris` is the name of the copy in her directory.

As you can see, these are useful, simple commands. Now we will take a more detailed look at each. Again, we urge you to try the commands as you read along. Use one of the editors or the redirected `cat` command to create some files to work with.

Directory Commands: *mkdir*, *rmdir*, *cd*, and *pwd*

Directories give you a place to keep your files. The first three commands let you create, remove, and move through directories. The last command tells you where you are.

The Make Directory Command: *mkdir*

The mkdir command lets you build your own directory subsystem. If you are on a UNIX system, you should have a *home* directory; this is the directory you are placed in when you log on. We will assume that your directory is a subdirectory of /home so that the full pathname of your directory is /home/yourname (that is, /home/roscoe, if your login name is roscoe). The procedure is simple and quick. To create a subdirectory called, say, Formletters, you enter

    mkdir Formletters

The general form of the mkdir command is

    mkdir name1 name2...

where *name1, name2,* and so forth, are the names of the directories you wish to create. You can make directories only within your own directory system (unless, of course, you have special privileges on the system). If *name1* is a tail and not a pathname, then the new directory is attached to the directory you are in when making the command. For example, if Bob is in his home directory and issues the command

    mkdir Foibles

the result is a new directory whose pathname is /home/bob/Foibles. After doing this, Bob could switch from his home directory to the Foible directory (see the cd command) and use the command

    mkdir Gambling

to create the directory /home/bob/Foibles/Gambling.

It is easy to make directories. The challenge is to design a directory system that is the most helpful to you. Again, experience is a great teacher. We suggest that you use capital letters to begin names of subdirectories. This naming technique will help you distinguish files and subdirectories (see Figure 9.4).

The Change Directory Command: *cd*

Once you have created a new directory, you would like to use it. The cd command lets you change from one directory to another. The general form of the command is

    cd directoryname

The change directory command was once called chdir, but it is used so often that newer versions of UNIX have shortened the name to cd. After it is executed, the named directory becomes your *working directory*. For example, if you enter the commands

```
cd /home/lola/Quarkdata
ls
```

the result will be a list of files in the directory /home/lola/Quarkdata. Of course, there is a question of permissions. If Lola gave this command, she would have the power to alter the files in this directory. If Bob gave the command, normally he could look but not touch. (The standard setup allows you to look at someone else's files but not alter them. However, you can copy the file and alter the copy.) The chmod command, discussed in Chapter 12, lets you change the permissions governing your files.

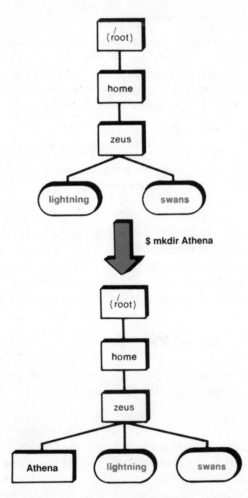

Figure 9.4.   The *mkdir* command: before and after.

The command

```
cd
```

with nothing following it will place you in your home directory.

mkdir Creates a New Directory		
Name	**Options**	**Arguments**
`mkdir`	**None**	*[directoryname...]*
Description:	The `mkdir` command creates a new subdirectory in the present directory.	
Example:	`mkdir Chapter4`	
	This command creates a new subdirectory called `Chapter4` that exists in the directory where you entered the command. *Note:* You should not use a blank space in your directory names; typing `mkdir Chapter 4` would create two directories. A handy convention is to name all directories starting with a capital letter.	

cd Change Directory		
Name	**Options**	**Arguments**
`cd`	**None**	*[directoryname...]*
Description:	The `cd` command makes the named directory your current working directory. If no directory is given, the command takes you to your home directory.	
Example:	`cd /home/reggie/Foods/Carbo`	
	This command would place you in the `/home/reggie/Foods/Carbo` directory.	

The Print Working Directory Command: *pwd*

Once you have the power to change working directories, you have the possibility of forgetting which directory you are in. The command `pwd` causes UNIX to print the full pathname of your current working directory. If, when you try to copy or move a file, UNIX claims that the file does not exist and you know it does, try pwd. You may find that you are in a different directory than you thought and that you need to use a full pathname for a file. The use of pwd is simple. If you type

```
pwd
```

and if UNIX replies

```
/home/src/cmd
```

then you are currently in the /home/src/cmd directory.

pwd **Print Working Directory**		
Name	**Options**	**Arguments**
pwd	**None**	**None**
Description:	The pwd command prints the pathname of the current working directory.	

The Remove Directory Command: *rmdir*

When you have no more use for a directory, the rmdir command lets you get rid of it. The standard form of the command is

```
rmdir dir1...
```

The rmdir command removes the one or more directories listed after the command. The command will not remove nonempty directories or, normally, directories belonging to others.

UNIX gives you the tools to organize your files efficiently and easily. We have given you the rules governing several useful commands, but it is up to you to make good use of them. The first step is to practice with them, creating new directories, populating them with files, and then copying and moving files. Get comfortable with the procedures.

Next, give thought to your own needs. Do not hesitate to create new directories. It is a good idea to use different directories to house different projects or different types of material. Give your directories and files names that tell you what the contents are. Use names like Chapter3 and UNIXbook rather than file1 and directory2. UNIX gives you the opportunity to make your directory system a model of clarity and convenience—take advantage of it!

rmdir **Removes Directories**		
Name	**Options**	**Arguments**
`rmdir`	**None**	`directoryname(s)...`

Description: The `rmdir` command removes the named directories, providing that they are empty.

Example: `rmdir Budget65 Budget66`

This command removes the directories `Budget65` and `Budget66` if they do not contain any files.

File Commands: *rm, cp, mv,* and *ln*

Handling old-fashioned files involved much paper shuffling. These four UNIX commands let you do the modern equivalent—electron shuffling—with much greater ease.

Sometimes electron shuffling is so easy it is dangerous. The commands `rm`, `cp`, and `mv` are prime examples. When you remove a file (`rm`) or copy a file (`cp`) or change the name of a file (`mv`), it is possible, even easy, to wipe out, destroy, and permanently lose valuable files. Please be careful! (We wanted to alert you right now about these possibilities and we will address them again in the following sections.) We will discuss ways to protect your files and yourself throughout this chapter and again in Chapter 11.

The Remove Command: *rm*

The `rm` command removes files. If you do not use it, your directories can become a jungle choked with unused and superceded files. The command is simple to use. You just follow `rm` with a list of the files you wish to be deleted. Each filename should be separated by a space from the others. Thus,

```
rm dearjohn dearjoe dearfred dearigor
```

removes four files.

As you can see, it is very easy to remove files. In fact, it is so easy and so irreversible that you should stop and ask yourself the following questions:

1. Am I sure I no longer want this file?

2. Is this the file I think it is?

3. Am I really sure about my answers to questions 1 and 2?

Special caution is needed when using `rm` with the wild card substitutions discussed later in this chapter. We'll remind you again when you reach that section. You may want to use the `-i` option (new to Release 4) described in the summary.

Ordinarily, you cannot remove directories with `rm`—use `rmdir` if that's what you want to do. The `-r` option given in the summary *does* let you remove directories, but you had better be certain that you really do want to remove *everything*. The `rmdir` command is safer because it removes only empty directories.

Normally, you are not allowed to remove files from someone else's directory. To make things fair, someone else can't remove yours.

---

rm Remove Files

Name	Options	Arguments
rm	-i, -r	*filename(s)...*

Description:	The `rm` command removes each file in the argument list.
Options:	`-i` For each file on the list, whether or not to delete it; the user responds with `y` or `n` for yes or no.
	`-r` Deletes a directory and every file or directory in it.
Example:	`rm -i rodgers`
	This will cause UNIX to query:
	`rm: remove rodgers?`
	You reply with `y` or `n`.

The Copy Command: *cp*

The `cp` command is used to create a copy of a file. There are several reasons why you should have a copy command. One is to create backup copies (a backup is a second copy) of files. A file you are working on can be wiped out by a system problem or (believe it or not!) by slips on your part. Thus, backups are a good idea.

Another reason is that you may wish to develop a second, slightly different version of a file, and you can use a copy as a convenient starting point. A third reason may develop from the fact that UNIX is a shared system. A colleague may write a program or collect some data you can use, and a copy function gives you an easy way to place it in your own directory. The simplest form of the copy command is

```
cp file1 file2
```

The command works from left to right; *file1* is the original and *file2* is the copy. This is how the command works. First, it creates a file called *file2*. If you already have a file by that name, it is *eliminated* and replaced by the new empty file. Then the contents of *file1* are copied into *file2*. You, of course, would use whatever names you want for the files; you are not limited to *file1* and *file2*. For example, Sam Softsell might use the command

```
cp buypasta buytacos
```

to copy the contents of his buypasta file into a buytacos file.

Sam should be careful that he does not already have a valuable file called buytacos, because it would have been wiped out by the last instruction. This is one of the less friendly aspects of UNIX, but you can use chmod (Chapter 12) to protect your valuables. You can also use the -i option (new to Release 4) described in the summary.

To copy a file from another directory into your own, you need to know the full directory name of the file. If you enter

```
cp bigthought idea
```

UNIX will search only your directory for a file called bigthought. If the bigthought file is in, say, Bob's directory (assumed to be /home/bob), then the proper command is

```
cp /home/bob/bigthought idea
```

Here, /home/bob/bigthought is the pathname of the original file. (At the end of this chapter, we will show you some abbreviations that will let you reduce the amount of typing you need to do when dealing with long pathnames.) Incidentally, Bob can use chmod to keep others from copying his files.

A second form of the copy command is

```
cp file1 file2... directory2
```

This copies the list of files given into the named directory, which must already exist. This instruction will become more useful to you once you begin establishing additional directories. The new files retain the tail name of the originals. For example, suppose Sam Softsell has a subdirectory called Backup in his home directory of /home/sam. The next command

```
cp pasta Backup
```

creates a file named pasta in the Backup directory.

There are two points to note here. First, although both files are named pasta, they exist in different directories and, thus, have different pathnames. For the preceding example, the pathname of the original file is /home/sam/pasta and the pathname of the copy is /home/sam/Backup/pasta. Second, if the directory named Backup did not exist, UNIX would assume that this command was in the first form we described. In other words, it would just copy the file pasta into a file called Backup, all in the original directory (see Figure 9.5).

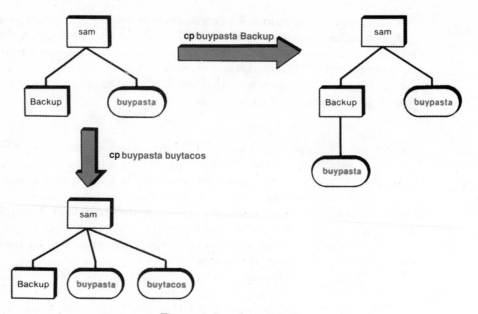

Figure 9.5.   Copying files.

Sometimes, UNIX may give you messages such as

```
cp: cannot create file2
```

or

```
cp: cannot open file1
```

This is UNIX's way of confessing bafflement at your instructions. Check to make sure that you typed the names correctly, that you are not trying to place files in someone else's directory, or that you have used the correct pathname (you may need to use a full pathname).

The Move Command: *mv*

The mv command lets you change the name of a file and lets you move a file from one directory to another. The simplest form of this command is

```
mv file1 file2
```

The effect of this command is to change the name of *file1* to *file2*. The file itself is left unchanged. Suppose that Lola LaLulu wants to change the name of a file from a.out to findanswer. She could solve her problem with the command

```
mv a.out findanswer
```

Suppose, however, she already had a file called findanswer. The mv command is as ruthless as cp; it would wipe out the old file in order to make the name available for the contents of a.out. However, the -i option (new to Release 4) described in the summary moderates this ruthlessness.

cp **Make Copies of Files**		
Name	**Options**	**Arguments**
cp	-i, -r	*file1 file2* or *file(s)...directory*

Description:
: The command cp *file1 file2* creates a copy of the first file (*file1*) and gives it the name *file2*. If a file named *file2* already exists, it will be replaced by the new one. The second form of the command (cp *file(s)...directory*) makes copies of all the files listed and places them in the named directory.

Options:
: -i   Protects you from overwriting an existing file by asking you for a yes or no before it copies a file with an existing name.

: -r   Can be used to copy directories and all their contents into a new directory.

Example:
: cp flim flam

This command makes a copy of the file flim and calls the copy flam.

cp   /home/snoopy/stormy   /home/ruff

This command makes a copy of the file stormy (from the /home/snoopy directory) and places the copy in the /home/ruff directory. The pathname of the copy is /home/ruff/stormy.

You can use the mv command to change the name of a directory, too. The form is

mv *Oldname Newname*

and is the same as that for changing a filename. In other words, mv does not care whether *Oldname* is a file or a directory; it will just proceed and give it the new name.

The final use of mv is to move files to an existing directory. The form is

mv *file1 file2... directory*

You can think of this command as moving one or more files to the specified directory. This is a very handy housekeeping command. For example, if Lola, an exotic physicist studying those exotic subatomic particles called quarks, has accumulated four files of quark data, she can create a directory called `Quarkdata` (using `mkdir`). Then she could type

```
mv quark1 quark2 quark3 quark4 Quarkdata
```

to gather the four files together in the new directory. This form of the command leaves the tail of the pathname unchanged. For example, the preceding command would change the pathname of `/home/lola/quark1` to `/home/lola/Quarkdata/quark1`. (At the end of the chapter, you will see a much quicker way to make the same move!) Of course, this use of `mv` will not work if the destination directory does not exist or if you do not have permission to write in that directory (see Figure 9.6).

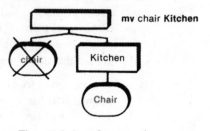

Figure 9.6.   A smooth move.

Suppose you give a command like this:

```
mv chair Kitchen
```

How does UNIX know whether you want `Kitchen` to be a file or to be a directory? Well, UNIX may be clever, but it isn't psychic—it does not know which you want. It *does* know, however, whether you already have a directory called `Kitchen`. If you do have such a directory, UNIX puts the `chair` file there. If you do not have a directory called `Kitchen`, UNIX assumes you want `Kitchen` to be a filename.

The Link Command: *ln*

With the `ln` command, you can assign multiple names to a single file. This allows you to refer to the same file by different pathnames (see Figure 9.7). This technique can be handy when you have many subdirectories because it lets you link one file to several different directories. (The names you assign are the links between the file and the directories.)

mv Move or Change a Filename

Name	Options	Arguments
mv	-i	*filename1 filename2* or *filename(s)* *directoryname*

Description: The mv command allows the user to change the name of a file. The first form of the command shown above changes the name of *filename1* to *filename2*. However, since filenames can include the full pathname, it is possible to use the command to move a file to a new directory as shown in the second form of the command.

Option: -i   Protects you from overwriting an existing file by asking you for a yes or no before it copies a file with an existing name.

Examples:

```
mv mrak mark
```

This changes the name of the file mrak to mark.

```
mv mark Hobo
```

This changes the name of the file mark (pathname /home/flisk/mark) to /home/flisk/Hobo/mark, thus moving the file to the Hobo directory.

```
mv mray Hobo/mary
```

This changes the name of the file mray (pathname /home/flisk/mray) to /home/flisk/Hobo/mary, thus changing the directory and the tail of the pathname.

A general form of this command is

```
ln file1 name2
```

where *name2* can be either a new name you wish to give to the file or it can be an existing directory name. If it is a proposed filename, the result of executing this command is that *file1* will now have two names: *file1* and *name2*. If *name2* is the name of a directory, then *file1* will also be known by the tail of its old name (*file1*) in the directory *name2*. Let's clarify these two cases with two examples.

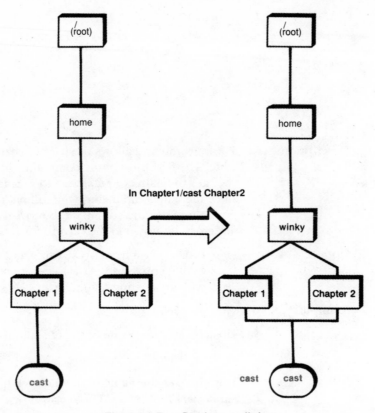

Figure 9.7.   Setting up links.

Suppose Tana, the Wonder Dog, is in her home directory (/home/tana) and gives the command

```
ln soupbone chews
```

UNIX checks to see if the name chews has been used yet. If it has not, then UNIX gives the new name to the file while still keeping the old one. (An ls command, for example, would show both, and an ls -l command would show that each had two links.) Tana then could call up the file by either name. What if there had already been a file called chews in the home directory? Then ln will first wipe out the old chews before making the link unless you use the -n option. What if chews already was a subdirectory? Then the situation would be like the next example.

Now suppose Tana has a subdirectory called Tidbit. The command

```
ln soupbone Tidbit
```

adds the soupbone name to the Tidbit directory, but it leaves the original name undisturbed. Thus, the same file is now in two directories and has two pathnames: /home/tana/soupbone and /home/tana/Tidbit/soupbone. These are the same file, not copies. When Tana is in her home directory and wants to see the file, she can type (after all, she is a wonder dog)

```
cat soupbone
```

which is short for `cat /home/tana/soupbone`.

If she switches to the `Tidbit` directory (see `cd`), she can see the contents of the file by typing

```
cat soupbone
```

which is short for `cat /home/tana/Tidbit/soupbone`.

Without the `ln` command, she would have had to type

```
cat /home/tana/soupbone
```

to see the `soupbone` file when in the `Tidbit` directory. When you have paws and have to type, you appreciate all the shortcuts you can get.

Suppose that Tana, while in her home directory, now issues the command

```
rm soupbone
```

The file `soupbone` disappears from her home directory. Does this mean that the contents of the file disappear? No! The file still exists in the `Tidbit` directory. Only when all of the names or links to the file have been removed will the file itself be erased.

Let's assume that you have established several subdirectories and that you want them to have access to the same mailing list. You could, of course, place a copy of the mailing list in each directory, but that would use too much disk space (see Figure 9.8). By using the `ln` command, you can link the file containing the list to a name in each of the directories. In effect, the same file will exist in each directory. An additional advantage is that if you update the file from one directory, you have updated it for all the directories.

There are limitations to `ln`. One is that you cannot use `ln` to assign two names to the same directory.

ln Make File Links		
Name	**Options**	**Arguments**
ln	-n, -s	*filename1 filename2* or *filename(s) directoryname*
Description:	The `ln` command lets you add one or more names to an existing file, thus providing a cross-reference system. Each name located in your directory has equal priority for reading or writing to the file. However, if a file is linked to	

another user, generally only the originator of the file can write in it (see the `chmod` command in Chapter 12).

The form `ln filename1 filename2` makes `filename2` a link to (or an alias for) `filename1`.

The form `ln filename(s) directoryname` lets you put new filenames or links into other directories.

Options: `-n`   If `filename2` is the name of an existing file, do not overwrite the contents of the file.

                `-s`   Create a symbolic link that lets you link across file systems.

Examples: (We will assume that the current working directory is `/home/francie/Spring` and that there is a file called `math` in the `/home/francie` directory.)

`ln /home/francie/math trig`

This command creates a filename `trig` in the current directory (`/home/francie/Spring`) and links that name to the file called `math` in the `francie` directory. The full pathname of the new link is `/home/francie/Spring/trig`.

`ln hist eng /home/francie`

This command puts the two filenames `hist` and `eng` from the current directory into the `/home/francie` directory. Each name is linked to the corresponding file in the current directory.

Comparing *cp*, *mv*, and *ln*

The three commands `cp`, `mv`, and `ln` form a family. All affect filenames, and they are used in a similar fashion. This similarity can occasionally confuse the new user. We think that a closer look at their workings can help prevent this, so let's take that look. Suppose you have a file called `jazz` in your home directory. To you the file is called `jazz`, but to the *computer* the file is known by an identification number. Normally, you don't need to know this number. However, you can find it by using the `-i` option of `ls`. For example, the command

```
ls -i jazz
```

could yield as output

```
2312 jazz
```

where 2312 is the ID number. This ID number, termed the *i-node* number, is the true, permanent name for the file. If, for instance, you change the name by typing

```
mv jazz cool
```

the ID number remains the same. (Try it and see!)

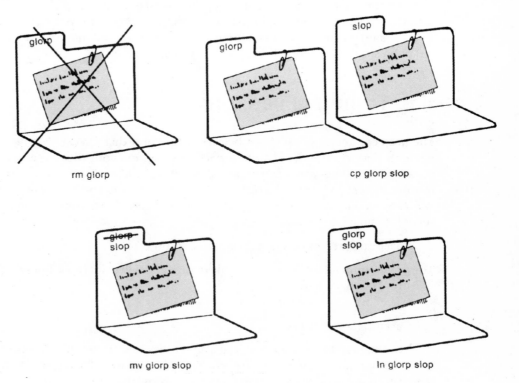

rm glorp

cp glorp slop

mv glorp slop

ln glorp slop

Figure 9.8.   A comparison of *rm, mv, cp,* and *ln.*

In the UNIX way of things, the name you choose (jazz, cool, or whatever) acts as a link between the file and your directory system. These links tie the files to the directories. Using the idea of links, we can visualize the effects of the three file manipulation commands:

1. The ln command establishes a new link between the file and a directory. All the old links (that is, names) continue to exist. No new files are created. Linking one file to different directories makes it appear as if several different files exist, but, in fact, there is just one file with multiple names. This is very useful when you want a particular file to be easily accessed from several directories without typing out pathnames.

2. The mv command establishes a new link while removing an old link. If the link is to be a different directory, it makes it appear as if the file has been

moved. However, only the link (or name) has been changed, and the file has the same ID number as before.

3. The cp command actually creates a new file with a new ID number and with its own link (name) to a directory. The old file continues to exist.

In summary, the cp command creates *new files* that are copies of the originals. The mv command creates *new names* for existing files and dumps the old names. The ln command creates new names for existing files and simultaneously maintains the old names. Neither mv nor ln creates new files.

Searching Through Files: *grep*

The grep command possesses a beauty of function that far exceeds its beauty of name. It performs the invaluable service of searching your files for a key word or phrase and telling you what it finds. Suppose, for example, you have several inventory files (infile1, infile2, infile3, and infile4) and you want to find out which one contains the description of your widget. The following command will serve that high purpose:

```
grep widget infile1 infile2 infile3 infile4
```

The grep command will search each file in turn and will print those lines that contain the string of characters widget.

The form of this command is

```
grep pattern file(s)
```

In Chapter 14, we explore grep's abilities much more fully. For the moment, we will point out just two more aspects. First, if the pattern has a space in it, enclose the pattern in single quotes so that grep will know that the second word is part of the pattern and not a file to be searched. For example, if you were interested only in a glaxon widget, you could type

```
grep 'glaxon widget' infile1 infile2 infile3 infile4
```

Second, the wild card substitutions described in the next section can make it easier to specify filenames. For instance, as you will soon learn, the first example could have been typed

```
grep widget infile?
```

The grep command is one of the most heavily used UNIX commands. As you become more involved with the system, you will find grep growing on you. Do not worry if it does; it is just a sign of a healthy relationship.

One of the pleasures of UNIX is the freedom it gives you in creating files and directories and in manipulating them. Whether you are a collector keeping an inventory, a businessperson dealing with accounts, a researcher working with experimental data and computer programs, or a homeowner monitoring the household budget, easy file handling is a key to happy computing.

What Can You Do with a UNIX File?

Files are the heart and soul of the UNIX operating system. They store everything from letters to programs to UNIX itself. Thus, it is not surprising to discover how many commands UNIX has for handling files. Table 9.1 provides a list of the most commonly used file-handling commands.

Table 9.1. What you can do with a UNIX file.

Task	Command Format
Read it	cat *filename* or more *filename*
Change or edit it	vi *filename*
Print it	lp *filename*
Simple formatting	pr *filename*
Make a copy	cp *filename newname**
Mail it	mail *loginname* < *filename*
Remove it	rm *filename*
Move it to a subdirectory	mv *filename directoryname**
Rename it	mv *filename newname**
Link a file	ln *filename newname*
Count it (see Chapter 12)	wc *filename*
Sort it (see Chapter 12)	sort *filename*
Search for key word	grep '*keywords*' *filename*
Check the spelling (see Chapter 13)	spell *filename*
Complex formatting (see Chapter 13)	nroff *filename*
Redirect the output from some commands to another file	sort *filename*> *newfile*
Combine files	cat *file1 file2*> *file3*
Append files	cat *file1*>> *file2*

Caution: The mv and cp commands are dangerous. If a file exists with the same name as the new filename, then the old file is wiped out.

Marvelous Metacharacters: Using Wild Cards and Symbolic Substitutions

You can get tired and bored punching in filenames and directory names, especially when you have to use the full pathnames. UNIX provides some tricky ways to save time. We will look here at some alternative ways to identify filenames.

One of the cleverer abilities of UNIX is *pattern searching*. That is, UNIX can find filenames that match a pattern which you supply. For example, you can have UNIX list all your files that start with chubby or remove all your files that end with old. Or you can have UNIX concatenate (cat) all your files having names with exactly four characters. The secret lies in the use of special characters, known as *wild cards*, that can stand for one or more characters in a filename. The wild cards are ? and *. The rules for using them are

1. A ? matches any one character.

2. An * matches any grouping of zero or more characters.

Some examples should make these rules clear. First, suppose that your directory contains the following files:

```
co.5    coward    hog    huge      part2.2    thug
cow     coy       hug    part2.1   start2.3
```

The command ls used by itself will list all these files, while the command ls cow will list only the cow file. The command

```
ls co?
```

however, will list cow and coy, but not co.5 or coward. We can describe the process this way. You provide the pattern co?, which means a co followed by exactly one character (any character). UNIX searches for filenames that match this pattern, and it finds cow and coy. It does not list co.5 or coward because they both have *more* than one character after the co.

Here are other examples of using ls and ? with the previous sample directory:

Command	Response
ls hu?	hug
ls hu??	huge
ls ???	cow coy hog hug
ls ?o?	cow coy hog

The process of finding out which of your files matches the pattern you give is called *filename expansion*. For instance, in the last example, we could say that the pattern ?o? was expanded to match cow, coy, and hog. Note that you use two ?'s to represent two characters, and so forth.

The * character is more general yet. As promised, it will represent any number of characters. Here are some sample commands and the responses:

Command	Response
ls h*	hog hug huge
ls *g	hog hug thug
ls hug*	hug huge
ls *hug	hug thug
ls *.*	co.5 part2.1 part2.2 start2.3

Let's take a closer look at how these examples work. The first example lists all files beginning with h. The second command lists all files ending in g. The third command lists all files starting with hug. Note that, in this case, the * even matches the *null character* (that is, no character at all). As you can see, the pattern hug? matches huge but not hug because hug? has exactly four characters. However, hug* matches both hug and huge.

The fourth command matches all names ending with hug. Again, the null character is matched. The final example matches all names containing a period in them, except for files whose name begins with a period. (Recall that ls does not show such files unless you use the -a option.)

The * and ? characters, as well as the > character, belong to a group of characters having special meanings and uses in UNIX. These characters are called *metacharacters*, an imposing term that hints at their latent power. Besides metacharacters, UNIX also possesses *metasequences*. An example is the pattern-matching sequence [ ]. Like ?, this sequence matches one character, but more restrictively. The trick is to place between the brackets a list of characters to be matched. Here are some examples:

Command	Response
ls co[xyz]coy	coy
ls [cdeg]o[gtw]	cow hog

The first example matches all 3-character names beginning with co and ending in x, y, or z. The second example would also have matched cog and how, among others, if they had been in your directory. Note that the [ ] sequence matches one character and *only* one character. For example, [nice] matches an n, an i, a c, or an e; it does not match ice or nice.

You can specify a range of characters using the [ ] notation. For instance, [2-8] represents the digits 2, 3, 4, 5, 6, 7, and 8; while [A-Z] represents all the capital letters. Thus,

    ls [A-Z]

would match all filenames consisting of a single capital letter, and

```
ls [A-Z]*
```

would match all filenames starting with a capital letter and ending in anything. The last example points out that you can combine the different pattern-matching operations into one command.

Very interesting, you say, but of what use is this? In part, the usefulness depends on what sort of names you give your files. Consider the earlier example that we gave of the mv command:

```
mv quark1 quark2 quark3 quark4 Quarkdata
```

Lola could have accomplished the same result with

```
mv quark? Quarkdata
```

or

```
mv quark[1-4] Quarkdata
```

Of course, the first instruction would also move any other files matching that pattern, such as quarky or quarkQ.

Here's another example. Suppose you created a directory called Backup and you wanted to place copies in there of *all* the files in your home directory. The following entry would do the job:

```
cp * Backup
```

In general, you should be cautious about using a solo *. Consider, for example, what the next command does:

```
rm *            ← caution: removes all files!
```

Since * matches anything, the command removes all of the files in your current working directory. Well, you are hardly likely to give that command unless you mean it, but it can crop up accidentally. Suppose that Lothario wishes to get rid of 20 files called hortense1, hortense2, and so forth. He could type

```
rm hortense*
```

and all would be well. But, if he accidentally hit the Spacebar and typed

```
rm hortense *   ← caution: removes all files!
```

UNIX would first look for a file called hortense, remove it if found, and then proceed to carry out the * and remove all files. Here is another example. You wish to *cat* the file fourtney.Bell. If you have no other files starting with f, you can type

```
cat f*
```

If you have other files starting with f, perhaps

```
cat fo*
```

or

```
cat f*1
```

will work, depending on the names of the other files.

Like many rules, these have exceptions. In particular, these metacharacters do not match an initial period, a slash, or a period immediately following a slash. There are good reasons for protecting an initial period. First, setup files, like `.profile`, often have names beginning with a period. This is to make the files unobtrusive, since `ls` does not list such files unless you use the `-a` option. If the metacharacters did match an initial period, you might accidentally remove a file that did not show up with the normal `ls` command. A second reason, which we discuss soon, is that the shell recognizes `.` and `..` as representing the current and parent directories. The slash is protected so that filename matching is confined to the current working directory. The slash, recall, serves to separate names in a pathname.

The wild cards are great time savers. The more you work and play with UNIX, the more often—and the more naturally—you will use their help.

Directory Abbreviations: ., .., and ~

UNIX offers you some useful abbreviations for directory names. We will unveil them here.

If Nerkie wants to copy two files called `tillie` and `max` from Bob's subdirectory `gossip` into his own subdirectory `lowdown`, he could type

```
cp /home/bob/gossip/tillie /home/bob/gossip/max /home/nerkie/lowdown
```

What a job! UNIX offers some shortcuts to those of you who desire less typing. They are abbreviations for particular directories as follows:

Directory	Command Shortcut
Your current working directory	. (a simple period)
The directory from which yours branches	.. (two periods)
A home directory (csh and ksh)	~ (a tilde)

The tilde abbreviation is available if you use either the `csh` shell or the `ksh` shell discussed in Chapter 11.

Here are some examples and what they stand for, assuming that Nerkie uses them while in the `/home/nerkie` directory:

Abbreviated Command	Meaning for Our Example
~	/home/nerkie
~bob	/home/bob
~lowdown	/home/lowdown
~bob/gossip	/home/bob/gossip

Notice the difference between `~lowdown` and `~/lowdown`. The first one would cause UNIX to look for the home directory of a user named `lowdown`, while the second would lead UNIX to look through Nerkie's home directory for a subdirectory called `lowdown`.

Here are some more examples showing how Nerkie could reduce his typing. Suppose he wants to copy the same two files as before (`tillie` and `max`) from Bob's subdirectory called `gossip` into his subdirectory `lowdown`:

```
cp ~bob/gossip/tillie ~bob/gossip/max lowdown
```

(Because Nerkie is in his home directory, UNIX will recognize `lowdown` as a subdirectory.)

An easier way to do the same thing would be to move into Bob's directory before giving the copy command:

```
cd ~bob/gossip
cp tillie max ~/lowdown
```

Yet another possibility would be to switch into his subdirectory and then give the copy command:

```
cd lowdown
cp ~bob/gossip/tillie ~bob/gossip/max .
```

These directory abbreviations can be combined with the wild card substitutions. For instance, Nerkie can copy the entire file contents of Bob's `gossip` directory into his own `lowdown` subdirectory with

```
cp ~bob/gossip/* lowdown
```

If Nerkie is already in the `lowdown` directory, he could have simplified this even more with

```
cp ~bob/gossip/* .
```

Here are some more examples and what they stand for, assuming that Nerkie uses them while in the `/home/nerkie` directory.

```
.            /home/nerkie
..           /home
./lowdown    /home/nerkie/lowdown
```

If Nerkie uses `cd` to switch to the `/home/nerkie/lowdown` directory, the meanings of the last two become

```
.            /home/nerkie/lowdown
..           /home/nerkie
```

The directory abbreviations often come in handy when you decide to make wholesale revisions in your directory system. They give you a convenient way to shift large blocks of files about. Suppose, for example, that Nerkie is working in his `/home/nerkie/Programs/Fortnerkie` directory and that he wishes to copy several files, all of which have names ending in `.f`, from `/home/nerkie/Programs` to his current directory. If he did not know about these directory abbreviations, he could use

```
cp /home/nerkie/Programs/*.f /home/nerkie/Programs/Fortnerkie.
```

But now that he knows better, he can just type

```
cp ../*.f .
```

That is, copy everything from the directory above that ends in `.f` into the current directory. Not only is this quicker to type, but it also offers fewer opportunities to make typing errors. Ah, how lucky Nerkie is to have a UNIX system at his service!

Review Questions

The hierarchical structure of the filing system is one of the major features of the UNIX operating system. Here are some exercises to give you confidence in using the system.

A. Matching Commands

Match the commands shown on the left to the functions shown on the right.

1. `cd ..`	a. Makes a new subdirectory named `D2`.
2. `pwd`	b. Lists contents of the working directory.
3. `mv dearsue dearann`	c. Changes the name of `dearsue` to `dearann`.
4. `mail sue`	d. Initiates sending mail to `sue`.
5. `cat part.? > final`	e. Prints all lines containing the word `sue` in the file `dearann`.
6. `ls`	f. Copies the file `stats` in `hoppy`'s home directory into a file called `stats` in the current working directory.
7. `mkdir D2`	g. Gives you your current working directory.
8. `grep sue dearann`	h. Concatenates all files whose names consist of `part.` followed by one character, and places the result in the file `final`.
9. `rm fig*`	i. Moves your working directory up one level.
10. `cp /home/hoppy/stats .`	j. Removes all files whose names start with `fig`.

B. Creating Commands

Use the hypothetical file structure shown in Figure 9.9 to create the commands that will accomplish the following actions (in some cases, there is more than one way). Assume that you are in the directory called `tinker`.

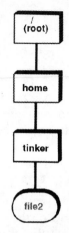

Figure 9.9.   Your hypothetical working directory.

1. List all files and directories in your account.

2. Read the filename `file2`.

3. Make a copy of `file2` and call it `file5`.

4. Make a subdirectory called `D2`.

5. Put yourself in subdirectory `D2`.

6. Move `file2` into `D2`.

7. While in subdirectory `D2`, list all files in directory `tinker`.

8. Assuming you are in the subdirectory `D2`, create a subdirectory `D3` at the same level as `D2`, that is, not a subdirectory of `D2`. (Hint: One method is a two-step sequence.)

9. Assume you are in the `home` directory. Place today's date in a file in `D3`, calling it `f8`.

10. Remove subdirectory `D3`.

Answers

A. 1—i, 2—g, 3—c, 4—d, 5—h, 6—b, 7—a, 8—e, 9—j, 10—f
B. 1. `ls`. 2. `cat file2`. 3. `cp file2 file5`. 4. `mkdir D2`. 5. `cd D2`. 6. `mv ../file2`. or `cd home` and `mv file2/D2/file2`. 7. `ls ../` 8. `cd` to go to your `tinker` directory; then `mkdir D3` or, in one step, `mkdir ../D3`. 9. `date > D3/f8` or `cd D3` and `date > f8`. 10. First, `cd D3`, second `pwd` to make sure you are there, then `rm *` (a powerful command!) then `cd` to get back `tinker`, and, finally, `rmdir D3`.

Exercises at the Terminal

Even if you have been following the chapter while sitting at a terminal, you might like to try these exercises illustrating the major commands and their use.

1. Find your full pathname.

2. List the contents of your home directory.

3. Some UNIX systems have games on them. Can you find the directory in which they are stored and list them?

4. Create a new subdirectory called D7. Put yourself in D7 and try to copy any two files into the D7 directory. You should use full pathnames for the experience.

5. Can you place a backup copy of your D7 files into a new subdirectory called D8 by using metacharacters?

6. Try creating a new filename using `ln`.

7. Use `grep` on your mailbox file (`mbox`) to find the occurrence of a word such as *dear* or *hello*.

8. Clean up your filing system by removing the files from D8 and then removing D8 itself.

10

Using Programming Languages: FORTRAN, Pascal, and C

Chapter 10

Using Programming Languages: FORTRAN, Pascal, and C

New UNIX user Wendell Turnbull Krumpnose rushed to the computer room clutching the magnetic tape that he had just received in the mail (ordinary mail, this time, not electronic mail). The tape contained a FORTRAN program that made home solar energy calculations.

"Here, guys, please load this on the system for me."

Since Wendell was such a nice guy, the technicians gladly dropped what they were doing and loaded the tape on a tape drive, which read the contents of the tape into a file called solcalc in Wendell's directory. Wendell sat down at his terminal, eager to use the new program.

But how? Wendell thought for a moment (that being the usual unit of time he devoted to thought). "Commands like cat and ls really are programs, and I run them just by typing their names. So maybe all I have to do is type solcalc." He did so, and UNIX replied with

```
solcalc: Permission denied.
```

Hmm. Maybe he should try typing the FORTRAN commands himself. He picked a line at random (real rval) from the program listing and typed it to see what would happen. UNIX responded with

```
real: not found.
```

Hmm. Perhaps a different approach was needed. "Help!" he cried, and the technicians hurried in with concerned looks upon their faces. "What can we do to assist you?" they chorused.

Wendell explained his problem, and they quickly set him straight. The computer has its own private language, and it isn't FORTRAN. UNIX systems, however, have a special program called f77 that translates FORTRAN into the simple instructions that the host computer can understand. This process is called *compiling*. Soon, under the benevolent tutelage of the staff, Wendell was able to master the needed skills. He changed the name of his file to solcalc.f so that f77 would recognize that it was a FORTRAN file. Next, he typed

```
f77 solcalc.f
```

and waited while f77 labored mightily for him. Finally, f77 produced a ready-to-go program and placed it in a file called a.out (a favorite UNIX name for such files). Now to use it! All Wendell had to do was type the word a.out, and the program ran. His original idea had not been that bad; he had just applied it to the wrong file.

Eventually, Wendell thought of modifications he wanted to make in the program. The program had many subsections called *subroutines*, and it seemed a shame to have to recompile the whole program when his changes were made to just one subroutine. Compilation uses a lot of computer time. Again, his friends helped him out and showed him how to use the UNIX editors to place each subroutine in a file of its own. Now, when he submitted the collection of files to f77, not only did the compiler give him a ready-to-run program (a.out), it also gave him a compiled version of each subroutine. From now on, if Wendell needed to change a subroutine, he needed to recompile only that one subroutine and let f77 combine it with his compiled versions of the rest of the program. With support like this, Wendell could not avoid fame and riches.

Running a Program

How do you run a program on a computer? This is a pretty important question for many people. Perhaps you know a computer language or two yourself. Perhaps you have purchased, borrowed, or otherwise acquired a program from elsewhere; or perhaps you are just learning to program. Once you get a program, it is a simple matter to run it using UNIX. In this chapter we will outline some of the basic concepts that concern programs, discuss some of the languages with which you can work, and explain how to run programs in C, FORTRAN, and Pascal. We will not tell you how to write programs, but this chapter will get you started in the process of using programs.

Languages, Compilers, and Interpreters

Once upon a time, not so long ago and not so far away, you needed to have mastered much terminal lore and have great skill to run a computer. Now, it is getting easier and easier every day to use computers. People have not gotten any smarter, and neither have the computers. (But computers have become faster, cheaper, more compact, and more powerful. They also can store more information than before, so they are not doing too badly!) What has changed is that clever people have written clever programs to make it easier for the nonspecialist to deal with computers. In particular, the development of programming languages, compilers and interpreters, and operating systems makes programming much simpler. What do all these terms mean? To clarify them, we will survey how a computer is used.

Computers are machines that follow instructions. If you devise a set of instructions to accomplish some particular task, that is a program. Thus, the trick to getting a computer to work for you is to give it the right instructions. This is not that easy to do because the computer itself understands only a limited set of rather basic instructions called the *instruction set*. Furthermore, it knows these instructions not by name but by a code (binary code) that uses only ones and zeros. The most basic way to program a computer, then, is to feed a string of these binary-coded instructions to the computer. This is called working in *machine language*. Programming in machine language is tedious and exacting; it certainly is not going to capture the imagination of the general public. Also, each type of computer would, in general, have its own machine language. Thus, every time a new machine was acquired, the users would have to learn the new language and rework their old programs. Users were driven by their own laziness to develop a universal language that could be used on many different machines.

Now that is an interesting problem. How do you create programs to run on any machine when each machine has its own primitive machine language? One way is to do it in two steps. The first step is to create a more universal language that humans can understand easily and, perhaps, even love. Such a language, of course, is incomprehensible to a computer. The second step is to write a translation program that translates the new language into the machine's own language. This translation program is called a *compiler*. Each kind of computer, then, would have its compiler written in its own machine language. The compiler will let the computer understand the universal language.

What universal language resulted from this plan of attack? By now, hundreds of languages have been created along these lines, but none is regarded as universal (except, perhaps, by its creator). Several, however, do have a widespread popularity, including such stalwarts as FORTRAN, COBOL, BASIC, Pascal, APL, PL/M, LISP, Logo, and C. UNIX systems usually are supplied with most of these languages and can have the others installed. This means that UNIX-compatible compilers or interpreters exist for these languages. (An *interpreter* is a particular kind of compiler used for interactive languages such as Logo and BASIC.)

Compiled Languages and Interpreted Languages

Compiled languages and interpreted languages represent two approaches to using languages on a computer. The compiling approach was developed in the days when the usual way of using a computer was to feed it punched cards, punched tape, or magnetic tape. This meant that the user had to prepare the complete program in advance and then submit the whole thing to the computer. A compiler would then take this entire block of programming and work it into a language acceptable to the computer. Thus, the end result of the compiler's toil was a complete program arranged in machine language. You could save this program and, next time, use it instead of the original. Hence, once your program was successfully compiled, you didn't have to compile it again unless you needed to change it. Since compilation was a slow process, you saved much time when you avoided compiling programs.

The development and rapid spread of the video keyboard terminal opened up a much more exciting way of communicating with a computer—direct interaction. Now you have an electronic "Simon says" machine. You tell the computer to do this, and it does; you tell it to do that, and it does. But, compiled languages do not fit into this scheme very easily. Nothing gets done until after you type the entire program and then have it compiled and run. Interactive languages, such as BASIC and Logo, get around this by translating each line *as you type it*. For example, suppose you type the following three lines in BASIC:

```
LET X = 6
LET Y = 2 + X
PRINT Y
```

Immediately after you enter the first line, the computer creates a storage area, names it X, and stores the value 6 in it. Immediately after you enter the second line, the computer creates a storage area, names it Y, adds 2 to 6, and stores the value of eight in Y. Immediately after you enter the third line, the computer prints the value eight on your terminal screen, letting you see how clever it is. The program that does the work of translating your instructions into machine actions is called an *interpreter*.

Suppose, though, you want to collect a few instructions into a program before having them acted upon. BASIC and Logo allow you to do this. However, when you do finally run the program, it is still interpreted line by line rather than as a block. That is, the interpreter looks at one line of instructions, converts it to an appropriate action, and only then does it look at the next line.

The chief difference, then, between a compiler and an interpreter is that the compiler translates entire program chunks at a time and an interpreter translates single lines at a time. Each method has its advantages and disadvantages. The main advantage of the interpretative approach is the direct and rapid feedback you get. Do it right, and you see your success immediately. Do it wrong, and you find out right away. Also, you get to correct it right away. The main disadvantage is that interpretative systems are relatively slow. For example, if a program cycles through the same instruction several times, that instruction has to go through the translation process each time. Compilers more or less reverse the situation. You do not get any feedback until you complete the program and try to compile and run it. On the other hand, once the program works properly, you have an efficient machine-language version. Compilers are fairly intelligent programs and, by looking at program segments larger than a line, they can put together a more efficient translation than an interpreter can.

We have indicated the role of languages and of compilers and of interpreters. Where do operating systems fit into the picture? Operating systems, such as UNIX, handle such tasks as feeding a program to a compiler, loading the resulting machine-language program into the computer, and running the program. Thus, modern computers are set up so that they can attend to all the grungy details while you act as the master planner.

Let's take a brief look at some of the more common languages.

FORTRAN

FORTRAN is an acronym for *FOR*mula *TRAN*slation. This language was developed in the 1950s to deal with scientific and engineering programming. As the name suggests, FORTRAN is particularly suited to working with equations and formulas. Since then, of course, computers have been used for a wider and wider range of problems, and FORTRAN has been modified to meet these new needs. The latest version, FORTRAN 77 (so named because its standards were defined in 1977), is a general-purpose language, capable of dealing with numeric and nonnumeric problems. Many people in computer science feel that FORTRAN is dated and is not state-of-the-art, but there is a tremendous body of programs and software available in FORTRAN. FORTRAN still is used widely in engineering, science, and education. Thus, the language will continue to be an important one for a long time.

COBOL

COBOL (*CO*mmon *B*usiness-*O*riented *L*anguage) was developed shortly after FOR-TRAN, and was intended to meet the needs of business programming. At that time, computers were huge and expensive so it was mainly only the giant companies that had them. Thus, much of the business programming for the major corporations has been done using COBOL. Small businesses, on the other hand, acquired computers when computers became smaller and cheaper. Business programming, on this smaller scale, more typically has been done in BASIC, because BASIC is better suited for small computers.

BASIC

BASIC (*B*eginners *A*ll-purpose *S*ymbolic *I*nstruction *C*ode) was developed in the 1960s at Dartmouth College to help students with no computer background learn to use a computer. It is an easy language to learn and use, and its simplicity and small memory requirements have made it a natural choice for microcomputers. It is probably the most widely used language in the world. BASIC is used for business applications, educational purposes, research, and computer games. It is an interactive language with all the advantages and disadvantages that the term implies. The original version had severe limitations, including highly restricted variable names, so now several enhanced versions are available. These versions are more powerful, but the existence of more than one version can cause problems when you try to shift a program from one machine to another.

Pascal

Pascal (named after the 18th-century mathematician Blaise Pascal) was developed in the 1970s by Niklaus Wirth, a Swiss mathematician. By that time, people had been programming long enough to develop good programming principles. Wirth developed Pascal to embody these ideas. His main intent was to provide a language that would help, even compel, computer science students to develop a good programming style. However, the use of Pascal has grown beyond education, and Pascal is now a very popular general-purpose language. Its use is being promoted in industry, where experience has shown it to produce programs that are more reliable and understandable than the older FORTRAN, BASIC, and COBOL programs.

C

C was developed in the 1970s by D. M. Ritchie at Bell Labs. In many ways, it is based on the same ideas as Pascal, but it was developed with an eye to *systems programming*, that is, the writing of programs to be used in running a computer system. For example, most of UNIX is written in the C language, including the FORTRAN and Pascal compilers. Although that is the orientation of the language, C can be used as a general-purpose language. On UNIX systems, programs written in C generally use less computer space than similar programs written in other languages.

The C compiler that came with earlier versions of UNIX implemented what has become known as K&R C, named after Brian Kernighan and D.M. Ritchie, who defined the first standard for the language. Recently, the American National Standards Institute (ANSI) has adopted a revised definition of the language called ANSI C. Version 4 of System V UNIX now makes ANSI C available in the UNIX environment.

C++

In the 1980s, Bjarne Stroustrup developed the C++ language at Bell Labs. As its name suggests, C++ is based on the C language. In particular, C++ adds to C the tools needed to make C++ an object-oriented programming (OOP) language. OOP represents a new programming paradigm that makes it easier to design and maintain large programs. Indeed, AT&T is rewriting the UNIX operating sytem in C++.

Logo

Logo was developed in 1966 with the design goals of being simple to use, yet extremely powerful. It grew from work in artificial intelligence and is used in educational research. It is an interactive language that integrates in a uniform manner the facilities for graphics, calculation, and list processing. It is not yet widely available on UNIX, but its use is expected to grow in the next few years.

Compiling and Using Programs

Writing a program involves several major steps. The first is deciding what you want the program to accomplish. The second is working out a logical approach to accomplish the goal. The third step, called *coding*, is expressing that approach in a programming language. We are not going to tell you how to do any of these things (we would like to, but that would take another book or two). We will show you what to do once you get that far.

Each language has its own compiler. They are all used in much the same fashion, so we will go through two examples in C and then outline the use of the FORTRAN and Pascal compilers.

Compiling a C Program: *cc*

To get the feel of UNIX compilers, you may want to run through this example at a terminal. We begin with a very simple example of a program in C. It is simple enough that you do not have to know C to work through this example.

```
#include <stdio.h>
main()
{
    char name [72];

    printf("Hi! What's your first name?\n");
    scanf(" %s", name);
    printf("Hello, %s!\n", name);
    printf("You have a very nice, intelligent-sounding name.\n");
}
```

To use this program, your first step is to call up an editor to create a file. If you have been good and have read the preceding chapters, you know how to do that. The name of the file should end in .c. This will identify the file as a C program to the C compiler. For example, you could call the file lets.c. If you copy this program into a file, be sure to type it exactly as it appears here. Do not substitute a parenthesis (()) for a brace ({) or for a bracket ([). Do not use uppercase letters where the program uses lowercase, and do not omit the semicolons. The indentions and blank lines are used to clarify the organization of the program to a human reader; they are ignored by the compiler. The #include statement tells the compiler where to find some standard input/output information.

Suppose that you now have this program in the file lets.c. Your next step is to feed the program to the C compiler. The UNIX C compiler is called cc (clever name, eh?), and the feeding consists of typing cc and following it with the name of the file you wish to compile. In this case, you would type

```
cc lets.c
```

There will be a brief wait while cc does its work. If you made a detectable error in typing the program, cc will tell you so. It even will tell you exactly what it thinks is wrong. Whether you can make sense out of the message depends on what you know about C. Of course, you may never make errors; if so, you need not worry about error messages.

Once cc is finished, the standard UNIX prompt will return. If you list your files, you will find a new one called a.out (see Figure 10.1). This is the name that cc gives to the file in which it places the machine-language version of your program. The program is ready to work. To run it, just type

```
a.out
```

If you want to save the program, it is a good idea to rename a.out so that you do not clobber your old program the next time you compile another program!

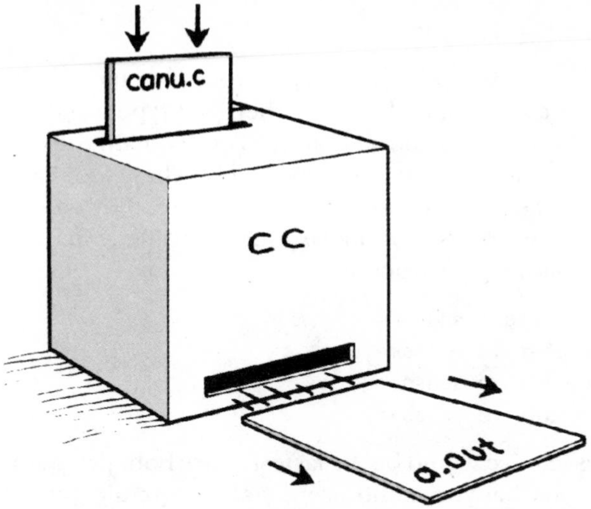

Figure 10.1.   Feeding a program to *cc*.

Let's extend the example a little. Use an editor to add a new line to lets.c:

```
# include <studio.h>
main()
{
    char name 72];

    printf("Hi! What's your first name?\n");
    scanf("%s", name);
    printf("Hello, %s!\n", name);
    printf("You have a very nice, intelligent-sounding name.\n");
    addsome();
}
```

The added line is the one with addsome() in it. Now create a new file called addsome.c and enter the following text in it:

```
addsome()
{
    printf("I am happy to have felt your fingers on me.\n");
}
```

Now you have two files: lets.c contains the main program, and addsome.c contains a subordinate program (called a *function* in C) that is used by the main program. To get this combination to work, compile both files simultaneously:

```
cc lets.c addsome.c
```

Once this is done, you can ls your files and see that you have three new files: lets.o, addsome.o, and a.out. When you type a.out, your new program will run. What about lets.o and addsome.o? They contain the object code (see the next box) for lets.c and addsome.c, respectively. They, too, can be fed to the cc compiler. Because they already are in machine code, they will be processed faster than the original files. Thus, if you lose your a.out file, you can reconstruct it with any one of the following instructions:

```
cc lets.c addsome.c
cc lets.c addsome.o
cc lets.o addsome.c
cc lets.o addsome.o
```

The last choice would be the fastest, since both programs already are in object code. Note, too, that you could use the addsome.o file with any other program that you devised that would call the addsome() function. If you want to change addsome.c and leave lets.c alone, you can edit addsome.c and use the third choice. Thus, you need to recompile only the parts you have altered.

Normally, cc produces permanent object files only when two or more files are compiled, but you can request an object file even if you compile only one file. The on-line manual will give you a complete outline of your options.

The cc compiler now is ANSI C compliant. You can select exactly how compliant through a series of three options: -Xt, -Xa, and -Xc. These options represent increasing degrees of conformity to the ANSI C standard.

cc C Compiler		
Name	**Options**	**Arguments**
cc	-c, -o, -Xt, -Xa, -Xc	*file1 file2* or *file(s)...directory*
Description:	The cc command compiles programs in the C language. If the input file is in C, its name should end in .c. If it is an object-code file, its name should end in .o. The submitted files are compiled (if necessary) to create an executable program file called a.out. An object-code file is created for each C file and is stored in a file whose name is the same as the original, except that .c is	

Options:	-c	Suppresses the loading phase (creating a.out) and forces an object file to be produced.
	-o *filename*	Causes the executable program to be given the name *filename* instead of a.out.
	-Xt	Uses ANSI C (transition level).
	-Xa	Uses ANSI C.
	-Xc	Uses strictly-conforming ANSI C.

replaced by .o. (The .o file eventually is deleted if only one program is submitted.)

Example:

```
cc -o poker straight.c flush.o
```

This command takes a C program from the file straight.c and the object code of a previously compiled C program from the file flush.o. The C program from straight.c is compiled, and the object code is placed in a file called straight.o. The two object codes are combined along with required C routines to form an executable program called poker. Typing poker will run the program.

The FORTRAN Compiler: *f77*

The UNIX FORTRAN compiler is called f77 to remind us that it can handle the latest version of FORTRAN (FORTRAN 77). A great mass of FORTRAN programming is in the preceding version (called FORTRAN IV or FORTRAN 66), and f77 accepts programs in that version, too. In fact, it accepts all sorts of files; the on-line manual will document the limits of its appetite. We will assume here that you are interested in running a standard FORTRAN program (either 77 or 66). (The f77 compiler replaces the fc compiler, which just did FORTRAN 66.)

The first step, once you have a FORTRAN program, is to place it in a file whose name ends with .f. This identifies the file as a FORTRAN file to the f77 compiler. (Incidentally, the column spacing in the files should be set up the same way that it is on punched cards; that is, columns 2 to 5 for line numbers, column 6 for the continuation mark, and columns 7 to 72 for statements.) Then submit the file to the compiler by typing f77 and the filename. For example, if your program is in a file called sun.f, you would type

```
f77 sun.f
```

Object Files and *a.out*

When you submit a program to one of the UNIX compilers, it generally produces two types of output files: object files (identified by their .o ending) and a loaded and executable file (called a.out by default). Both contain machine-language versions of your programs, so you may wonder what the difference is. (If you don't wonder, you have our permission to skip this box.)

An object file contains the machine-language code for your program. It is, however, an incomplete file. First, your program will probably use one or more system *library* functions. By that, we mean programs provided by the system. Examples would be print or write statements, trig functions, and the like. The printf() and scanf() functions in the C program example are two such library functions. Your object file will not contain the code for these functions; it just has the code for the part of the program that you wrote. Second, you may have spread your program over two or more files. The object files would not contain the instructions needed to tie the files together. Third, an object file is not set up to run; it is just a passive storehouse of information.

The a.out file, on the other hand, *is* ready to run. It includes the code for system functions, it combines your files if you have more than one, and it is set up to execute when you type its name. It contains the same sort of code as the .o files; it is just more complete.

Well, you may wonder, why bother with object-code files if a.out is all you need to run a program. The reason is that object files become very handy if you modularize your programs. In FORTRAN, you should give each subroutine its own file. In C, you should give individual functions their own files. In this manner, you can build up your personal library of little task-solvers and construct programs from various combinations of files. Even if you don't have such ambitions, this approach of separating programs into several files allows you to update individual files without having to recompile the entire program. An object file compiles much more quickly than does the original code.

Can you mix object-code files from different compilers? You can to some extent, but not in a casual manner. It takes a special blend of information to do so—a blend beyond the scope of this book. A Bell Labs pamphlet, *A Portable FORTRAN 77 Compiler*, by S. I. Feldman and P. J. Weinberger, explains how to make C and FORTRAN programs compatible.

If your program is acceptable, f77 then produces two files. The first is called a.out and the second, sun.o. The sun.o file contains the object code for your program, and a.out has the executable version. (See the preceding box if you have forgotten the difference.) To run your program, just type

```
a.out
```

If your program is spread over more than one file (in subroutine files, for example), just enter all the filenames after the f77 command. These files can be FORTRAN files, object-code files, or a mixture of the two. For example, suppose you had already compiled the three files sun.f, moon.f, and earth.f, and had saved the corresponding object-code files. If you then changed moon.f and needed all three files for a complete program, you could type

```
f77 sun.o moon.f earth.o
```

to get a new a.out file. As we have mentioned earlier, it is a good idea to change the name of the a.out file if you plan to use the program again.

f77	**FORTRAN Compiler**	
Name	**Options**	**Arguments**
f77	-o, -c	*file(s)*
Description:	The f77 compiler compiles programs written in FORTRAN. If the program is written in FORTRAN, it should be placed in a file whose name ends in .f. If the program is in object-code form, it should be in a file whose name ends in .o. The compiler takes .f files, compiles them, and stores the object code in files of the same name, but with the .f replaced by .o. The object code and required support routines are loaded into an executable file called a.out.	
Options:	-o *filename* This option causes the executable program to be called *filename* instead of a.out.	
	-c This suppresses loading but still produces object files for each source.	
Example:	f77 -o porker slop.f	
	This command takes the FORTRAN program in the file slop.f, compiles it, and places the object code for it in a file named slop.o. It then takes the object code, combines it with the required FORTRAN support programs, and loads them into an executable file named porker. The program can be run by typing porker.	

The Pascal Compiler: *pc*

The cc and f77 compilers are standard components of the UNIX system, but there is no standard Pascal compiler. Many systems, however, have the Pascal pc compiler developed at Berkeley, and we will use it as a typical example. It is used in the same fashion as cc and f77. Pascal programs should be stored in files whose names end in .p. Suppose, for example, you have a Pascal program stored in a file called rascal.p. To compile your Pascal rascal, type

```
pc rascal.p
```

If the compiler finds no major errors, pc will provide you with a file called a.out, which will contain the executable version of your program. To use it, type

```
a.out
```

Again, we remind you that it is a good idea to change the name of the a.out file so that some new a.out does not come along and clobber it.

Like cc and f77, pc generates object-code files in addition to a.out. Normally, it does so only if you compile two or more files at the same time, but you can request object code even for a single file. The UNIX on-line manual will outline your options.

Once you have object-code versions of your Pascal procedures, you can combine them with Pascal files. There are some details of referencing that you will have to attend to. Check with your system's manuals or staff to learn the specific requirements.

Compilers: Summing Up

As you probably noticed, the compilers cc, f77, and pc are all used in much the same way. Each accepts language files (whose names should end in .c, .f, and .p, respectively) and object-code files (whose names should end in .o). Each will accept several files simultaneously and will combine them into a complete program (see Figure 10.2). Each can generate object-code files from the language source files. Each loads the assembled program into a file called a.out, which can then be run by typing its name. The only caution that we might raise is that you cannot routinely feed object-code files produced by one compiler to a compiler for a different language. (This task is not impossible, but it is definitely beyond the scope of this book.)

The compilers are easy to use and will produce efficient programs, so if you know one of these languages, get in there and write a great program!

pc **Pascal Compiler**		
Name	**Options**	**Arguments**
pc	-c, -o	*file(s)*

Description: The pc command compiles programs written in Pascal. Pascal filenames should end in .p. The compiler also accepts object-code programs contained in files whose names end in .o. The object code produced for a .p file is placed in a file of the same name but with the .p replaced by .o. A complete program is assembled from all the files and is loaded along with the required system routines into an executable file named a.out. This file can be run by typing its name and pressing Return.

Options:

-c   This suppresses the loading phase (creating a.out) and forces an object file to be produced, even if only one program is compiled.

-o *filename*   This option causes the executable program to be called *filename* instead of a.out.

Example: f77 -o porker slop.f

This command compiles the Pascal program in mask.p and places the object code for that program in the file mask.o. It then combines this object code with the code in sword.o and with the system code to produce a complete program which is loaded into the file zorro.

Running a Program in the Background

Has this happened to you? You start a program running at a terminal. Then you think of something else you want to do on the computer, but the program seems to take forever (for example, more than 60 seconds) and you have to sit twiddling your thumbs until the program is done. If you enjoy that sort of situation, read no further. But if you think you deserve better, UNIX agrees. That is why UNIX offers the *background* job option, which lets the system work on a problem out of view, freeing the terminal for other tasks or games.

Compiler	Accepts* filenames ending with	Produces† .o files	Executable program† placed in file
cc	.c, .o	If more than one file is submitted.	a.out
f77	.f, .o	Yes	a.out
pc	.p, .o	If more than one file is submitted.	a.out

* partial list
† assuming no options specified

Figure 10.2.   Compilers and files.

The way to run a program in background is simple. Suppose, for example, you have a program called a.out that reads information from one file, does a bunch of amazing things, and then prints brilliant results into a second file. To run this program in background, type

```
a.out &
```

The & symbol following the command is the instruction that tells UNIX to run the program in background. Once you enter this command, you will get a response, but the response will depend on the system you are using. If you are using the Bourne shell, the response you get will look like this:

```
6784
$
```

The 6784 is a job identification number assigned by the system to this particular job. The actual number assigned will depend on what the computer is doing just then. (Every job running on the system, background or not, is assigned its individual job identification number.) Do these numbers have any uses? Yes, and we will tell you one of them before this chapter is done.

The second line, the usual UNIX prompt, tells you that UNIX is ready for your next command. Now you can continue your work while your program works away unseen by you. Neat!

There are some things you should know before doing background jobs. First, if the system is heavily loaded with tasks, background jobs will only bog it down further. Second, you cannot give a background job any input from the terminal. If your job needs terminal input, it will just get stuck and stop when it reaches that point. Third, if your program normally sends output to the screen, it still will when in background. This means that you could find yourself inundated by a string of numbers while you are editing one of your sensitive poems. There are remedies for these situations. If the system is heavily loaded, do not run background jobs. If your job normally takes input from the terminal, you can use redirection (see Chapter 11) to get the program to take its input from a file. Just remember to put the right data in the file. Finally, you can use redirection to channel the output to a file instead of to the screen.

Sometimes, it can happen that your job gets stuck or is taking too long and you want to stop it. Here's where you get to use the identification number. For example, to end the job we mentioned previously, you can type

```
kill 6784
```

and the job is "killed." Don't worry, the job doesn't feel a thing. (In the language of UNIX, *stopping* a job merely suspends it and it can be resumed at a later time. *Killing* a job aborts it and gets it off the system.)

Release 2.0 of System V added a new and useful command that lets you shift a job between background and foreground. We will talk a little more about this command (shl) and stopped jobs in Chapter 11.

Additional Programming Features

UNIX has much more language support than we have described so far. Here, we would like to point out some additional options just so that you will know what is there.

Many UNIX systems carry one or more interactive languages such as BASIC or Logo. Several versions are available. You usually initiate an interactive language by typing in a keyword, such as

```
basic
bas
```

or

```
logo
```

The keyword calls up the interpreter and changes the user prompt (perhaps to > or *) to remind you that you are working in that language now. Once this happens, you can then communicate with the computer in that language. When you are finished, typing another keyword (perhaps goodbye or bye) returns you to the usual UNIX mode and gives the usual UNIX prompt.

Other programming aids include lint (which checks out C programs), cb (which beautifies C programs with proper indentions and the like), sdb (a symbolic debugger for C and FORTRAN), and make (which helps you maintain large programs). If you revise a subroutine, make puts together the whole program with minimum recompilation.

Two other languages commonly found on UNIX systems are APL and LISP. The former is handled by the interpreter apl, and the latter is handled by the compiler liszt and the interpreter lisp.

There is one other language that you may wish to program in—UNIX itself. Not only does UNIX have a large number of commands, but it also has some control statements that allow you to use UNIX programs to perform loops and make logical decisions. You can construct a program from a series of such commands, store them in a file, and use the chmod command to make that file into a program that you can run just by typing the filename. We will discuss such *shell scripts* in Chapter 11.

A Final Word

Actually, there is no final word. UNIX is an open-ended system, and you can go as far as your knowledge and imagination can take you. If you obtain a compiler or interpreter (written in C) for some other language, you can install it in your directory and use it. If you want to create your own computer language, go ahead. Not only can you install it in your own directory, but UNIX supplies yacc (*y*et *a*nother *c*ompiler *c*ompiler) to help you put together a compiler for it!

Review Questions

A. Matching Compilers with Languages

Match the compiler with the language it compiles.

1. cc	a. Pascal
2. f77	b. French
3. pascal	c. FORTRAN
	d. C

B. Questions

1. Which of the following is a proper name for a file containing a C program?

   a. blaise.c

   b. blaise.p

   c. blaise.o

   d. blaise

2. What two files are produced by the command: f77 henry.f?

3. Assume that you have the object code of a C program stored in a file named red.o. Will typing the filename cause this program to run?

Answers

A. 1—d, 2—c, 3—a
B. 1. a; 2. a.out and henry.o; 3. No, you type the name of the executable file (a.out by default), not the object-code file, to run a program.

Exercises at the Terminal

If you know how to use FORTRAN or C, write a simple program in one of those languages. Then try the following:

1. Make a programming error deliberately and see what the compiler says about it.

2. Correct the error and compile the program.

3. Run the program.

4. Obtain the object-code file for the program.

5. Feed the object code to the compiler and see how that works.

11

The UNIX Shell: Command Lines, Redirection, and Shell Scripts

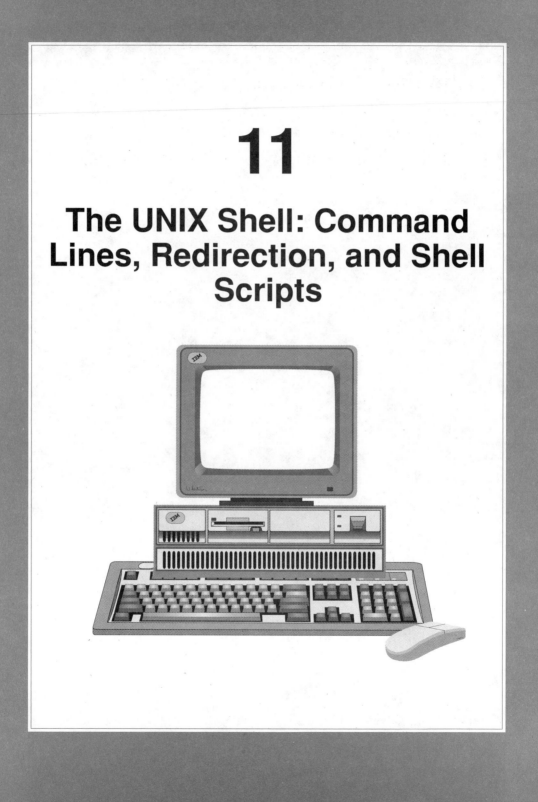

Chapter 11

The UNIX Shell: Command Lines, Redirection, and Shell Scripts

Much of UNIX's awesome strength comes from its *shell*, the program that handles your interactions with the computer system. The UNIX shell plays two roles. First, it acts as a command interpreter. Second, it is a programming language. Sounds good, but what do these terms mean? By calling the shell a *command interpreter*, we mean that it interprets your commands. If, for example, you type the date command, the shell tracks down where the date program is kept and then runs it. By calling the shell a *programming language*, we mean that you can string together a series of basic commands to perform some larger task. The pipelines and the shell scripts we will discuss in this chapter are examples of that ability.

Nowadays, with Release 4 of UNIX System V, you have your choice of shell programs. The original shell program, developed at Bell Labs, is called the sh shell or, after its creator, the Bourne shell. It usually is set up as the default shell on System V systems, so most likely it is the one you have been using. The csh shell (or C-shell), developed at Berkeley, was the next shell to gain widespread use. It is the default shell for BSD (Berkeley Software Development) UNIX and now is available in System V. Recently, the ksh shell, also called the Korn shell after its Bell Labs creator, has become popular. The Korn shell is upwardly compatible with the Bourne shell; that means it duplicates the behavior of the Bourne shell, then adds new features. The C-shell, on the other hand, is not always compatible with the other two shells.

Clearly, if you want to know UNIX, you should get to know at least one of the shells. We hope to help you do that in this chapter. All three share many basic properties, including the usual forms for commands to the shell, redirection, and pipes, and we will discuss these topics first. Next, we will look at *job control* techniques for running more than one task at a time. Here the methods do depend on the shell. Then we will examine how csh and ksh offer *history* facilities that let you repeat earlier commands without retyping them. Finally, for those of you who wish to delve more deeply into shells, we will present shell scripts, shell variables, shell metacharacters, and your .profile, .login, and .cshrc files. Okay, let's begin by looking at the command line.

The Shell Command Line

When you sit down to a UNIX system, you have hundreds of UNIX commands at your call. Many will become indispensable to you, some you will use occasionally, and some you may never see. There are some basic commands that almost every user needs to know, and frequent use will burn them into your brain. The more you use the system, the more commands you'll know by heart, but with so many commands available, remembering the details can be a problem. Fortunately, most UNIX commands are used in a similar fashion. Unfortunately, there are many exceptions, but we can view this as a sign of the vibrant vitality of the UNIX system.

You have seen the main elements of a command in Chapter 3, but you probably would enjoy seeing them again. The elements are the command name, the options, and the arguments. (Technically, anything following the command name is an argument, but we will use the term *argument* to mean the file, the directory, or whatever it is that the command acts upon, and we will use the term *option* to indicate a modification of the command.) When put together on one line, these elements constitute the *command line*. An example of a command line is

```
ls -l /home
```

Here the command name is ls, the option is -l (that is, the *long* form), and the argument is the directory name, /home (see Figure 11.1).

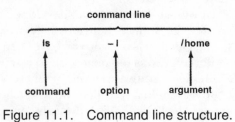

Figure 11.1. Command line structure.

Computers, being the simple-minded machines they are, require that you follow rules when typing in a command line. Here are some of them:

1. *Each element should be separated from the others by at least one space.* UNIX uses the spaces to tell when one element ends and another begins, so if you type

   ```
   ls-l /home
   ```

   UNIX will think you are looking for a command called `ls-l`, and if you type

   ```
   ls -l/home
   ```

   UNIX will think you are looking for an option called `-l/home`. In either case, you will leave UNIX dumbfounded. Why can't UNIX figure out what you really meant? After all, there are not any other command names beginning with `ls`, so UNIX should have known that you intended `ls-l` to be `ls -l`. Ah, but UNIX is so flexible that you could have *created* a new command called `ls-l`. Thus, UNIX takes the safe route and doesn't try to second-guess what you meant. Since many users forget to put a space between a command name and the option flag, we remind you once again—*put a space after the command name*. On the other hand, *don't* put spaces within an element:

   ```
   ls -l /home          ← RIGHT
   ls - l /home         ← WRONG

   ls -s /bin           ← RIGHT
   ls-s /bin            ← WRONG
   ```

2. *The proper order of elements is command name, options, and arguments.* Often, you do not need any options and, sometimes, you do not need an argument; just omit the elements you do not need. Here are some examples of right and wrong command line orders.

   ```
   cat -n hobo          ← RIGHT
   cat hobo -n          ← WRONG

   cat hobo             ← RIGHT
   hobo cat             ← WRONG

   ls -a                ← RIGHT
   -a ls                ← WRONG
   ```

   Note that a few commands may violate this sequence.

3. *Options usually are indicated with the flag notation, where one or more characters follow a hyphen.* Typical examples are the `-n`, `-a`, and `-l` flags that you just saw. More than one option can be used at a time (unless they contradict each other), and the order usually is not important. Multiple option flags may be separated from each other by spaces or, if they require no further input, may be strung together on the same hyphen. (In some instances, only one of these two approaches may work, depending on the particular command.) For example, if you wished to get a long listing (`-l`) of all files (`-a`) in reverse order (`-r`), you could type any of the following RIGHT examples:

```
ls -l -a -r            ← RIGHT
ls -l-a-r              ← WRONG

ls -lar                ← RIGHT
ls -l a r              ← WRONG

ls -r -al              ← RIGHT
ls -r -la              ← RIGHT
```

What do we mean by "require no further input?" We mean an option that is called up just by giving a letter or symbol alone. For example, the `-l` and the `-a` options of `ls` need no further input. On the other hand, the `-o` option of `cc` (see Chapter 10) must have a filename supplied with it.

4. *Some commands take, or can take, more than one argument.* These should be separated from each other by spaces:

```
cat cabbage king walrus        ← RIGHT
cat cabbagekingwalrus          ← WRONG
cat cabbage, king, walrus      ← WRONG
```

5. *You can combine several commands on one line by separating them with semicolons.* For example, if you wanted to compile the FORTRAN program in the file `lulu.f` and run the resulting `a.out` program, you could type

```
f77 lulu.f; a.out
```

6. *You can spread a command over more than one line by typing a backslash (\) just before you press the Return key.* Once you type a Return without a backslash, the `csh` shell executes the command. Here we `cat` the file `dolphins`, splitting the command line:

```
$ cat \
> dolphins
Dolphins can use their sonar to observe the heart and
lungs of a human swimmer. Thus, to a dolphin, a human
```

```
looks more like a dolphin (albeit a sickly one) than
does a fish.
$
```

What we have just described applies to the sh and the ksh shells. The csh shell is slightly different in that it normally uses a % instead of a $ as a prompt and in that it does not show a > (or, indeed, any other secondary prompt) for the continued line.

A command can be your own creation. For example, you saw in the last chapter that you can run a computer program simply by typing the name of the file in which the executable program is stored. Later in this chapter you will see how to use shell scripts to produce your own commands. First, though, let's take a fuller look at redirection.

Redirection

Redirection is one of those features that makes UNIX pleasant to use. You have already seen one type of redirection in Chapter 4 when we discussed the > operator. Now we will trot out a full stable of redirection operators for your appreciation. They are >, >>,<, and ¦. (For good measure, we will throw in the tee command.) As you can see, they are fine looking operators, but what do they do? Read on and see.

Redirecting Output to a File: >

You have seen the > operator before. It allows you to redirect the output of a command or program to a file. An example is

```
cat list1 list2 > list3
```

In this case, the output of cat is the joined contents of the files list1 and list2. The file list3 is created, and this file then is filled with the joined contents of list1 and list2. For instance, if the contents of file1 are

```
milk 2 qt
bread 1 loaf
hamburger 2 lb
```

and if file2 contains

```
lettuce 1 hd
spaghetti 1 lb
garlic
basil
butter
```

then the newly created `file3` will contain

```
milk 2 qt
bread 1 loaf
hamburger 2 lb
lettuce 1 hd
spaghetti 1 lb
garlic
basil
butter
```

The general format for using the > operator is

```
command > filename
```

The *command* (which can include options and arguments and which can be an executable program of your own) should be one that produces some sort of output normally routed to the screen. It could be something like `ls`, but not something like `rm list1`, for this second command performs an action but does not produce an output to the screen.

Perhaps the most important point to remember is that the right-hand side of the command should be a file. (However, UNIX treats I/O devices as files, so the right-hand side of the command could represent a printer or another terminal.) Using this command automatically causes a file to be created and given the name you choose. If you already have a file by that name, it will be wiped out and replaced by the new one, so be careful.

I/O Devices and Files

UNIX's marvelous redirection operators are made possible by the fact that UNIX treats I/O devices (input and output devices) as files. This means that each device is given a filename. These files usually are kept in the directory `/dev`. This directory contains a separate file for each terminal, printer, phone hookup, tape drive, floppy disk, and so forth. For example, this text is being typed on a terminal named `/dev/tty06`. (How can you tell what your terminal's filename is? Type the command `tty` and UNIX will tell you the device name.) If you `ls` the contents of `/dev`, you will get to see all of the device filenames.

How can you make use of these names? Normally, you do not have to. For instance, remember how you got the `cat` command to use the terminal for input? You typed

```
cat
```

---

and UNIX interpreted the lack of a filename to mean that it would use the terminal as an input. However, you could also have used

```
cat /dev/tty06
```

if you were using tty06. This would be using the filename directly, but omitting a filename is simpler in this case.

When you give a command like ls, it is really the same as

```
ls > /dev/tty06
```

if you are using tty06. Thus, when you use a command like

```
ls > save
```

you are just replacing one file with another as far as UNIX is concerned. This equivalence is what makes it simple to include the redirection feature.

When you use the redirection operators, you do not need to make use of device filenames. UNIX itself takes care of the bookkeeping, but it is the file system that makes redirection convenient.

Redirecting and Appending Output to a File: >>

Suppose you want to add information to an existing file. The >> operator was designed to do just that. To add the contents of the file newpigs to the file pigs, just type

```
cat newpigs >> pigs
```

The new material is appended to the end of the pigs file. Suppose there was no pigs file. Then the file named pigs would be created to receive the contents of newpigs.
The general format for using >> is

```
command >> filename
```

where *command* is a command or sequence of commands that produce an output, and *filename* is the name of a file.

Redirecting Input from a File: <

The last two operators send data to files; this operator gets data out of files. You can use it with commands or programs that normally take input from the terminal. For example, you could use one of the editors to write a letter and store it in a file called letter. You could then mail it to another user (let's assume a login name of hoppy) with the following command:

```
mail hoppy < letter
```

The < operator tells mail to take input from the file letter instead of from the terminal.

The general form for using this command is

```
command < filename
```

The *command* should be one that would normally take input from the keyboard.

This form of redirection is particularly useful if you are running a program originally designed for punched cards. In FORTRAN, for example, a READ statement normally causes a punched card system to look for data on punched cards. (Where else!) The same program run on a UNIX system causes the system to expect *you* to type in that data from the keyboard when the program is run. You can get around this with the < operator. Suppose, for instance, that the executable program is in a file called analyze. You could place the data in a file called, say, datafile, and run the program this way:

```
analyze < datafile
```

When the program reached the part where it read data, it would read the data in datafile. The data would need to be entered in datafile in the same format used for the punched cards.

Combined Redirects

Suppose the program analyze produces some output that you want to save in a file called results. At the same time, you want analyze to get its inputs from the datafile file (see Figure 11.2). You can do that with the command sequence

```
analyze < datafile > results
```

This command causes the program analyze to look for input in the file datafile and to place its output into the file results. The redirection instructions can be in either order. The next example would work also:

```
analyze > results < datafile
```

Do not use two or more inputs (or outputs) in the same command:

```
analyze < data1 < data2          ← WRONG
```

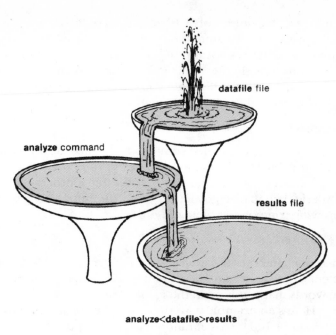

Figure 11.2.   Combined redirects.

The Pipeline: |

Sam Nifty has lots of files in his directory. He wants to know how many, but he feels (rightly so) that the computer, not he, should do the counting. The `ls` command, he knows, lists the names of his files, and the `wc` command (see Chapter 12) counts words. Can he use the > and < operators to somehow link these commands together? Not really, for these operators always link a command to a file, never a command to a command. He could create a temporary file and do it this way:

```
$ ls > temp          ← list files, store in temp
$ wc -w temp         ← count words in temp
$ rm temp            ← remove temp
```

However, this is a little awkward, and there is a real need for an operator that links a command to a command.

    If there is a need, UNIX tries to fill it. For this particular need, UNIX provides the *pipeline* operator, represented by the symbol |. (On some keyboards, this is a solid vertical line; on others, it is a vertical line with a small gap in the middle.) This operator *pipes* the output of one command into a second command. For example, Sam can solve his problem with this combined command:

```
ls ¦ wc -w
```

In this case, the *output* of ls (that is, a list of filenames) is accepted as the *input* of wc -w, which then counts the number of words. Because the list of filenames is shunted to wc, it does not appear on the screen. All that Sam will see is the final output of wc. Thus, this simple command that uses a pipe replaces three commands and counts the number of files that you have in your directory.

The general format for using the pipe is

```
command ¦ command
```

The output of the first command becomes the input of the second command. You can string together as many pipes as you need, and you can use > and <, too. Suppose, for example, that you have written a program called bigword that selects words longer than eight letters from its input and prints them. What will the following compound command do?

```
bigword < MyLife ¦ wc -w
```

This command causes bigword to search the file MyLife for words longer than eight letters. These words are then counted by wc -w, and the end result is the number of big words that you have in the file MyLife.

Here's an example with two pipes. Suppose you have a program randomword that chooses 100 words at random from its input. (Perhaps you are an author who needs a few extra words to sprinkle through your work.) You want to sort these words alphabetically and process the list with a program of your own called caps. Here's how to do it:

```
randomword < MyLife ¦ sort ¦ caps
```

In this example, the output of randomword is sent to sort (Chapter 12), and the output of sort is then sent to caps. Only the output of caps is sent to the terminal, so the rest of the process is invisible to the user.

Split Output: *tee*

Suppose you are running a program and want to see the output as it is produced and want also to save the output in a file. One way is to run the program twice: once without using > and once using it. This is a bit wasteful and, thanks to tee, is unnecessary. Actually, tee is not an operator like > or ¦ but is a command. It takes its input and routes it to two places—the terminal and the file of your choice. You can think of it as a tee fitting to the pipeline. It is used this way:

```
ls ¦ tee savels
```

The pipe relays the output of ls to tee; tee then sends the output to the terminal and to savels, the file that you chose for saving the output.

The output to the terminal can be piped further without affecting the contents of the file. For example, you can try this command:

```
ls | tee savels | sort -r
```

The file savels will contain a list of your files in alphabetical order (since that is what ls produces), but your terminal screen will show your files in reverse alphabetical order, for the other output of tee has been routed to sort -r, which sorts in reverse order (see Figure 11.3).

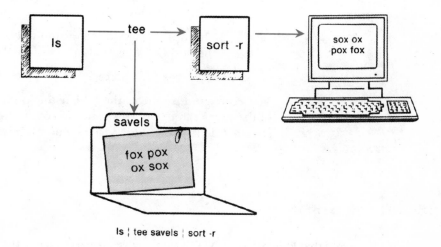

ls | tee savels | sort -r

Figure 11.3.   Using the tee command.

The general format for using the tee command is

```
command | tee filename
```

Here the output of *command* is piped to tee, which routes copies of *command*'s output to the terminal and to the file, *filename*. Actually, tee has two options, which are described in the following summary.

As you have seen, the redirection operators give you some very flexible means for routing data through the system. They are an important component of the design of UNIX, so make yourself familiar with them.

UNIX redirection offers one form of controlling how your tasks are performed. The UNIX job control systems offer another way with different possibilities. We will look at it after first seeing how to change shells.

tee Splits Output		
Name	**Options**	**Arguments**
tee	**[-i, -a]**	*filename(s)*

Description:	The tee command routes its input to the terminal and also to the named file or files.
Options:	-c This option ignores interrupts.
	-a This option causes the output to be added to the end of the named file.
Example:	`la -l /home ¦ tee -a clutter`
	This command produces the long listing of the contents of the /home directory. This listing is sent to the terminal screen, and it also is added to the end of the file, clutter.

Selecting a Shell

We have said that Release 4 of UNIX System V gives you a choice of three shells. What determines which one you actually use? When you log in, the system checks the /etc/passwd file. This file lists information about system users, including which shell to use. So if this file says you use the sh shell, then the system starts up that shell for you. (Also, if no shell is mentioned, the system will use the sh shell for you.) To see what this file says about you, you can use the grep command. For instance, if your login name is nessie, the following command will print the line describing you:

```
$ grep nessie /etc/passwd
```

Suppose you want to switch to a different shell. Then you can request that your system administrator change the setting in the /etc/passwd file. But if you just want to experiment, you can start up a shell by typing its name. For instance, to start up the csh shell, give the csh command:

```
$ csh
%
```

To return to your original shell when you are done, type exit or press Ctrl-D at the beginning of a line:

```
% exit
$
```

By the way, if you are in, say, the csh shell, do not type sh to return to the sh shell. Typing the name of shell always starts up a *new* shell. If you started in the sh shell, typed csh, then sh, you would wind up with the sh shell running a csh shell running a second sh shell. To quit, you would have to exit the second sh shell, then exit the csh shell, then log out.

UNIX Job Control

A *job* is a task that you have the computer do for you. Editing a file is a job, compiling a program is a job, and listing your files is a job. UNIX gives you control over the jobs you ask it to do. For instance, Chapter 10 shows how you can use the & command to run a job in the background. Here we will review the & command, as well as learn how to keep a job running after you log off, check the status of a job, and terminate jobs that have gotten out of hand. All three shells share these aspects of job control. After discussing them, we will look at special features each shell provides.

Background Jobs: &

To run a job in background, just follow the command with the & symbol:

```
$ sort biglist > newlist &
 4242
$
```

The *sort* command (Chapter 12) can take time for a very large file. Placing it in background means that your terminal is freed so that you can do other tasks while the sorting process goes on. The 4242 is the particular process identification number assigned to this background job. Every job running on the system has its own unique ID number, and we will check out some uses for these numbers in a moment. (The csh and ksh shells additionally print a *job control* number when displaying the ID number—we will talk about that later.)

Keep in mind that a job running in background still normally sends its output to the screen, where it can surprise you amidst some other activity. Just use redirection (as you did previously) to avoid that problem.

Suppose your background job is a long one and that you do not feel like waiting around for it to finish. But if you just log out or hang up, the job will be arrested and killed when you do. UNIX has a way out of that difficulty—the nohup command.

No Hangups: *nohup*

The nohup command tells UNIX to ignore the terminating signals generated when you log out or hang up. Thus, a job started under the protection of this command will keep running even after you sign off. (The csh shell behaves in this manner automatically, so it does not require using the nohup command.) If you are using a phone line to communicate with the computer, this can save you money. To use this feature, just precede the desired command with nohup:

```
nohup sort biglist > newlist &
```

Notice that you use nohup in conjunction with &. If you run a nohup job in foreground, you will not be able to start the logout procedure until the job is finished, so you save nothing.

What if you forget to use redirection to collect the output of the job? Then UNIX will send you a message like

```
output sent to 'nohup.out'
```

When you next log back on, just check for a file called nohup.out; it should hold the output. Even if you do use redirection, UNIX will create and use the nohup.out file if any error messages were generated by your job.

Okay, we can now get background programs to run even when we sign off. Another useful skill would be to stop a background program that was turning out badly. That's the next topic.

nohup Continue Running a Program After Hang Up

Name	Options	Arguments
nohup	None	*command*

Description: The nohup command lets you initiate a command that will continue running even if you hang up your phone connection or otherwise log off the system. It should be run as a background process. Unless you use redirection, output will be placed in a file called nohup.out. Error messages also are sent to that file.

Example:
```
nohup spell ch23 > sp.ch23 &
```

This spell command checks the spelling of the file ch23 in background. Misspelled words are redirected to the sp.ch23 file. If the program generates any error messages, they are sent to a file called nohup.out.

Terminating Unruly Jobs: *kill*

Into every computer user's life comes the program that just won't quit. The computer insists on taking some trivial error seriously and expends considerable time doing useless things with great speed and accuracy. Ordinarily you can use an interrupt (a Delete key or Break key) to stop such a program, but that will not work for a program running in background. You need a special tool, and that tool is `kill`. To use `kill`, type the command and follow it with the process ID number. For instance, earlier we gave the example

```
$ sort biglist > newlist &
 4242
$
```

To stop this background program, just type

```
kill 4242
```

and your program will terminate. Or, at least, it usually will. Some resistant processes may ignore the ordinary `kill` signal, and you may have to use the potent *sure kill* option:

```
kill -9 3452
```

Here we invoke the -9 option, which brooks no opposition.

Some tasks, when run in background, ultimately generate more than one background program, or *process*, each with its own ID number. Tracking down all the IDs and killing them all can become an unsatisfactory experience. But `kill`, has a means of dealing with this situation: use an ID value of `0`. This terminates all background jobs that you have started up during the current session:

```
kill 0
```

To kill even those jobs that ignore the ordinary kill request, you can use

```
kill -9 0
```

Be WARNED, however, that this will also kill your login shell program, thus logging you off the system. But sometimes that may be what you need.

But what if you have forgotten the process ID's? Then you can use the `ps` command to find it.

kill Terminates Job		
Name	**Options**	**Arguments**
kill	[-9]	*process ID number*
Description:	The `kill` command terminates the specified job. You can obtain the process identification number by using the `ps` command. The form is `kill` number, where number is the process identification number. If number is 0, all background jobs are sent the kill signal.	

Option:	-9	This is a *sure kill* which can be used if an ordinary kill fails. (This is a special case of a more general option that you can study in the manual.)
Example:		Suppose the job `spell essay > err &` has a PID of 3492. Terminate the job with `kill 3492`.

Process Status: *ps*

The ps command reports on the processes currently going on in the computer. As a beginning UNIX user, you do not have to be overly concerned with processes. But we will look into the ps command for two reasons: to see how to find a process ID number if you need to kill a background job, and to provide insight into how shells work. Let's see what happens when you give the command

```
$ ps
  PID TT TIME COMMAND
 5863 30 0:11 sh
 5922 30 0:01 ps
$
```

Aha! Two processes! The ps command, of course, is the one you just ran. But what is this sh? It is the shell program itself! When you log in, UNIX starts up a shell process to handle your needs. This reminds you that to the computer, the shell is just another program. For each process ps lists the process ID (PID), the terminal number (TT) of 30, the time used so far, and the name of the process. Now let's put a process into background and repeat the command:

```
$ sort bigfile > newfile &
 6234
$ ps
  PID TT TIME COMMAND
 5863 30 0:11 sh
 6234 30 0:03 sort bigfile
 6235 30 0:01 ps
$
```

Here you used a file big enough so that the sorting is still going on when you invoke ps. Now you get the PID for the sorting process as well as for the ps process itself. Wait a bit and repeat the command:

```
$ ps
  PID TT TIME COMMAND
 5863 30 0:11 sh
```

```
6258 30 0:01 ps
$
```

Since this is a new invocation of ps, it has a new process number. It is still the same shell, so that PID is unchanged. In the meantime your sorting job has finished, and other users have created processes 6236 through 6257.

What about those other users? You can learn what they are up to by using the -a option:

```
$ ps -a
  PID TT TIME COMMAND
 4347 03 0:53 sh
 5288 03 0:22 sh
 6321 03 0:00 lpd
 6238 07 0:11 sh
 6514 07 0:01 vi .remind
 5553 08 0:23 sh
 6494 08 0:08 vi mbox
 5698 28 0:13 sh
 6405 28 0:13 vi menu5.c
 5863 30 0:11 sh
 6527 30 0:02 ps -a
 6245 32 0:12 sh
 6374 32 2:46 nroff -mm
$
```

This sums up what is happening at the six active terminals. Note that each user has his or her own shell process. (There you are on terminal 30.)

ps Process Status Report		
Name	**Options**	**Arguments**
ps	[-a, -f]	None
Description:	The ps command prints information about processes currently in the system. The output consists of the process identification number (PID), the terminal (TT), CPU time used (TIME), and the command (COMMAND). The PID is a number uniquely assigned to the process. By default, ps reports on processes initiated at the user's terminal.	

Options:	-a	This option displays ps information for all terminals, not just the user's.
	-f	This option prints a full list of information about each process, including status, priority, and size information.

The *at* Command

Suppose you have a big job to run but the system is heavily loaded at the time. You would like to run the job at, say, 2 am, when the work load is low, but you do not want to wait around until then. You may be able to use the at command to ask the system to run your job at a later time. (We say *may* because the system administrator may limit access to the at command. He or she can let everyone use it, let no one use it, let only people on a special list use it, or let everyone except those on a special list use it.)

Let's assume you do have access to the at command. How do you use it? An example is

```
$ at 02                          ← Give time, using 24-hr clock
f77 -o wm worldmodel.f           ← Give list of commands
sort -o wm.data wm.data
<Ctrl-d>                         ← Terminate list
537271200.a                      ← Job number assigned by at
$
```

You type at, then the time you want the job run. If the time is two digits, at interprets it as the hour. If the time is four digits, at interprets it as hours and minutes. Thus 0215 would be at 2:15 am.

After entering the command line, you type the command(s) you want run at that time. To indicate that the list is finished, type Ctrl-d at the beginning of the line. Then at returns a job identification number for your request. When 2 am rolls around, your job is executed.

What if your request produces output? Since you may not be logged on when the task runs, the output cannot be sent to your terminal. The sensible thing to do is to use redirection to collect any output. If you fail to do that, at will send the output to you via the mail command.

What if you want to run the command on a particular day? Then you can add a date to the time on the at command line:

```
$ at 0900 April 1
mail mark                        ← new_duties
```

```
<Ctrl-d>
537271322.a
$ at 1430 Wednesday        ← commandlist
537271630.a
```

The first example uses a month-day date, and the second uses the day of the week. Note that if you already have the commands in a file (here commandlist), you can use redirection instead of keyboard input to supply the commands. The UNIX manual discusses other forms that can be used to specify the time.

What if you have second thoughts? Then you can use the -r option to remove the request:

```
$ at -r 537271630.a
```

If you have forgotten the ID number, use at -l to get a list of all tasks currently scheduled for you by at.

at Execute Commands At A Later Time		
Name	**Options**	**Arguments**
at	[-r job(s)]	*time* [date]
at	[-l job(s)]	
Description:	The at command is used to schedule commands to run at a given time. The time is typed on the command line, following at. The commands to be run are typed on the following lines, and Ctrl-d at the beginning of the line is used to terminate the list of commands. Or you can use redirection on the command line to provide input of commands from a file.	
	The time is specified as a two-digit number (the hour time) or as a four-digit number (hours and minutes); a 24-hour clock is assumed, but you can have an am or pm prefix.	
	The *date* argument can be a month name (or three-letter abbreviation) followed by a day: for example, Jan 30 or june 27. Or it can be a day of the week or three-day abbreviation, as in Tuesday or fri.	
	The at command returns a job identification number for reference.	

Options:	-r job(s)	Remove the indicated job(s) from at's list of tasks. The *job* is the identification number returned by at when a request is made and also by the -l option.
	-l job(s)	List the jobs scheduled by at for the requestor, showing when they are scheduled to be done. If the optional list of jobs is used, then just those jobs are listed.
Examples:	`$ at 23 < cmdlist`	

Run the commands in the file `cmdlist` at 23 hours, that is, 11:00 pm.

`$ at 1115pm Fri < cmdlist`

Run the commands in the `cmdlist` file at 11:15 pm, next Friday.

```
$ at 1 mar 3
cc task?.c
<Ctrl-d>
```

Compile some C files at 1 am, March 3.

Next let's look at some of the more advanced job control features. You may not need them as you first explore UNIX, but after you start using UNIX regularly, you will probably appreciate the convenience these features offer.

Bourne Shell Job Control: *shl*

Release 2.0 of System V introduced a new command designed to facilitate job control. The command is termed a *shell layer manager*, and its name is shl. It gives you the ability to run several programs simultaneously, shifting each from foreground (keyboard control) to background, and from background to foreground as needed.

The shell, recall, is a program that handles your interactions with the computer system. When you log in, a *login* shell is started up for you. This program puts the prompt on your screen, interprets what you type (including wild card expansions), and performs other useful tasks. The shl command allows you to initiate up to seven additional subshells and to switch between them. The subshells are called *layers*. At any one time, just one layer will be active, but you can easily change to another layer. It is something like logging in on several different terminals, then moving from one terminal to the next to work. The difference is that you use just one terminal and use special keystrokes to switch from one layer to another.

Let's see how shl works. To start the program up, type its name:

```
$ shl
>>>
```

Here >>> is the shl prompt; it tells you that you are in the shl command mode. To start up a layer, use the create command:

```
>>> create
(1)
```

Here we get a new prompt—the (1) is the default prompt for layer number 1. Once you have that prompt, you can proceed as you normally do in UNIX, sending mail, writing reports, running programs, and so on. To suspend the layer and return to the shl command mode, you type the swtch character, which usually is set to be Ctrl-z:

```
(1) <Ctrl-z>
>>>
```

Once in the command mode, you can create another shell:

```
>>> create pascal
pascal
```

This time we named the shell pascal by typing that word after the create command. Now the prompt is the word pascal. This feature makes it easier to remember what you are using a particular shell for. Again, you can use the swtch character to switch back to the command mode:

```
pascal <Ctrl-z>
>>>
```

How do you return to layer 1? Once a layer has been created, you merely need to type its name while in the command mode. Here, for example, we switch from the command mode to layer 1, then back to the command mode, then to the pascal layer:

```
>>> 1
resuming 1
<Ctrl-z>
>>> pascal
resuming pascal
```

To leave shl, use the quit command:

```
pascal <Ctrl-z>
>>> quit
$
```

Here we went from the pascal layer to the shl command level to the shell.

We have discussed the most essential commands, but there are several others, including a `help` command that summarizes the available commands.

The `shl` program is very useful when you are working on several tasks at once. For example, if you are editing in one layer, you can give the `swtch` character while in the editing command mode and leave the layer to work on something else. Then, when you resume running the editing layer, you will not have to reinvoke the editor. Instead, you can simply resume editing where you left off.

---

shl Shell Layer Manager

Name	Options	Arguments
shl	None	None

Description: The `shl` command allows you to set up several interactive shells, or *layers*, to exist concurrently. Only one layer will be interactive, or current, at a time, but you can switch between layers. Typing `shl` places you in the `shl` command mode. The available commands allow you to create layers and to switch to various layers. Up to seven layers can be created. Typing a `swtch` character (typically set to Ctrl-z) lets you switch from a layer to the command mode.

Commands: (partial list)

create (name)	This command creates a new layer. If name is provided, it is used as the layer name and for the layer prompt. If it is omitted, the first layer is called 1 and (1) is used for the prompt, and so on.
delete *name(s)*	Delete the named layer(s), killing the corresponding jobs.
help	Display a summary of commands.
quit	Quit shl.
name	Resume the layer called *name*.

Example:

```
$ shl                         ← Start shl up
>>> create eve                ← Start layer called eve
eve date                      ← Give command in eve
Tue Dec 23 12:12:03 PST 1986
eve <Ctrl-z>                  ← Go to command level
>>> quit                      ← Go to shell
$
```

Job Control with the C Shell and the Korn Shell

As you have seen, the Bourne shell uses the `shl` command to provide the ability to switch between different jobs. The C shell and the Korn shell, on the other hand, have similar abilities built directly into the shells. Although different from each other in many respects, the C shell and the Korn shell provide essentially the same job control services, which we will examine now.

The Job Shell

Release 4 also supplies a shell known as the Job shell, or `jsh` shell. It is the `sh` shell extended to provide the same job control features as the `ksh` shell, but without the other `ksh` shell features, such as history and aliasing.

Stopping and Restarting a Job: *Ctrl-z* and *fg*

You are in the midst of editing a large file or of running an interactive program when you receive mail that you want to reply to immediately. You can stop your current job by typing

```
Ctrl-z
```

and you can then attend to your mail. When you want to restart the job, type

```
fg
```

(for *f*oreground), and your job resumes where you left off. If you were editing a file in `vi`, you would be returned to the line you were working on.

Simple? Simple! Type Ctrl-z to stop the job and `fg` to resume it. What if you stop a job and forget about it? If you do, you will be given a warning when you try to log off. The `csh` shell will say

```
Stopped jobs
```

and not let you log out. However, if you persistently try to log out, `csh` will eventually let you and will kill your stopped jobs. A better idea is to bring the job to foreground and terminate it properly.

Incidentally, with some keyboards, many people accidentally press Ctrl-z instead of `ZZ` when attempting to leave `vi`. This leads to some mysterious "Stopped jobs" messages. Of course, once they read this section, those users won't find the messages so mysterious.

Background Jobs: *&* and *fg*

Earlier, you saw how the Bourne shell let you use the & operator to run jobs in background. You can do the same with the C shell and the Korn shell. For example, to save a list of your files, you could type the following:

```
ls -la > listing &
```

The Bourne shell responds to this request by running the command in background and by displaying a process ID number. The C shell and Korn shell do this too, but they additionally display a *job control number* in brackets:

```
[1] 1606
```

Here, the 1 is the job control number, and the 1606 is the process ID. The job control number as you will soon see, is the key to managing multiple jobs.

Meanwhile, suppose you decide you want to move the background job back to the foreground again. With the C shell and the Korn shell, you can give the fg (for foreground) command:

```
fg
```

This puts the program running in the foreground on your terminal (see Figure 11.4).

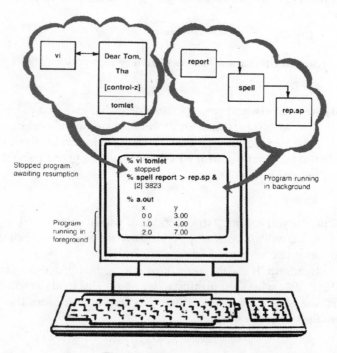

Figure 11.4.   Job types.

Multiple Jobs: *jobs* and *bg*

You are a blur of activity. You have stopped a job, started two jobs in background, started and stopped another job, and then started yet another job. But, what was the first job you started? And, what job is going to come into foreground the next time you type fg? You need some way to check on what you've done and to identify the various tasks you have underway. Perhaps you also need a vacation. Well, UNIX may not help with the vacation, but it can deal with the other problems.

The simplest, quickest way to review what you are doing is to type

```
jobs
```

This command will then list and label the jobs that you have initiated at your terminal. (If you are using two terminals simultaneously, each will have its own job list.) Here is a sample response:

```
[2]     Stopped      vi whatamess
[3]     Stopped      vi *7
[4]  -  Stopped      f77 /home/wiseone/bigprograms/begin.f
[5]  +  Stopped      vi fing
[6]     Running      ls -R / ¦ sort -o jnk
```

The first column identifies the job with a number in brackets; we will call this the *job number*. The + in the fourth line indicates the *current* job, and the - in the third line marks the next most current job. (The jobs command has an interesting conception of "current." All stopped jobs are more current than running jobs. The most recently stopped job is the most current. Of running jobs, the least recently initiated job is the most current.) Jobs labeled Stopped are, indeed, stopped. A job labeled Running is running in background. The final column gives the name of the job.

How do you use this information? Suppose you want to resume work on job [2]. One way is to type

```
fg %2
```

The % character is used to introduce a job number, so this instruction means to bring job [2] into foreground. (The csh shell lets you omit the fg.)

What happens if you type fg with no further information? Then the job labeled with the + sign will be brought into foreground.

You can also take a stopped job and start it up in background, and you can stop a job already running background. Use the bg (for background) command with the job identifier:

```
bg %4
```

Or, using the csh shell, you can do this:

```
%4 &
```

The job is placed in background and you receive a message such as

```
[4]  f77 /home/wiseone/bigprograms/begin.f &
```

telling you the name of job [4] and that it now is running in background.

To stop job [6] running in background, just type

```
stop %6
```

Job Numbers and Process ID Numbers

Earlier, we mentioned that each job you stop or put into background is given a job number (in brackets) and also a process ID number. Why two numbers? And what are their uses?

First, the job numbers assigned by job are personal to you and your terminal. The first job you stop or put in background after logging in on a given terminal is called [1], the next one [2], and so on—the sequence is fairly predictable. They are small integers that are easily typed, and they are the labels recognized by the csh and ksh job control systems. However, these numbers are not unique; your neighbor could very well also have a job [1] and a job [2]. To keep things straight, the computing system needs a method to assign each job a unique identification; that is the purpose of the process ID number. Another difference is that only jobs that you stop or place in background are given job numbers, but every job you run is assigned an ID number. In short, a job number is a local, useful-to-you label, and the process ID number (PID) is a system-wide, useful-to-UNIX label (see Figure 11.5).

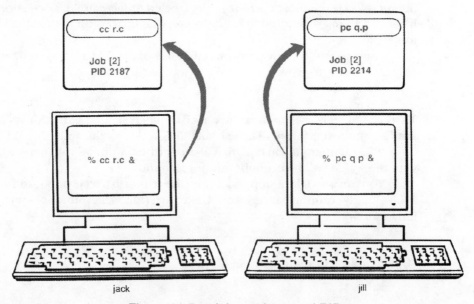

Figure 11.5.   Job numbers and PIDs.

You can get both labels displayed by using the -1 option on jobs; see the upcoming jobs summary.

Using *kill* in the C Shell and the Korn Shell

If you are using the C shell or the Korn shell, the kill command recognizes job control numbers as well as the usual process ID number. You have to precede a job control number with a % so that kill can tell that it is a job control number. That is, the command

```
kill %8
```

means kill the job with the job control number of 8, but the command

```
kill 8
```

means kill the job with the process ID number of 8.

A Summary of the *csh* and *ksh* Job Control Systems

Table 11.1 lists the operations we have discussed for controlling jobs when using the csh or ksh shells—the jobs command summary follows.

Table 11.1. Job control commands.

Command	Definition
Ctrl-z	Stops the job you are working on.
command &	Makes *command* run in background.
jobs	Lists stopped and background jobs, assigning them job numbers. The job numbers are given in brackets, as [1]. The *current* job is identified with a + and the next most current with a -. Since you can go back and forth between jobs, the current job may not be the last one on the list.
fg	Brings the + marked job from the jobs list into the foreground, starting it if stopped.
fg %*n*	Brings job *n* from the jobs list into foreground, starting it if stopped.
%*n*	Short for fg %*n*. (csh only)
%*n* &	Restarts job *n*, placing it in background. (csh only)

continues

Table 11.1. continued

Command	Definition
bg	Puts the + marked job from the jobs list into background, starting it if stopped.
bg %*n*	Puts job *n* from the jobs list into background, starting it if stopped.
stop %*n*	Stops the specified background job.
kill %*n*	Kills job *n*, that is, terminates the job rather than merely suspending it.

jobs **List and Identify Stopped and Background Jobs**

Name	Options	Arguments
jobs	[-1]	None

Description: The jobs command prints a list of stopped jobs and jobs running in background. The format is as follows:

```
[1] + Stopped   vi whatamess

[2] - Stopped   vi fing

[3]   Running  ls -R / ¦ sort -o jnk
```

The first column is the assigned job number enclosed in brackets. The second column contains a + for the *current* job and a - for the next most current job. The third column states whether the job is stopped or running in background. The final column gives the name of the job.

The job command ranks by *currency*. From most current to least current, the order is as follows: most recently stopped job to least recently stopped job followed by the first initiated background job to the most recently initiated background job. In the example, the user went back to [1] after stopping [2] and then stopped [1] again.

The job numbers are assigned for a given terminal; if you use two terminals simultaneously, each will have its own list of job numbers.

Option:	-l	This option gives a long listing that also includes the process identification number (PID. This is a unique system-wide number. Different users may have jobs with the same job number, but no two jobs have the same process ID number.

Both the Korn shell and the C shell provide history facilities for tracking and recalling your prior commands. However, they take quite different approaches. We will examine the C shell approach first because, historically, it came first.

The *csh* Shell History Facility: A System That Remembers

The csh shell has the remarkable ability to keep a history of the commands you have used. The number of commands that it remembers is usually around 20, but you can change that number if you like. The *history* function makes it easy to repeat earlier commands. It also makes it possible to modify them before repeating them.

Initiating Your History Service

Your system administrator may not have enabled the history feature for you. If the forthcoming examples do not seem to work, you may have to activate the history service yourself. You can use the following command to start up the history service:

```
set history=20
```

Here 20 represents the number of command lines that will be recalled. You can use another value for this number, but 20 is the standard. Version 4.3 of BSD UNIX lets you use spaces on either side of the equal sign, but some earlier versions do not allow them.

If you type history at the UNIX prompt, the command will stay in effect until you log out. To have history turned on automatically each time you log in, place this command in your .cshrc file, as we will describe later.

Repeating an Earlier Command: Event Identifiers

We will look at an example to see how the history function lets you easily repeat commands. Hilary Dale, after doing a few things on the system, types the following command:

```
history
```

UNIX responds with the following list:

```
1 mail
2 cd energy
3 vi walls.f
4 f77 walls.f floors.o windows.o roof.o temp.o
5 a.out
6 vi checkfile
7 vi walls.f
8 history
```

This, obviously, is a list of the commands that she has executed. (UNIX refers to each command line as an *event.*)

Apparently (starting at command 3), she modified part of a FORTRAN program, compiled it along with the unchanged portions, ran the new version, checked it, found something wrong, and then fixed up the walls.f program. Her next step will be to repeat command 4. She can, of course, retype the entire command, or she can use some nifty history features. She can type any of the following entries to return that command:

!4   ← *identification by command number*

or

!f   ← *identification by command name*

or

!-5   ← *identification by relative position*

or

!?77?   ← *identification by pattern*

Each of these commands (which we will call *event identifiers*) will repeat command 4 by first printing what the command was. The ! · character alerts UNIX that the command uses the history list.

The first form means, "Run the fourth command from the history list." The second form means, "Run the most recent command from the history list beginning with the character f." The third form means, "Look back five commands and run that command." The fourth form means, "Find the most recent command line with the pattern 77 in it, and run that command." The question marks on either side identify the pattern. The two commands that use patterns, !f and !?77?, have the advantage that you probably will not have to look up the history list numbers to use them.

The second form of event identifier need not be limited to one character after the !. Suppose that a history list had a mkdir command followed by a more command. Since it was most recently executed, the !m would rerun the more command, and a !mk command would run the mkdir command. You can use as many letters as you need to identify your chosen command unambiguously.

The fourth form can use a pattern from anywhere in the line; the commands !?oof? or !?wind? would have worked just as well. The command ?wall?, however, would have rerun command 7 instead of command 5, since it was the most recent command line containing that pattern.

A special case of a history repeat command is

```
!!
```

Not only does this command look very assertive, it repeats the previous command. Thus, it is the same as !-1, but it can be typed more quickly.

Because the ! symbol has a special meaning to the C shell, you have to use the combination \! if all you want is an ordinary, nonhistory exclamation point. The backslash tells the C shell to interpret the following character as an ordinary character instead of as a special character. For example, the USENET system for transferring mail between UNIX sites uses the exclamation point to separate site names in a mail address. If, for instance, you wish to send mail to well!unicom!don, you would use this command from the C shell:

```
mail well\!unicom\!don
```

Adding to a History Command

History substitutions (that's the official term for translating event identifiers into ordinary commands) do a lot more for you than just repeat earlier commands. For one thing, they can be incorporated into longer commands. Suppose, for example, you have just run the following command:

```
sort namelist1 namelist2 namelist3 namelist4
```

As the output begins pouring down the screen, you realize that you forgot to redirect the output. You can press the Ctrl-c key or whatever key generates an interrupt signal for your system. This does not count as a command and does not go on the history list. Then, you can type

```
!! > finallist
```

UNIX translates this as

```
sort namelist1 namelist2 namelist3 namelist4 > finallist
```

and you are in business! Similarly, the command:

```
!5 | more
```

would rerun your fifth command and pipe its output through more.

The history reference needn't be the first part of your command line. For example, if you wanted to time a command that you had just run, you can give the command

```
time !!
```

You can also make !! part of a single command string. For example, suppose your last command was

```
ls -F /home/doc
```

and that you next wanted to see what was in the directory /home/doc/csh. You could type

```
!!/csh
```

and the history facility will interpret this as

```
ls -F /home/doc/csh
```

Whenever UNIX sees the special character ! in a command line (with some exceptions, such as in > >!), it checks the history list and makes the appropriate substitution, putting spaces where you put them and omitting spaces where you omitted them.

Simple Command Line Editing

You are putting a C program together and have just typed

```
cv peter.c piper.c picked.c a.c peck.c of.c pickled.c
```

You press Return, and UNIX replies

```
cv: not found
```

Then you realize that you typed cv instead of cc. Cheer up, you do not have to retype the whole line. This next command line will patch it up:

```
^cv^cc
```

The caret character ^ at the beginning of a command line tells UNIX that you wish to make a correction in the preceding command. (On some terminals, the ^ character is represented by a vertical arrow.) The characters between the first and second ^ are then replaced by the characters following the second ^. UNIX will print the corrected line,

```
cc peter.c piper.c picked.c a.c peck.c of.c pickled.c
```

and then execute it.

Substitution occurs at the first instance of the pattern, so make your pattern unambiguous. Suppose, for example, you enter

```
cc that.c old.c black.l magic.c
```

You want to correct black.l to black.c. The command

```
^l^c
```

is no good because it will change the first l to a c; for example, the "corrected" version will read:

```
cc that.c ocd.c black.l magic.c
```

The correct solution is to type

```
^.l^.c
```

or

```
^k.l^k.c
```

which identifies the l as being the one that is at the end of black.l.

Selecting Parts of a Command Line: Word Identifiers

Sometimes you may want to use just part of an earlier command. For instance, you may want to vi a file that you catted earlier (that's UNIX lingo). The history system has a way for you to specify not only the command line but also individual words from the line. The words are numbered from left to right, and the first word (the command name) is number 0. To avoid confusion with command line numbers, the word numbers are preceded by a colon (:). There also are some special symbols used: ^ is word number one, $ is the last word, and * stands for all the words after word 0. The : can be omitted with these last three symbols. A *word identifier*, then, is a construction such as :2 or $. A word identifier is not used alone but is appended to an event identifier so that UNIX will know which command to look at (see Figures 11.6 and 11.7).

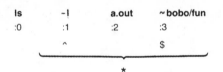

Figure 11.6.   Historical representation of words of an event.

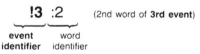

Figure 11.7.   Structure of a complete word specification.

Suppose, for example, your fourth command was

```
cat that.c doormat.c hat.c pat.c
```

Here's how different history references would be translated:

Reference	Meaning
!4	cat that.c doormat.c hat.c pat.c
!4:0	cat (0th word of 4th command)
!4:1	that.c
!4^	that.c
vi !4:2	vi doormat.c
edit !4$	edit pat.c
more !4:2-4	more doormat.c hat.c pat.c
lpr !4*	lpr that.c doormat.c hat.c pat.c

Notice that you can use the hyphen (-) to give a range of words. The special symbol * means much the same as ^-$. The difference is that ^-$ can represent one or more arguments, while * can represent 0 or more arguments. Let's clarify that. Suppose that this is part of your history list:

```
cat dwarf giant
cd dungeon
ls
```

Then these are some history substitutions:

Reference	Meaning
more !1:^-$	more dwarf giant
more !1*	more dwarf giant
cat !3*	cat (with no argument)
cat !3^-$	error (looks for at least one argument for ls and finds none)

There is one other convention that can simplify life a bit. If you are referring to the immediately preceding command, you can omit the line identifier. For example, if the last command were number 5, then the following would be equivalent:

```
cat !5:2
cat !!:2
cat !:2
```

However, a solitary ! without following characters means nothing.

history Prints a List of Last Commands Given

Name	Options	Arguments
history	None	None

Description: The history command prints a list of the last *n* commands or events run by the C shell. To set *n* in the .cshrc file, add the line

```
set history=n
```

The history list can also be used to substitute for commands using the ! symbol as shown next.

Identifying commands or events:

!*n*	Command number *n* from the history list.
!-*n*	The *n*th command before the present one.
!*c*	The most recent command beginning with the character *c*.
!?*pat*?	The most recent command containing the pattern *pat*.

Identifying words within an event: the first word is number 0:

:*n*	The *n*th word in an event.
:^ or ^	Same as :1.
:$ or $	The last word in an event.
:*n1*-*n2*	The *n*1 through *n*2 words.
^-$	Words 1 through the last word.
*	Words 1 through the last, or no word at all if there is no word 1.

Special notations:

!!	The preceding command line.
!	The preceding command line (must be followed by a word identifier).
!*	The options and arguments, if any, of the preceding command.

Examples: !!

This command repeats the previous command.

!5

This command causes event 5 on the history list to run.

^ls^ls-1

The previous command is run, substituting ls -1 for ls.

more !5:3-$

The command more is run on history event 5, from word 3 to the end of event 5.

Note that there are several modifiers that you can add to history substitutions. They consist of letters or symbols preceded by a colon. We will leave it to you to investigate the on-line manual for details—see the sections on csh and newcsh. Most of the modifiers are more useful as components of UNIX programming than as casual aids.

History with the *ksh* Shell

The Korn shell also provides a history facility, but its design differs from the csh facility. By default, it stores your commands in a file in your home directory called .sh_history. By default, the shell saves the last 128 commands. Because these commands are saved in a file, they are not lost when you log off. The shell then provides methods letting you repeat these commands, editing them if necessary. Let's take a look at the basic capabilities that the Korn shell provides.

In-line Editing

The simplest method for availing yourself of the Korn-shell history service is to use the *in-line* editing option. In-line editing means you can edit current and past command lines without having to retype them completely. To activate this option, you need to issue the following command:

```
set -o vi
```

If the Korn shell is your login shell, you can place this command in your .profile file. Otherwise, you can type it after you start up the Korn shell. This service makes the shell act something like the vi editor. Normally, you are in text, or input mode. But pressing the Escape key places you in the edit mode, and you can use vi-style commands for moving the cursor and changing text. While in that mode, you can edit a command line. When done, press the Return key, and the shell executes the edited version of the command line. For instance, suppose you have typed the following command line but have not pressed Return:

```
cay finsertfile > toflimsot
```

Gosh, you have mistyped cat. Just strike the Escape key, use the usual vi movement keys to place the cursor over the y (the h-key moves the cursor to the left, the l-key moves it to the right), type rt to replace the y with the t, then press Return. The Korn shell then executes the corrected command.

Suppose you entered the erroneous command before noticing the error. After the shell complains about not being able to cay, you still can use in-line editing. Just press Escape to enter the edit mode, then use the vi movement key for going up a line (the k-key), and the mistyped line appears as the current command. Correct it, then press Return to run it. In fact, while in the edit mode, you can use the k and j keys just as in vi to move back and forth through your recent command lines. You can even use the / and ? commands to search for strings containing a particular string or pattern, much as in vi. (One difference is that in in-line editing, / searches backwards and ? searches forwards, the opposite of vi. That is because one usually searches backwards for past commands but usually searches forward in a text file.)

The *fc* Command

The second Korn shell history technique uses the fc command. This command lets you list, edit, and invoke command lines from the history file. For editing purposes, this command uses the editor specified by the FCEDIT shell variable. We will discuss shell variables later in this chapter, but you can type the set command to see what variables already are defined. For instance, suppose you type the set command and see the following setting:

```
FCEDIT=/bin/vi
```

Then fc will use the vi editor. If FCEDIT is undefined, fc will use the ed editor. (Unless you are familiar with ed, you will probably find this default editor a bit baffling, so set FCEDIT to an editor you like. We will discuss the technique soon in the section on shell variables.)

Suppose, for example, you want to see a numbered list of your recent commands. Then invoke the fc command with the -l option:

```
$ fc -l
51      cat todo
52      vi fortunecookie
53      mail bessiemay
```

299

```
54      ls
55      rm todo
56      cat canary
57      cwd
$
```

If you want to see more of the list, you can specify the first line number you want shown. For instance,

```
fc -l 20
```

would list past command beginning with the twentieth one.

Suppose you want to edit fortunecookie again. You can identify the command by line number or by the first few letters in the command line. You can use either of the following constructions:

```
fc -e 52
fc -e - v
```

The -e option specifies an editor to use, but the combination -e - means to skip the editing and to rerun the command. What command? The 52 means command 52 in the list. The v indicates to execute the most recent command beginning with a v. In general, you need to type just enough of the command name to distinguish it from other commands. For instance, given the history list you just saw, the command

```
fc -e - c
```

would invoke the cwd command, but

```
fc -e - ca
```

would invoke the cat canary command, since it was the most recent command line beginning with ca. (The Korn shell alias facility, discussed next, simplifies evoking the fc -e - command.)

To edit a command line first before executing it, identify the command line by its initial letters or by number:

```
fc v
```

This will place you in the FCEDIT-specified editor on the line containing the most recent command line beginning with a v. You then can edit the line. When you exit the editor, the Korn shell will execute the edited command line.

The UNIX history service may not tell you when Hannibal crossed the Alps or the essential features of feudalism, but it can reduce the amount of typing that you do and thus reduce the number of keyboard errors. It also can be used in UNIX programming and, in the next section, we will show how it can enhance the alias system.

Aliases: Short-cut Names

The Korn shell and the C shell both provide an alias facility that lets you create abbreviations for longer commands. For instance, suppose you want to make L represent the ls -Fla combination. Here's how you would do it in the C shell:

```
alias L ls -Fla                          ← csh shell
```

This `alias` command defines L to represent the `ls -Fla` combination. You can continue using this short cut until you log out. To make this abbreviation permanently available, put this command into your `.cshrc` file, which we will describe soon.

The Korn shell equivalent has a slightly different syntax:

```
alias L = 'ls -Fla'                      ← ksh shell
```

Again, the definition persists until you log off, but if you place this definition in your `.profile` file, the definition will go into effect automatically when you log in.

For either shell, typing `alias` by itself causes the shell to print a list of currently defined aliases. The Korn shell predefines some alias for you. History users will find two of the predefined aliases particularly useful:

```
r='fc -e -'
history='fc -l'
```

Thus, if you want to see a list of your recent commands, you can type `history`. Admittedly, that's longer than `fc -l`, but its meaning is a bit more intuitive. And r (for *r*epeat) certainly is more convenient than `fc -e -`.

The *csh* Shell Filename Completion Service

Suppose that you have created a nice, descriptive filename such as `garlic.division.report`. You may find yourself not wanting to type the entire name when you go to edit the file. If the `csh` filename completion service is active, you can type a few initial letters, press the Esc key, and `csh` will complete the rest of the name for you:

```
% vi gar<Esc>                    ← you type this
% vi garlic.division.report      ← the shell completes the name
```

Of course, there are some restrictions. The shell is not omniscient, so you must type enough characters to distinguish the name from others. If `garlic.division.report` is the only file beginning with a g, then you have to use only one character. But if you also have a file called `garfish.division.report`, you will have to type `garl` and press Esc.

Suppose you have a file called `garlic.division.debts`. Filename completion still can help. If two files match the pattern you type, the shell will extend the name for as many characters as the names have in common and then beep. You can type the rest of the name, or enough of it to choose between the two:

```
vi garl<Esc>                    ← you type this
vi garlic.division.             ← shell extends name
vi garlic.division.r<Esc>       ← you add the r
vi garlic.division.report       ← shell completes name
```

If the system administrator has not turned on this feature for you, you can use this command:

```
set filec                       ← csh shell feature
```

As with similar examples we have discussed, you can place this command in your `.cshrc` file to activate file completion automatically.

Shell Scripts

UNIX lets you use standard UNIX commands as building blocks to construct new commands of your own devising. The shell makes this possible. (We will use the `sh` shell as the basis for our discussion, but what we will say applies equally well to the `ksh` shell. The `csh` shell has its own brand of shell scripts, but it also recognizes the `sh` variety.) Normally, the shell takes its input from the terminal. (Its normal input consists of the commands you type.) But, like other UNIX programs, the shell also can take input from a file. A file containing UNIX commands is called a *shell script*. For example, you can use an editor to create a file with the following command line:

```
ls -l
```

Suppose you name this file `ll` (for `long list`). Then you can have the shell run this command by typing

```
sh ll
```

and the command in the `ll` file is executed. The `sh` command invokes the shell, and the shell runs the instructions found in the `ll` file. (Actually, using `sh` creates a new shell which then takes over control. When it finishes running the shell script, the new shell "dies," returning control to your original shell. See the upcoming box on multiple shells.)

Now suppose you type

```
ll
```

You are informed

```
ll: cannot execute
```

but you need not accept this. Just type

```
chmod u+x ll
```

and try typing `ll` again. Now the command runs just by typing the filename! We will discuss the `chmod` (change mode) command in Chapter 12, but what it does here is rather simple: It changes the mode of the `ll` file so that you (u) add (+) executable (x) status to the file. You now have a convenient abbreviation (`ll`) for a lengthier command (`ls -l`).

Let's summarize the main points before we move on to more interesting examples.

- A shell script consists of a file containing UNIX commands.

- A shell script can be run by typing `sh` *filename*.

- If you use the `chmod` command (Chapter 12) to make the file executable, you can type just the filename to make it work:

filename

Shell scripts are quite versatile and flexible. First, you can include more than one command in a script. Second, you can have your script use command line arguments, just like the built-in commands do. Third, you can create loops and other programming features in a script. We will look at the first two features now, and in Chapter 14 we will look at some more advanced uses of shell scripts.

Multiple Shells

There is just one shell program in UNIX System V, but there are many instances of the shell. Each time you log in, the system starts up a shell process for you. (A *process* is a program being run.) Each other user has his or her own shell process. Of course, only one program runs at any moment, but UNIX switches from running your shell to running Laura's shell to running Pete's shell, and so on, attending to each of your needs in turn. Your shell process knows about your commands, but not Pete's, and vice versa. Thus, the separate shell processes keep your work from getting muddled up with the work of others.

More remarkable, perhaps, is the fact that you yourself can have more than one shell process going for you. For example, executing a shell script creates a new shell which runs the script and expires when it finishes. You can use `ps` to test this claim. First, create a file called, say, `do.ps` and containing this command:

```
ps
```

Next, run this script, doing a ps before and after:

```
$ ps
  PID TTY       TIME COMD
 5004 30        0:02 sh
 5023 30        0:01 ps
 $ sh do.ps
  PID TTY       TIME COMD
 5004 30        0:03 sh
 5090 30        0:01 ps
 5089 30        0:00 sh
 $ ps
  PID TTY       TIME COMD
 5004 30        0:03 sh
 5099 30        0:01 ps
```

The shell you were granted at login has a PID of 5004. The temporary shell that ran the shell script had a PID of 5090. Similarly, each invocation of ps has its own PID. If you make the script executable and type its name, that, too, creates a temporary shell. Try it and see.

You do not have to run a shell script to create a new shell. Just type sh and press Return. The screen may look the same, but you are using a new shell.

You can continue typing sh's, creating a shell with a shell within a shell . . . . To reverse the process, type Ctrl-d. Each Ctrl-d kills off the most recently created shell. Try it. Of course, if you lose count and press too many Ctrl-d's, you will exit the original shell and find yourself logged out!

Multiple Commands

You are not limited to one command per script. For example, when you have spent too many hours at the terminal, you might need a script like the following:

```
who am i
pwd
date
```

Just put one command per line, as if you were typing instructions from the terminal. Or you can put several commands on the same line by using the semicolon as a separator:

```
who am i; pwd; date
```

Place either version in a file called huh, and typing huh will produce an output such as

```
$ sh huh
fleezo    tty7    Apr 16   11:55
/home/fleezo/stocks
Thu Apr 16 11:55:21 PST 1992
$
```

It would be nice if the script could print descriptive messages. UNIX does not let you down here, for the echo command gives you the means. In its simplest form, which is all we need here, echo sends a copy of its arguments to the screen, for example,

```
$ echo 34
34
$ echo He spreads the burning sands with water.
He spreads the burning sands with water.
$
```

Now you can upgrade huh to the following:

```
echo You are
who am i
echo The directory you are in is
pwd
echo The date is
date
```

Running the new huh produces this sort of output:

```
$ sh huh
You are
fifi    tty14   Apr 16   12:08
The directory you are in is
/home/fifi/cosmology/gravity
The date is
Thu Apr 16 12:08:23 PST 1992
$
```

(The output would be neater if we had a command that just gave the user's name without the other information. We will show one possibility later in this chapter and a second version in Chapter 13.)

What if you want one of your scripts to use an argument? For instance, suppose you are in the directory /home/me and you want a long listing of the /home/me/profits directory. Can you type

```
ll profits
```

to get that listing? Well, you can type it, of course, but the shell will ignore the `profits` and just list your current directory. That is, your command will be interpreted as

```
ls -l
```

and not as

```
ls -l profits
```

But there is a scheme that will not ignore your profits; it is our next topic.

echo Echo Arguments		
Name	**Options**	**Arguments**
echo	**None**	*[any string of characters]*
Description:	The echo command writes its arguments on the standard output. Without arguments it produces an empty line.	

Example:	`$ echo say New York unique 10 times fast`
	`say New York unique 10 times fast`
	`$`	

Command Line Arguments for Shell Scripts

When you use the shell script, the shell does keep track of any arguments you type after the script name. Your script can use these arguments by referring to them by the following scheme: $1 is the first argument, $2 is the second argument, and so on. In addition, $* is short for all the arguments, and $0 is short for the name of the shell script itself. The $1 and its companions are called *positional parameters*, for the number indicates the position of the original argument. Figure 11.8 is an example illustrating how the scheme works. First, here is the script itself, stored in the file `i.remember`:

```
echo This is the $0 command
echo My first argument is $1
echo My third argument is $3
echo Here are all my arguments: $*
```

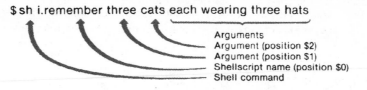

Figure 11.8.   Scripts and arguments.

Next, here is a sample invocation:

```
$ sh i.remember three cats each wearing three hats
This is the i.remember command
My first argument is three
My third argument is each
Here are all my arguments: three cats each wearing three hats
$
```

Thus, $1 is three, and so on. Incidentally, the explicit numbering scheme extends only to $9, but the $* will encompass however many arguments you give.

Now you can modify 11 to make it more useful. One version would be

```
ls -l $1
```

Another possibility is

```
ls -l $*
```

How do they differ? The first version will list just one directory (the first one fed to it), while the second will list all the directories given to it.

Here is another example. Suppose you create a shell script containing the following command:

```
mv $1 $1.$0
```

Call the script pig. Then, assuming that you have a file called porky, what will the following command do?

```
sh pig porky
```

Well, $1 is the first argument (porky), and $0 is the name of the script (pig), so this command is interpreted as

```
mv porky porky.pig
```

You now have a command that will add .pig to the name of any file! This could be quite useful to swinologists and to users of PIGTRAN (OGAY OTAY . . .).

Another important feature of shell scripts is that they can use redirection and pipes. See if you can tell what the following shell script does (the lp command sends stuff to be printed on a line printer):

```
cat $* ¦ lp
date >> prfile
echo $* >> prfile
echo >> prfile
```

The best way to check what this does is to run it on your system. But if you cannot wait for that, here is what happens. The first line concatenates all the files that you feed to the shell script as arguments. (Recall that $* stands for all the arguments to the shell script.) This combined file then is piped to the printer and printed. The next line adds the current time and date to the end of a file called prfile. (If no such file exists, it is created.) The next line adds the names of the files you printed to the end of prfile. The final line adds a blank line to prfile. Thus, the net effect of this shell script is to print some files and to keep a record of which files you printed and when. Note that the script uses a prfile in your current directory. If you want to use this command in various directories, you should be more specific about the name. For instance, Ben could establish an Accounting directory and use /home/ben/Account-ing/prfile as the storage file.

This should be enough to get you started with shell scripts. We will develop more examples in Chapters 13 and in Chapter 14 we will unveil further delights of this topic. Now let's look at another shell feature, shell variables.

Shell Variables: *sh* and *ksh* Shells

As the shell carries on its activities on your behalf, it has to keep track of a number of things, including the name of your home directory, which prompt you use, and where to look for commands. To do this, the shell uses *shell variables*. You can think of variables as names that can have values assigned to them. The shell has built-in variables that keep track of your home directory, etc. It uses other shell variables to control features such as history and filename completion. And it also lets you define variables of your own. First we will look at some of the built-in variables, and then we will see how you can create and use your own variables. We will begin by looking at how the sh and ksh shells handle shell variables, then look at the csh approach.

Built-in Variables

To find out what variables your shell is using, just type the command set:

```
$ set
HOME=/home/zeke
IFS=
```

```
MAIL=/usr/mail/zeke
PATH=.:/bin:/usr/bin
PS1=$
PS2=>
TERM=adm5
$
```

The shell prints out the variables it knows. The name to the left of each equals sign is the name of a variable, and the stuff to the right is the value of the variable. Thus, the variable TERM has the value adm5. It is a UNIX tradition (but not a requirement) that variable names be in uppercase. You may not have the exact set of variables we have here, but this collection is typical. Let's describe what each one is. Then we can talk about how they are used and how they can be changed.

Standard Shell Variables

HOME: This is set to the pathname of your home, or *login*, directory.

IFS: (Internal Field Separator) This is set to a list of the characters that are used to separate words in a command line. Normally, this list consists of the space character, the tab character (produced by pressing the Tab key), and the newline character (produced by pressing the Return key). They are *invisible* characters, so you do not see them. But you can see, for example, that the newline character produced a blank line.

MAIL: This variable's value is the name of the file to which your mail is sent. The shell checks the contents of this file every so often, and when something shows up, you are notified that mail has arrived for you.

PATH: This names the directories that the shell will search to find commands. A colon is used to separate the directory names; there are no spaces. The directories are searched in the order given. For example, if you give the command cat, the shell first searches your current directory (.) for an executable file by that name. If it does not find one there, then it looks in /bin. If it still has not found cat, it looks in /usr/ bin. And if it still has not found a cat program, the shell reports back that it cannot find that command. Note that this particular sequence of directories in PATH means that if you have an executable file called cat in your current directory it is executed rather than the standard system cat, which would be in one of the subsequent directories. (Note: if the very first character in the string is a colon (:), the shell interprets that as .:, that is, as if the current directory is first on the list.

PS1: (Prompt String 1) This is the string used as your prompt. Normally (as in this example), it is set to $, but you can redefine it if you like.

PS2: (Prompt String 2) This prompt is used when UNIX thinks you have started a new line without finishing a command. You can continue a line, for example, by using a backslash (\) before pressing the Return key:

```
$ echo O give me a ho\
> me where the buffalo roam
O give me a home where the buffalo roam
$
```

See the section on metacharacters in this chapter for more information on \ and other special characters.

TERM: This identifies the kind of terminal you habitually use. Knowing this, the shell knows what to interpret as a backspace key, and so forth.

To use these variables we need a convenient way to specify the value of a particular variable, and we need a way to change that value. Let's look at these two points next.

Specifying the Value of a Variable

The shell uses the metacharacter $ to specify the value of a variable. (What could be more American than denoting value with $?) Compare these two commands and responses:

```
$ echo TERM
TERM
$ echo $TERM
adm5
$
```

Using TERM prints the word literally, but using $TERM causes the *value* of TERM to be echoed (see Figure 11.9). By using echo and $ we can print out the value of any particular variable.

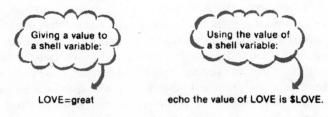

Figure 11.9. Using shell variables.

We also can use the $ construction as part of other expressions. Suppose, for example, Zeke is working in a distant directory and wants to copy a file into his home directory. He could type

The shell would see $HOME and know that Zeke wanted the value of the HOME variable, which is /home/zeke. Then it would make that substitution.

That may not seem like much of a savings, but consider the possibilities for shell scripts. If Zeke wrote a shell script with the line

```
cp $1 /home/zeke
```

only he could use it. But if he used

```
cp $1 $HOME
```

then anyone could use this script, and the copy would go to the home directory of the user. (Actually, you need to use the export command to make this use of the HOME variable work. We discuss export later in this chapter.)

Here is another example. Remember that in discussing our huh script, we hankered for a command that yielded just the user's name. You can construct such a command very simply on those systems that carry a built-in variable set to the user's login name. If your system uses such a variable, it may have a name like USER or LOGNAME. Then you could create an executable file called myname containing the simple line

```
echo $LOGNAME
```

We will assume you have a myname function available from now on. If you don't have the proper shell variable, you can create one, using the information in the rest of this chapter. Or you can use the approach we give in Chapter 13. In the meantime, remember that the myname command outputs the user's login name.

Calling something a variable implies that you can change its value. And that we can do.

Setting Shell Variables

To create shell variables and to give them values, you give commands like these:

```
AGE=65
NAME=Scrooge
```

The form is

```
name=value
```

where *name* is the name of the variable and *value* is the value of the variable. Note that there must be no spaces between these items and the equals sign.

The shell variables you create are added to the list. You can check this by typing set to get the full list of shell variables:

```
$ set
AGE=65
HOME=/home/zeke
IFS=

MAIL= /usr/mail/zeke
NAME=Scrooge
PATH=.:/bin:/usr/bin
PS1=$
PS2=>
TERM=adm5
$
```

Usually, there should be no blanks or other IFS characters in the value-giving command:

```
$ LUNCH=hot and sour soup
and: not found
$
```

This example just confused the shell. Use single quotes to get the whole expression:

```
$ LUNCH='hot and sour soup'
$ echo $LUNCH
hot and sour soup
$
```

As hinted earlier, you can redefine the built-in variables. Suppose you tire of the usual $ prompt. Then change it!

```
$ PS1=~~
~~myname
zeke
~~
```

(Recall that myname is a shell script that returns the user's login name.) If you want spaces in the prompt, use single quotes:

```
~~PS1='Your wish is my command: '
Your wish is my command: myname
zeke
Your wish is my command:
```

Of course, this new arrangement ends when you log out. In the next section we will see how to make such arrangements more permanent.

Customizing Your Environment: Your *.profile* File

When you log in, a shell is created for you (see Figure 11.10 for a condensed login procedure). Some shell variables (such as PS1 and PATH) are given to it at this time. Then the shell looks in your home directory for a file called .profile and follows the instructions it finds there. (The system treats .profile as a shell script.) Usually, the system administrator provides you with a standard version of this file. (Remember, filenames beginning with a period are not listed by a simple ls. You need to use ls -a to see them.) The contents of this file will vary from system to system, but here is a typical example:

```
$ cat .profile
export MAIL PATH TERM
umask 22
MAIL=/usr/mail/bess
TERM=adm3
$
```

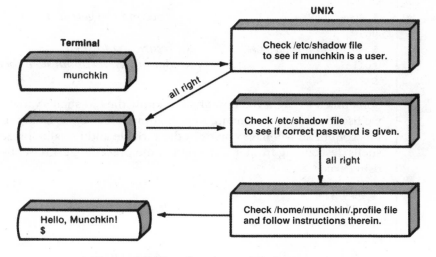

Figure 11.10.   Condensed login procedure.

The export command makes the listed shell variables available to subshells. The unmask command affects who can read, write, and execute files you create. (The chmod command in the next chapter lets you change these permissions for individual files.) Next we have the two shell variables MAIL and TERM assigned values. Your file might have other entries. For example, it may have a shell variable called EXINIT which is used by the vi and ex editors to set up options.

Using *export*

Your login shell knows certain shell variables such as HOME, MAIL, and any variables you may have defined. When you start a new shell, however, (by running a shell script, say), that shell is ignorant of the old shell's variables. You can create a new variable in the new shell using one of the old names, but it will be a distinct variable, and old shell will not know it. The rule, you see, is that each shell's variables are private to itself. This exchange illustrates the point:

```
$ CAR=rolls              ← first CAR gets its value
$ echo $car
rolls
$ sh                     ← create new shell
$ echo $CAR

                         ← shell equivalent to huh?
$ CAR=vw
$ echo $CAR              ← a second CAR gets its value
vw
$ <Ctrl-d>$ echo $CAR    ← return to old shell
rolls                    ← doesn't know about new shell's CAR
$
```

Sometimes we want the new shell to know the old shell's variables. Then we use the export command. Any shell variable used as an argument for this command will have copies of the variable and its value presented to all shells descending from it. Let's repeat the preceding exercise, but this time using export.

```
$ export CAR
$ CAR=rolls              ← first CAR gets its value
$ echo $CAR
rolls
$ sh                     ← create new shell
$ echo $CAR
rolls                    ← the new shell has a copy of the 1st CAR
$ CAR=vw                 ← the copy gets a new value
$ echo $CAR
vw
$ <Ctrl-d>$ echo $CAR    ← return to old shell
rolls                    ← original CAR has original value
$
```

> As you can see, variables can be exported down to subshells, but they cannot be exported back up to parent shells.
>
> To find out what variables are already exported, just type `export` without any arguments.

The neat thing about `.profile` is that you can use an editor to put in your own entries. If you want to have a different prompt, insert a line like this:

```
PS1='What next, Bess? '
```

If you do not have a variable set to your login name, you can create one:

```
LOGNAME=bess; export LOGNAME
```

Then you can use this shell variable in the `myname` script.

If you want to keep your own record of when you log in, insert a line like this:

```
date >> loginlog
```

Then each time you log in, the `date` command is run, and its output is diverted to the `loginlog` file, giving you a record of the date and time of your logins.

If you have a supply of shell scripts or other programs that you use often, here is a useful practice. First, establish a subdirectory to hold these executable files. Then add that subdirectory to your PATH search list. Then, no matter what directory you are in, you can run those programs just by typing the name. For example, Bess could establish a `bin` subdirectory and add this line to her `.profile`:

```
PATH=.:/bin:/usr/bin:/home/bess/bin
```

A trickier way of doing the same thing is

```
PATH=$PATH:$HOME/bin
```

$HOME is converted to /home/bess, then :/home/bess/bin is added to the end of the original PATH. The advantage of this form is that it can be used in anyone's `.profile` without using the user's name explicitly.

Let's have one more example. If you like the personal touch in computers, you can add a line like

```
echo Welcome, Bess! I am glad you are back!
```

As you grow more familiar with the system, you will get your own ideas about what to put in your `.profile`. Feel free to use this opportunity; it's there for you.

Shell Scripts and the *csh* Shell

The csh shell has a dual personality—it can run sh shell scripts, and it can run scripts that use the csh scripting language. Because sh scripts are more universal, we will stick with them and show you how to use them within the csh shell. However, there are some aspects of csh scripting you may need to know. For example, the csh shell handles shell variables differently. Also, instead of using the .profile file (as the sh and ksh shells do), the csh shell reads the .login and the .cshrc files when you log in, and these files will use csh-style environment variables.

Running *sh* Shell Scripts from the *csh* Shell

Suppose you have written or acquired a sh shell script but that you use the csh shell. You have two ways to run the script. First, you can invoke the sh shell explicitly:

```
% sh huh
You are
boxo      tty12   Apr 18  14:08
The directory you are in is
/home/boxo/hoppers/frogs
The date is
Sat Apr 16 14:08:44 PST 1992
```

Secondly, if you use chmod to make the shell script executable, then the csh shell automatically uses the sh shell to run the script! That is, suppose you are in the csh shell, that huh is an executable script file, and that you enter the huh command:

```
% huh
```

Then the csh shell invokes the sh shell and has it execute the instructions in the huh script. The designers of the csh shell made it work this way so that the shell would be compatible with the enormous number of sh scripts already available in the UNIX world. (For those of you curious about such matters, you can get the csh shell to execute a script using csh instead of sh by making the first line of the script file start with the # character—the rest of the line is ignored.)

Shell Variables in the *csh* Shell

Like the sh and ksh shells, the csh shell maintains shell variables. Some variables are built into the shell, and you also can define your own. However, the csh shell does not handle shell variables in quite the same fashion. In particular, it uses a different syntax for assigning values, and it uses special variables called environment variables instead of using the export command. We will look at these matters next.

Built-in Variables

The csh shell maintains two kinds of shell variables. One kind is the ordinary shell variable, and the other is the *environment* shell variable. The difference is that an ordinary variable is known just to the shell in which it is created. If you start up a new shell, it does not know (aside from special exceptions) the shell variables of the original shell. Environment shell variables, on the other hand, are known to the shell in which they are defined and all descendant shells. In other words, the csh environment variables work like exported variables in the sh and ksh shells.

To find out which ordinary shell variables your shell knows, type the command set:

```
% set
filec
history 20
home    /home/goofus
mail    /usr/spool/mail/goofus
noclobber
path    (. /bin /usr/bin)
shell   bin/csh
user    goofus
%
```

The shell prints the variables it knows. The list you get may very well be longer than this. The name on the left is the name of a variable, and the stuff to the right is the value of the variable. Thus, the variable user has the value goofus.

You should recognize some of these variables. The history shell variable, recall, turns the history service on and specifies the number of command lines to remember. The noclobber and filec variables turn on file protection and filename completion. So our example shows that all three of these services are active. *Note:* Some shell variables, like noclobber, have no value. In that case, we say the variable is set.

Next, to see the list of environment variables, type the setenv command:

```
% setenv
HOME=/home/goofus
SHELL=/bin/csh
TERM=adm5
USER=goofus
PATH=.:/bin:/usr/bin
%
```

It is a BSD UNIX tradition to use uppercase names for environment variables and lowercase for regular shell variables. Also, note that the setenv command lists put an equal sign between the variable name and its value.

You probably noticed that there seems to be a sort of overlap. One list has home, and the other has HOME, and so on. What happens is that each time you create a new shell, BSD UNIX automatically creates shell variable copies of certain important environment variables. So home is a copy of HOME, user is a copy of USER, and so on. What are these certain important environment variables? They are the same built-in variables we described for the sh and ksh shells.

To use these variables, you need a convenient way to obtain the value of a particular variable, and you need a way to change that value. Let's look at these two points next.

Obtaining the Value of a Variable

To find the value of a particular csh shell variable, apply the same method as for sh shell variables: use the $ metacharacter as a prefix to the variable name. For instance, consider the following example:

```
% echo history
history
% echo $history
20
```

Echoing history displays the word "history," but echoing $history displays the value of the history variable.

Setting Shell Variables

The csh handles creating shell variables differently from the sh shell. You must use the set command to create a shell variable and, optionally, to give it a value:

```
set age = 65
set name = Scrooge
set bebop
```

The format is

```
set name = value
```

where *name* is the name of the variable and *value* is the value of the variable. The value can be a number or a word, or it can be omitted entirely. For instance, the last example creates, or sets, the variable bebop, but does not give it a value. (Unlike the sh shell, you can use spaces around the equal sign.)

The shell variables you created are added to the list. You can check this by typing set to get the full list of shell variables:

```
% set
age     65
bebop
history 20
home    /home/goofus
mail    /var/spool/mail/goofus
name    Scrooge
noclobber
path    (/bin /usr/bin)
shell   bin/csh
user    goofus
%
```

Normally there should be no blanks in a value-giving command, but you can use quotation marks (single or double, but not mixed) to assign a phrase to a variable:

```
set lunch = "hot and sour soup"
set dinner = 'rack of lamb'
```

To get rid of a variable, use the unset command. For instance,

```
unset noclobber
```

turns off overwrite protection for redirection.

The environment variables work in a similar, but not identical, fashion. First, you use setenv instead of set. Second, you do not use an equal sign:

```
setenv COLORS 8
setenv EXINIT "set noai wm=15"
```

This creates an environment variable called COLORS and gives it the value 8. It also creates an environment variable called EXINIT, which is used to modify how the vi editor behaves. Use unsetenv to delete an environment variable.

We have mentioned how some UNIX features, such as history and redirection, are modified by shell variables. If you have some settings you prefer, you probably do not want to have to type them each time you log on. Fortunately, UNIX lets you have your favorite variables set automatically.

Customizing Your Environment: Your *.login* and *.cshrc* Files

When you log in, recall, UNIX checks the /etc/passwd file to see which shell you use. If that file states you use the csh shell, then UNIX starts up that shell for you, setting some shell variables and environment variables, such as home and PATH at that time. Unlike the sh and ksh shells, the csh shell does not check your .profile. Instead, it looks in your home directory for a file called .cshrc and follows the instructions it finds there. Next it looks for a file called .login and follows the instructions in it. (The system treats .cshrc and .login as shell scripts.) The difference between the two files is that the .cshrc file is executed each time you start up a new csh shell, while the .login file is executed only when you log in. Usually the system administrator provides you with standard versions of these files. (Remember, filenames beginning with a period are not listed by a simple ls. You need to use ls -a to see them.) The contents of these files will vary from system to system, but here are typical examples:

```
% cat .cshrc
set history=20
set noclobber
set filec
set mail=/var/spool/mail/$user
% cat .login
set noglob
set term=(tset -S -n -m 'dialup:?tvi920')
setenv TERM $term[1]
setenv TERMCAP "$term[2]"
unset term
unset noglob
mesg y
set path=(/bin /usr/bin .)
setenv EXINIT 'se noai wm=15 terse nowarn sm'
set ignoreeof time=15
%
```

Let's look at a couple of high points. Both files use csh-style shell variables, which is why we spent some time discussing them. Typically, environment variables are defined in the .login file. Because they carry over to subsequent shells, they need be defined just once. Regular shell variables, however, are defined in the .cshrc file so that they get defined each time you start a new shell. Because both .login and .cshrc are ordinary text files, you can edit them and add to them. For instance, if your setup does not have the history feature turned on, just add the line

```
history=20
```

to your .cshrc file. Or you can change 20 to 40 if you want the system to recall more command lines.

Let's look at some commands you can add to these files. Suppose you want to be greeted when you log on. Then you can put an echo command in the .login file:

```
echo Welcome back, $user!
```

To control various csh services, you can modify your .cshrc file by adding or deleting lines to set noclobber, history, and filec, for example:

```
set noclobber
```

You could put them in .login, but then they would affect only your login shell and not any subsequent shells you might create. (Remember, some actions, such as certain commands from the vi editor, create a new shell without you having asked for one.)

If you want to keep your own record of when you log in, insert a line like this:

```
date >> loginlog
```

Then each time you log in, the date command is run, and its output is diverted to the loginlog file, giving you a record of the date and time of your logins.

If you have a supply of shell scripts or other programs that you use often, here is a useful practice. First, establish a subdirectory to hold these executable files. Then add that subdirectory to your path search list. Then, no matter what directory you are in, you can run those programs just by typing the name. For example, Bess could establish a bin subdirectory and add this line to her .login:

```
path=(/bin /usr/bin /home/bess/bin .)
```

Tired of the % prompt? The csh recognizes a shell variable called prompt. If you set it to some value, the shell will use that value for your prompt. For example, you can place the following in the .cshrc file:

```
set prompt="Yes, O wise one? "
```

This change will not take place until the file contents are executed. That happens automatically the next time you log in. Or you can use the source command to put it into effect immediately:

```
source .cshrc
```

The phrase Yes, O wise one? is called a *prompt string*. Note that we included a space at the end of the string. That's to separate the prompt string from your typed commands.

If you use ! as part of the prompt string, it is replaced by the command number used in the history list. This results in numbering your command lines on screen.

In this chapter we have used several special characters, including $ and !. At this point it may be useful to summarize the special characters encountered so far and to add a few more to the list.

Shell Metacharacters

The various UNIX shells recognize several characters (*metacharacters*) as having special meaning, such as * and ¦. Each shell also has ways to remove these special meanings. We will summarize the more common metacharacters now and then show how to neutralize them.

Function	Metacharacter
Wild card substitution	* ? [ ] (Chapter 7)
Redirection	> >> < ¦ (This chapter)
Background process	& (This chapter)
Command separator	; (This chapter)
Continue command on next line	\ (This chapter)
Value of a variable	$ (This chapter)
History prefix (csh shell)	! (This chapter)

To this list add the backquote: `. Do not confuse this with the regular quote ('), which leans the opposite way. A pair of backquotes does for commands what the $ does for shell variables. That is, a command name in backquotes is replaced by the output (or value, so to speak) of the command. Compare these two command-response pairs:

```
$ echo date
date
$ echo `date`
Mon May 21 11:22:05 PDT 1984
$
```

The backquotes are useful in shell scripts; see the Review Questions section for examples.

Neutralizing Metacharacters

Now suppose you want to use some of these symbols literally, perhaps in a command like

```
echo Type a * if you are happy
```

Try it. You will find that the * is replaced by a list of all your files! After all, that is what * means to the shell. To get around this difficulty, UNIX offers metacharacters that neutralize metacharacters. For this purpose it uses the backslash (\), single quotes ('), and double quotes ("). Let's see what each does.

The backslash negates the special qualities of whatever character immediately follows it. Unspecial characters are left that way. Here is an example:

```
$ echo \* \I \ \\ \[
* I \ [
$
```

Note that it even negates itself, so \\ is rendered \. The single \ is read as *blank*\ and is printed as a blank, just as \I is printed as I.

Now suppose you wish to print the sequence *?*. You could use

```
echo \*\?\*
```

or you could type

```
echo '*?*'
```

The single quotes turn off the special meaning of every character between them:

```
$ echo 'Send $100 to whom?'
Send $100 to whom?
$
```

The double quotes are slightly less restrictive. They turn off all the metacharacters *except* $, `, and \. Thus,

```
$ echo 'myname'
mariella
$ echo '`myname` is nice & sweet'
'myname' is nice & sweet
$ echo "`myname` is nice & sweet"
mariella is nice & sweet
$
```

The single quotes cause the backquotes and the & to be printed literally. The double quotes also cause the & to be printed literally, but the 'myname' is replaced by its output, mariella.

Once you use an opening single or double quote, the sh and ksh shells expect you to provide a closing quote, too. If you press Return before doing so, these shells shift to their second prompt, telling you they expect more to the command:

```
$ echo 'The morning fog
> flowed into the
> low valleys.'
The morning fog
flowed into the
low valleys.
$
```

This gives you a means to print several lines with a single echo.

Another use for quotes is to combine several words into one argument. Suppose, for instance, that additon is a shell script. If we give the command

```
additon five fleet fools
```

then $1 is `five`, $2 is `fleet`, and so on, as usual. But if we say

```
additon 'five fleet fools'
```

then $1 is the whole phrase `five fleet fools`.

There is another metacharacter useful in shell scripts. It is the # symbol, and it tells the shell to ignore what follows. You do not need a script to use it. For instance,

```
$ # this computer is not playing with a full stack
$
```

See! No reaction. The value of this metacharacter is that it lets you place explanatory comments in a shell script. For example, your `myname` script could look this way:

```
# myname:Ia command that returns the user's login name
echo $LOGNAME
```

If you use the `csh` shell, keep in mind that using such a comment as the first line in a shell script causes that shell to interpret the script as a `csh`-shell script instead of an `sh`-shell script.

Farewell, Dear Shell

This ends our discussion of the shell for a while. You have encountered many shell features in this chapter: command lines, redirection, job control, shell scripts, shell variables, the `.profile`, `.cshrc` and `.login` files, and shell metacharacters. Using them can greatly enhance your UNIX powers and pleasures. You will use them in subsequent chapters, and we suggest you play with these features until they become familiar. Using them will do much more for your understanding than just reading about them.

But now it is time to return to the nitty-gritty of learning some of the multitudinous commands known to the shell. We will resume that task in the next chapter.

Review Questions

1. Of the following commands, some are correct and some have errors in them. Identify the incorrect commands and then fix them.

   a. `ls-1 blackweb`

   b. `ls rupart -s`

   c. `ls -s-1`

d. `ps -a`

e. `cat duskhaven > lp`

f. `jolly > cat`

g. `PAL = ginny mae`

h. `NETWORTH = 45`

2. The file `exc` contains the line: `chmod u+x $1`. What will the following commands do?

```
sh exc fopman
sh exc exc
```

3. Our `huh` shell script had output like

```
you are
godzilla tty92 Feb 21 23:24
```

Modify the script so that the output is

```
You are godzilla
```

4. Suppose you often `cd` to the `/home/lisa/progs/pasc/proj` directory. What could you put into your `.profile` to make this easier to do?

5. Devise a shell script that will set a shell variable called `NAME` to the name of whatever user uses the script; assume the user is logged into his or her own account.

Answers

1. a. `ls -l blackweb`; should be a space before the `-`.
   b. `ls -s rupart`; put the option in the right place.
   c. `ls -s -l` or `ls -sl`
   d. fine
   e. `cat duskhaven ¦ lp` or `lp duskhaven`; either sends the file `duskhaven` to the printer. The original command in this question would create a *file* called `lp` and place a copy of the contents of `duskhaven` there.
   f. `cat jolly` or `cat < jolly`; the filename should be to the right of the redirection operator.
   g. `PAL='ginnie mae'`
   h. `NETWORTH=45`; remember, NO SPACES

2. The first command makes `fopman` into an executable file. The second makes `exc` into an executable file. Hereafter, the user can give commands like `exc nosecount`.

3. One way is to replace

```
echo You are
who am i
```

with

```
echo You are 'myname'
```

The backquotes cause 'myname' to be replaced by its value.

4. One possibility is to put in the line

```
PROJ=/home/lisa/prog/pasc/proj
```

Then to reach that directory, just type

```
cd $PROJ
```

5. `NAME='myname'`

Exercises at the Terminal

1. Try out some pipes. To provide suitable tools, you can use the commands `wc`, which counts the words in its input, and `sort`, which sorts its input alphabetically. Create a file of text called `mystuff` and try these commands; then devise your own.

```
wc mystuff > savecount
cat mystuff ¦ sort
sort mystuff ¦ tee sorted ¦ wc
```

2. Put a `ps` command in your `.profile` file and find out the process number of the shell that reads that file. Is it the same shell that later interprets your commands?

3. Devise a shell script that `cats` a file and also copies it into your home directory. Make the copy have a name that adds `.cpy` to the original name.

4. Implement the personal command directory approach we outlined in the section on `.profile`.

12

File Management Commands and Others: *wc*, *sort*, *lp*, and *chmod*

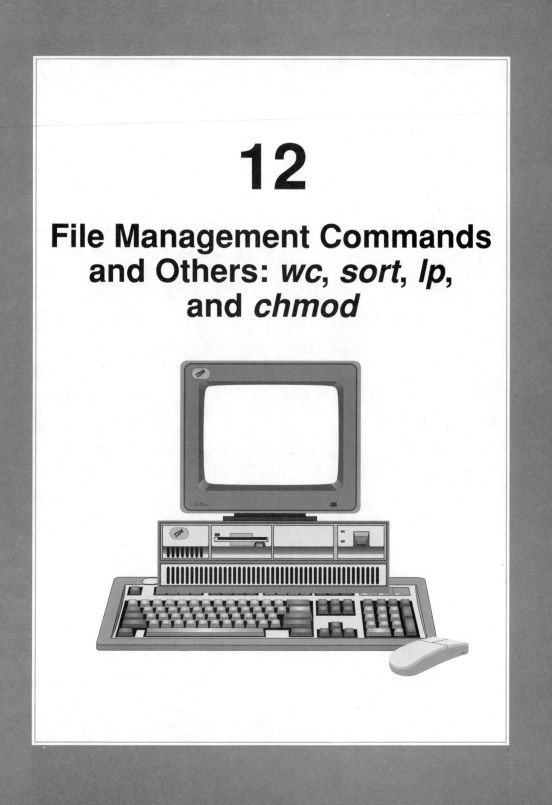

Chapter 12

File Management Commands and Others: *wc*, *sort*, *lp*, and *chmod*

Files are the heart of UNIX's storage system, so it is no surprise that UNIX has many commands for managing and manipulating files. This chapter will look at commands for counting the number of words in a file, for looking at the beginning or end of a file, for sorting files, for comparing files, for printing files, and for modifying file permissions. It also will mix in a few miscellaneous commands. As you read through the descriptions, remember to sit down and try out the commands.

File Management Commands

Word-Counting: *wc*

The wc command tells you how many lines, words, and characters you have in a file. If you have a file called gourd, you can find this information by typing

    wc gourd

and UNIX responds with, say,

```
79   378   2936 gourd
```

This response tells you that there are 79 lines, 378 words, and 2936 characters in the file gourd. You can have more than one file as an argument. For example, the command

```
wc gourd mango
```

would produce a result like this:

```
 79   378   2936 gourd
132   310   2357 mango
211   688   5293 total
```

Not only does wc count the lines, words, and characters in each file, it also finds the totals for you!

The most commonly used options for wc are -l, -w, and -c. The first one counts lines only, the second counts words only, and the last option counts characters only. Of course, you can combine them:

```
wc -lw darkeyes
```

This command would count the number of lines and words in darkeyes but not the number of characters.

wc **Word Count**		
Name	**Options**	**Arguments**
wc	**[-1wc]**	**[*filename(s)*]**
Description:	The wc command is actually a counting program. By default, it works in the -lwc option, counting the lines, words, and characters in the named files. If more than one file is given, wc gives the counts for each file plus the combined totals for all files. If no file is given, wc uses the standard input—the terminal. In this case, you should terminate the input with a Ctrl-d. Multiple options should be strung together on the same hyphen.	
Options:	-l Counts lines	
	-w Counts words	
	-c Counts characters	
Example:	wc -w essay	
	This command would count the number of words in the file essay.	

File Checking: *head*, *tail*, and *sed*

These three commands give you a quick way to check the contents of a file without viewing the whole file. The head command (see Figure 12.1) lets you investigate the beginning of a file. For instance, the command

```
head overheels
```

displays the first ten lines of the overheels file. Or, to see the first fifteen lines of the file, type this,

```
head -15 overheels
```

The head command is one of several BSD UNIX commands newly incorporated into Release 4 of System V UNIX. The tail command shows you the last 10 lines of a file. For example, to see the last 10 lines of the file feathers, just type

```
tail feathers
```

The summary for the tail command shows how to select more or fewer lines.

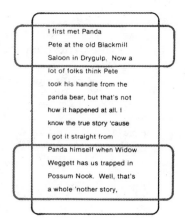

```
I first met Panda
Pete at the old Blackmill
Saloon in Drygulp. Now a
lot of folks think Pete
took his handle from the
panda bear, but that's not
how it happened at all. I
know the true story 'cause
I got it straight from
Panda himself when Widow
Weggett has us trapped in
Possum Nook. Well, that's
a whole 'nother story,
```

Figure 12.1.   Head and tail look at a file.

Our third aid, sed, actually is an editor that we will discuss in Chapter 13. But it does no harm to jump the gun a bit and tell you that this command displays the first 10 lines of the file feathers.

```
sed 10q feathers
```

You can replace the 10 with a different number if you wish to display a different number of lines.

head Gives the Head of a File (New with Release 4)

Name	Options	Arguments
head	[-number]	filename(s)

Description: The head command shows the first 10 lines of the named files, unless the number option specifies a different number of lines. If you provide more than one filename, head displays the name of each file before displaying the contents.

Option: -number For number, substitute the number of lines you wish to have printed.

Example: head -15 hunter

This command displays on the screen the first 15 lines of the hunter file.

tail Gives the Last Part of a File

Name	Options	Arguments
tail	[+/- number][lbc]	filename(s)

Description: The tail command shows the tail end of a file. By default, it delivers the last 10 lines. The tail command will work with only one file at a time.

Options: + number Start number from the beginning.

- number Start number from the end.

-lbc Indicates whether number is to be counted in lines (l), blocks (b), or characters(c). Option l is assumed if no letter is given.

Example: tail -20 gate

Prints the last 20 lines of the file gate.

tail +30c gate

Prints the file gate starting with the 30th character.

Note: Constructions of the form tail -15 -c gate are not allowed. All options have to be strung after one + or -.

Sorting: *sort*

One of UNIX's great labor-saving commands is sort, which can sort files numerically or alphabetically. The sorting function can be used simply or with some fancy options. We will just take a basic look this time and will save the fancy stuff for Chapter 13. The sort function, when used without options, sorts files alphabetically by line. Actually, the idea of "alphabetical" order has to be extended, since a file may contain nonalphabetic characters. The basic order used is called the *machine-collating sequence*, and it may be different on different machines. For UNIX, the following points are generally true:

1. Uppercase letters (capitals) are sorted separately from lowercase letters, with all uppercase characters appearing before the lowercase characters. Within each case, the standard alphabetical order is used.

2. Numbers are sorted by the first digit. The sorting order is 0,1,2,3,4,5,6,7,8,9.

3. The remaining symbols—ones like), %, +, and !—are not grouped together. Some may come between the numbers and the alphabet, and others before or after all numbers and letters.

Let's look at how a particular example might work. Suppose that the contents of grabbag are

```
Here is a small
file with some
words in it
and also
some numbers like
1
23
and
102.

 The first line is blank; this one begins with a blank.
```

This is how the command

```
sort grabbag
```

would arrange the contents on one system:

```
 The first line is blank; this one begins with a blank.
1
102.
23
Here is a small
```

333

```
and
and also
file with some
some numbers like
words in it
```

Note that the line beginning The first... was not placed with the other alphabetical lines. The reason is that the first character of that line is not the letter T but a blank. Thus, the line was placed according to where blanks go. (The -b option will cause blanks to be ignored.) Also note that 102 is listed before 23! This is because sort treats numbers as words and sorts them by their first digit. (The -n option treats numbers as numbers and sorts them arithmetically; it would place the numbers in file1 in the order 1, 23, 102.) Finally, notice that sort lists capital letters before it lists lowercase letters.

If you feed more than one file to sort, it will sort the files *and* merge the results. This is great for combining, say, inventory lists.

Normally, the sort function sends its output to the terminal. To save the results, you can use redirection. For example, to sort and merge the files redsox and whitesox and then store the results in a file called pinksox, type

```
sort redsox whitesox > pinksox
```

Or, you can use the -o option described in the sort summary.

sort **Sorts and Merges Files**		
Name	**Options**	**Arguments**
sort	[-d, -f, -n, -o, -r]	*filename(s)*
Description:	The sort command sorts and merges the lines from the named files and sends the result to the screen (see Figure 12.2). In the default mode, lines are sorted by the machine-collating sequence, which is an extended alphabetical order encompassing letters, digits, and other symbols. Capital letters are sorted separately from lowercase letters.	
Options:	-d	"Dictionary" order, using only letters, digits, and blanks to determine order.
	-f	Ignore the distinction between capital and lowercase letters.
	-n	Sort numbers by arithmetic value instead of by first digit.

-o *filename*	Place the output in a file called *filename* instead of on the screen. The name can be the same as one of the input names.
-r	Sort in reverse order.

Example: `sort -fr -o sortbag grabbag`

This command would sort the lines of the file `grabbag`. Capitalization will be ignored by the sorting process, and the lines will be in reverse alphabetical order. The results will be stored in the file `sortbag`.

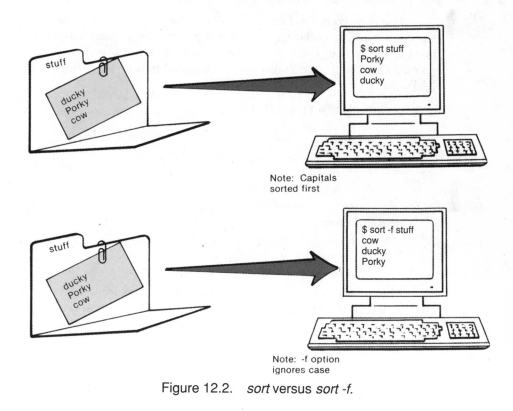

Figure 12.2.   *sort* versus *sort -f.*

File Comparison: *cmp*, *comm*, and *diff*

While cleaning up your filing system, you find two files with the same name but in different directories. Are they really the same? Or, let's say that you have two similarly named files. One is updated, but you do not remember which. Can you quickly compare the two? This is a small sample of the potential uses for some sort of system function that compares files. We will look at three UNIX possibilities.

The first is cmp. It is the simplest and tells you the least. It compares two files and finds the location (line and byte) of the first disagreement between the two. An interchange between you and UNIX might look like this:

```
$ cmp rascal.p rascall.p
rascal.p rascall.p differ: char 48, line 21
```

The comm command tells you more, but it works successfully only with files sorted in the ASCII collating sequence. It prints three columns. The first column lists lines found only in the first file. The second column lists lines found only in the second file. The third column lists lines found in both files. Here is a typical user-UNIX dialogue:

```
$ comm giftlist1 giftlist2
       Android, Arnold
          Falpha, Alpha
          Filename, Ronald
          Gossens, Waldo
          Goto, Dmitri
       Spumoni, Brunhilda
Spumoni, Hopalong
          Vlug, Merrimee
Yeti, Milo
          Zazzy, Quintus
```

The columns overlap, but you can see which lines are shared and which are not. In this case, only giftlist1 contains Spumoni, Hopalong, and Brunhilda. The rest of the names are in both lists. You can suppress the printing of any column you choose. The details for the comm command are in the summary.

The diff command is the most powerful of the three (see Figure 12.3). It finds the difference between two files and then tells you the most efficient way to make the first file identical to the second! It is a big help in updating files.

If you run diff on the same two files you used comm on (that is, you type diff giftlist1 giftlist2) you get this result:

```
0a1
> Android, Arnold
5c6
< Spumoni, Hopalong
- - -
```

```
> Spumoni, Brunhilda
7d7
< Yeti, Milo
```

cmp	Any two files (text or binary code).	Location of first difference, if any.
comm	Two sorted text files	Column 1: Lines only in first file. Column 2: Lines only in second file. Column 3: Lines in both files.
diff	Two text files.	Changes needed to make the first file just like the second file.

Figure 12.3. *cmp, comm,* and *diff.*

This needs some interpretation. The a, c, and d stand for append, change, and delete. The numbers are line numbers, the < means a line from the first file, and the > means a line from the second file. We can paraphrase the output this way:

Add to the beginning (line 0) of the first file, line 1 (Android, Arnold) of the second file.

Change line five of the first file (Spumoni, Hopalong) to line six (Spumoni, Brunhilda) of the second file.

Delete line seven (Yeti, Milo) of the first file.

Keep in mind that the goal of diff is to show how to make the first file identical to the second. For instance, if you revised a standard document used by several colleagues, you could email them the diff information needed to update their copies of the document.

cmp Compares Two Files, Finding Location of Difference

Name	Options	Arguments
cmp	-1	*filename1 filename2*
Description:	The cmp command looks through two input files and prints the byte and line number of the first difference between the two files. You can use - for *filename1* if you want one of the files to be the standard input.	

337

Option: -l   The long option prints the byte number (decimal)
                  and the differing bytes (octal) for each difference.

Example: cmp -l remember

This command will print the location of the first difference between what you type on the terminal (terminated by a Ctrl-d) and what is in the file remember.

comm Finds Lines Common to Two Sorted Files

Name	Options	Arguments
comm	[-1, -2, -3]	*filename1 filename2*

Description: The comm command reads the two named files which
                should be in ASCII collating sequence) and produces
                three columns of output. The first column contains lines
                found only in the first file, the second column contains
                lines found only in the second file, and the third column
                contains lines found in both files.

Options: -1   Do not print the first column.

            -2   Do not print the second column.

            -3   Do not print the third column.

Example: comm -12 listA listB

This command will print only those lines found in both
listA and listB.

diff Finds the Difference Between Two Files

Name	Options	Arguments
diff	[-b, -e, -i, -w]	*file1 file2*

Description: The diff command compares two text files and pro-
                duces output showing what changes to make in the first
                file in order to make it identical to the second file.

                The output format uses a for *append*, c for *change*, and
                d for *delete*. The symbol < means a line from the first file,

and > indicates a line from the second file. Numbers denote the lines affected. The following is an example.

```
8a10,12

  >Barth, Garth

  >Cuddles, Misty

  >Dollar, Petro
```

This means to append line 10 to line 12 of *file2* after line 8 of *file1*. Then, the three lines from *file2* are shown.

Options:	-b	Ignores trailing blanks in a line. Other blank strings are considered equal regardless of length. This option would consider the following two lines to be the same:

```
    eye of a newt

    eye   of   a   newt
```

-e   Produces output in the form of `ed` editor commands.

-i   Ignore the case of letters, causing `Bingo` to be considered equivalent to `bingo`.

-w   Ignore all blanks (spaces and tabs), causing `seethecat` to be considered equivalent to

```
    see the cat.
```

Examples: `diff -e giftlist1 giftlist2`

This command causes the output to be expressed as `ed` commands. If the files are the same as the example in the text, then the output would be:

```
7d

5c

Spumoni, Brunhilda

.

0a

Android, Arnold

.
```

Notice that the commands include the period symbol
that is needed to return to the command mode in ed.

Redundancy Elimination: *uniq*

Suppose you have two mailing lists that you have sorted and merged. You notice that some of the addresses are duplicated, and you want to get rid of the repeated versions. You can do this with uniq. It will read a file, compare adjacent lines, reject repetitions, and print the remaining lines on the terminal or into a file that you choose.

Assume that the merged file weelist has the following contents:

```
anchovies
apiaries
artichokes
artichokes
aviaries
```

The command

```
uniq weelist
```

will produce the following output:

```
anchovies
apiaries
artichokes
aviaries
```

As you can see, uniq eliminated one copy of the word artichokes from the file. If you want to direct the output to a file, just give the name of that file after the name of the file that is to be processed. Thus, the command

```
uniq weelist newfile
```

would produce the same output but would route it to the file newfile instead of to the screen.

Because uniq works by comparing adjacent lines, the duplicate lines must be next to the originals or else uniq will not spot them. Sorting the file first, using sort, will ensure that uniq works.

Making a Printed Copy

Video terminals are fun, but for some purposes (conducting inventories, wrapping fish, and so forth), you really need printed paper output. You can use the commands in this section to give you a printed output.

---

uniq **Removes Duplicated Lines from a File**

Name	Options	Arguments
uniq	[-u, -d, -c]	*inputfile [outputfile]*

Description: The uniq command reads the input file, compares adjacent lines, and prints out the file minus the repeated lines. If a second *filename* is given, the output is placed in that file instead of on the screen.

Options:

-u   Prints only those lines that have no duplicates. That is, a line that appears two or more times consecutively, in the original file, is not printed at all.

-d   Prints one copy of just the lines with duplicates, that is, unique lines are not printed.

-c   Prints the usual output, but precedes each line with the number of times that it occurs in the original file.

Example: uniq -d ioulist urgent

This command would scan the files ioulist for lines that appear more than once consecutively. One copy of each such line would be placed in the file urgent.

---

lp, cancel, and *lpstat*

The lp (for *l*ine *p*rinter) command sends one or more files to a line printer (see Figure 12.4). To have the file Fallreport printed, type

```
$ lp Fallreport
request id is pr2-46 (1 file)
$
```

(The line following the command provides a *request identification* for your printing job—more on that in a moment.)

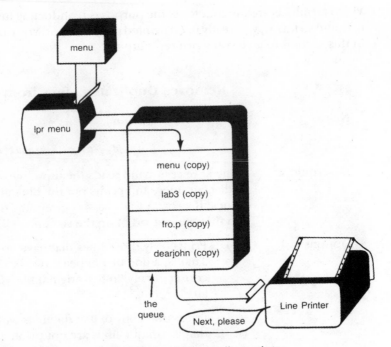

Figure 12.4.   Using a line printer.

Chaos would result, however, if this command sent your file directly to the printer because other lp commands might arrive in the middle of your print job and interrupt it. Instead, this command sends a copy of your file to a printer *queue*, where it waits its turn to be printed.

What if you sent the wrong file? Then use cancel to remove it from the queue or to halt the printing. Just use the request ID:

```
cancel pr2-46
```

Many installations have more than one printer. For example, a system might include a high-speed dot matrix printer and a slower, letter-quality printer. The lp command lets you specify which printer you want by using the -d option. For example, if a letter-quality printer were designated pr1, then you could send a letter to it with this command:

```
lp -d pr1 dearpres
```

If you do not specify the printer, the system will use a default value. For instance, our attempt to print Fallreport sent the text to pr2, as shown by the request ID assigned to it. If you like, you can establish your own default value by setting the shell variable LPDEST to the appropriate value.

To check up on the status of a printing request, just type

```
lpstat
```

To print several files, list them all after the command:

```
lp Winterreport Springreport Summerreport Fallreport
```

Each file will begin at the top of a page. If you want the files printed as one unit, you can do something like this:

```
cat Winterreport Springreport Summerreport Fallreport ¦ lp
```

lp, cancel, and lpstat **Using the Line Printer**		
Name	**Options**	**Arguments**
`lp`	`[-d]`	`[filename(s)]`
`cancel`		**request ID**
`lpstat`	`[-p, -t]`	

Description: The `lp` command sends the named files to a line printer queue where they are printed in an orderly fashion. If you omit a *filename*, `lp` accepts input directly from your terminal—terminate the input with Ctrl-d. The `lp` command returns a request ID that can be used with `cancel`. The `cancel` command removes files from the queue and even halts the printer if necessary. Type `cancel` and follow it with the request ID. The `lpstat` command reports on the status of your requests when used without options.

Options: -d   (for `lp`) Lets you select a printer.

        -p   (for `lpstat`) Reports on printer statuses.

        -t   (for `lpstat`) Provides a total status report, covering printers and the printer queue.

Example: `lp some stuff`

This command prints the contents of the files `some` and `stuff`.

Permissions: *chmod*

The chmod (for *ch*ange *mode*) command gives you the final say on who can read and use your files and who cannot. This command considers the UNIX users' world to be divided into three classes:

1. You, the user (u).

2. Your group (g).

3. Others (o).

What's this bit about a group? UNIX was developed at Bell Labs for use there in research. So, originally, a *group* would correspond to a particular research group. What constitutes a group for you will depend on your system. Perhaps it might be students in the same class or workers in the same department, or it might be arbitrary. Whatever the system, users in the same group are assigned the same *group number*, and this number is stored in the /etc/passwd file, which also contains your login name, your home directory assignment, and your login shell. So UNIX knows which group you are in and who else is in it (even if you do not).

In addition to three classes, there are three kinds of permissions that chmod considers:

1. Read permission (r)—this includes permission to cat, more, lp, and cp a file.

2. Write permission (w)—this is permission to change a file, which includes editing a file and appending to a file.

3. Execute permission (x)—this is permission to run an executable file, for example, a program.

You can check to see what permissions are in effect by using the -l option for ls on the pertinent files. For example, the command

```
ls -l a.out expgrow.f
```

could produce this output:

```
-rwxr-xr-x 1 doeman       25957 Jan 27 15:44 a.out
-rw-r--r--- 1 doeman         671 Jan 27 15:17 expgrow.f
```

The symbols on the left (-rwxr-xr-x) contain the information about permissions. There are ten columns. The first, which contains a hyphen for these examples, has a d for directories and other letters for special kinds of files. Do not worry about that column.

The next nine columns are actually three groups of three columns each. The first group of three reports user permissions, the second group of three reports group permissions, and the final group of three reports other permissions. We can spread out the three groupings for a.out like this:

```
rwx      r-x      r-x
user     group    other users
```

Within each grouping, the first column shows an r for read permission, the second column a w for write permission, and the third column an x for execute permission. A hyphen (-) means no permission.

Thus, for the preceding a.out file, the user has read, write, and execute permissions (rwx) for the file a.out. Members of the same group have read and execute permissions (r-x) but no write permission. Other users also have read and execute permissions (r-x) but no write permission. Permissions for the expgrow.f account are similar, except no one has execution permission.

What does this all mean? It means that anyone on the system could read or copy these two files. Only the user, however, could alter these two files in this directory. (However, if you copied this file into your directory, you would then be able to write as well as read and execute.) Finally, anyone who wanted to could run the program a.out by typing the name of the file. (If the other user were in a different directory, he or she would have to use the full pathname of the file.) In most systems, these particular permissions are established by default; chmod lets you change them.

The chmod command is used a bit differently from most other UNIX commands. The simplest way to use it is to type chmod and then type a space. Then comes an *instruction segment* with three parts and no spaces. The first part of the segment consists of one or more letters identifying the classes to be affected. The next part is a + or – sign for adding or subtracting permissions. The final part is one or more letters identifying the permissions to be affected (see Figure 12.5). After the instruction segment is another space and the name(s) of the file(s) to be affected by the changes. This may sound a little confusing, but it is simple once you see a few examples. So, here are some examples:

```
chmod g+w growexp.f
chmod go-rx a.out
```

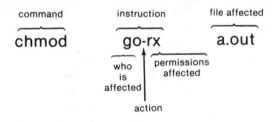

Figure 12.5.   Parts of a *chmod* command.

The first example grants other members of your group (g) the right to write (w) in the file growexp.f. The second example takes away both read (r) and execute (x) privileges from members of your group (g) and from others (o). If you repeated the ls -l command now, the result would be

```
-rwx------ 1 doeman      25957 Jan 27 15:44 a.out
-rw-rw-r-- 1 doeman        671 Jan 27 15:17 expgrow.f
```

You can include more than one permission instruction by separating the permissions with commas. For instance, the command

```
chmod g+w,o-r project.big
```

would let other group members write in the project.big file and would deny other users permission to read that file. There should be no spaces within the instruction segment.

You can use chmod on your directories. Just use the directory name instead of the filename. What are the effects of these permissions on directories? *Read permission* for a directory lets you read (using ls, for example) the names of the files in the directory. *Write permission* lets you create new files in the directory and remove files from the directory. Finally, *execute permission* for a directory lets you cd to that directory.

Perhaps you wonder what the point is in changing permissions for yourself (u). First, you can create a shell script file of UNIX commands. If you give that file *execute* status, then typing that filename will cause the commands in the file to be executed. We talked about that in Chapter 11. Second, by removing write permission, you can protect yourself from accidentally changing a valuable file.

---

chmod Change Modes or Permissions on Files

Name	Options	Arguments
chmod	ugo, +/-, rwx	filename(s) or directory name(s)

Description:	The chmod command grants or removes read, write, and execute permissions for three classes of users: user (you), group (your group), and others. A chmod command has three parts: the command name (chmod, of course), the instruction string, and the name of the file to be affected. The instruction string also has three parts: letter(s) indicating who is affected, a + or - symbol indicating the action to be taken, and letter(s) indicating which permissions are affected. The code is as follows:

Who:

u	The user
g	The user's group
o	Others (everyone other than u or g)
a	All (short for ugo)

> *Action:*
>
> +   Add permission
>
> -   Remove permission
>
> *Permission:*
>
> r   Read
>
> w   Write
>
> x   Execute

Example: Suppose you (login name booky) gave the command ls -l and found the following permissions for your payroll file:

```
-rwxrwxrwx 1 booky  1776 Jan 4 9:33 payroll
```

If you wanted to remove the write and execute permissions for your *group* and *other* users, type:

```
chmod  go-wx  payroll
```

The g refers to group, the o to others. The - means remove permissions w and x.

Messages: *mesg*

Usually, accounts are set up so that if someone tries to write to you while you are on a terminal, you will get a message to that effect. This makes UNIX a friendly and neighborly environment. Sometimes, however, you may not want to be interrupted. For those times, UNIX gives you ways to turn off the messages. The mesg command controls attempts to write or talk to you.

To prevent people from reaching you with write or talk, type

```
mesg n
```

When you feel more open to the world, you can reestablish your communication links with

```
mesg y
```

If you forget your state, just type

```
mesg
```

and UNIX will let you know your current state. The command will endure until you log out.

The mesg y command may be included in the standard .profile file or, for csh shell users, in the .login file. You can change it if you like, so that you can login with mesg n (see Figure 12.6).

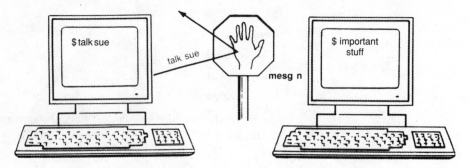

Figure 12.6.   *mesg* at work.

mesg **Permit or Deny Messages from *write* or *talk***		
Name	**Options**	**Arguments**
mesg	**None**	[-y, -n]
Description:	Typing mesg y allows other users to communicate with you using write or talk.	
	Typing mesg n forbids other users from communicating with you using write or talk.	
	Typing mesg will cause UNIX to reply with is y or is n as the case may be.	

Commands for Your Terminal: *tty* and *stty*

The tty command tells you the pathname of your terminal. For example, the command

    tty

might elicit the response

    /dev/tty08

This means you are using terminal number 8 and the terminal is treated as a file in the /dev (for device) directory.

The stty command is used to set terminal options, such as the *baud rate* (transmission speed), parity, and echo, and to set which key is the erase key. Much of stty concerns the interface between the terminal and the computer, but we will just look at some of the less technical aspects. Normally, the system takes care of these matters for you, but you might want to change some of the choices.

The first step is to determine the current situation. Type

```
stty
```

and UNIX will report back the baud rate and option settings that are different from the default (standard) values. Here is a sample response to that command:

```
speed 9600 baud; -parity
erase = ^h; kill = @
brkint inpck icrnl onlcr tab3
echo -echoe echok
```

What does this all mean? First, the speed 9600 baud indicates the rate at which information is sent back and forth between the terminal and the computer.

Next, the single words, with or without a leading hyphen, refer to various communication conventions and modes. For instance, echo means that each character you type is echoed back to the terminal. Thus, when you type the letter Q, the letter Q appears on the screen. Preceding one of these words with a hyphen reverses its meaning. Hence -echo would tell the computer not to echo back the characters you type. (Some terminals handle echoing internally, so the echo mode would produce a double echo for them.) Chances are you do not need to tamper with these modes.

Finally, there are entries of the form erase = ^h. This particular entry means that the erase character has been set to Ctrl-h.

Suppose you want to change some of these values. You can use the stty command to do so. (However, don't make such changes without good reason. You may wind up making your terminal unable to communicate!) Here are some examples:

```
stty 2400      ← set the baud rate to 2400

stty -echo     ← set the no echo mode

stty erase %   ← set the erase character to %
```

Note that setting the baud rate instructs the *computer* which rate to use and to expect. It does not set the *terminal's* rate. In general, both computer and terminal have to be set to the same rate. Setting the terminal may involve special keystrokes or setting physical switches.

To set erase or kill to a control character, you can type first an escaped caret (\^) then the corresponding letter. Thus, to set the erase character back to Ctrl-h, type

```
stty erase \^h
```

Alternatively, you can type a backslash, then type Ctrl-h directly.

You should be cautious with such changes. For example, changing the baud rate just changes the computer end. You would also have to change the rate at the terminal end, perhaps by resetting switches.

To make such a change permanent, place the instruction in your .profile file, as described at the end of this chapter.

Using the UNIX Clock: *time* and *calendar*

Never let it be said that UNIX won't give you the time of the day. It gladly informs you whenever you give the date command. UNIX can support the date command because it keeps track of the time internally. This ability helps it to perform such diverse tasks as timing commands (time) and providing you with a reminder service (calendar).

time

The `time` command tells you how long a simple command takes. Its general form is

```
time COMMAND
```

After you give this instruction, the `COMMAND` (which can be any UNIX command or program execution) is run, and when it is finished, you are given a breakdown of how much time was used. The output of `time` looks like this:

```
15.0 real
5.2 user
2.1 sys
```

These times are in seconds. The time labeled `real` is the elapsed time from when you first give the command until the command is completed. Because UNIX is a time-sharing system, it may have been doing some other tasks during that time period, so `real` time does not really represent how much time was devoted to your needs. The next two times relate just to the CPU time spent on your command. The `user` time is time spent executing the command, and `system` time is the additional time spent in the system as a result of the command.

These `time` commands are very important when you are renting CPU time that can cost $180 per hour or more.

calendar

The `calendar` command provides a built-in reminder service. (Do not confuse it with the `cal` command, which generates monthly and yearly calendars.) Actually, you do not even execute the `calendar` command. Your responsibility is to create a *file* named `calendar` in your login directory. In this file, you place dated reminders such as:

```
September 22        Dentist at 2:30
9/24         dinner at Antoine's, 8pm
PAY AUTO INSURANCE Sept 28
```

Early each morning, UNIX will look through all the login directories for files named `calendar`. Whenever it finds one, it will read the file and look for lines containing the date for today or tomorrow. The lines that it finds, it will mail to the directory's owner. Thus, you receive a reminder via `mail` the day before the date and then on the day itself.

The date can be anywhere on the line, and you can use recognizable abbreviations. However, `calendar` does not recognize dates in which the day precedes the month. Thus, you will not be reminded of lines containing dates such as "25 December" or "25/12."

time Time a Command		
Name	**Options**	**Arguments**
`time`	None	*commandname*

Description: The `time` command, when followed by a command name, runs the named command and gives you a breakdown of the time used. Three times are given:

Real, or elapsed time—This is the actual time that passes from the moment you initiate the command until the command is finished. If UNIX is switching back and forth between your demands and those of other users, all that time is included, too.

User time—This is the CPU time used solely for the execution of your command.

System time—This is additional CPU time spent in the system in the course of setting up and servicing the command.

Example: `time cc woo.c`

This command will cause command `cc woo.c` to run. When execution of the command is finished, UNIX will print the time summary for `cc woo.c`:

```
4.0 real
```

```
1.1 user
```

```
0.9 sys
```

1.1 seconds were used to execute the command and another 0.9 seconds were spent in the system supporting the command execution. 4.0 (that is, 6.0 - 1.1 - 0.9) seconds were spent time-sharing.

File Compression and Expansion: *compress*, *uncompress*, and *zcat*

Typically, a UNIX system stores your files on one or more hard disks. Technology keeps making more and more space available to store files, but humanity has had no problem filling this space as it becomes available. So it is not improbable that you may eventually get a message from your system administrator to trim your disk space usage. One approach is to delete files you no longer need, but with Release 4 of UNIX System V, you now have the option of compressing files, then expanding them later as needed. These commands also are handy for transmitting files by mail or over a network. You can compress a file before sending it, and the recipient can expand it.

---

calendar **A Reminder Service**

Description: To use this service, create in your login directory a file called calendar. Put notes to yourself in this file. Every line in this file containing a recognizable date is mailed by UNIX to you twice: (1) on the day before the date listed and (2) on the date itself. The date can be anywhere on the line. It should include the month and the day *in that order*, and you can use reasonable abbreviations.

Example: The calendar file can contain entries such as:

```
Buy goose March 19

call gus mar. 20 at 3 pm

3/23 Report due
```

The compress command compresses a file, replacing the file with a compressed version that has .Z added to its name. For instance, the command

```
compress keynote
```

replaces the keynote file with a compressed version called keynote.Z. Typically, the compress command reduces the size of a file containing English text by 50% to 60%.

The uncompress command reverses the effect of the compress command. For example, the command

```
uncompress keynote.Z
```

replaces the compressed keynote.Z file with an uncompressed version called keynote.

Once you have compressed a file, you do not have to uncompress it to view it. The zcat command uncompresses the contents of a file and displays them on screen without actually altering the compressed file. That is, if turkey.Z is a file that has been compressed by the compress command, then the command

```
zcat turkey.Z
```

displays the uncompressed file contents on-screen, leaving the turkey.Z file intact and still compressed. If the file is long, you can pipe the output through more or pg:

```
zcat bigturkey.Z ¦ more
zcat excuseme.Z ¦ pg
```

compress, uncompress, and zcat
Compress and Uncompress Files

Name	Options	Arguments
compress, uncompress, zcat	**None**	*filename(s)*

Description:	The compress command replaces a file by a compressed version that has .Z appended to the original file name. Text files typically are reduced 50% to 60% in length.
	The uncompress command undoes the work of compress, restoring a compressed file to its original form and removing the appended .Z from the file name.
	The zcat command displays an uncompressed version of a file on screen while leaving the compressed version of the file unaltered.
Examples:	compress waist
	Replaces the waist file with a compressed version named waist.Z.
	uncompress waist.Z
	Replaces the waist.Z file with an uncompressed version named waist.
	zcat waist.Z
	Displays the uncompressed contents of the waist.Z file while leaving waist.Z unaltered.

Conclusion

We have examined quite a few UNIX commands in this chapter, and they should give you an idea of the power and variety of the UNIX system. Once again we urge you to try them out and to experiment. You may even wish to look through the manual, for in many cases we have given only the more common options.

Review Questions

Explain what each of the following commands is used for.

1. chmod

2. mesg

3. time

4. calendar

5. sort

6. tty

7. lp

8. compress

9. head

Some of the commands in the following list are correct; some have errors in them. Identify the incorrect commands and then correct them. Describe what the command does, too.

10. wc-w blackweb

11. tail blackweb

12. sort -f- n iou.list

13. tail blackweb -15

14. comm -3 stallion Stallion

15. cat Rupart > lp

16. blackweb > wc

Answers

1. Changes modes or permission on files; 2. Permits or denies messages from write; 3. Times a command; 4. A reminder service; 5. Sorts a file; 6. Finds differences between two files; 7. Sends material to a line printer; 8. Compresses a file; 9. Shows the beginning of a file; 10. wc -w blackweb counts words in the file blackweb;

11. Correct—shows the last ten lines of the file `blackweb`; 12. `sort -f -b iou.list` or `sort -fb iou.list` sorts the contents of `iou.list` in machine-collating order, but ignores the difference between capital and lowercase letters and ignores the initial blanks; 13. `tail -15 blackweb` shows the last 15 lines of `blackweb`. (The incorrect version given in question four would show the last ten lines of `blackweb` and would then look for a file called `-15`, of course, if you had a file by that name, then the original instruction would be correct.); 14. Correct—shows in column 1 those lines that are only in the file `stallion` and shows in column 2 those lines that are only in the file `Stallion`; both files, however, need to be sorted for this to work correctly; 15. `cat Rupart ¦ lp` or `lp Rupart` sends the file `Rupart` to be printed on the line printer. The original command given in question six would create a file called `lp` and would place a copy of the contents on `Rupart` there; 16. `wc < blackweb` or `wc blackweb` counts the lines, words, and characters in the file `blackweb`. The `<` and `>` operators require a command or executable file on the left, and a filename on the right.

Exercises at the Terminal

1. While in your home directory, do the following:

    a. List the contents of your home directory.

    b. Count the number of files you have using the command sequence shown earlier in the chapter (with pipes).

    c. Find your longest file.

    d. Read the beginning of three files using `sed` and pipe the results through `more`.

2. a. Use your favorite editor to create two new files as follows:

    file `aha` contains the following text:

    ```
    since
    you
    went
    away
    ```

    file `bah` contains the following text:

    ```
    since
    your
    last
    stay
    ```

b. Now try the following commands:

```
head aha bah
head -2 aha bah
tail -2 aha bah
sed 3q aha bah
cmp aha bah
com aha bah
diff aha bah
sort aha
sort aha bah
wc -l aha bah
compress aha
ls aha*
cat aha.Z
zcat aha.Z
```

3. Try a few commands like:

```
who ¦ sort ¦ more
who ¦ sort ¦ tee CC
sed CC
```

13

More Text Processing: *cut, paste, sed,* and *nroff*

Chapter 13

More Text Processing: *cut, paste, sed,* and *nroff*

Today, much computing effort goes into the creation and the alteration of text. Therefore, it is not surprising that UNIX has many facilities dealing with text processing. There are several aspects to this subject. First, there is the basic process of creating text files. You have seen how to use editors such as emacs and vi to do this. Second, there is the process of modifying a file, perhaps to correct the spelling of a word you have persistently misspelled or to change a name in a form letter. Or you may wish to rearrange text. A third aspect is formatting the file, that is, setting margins, lining up the right-hand side of the text, controlling line spacing, etc. These tasks can be accomplished using the standard editors, but often they can be done more conveniently and efficiently using the UNIX commands cut and paste for rearranging, spell for proofreading, sed for editing, and nroff for formatting. All four of these tools are designed to work as *filters*, so let's discuss this unifying feature before we move to the individual commands.

UNIX Filters

Many UNIX utilities, including pr, wc, sort, and those discussed in this chapter, are designed to be *filters*. Typically, a filter takes input from the standard input (usually your terminal), processes it somehow, and sends the output to the standard output (usually your screen). By using UNIX redirection and pipes, a filter can just as easily take its input from a file or from another command instead of from the terminal. (Also, most filters can take input from files used as arguments.) Similarly, you can use UNIX redirection and pipes to route the output of a filter to a file or to another command. This agility makes for a flexible, powerful system. You do not need one command for keyboard input and a separate command to handle files. You do not need a carload of complex programs when you can achieve the same results by linking the right combination of filters together with pipes. Designing programs to act as filters is an important part of the UNIX philosophy.

Note that a filter adds nothing superfluous to its output; *sort* does not preface its output with a merry

```
All right, sweetheart, here's your output!
```

This may make UNIX utilities seem a little cold and impersonal, but you would not want a message like that piped along to wc or lp along with the rest of the output.

Note: If you do not use pipes and do want the personal touch, you can make shell scripts like this:

```
echo There! It\'s all sorted.
sort $*
```

You use a backslash before the single quote metacharacter because you want it to be a simple apostrophe.

Now let's get on to particulars by looking at cut and paste.

Rearranging Text: *cut* and *paste*

The traditional cut-and-paste method consists of cutting up a manuscript and pasting the parts together in a new order. The UNIX commands accomplish a similar aim. They do, however, concentrate on vertical cuts and pastes.

Extracting Vertical Slices: *cut*

The cut command has two modes. One (the -c option) selects columns from a file, with each column being one column wide. The second mode (the -f option) selects out fields (see Figure 13.1). Let's take the first mode first. To use it, follow the -c (no intervening spaces) with the numbers of the columns to be passed on. Use a hyphen to indicate ranges and a comma to separate entries. Here are some examples:

```
cut -c2,4,6          ← Pass columns 2, 4, and 6
cut -c2-6            ← Pass columns 2 through 6
cut -c2-6,10-12      ← Pass columns 2 through 6 and 10 through 12
```

The numbers must be in increasing order.

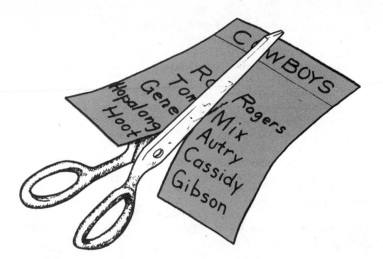

Figure 13.1.   The *cut* command can select fields from a file.

This form of cut is useful for tables or files in which data is organized by columns, for example, data left over from the punched card era. Suppose the file stuff looks like this:

```
Owen        Danny      234 606 899833
Gershwin    Matthew    543 105 229381
Plaut       Julie      423 636 596215
```

Then you could have this exchange with the computer:

```
$ cut -c1-15,31-33 stuff
Owen            234
Gershwin        543
Plaut           423
$
```

You get back columns 1 through 15 and columns 31 through 33. Because cut is a filter, you could pipe the output to sort if you wanted the output sorted.

The -f option works similarly, but now the numbers refer to fields rather than columns. That is, the command

```
cut -f1-3,5
```

means to print fields one through three and five. And what is a field? It is a string of characters marked off by a *delimiter*. A delimiter is a character used to indicate the boundaries of a field. For cut, the delimiter is assumed to be the tab character, but you can use the -d option to reset the delimiter. Let's give an example. Since a tab character is difficult to see, let's use a colon for a delimiter. First, you create a file morestuff with colon-delimited fields:

```
Fennel:Douglas:Saint Bernard:55
Snapp:Ginger:Collie:43
```

Then feed the file to cut, specifying the delimiter and the desired fields:

```
$ cut -f2,4 -d: morestuff
Douglas:55
Ginger:43
$
```

Here you print the second and fourth fields. Note that there are no spaces in the options. If you want a space or a shell metacharacter to be a delimiter, quote it:

```
cut -f1-4 -d" "
```

Remember your shell script myname in Chapter 11? You can use cut to construct another version:

```
who am i ¦ cut -f1 -d" "
```

This prints the first field of the who am i command, and that is just the user's login name.

cut Cuts Out Selected Fields of a File		
Name	**Options**	**Arguments**
cut	**-c or -f, [-d]**	*filename(s)*
Description:	The cut command passes through the requested columns (-c option) or fields (-f option). Columns are one character wide and are identified by number. Fields are recognized by a field delimiter (default is a tab) and identified by number. In either case, a hyphen is used to indicate a range of numbers and a comma is used to separate individual numbers or ranges. The list of identifying numbers follows the appropriate option without spaces.	
Options:	-clist	Pass on the columns in the list.
	-flist	Pass on the fields in the list.
	-d	Change the delimiter character to the one immediately following the d. A space or a shell metacharacter should be enclosed in double quotes.

Examples:
```
cut -c2-5,8 frip
```
This command prints columns two through five and column eight of the file `frip`.

```
cut -f3,6 -d: fnip
```
This command prints fields three and six of the file `fnip`. The fields are separated by a colon.

Putting It Together: *paste*

The `paste` command is the reverse of `cut`. It takes two or more input files and pastes them together, side by side. If two files are pasted, then the first line of the first file is pasted to the first line of the second file, and so on. The default *glue* that holds the lines together is the tab character. For instance, suppose you have the following two files, as revealed by `cat`:

```
$ cat fname
gene
fred
elmo
brinleigh
$ cat lname
smith
flint
jardine
snerch
$
```

Then `paste` does the following:

```
$ paste fname lname
gene      smith
fred      flint
elmo      jardine
brinleigh     snerch
$
```

The tab between `gene` and `smith` causes `smith` to start in column nine (one tab from the margin). But the last letter of `brinleigh` already is past the first tab stop, so the tab character pushes `snerch` to the next tab stop, column 17.

The `-d` option lets you change the pasting character. Here you change it to a space (you need to use quotes for a space character):

```
$ paste -d" " fname lname
gene smith
fred flint
elmo jardine
brinleigh snerch
$
```

The paste command also can accept input from the terminal or a pipe. For these cases, use a hyphen for one or more filenames. For instance, this would paste keyboard input between two other files:

```
paste fname - lname
```

You would type a Ctrl-d to indicate the end of the keyboard input.

A typical use for cut and paste in conjunction would be to extract some fields from a table of data and to paste them together in a different order.

paste Horizontally Merges Lines of Files		
Name	**Options**	**Arguments**
paste	**[-d]**	**filename(s)**

Description:	The paste command sticks together corresponding lines from the files given as arguments. All first lines are joined into one first line, and so on. Within the compound line, the original lines are separated by a tab character by default. A hyphen (·) can be used as a filename to indicate input from the standard input.
Options:	-d The character following the d is used to link together the input lines. If more than one character is given, they are used circularly; that is, the first character is used, then the second, to the end of the list, and then that order is repeated.
Example:	paste -d: fnip fnop
	This command adds each line in fnop to the end of the corresponding line in fnip, separating the two with a colon.

Combining Files: *join*

The cat command lets you combine files vertically; that is, it enables you to append one file to another. The join command lets you combine files horizontally, with the lines of one file being tagged to the end of the corresponding lines of another file. The `join` command is more demanding however. First, the lines in a file must be in sorted order. More specifically, they should be in ascending ASCII sequence, such as the `sort` command produces. Second, for two lines to be combined, they must have the same *join field*. Normally, `join` uses blanks and tabs to divide a line into fields, and the first field is taken to be the join field. The `join` command then prints the join field, the rest of the fields from the first file, and the rest of the fields from the second file. Let's try it. First, suppose you begin with the files shown by the following `cat` commands:

```
$ cat rbi.and.ba
Abe Booth        88           .332
Billie Hays      82           .345
Tank Derron      73           .302
$ cat pos.and.fld
Abe Booth        RF           .978
Billie Hays      CF           .989
Tank Derron      LF           .982
$
```

Although you cannot tell from the appearance, this file uses tab characters (see the upcoming box) to align the fields.

Now let's use the `join` command:

```
$ join rbi.and.ba pos.and.fld
Abe Booth 88 .332 Booth RF .978
Billie Hays 82 .345 Hays CF .989
Tank Derron 73 .302 Derron LF .982
```

In this case, the join field was the column of first names. That is why the last names appear twice—they belong to a different field. Also note that the `join` command uses a space character to separate the fields on output.

You can modify that behavior by using the `-t` option. If you use, say, `-tc` in the command line, where *c* is some character, then `join` will use the *c* character to identify fields during input and to separate fields during output. For the last example, you should use the tab character. That way, the first and last names would be in one field, and the output would line up better. To use a tab with the `-t` option, however, you have to enclose it in single quotation marks. Otherwise, the shell will think that you are just spacing out the command line. Let's try it. We have used `<Tab>` to indicate where you press the Tab key. Note that you still have to type a space after the tab in order to separate it from the filenames.

```
$ join -t'<Tab>' rbi.and.ba pos.and.fld
Abe Booth        88           .332     RF        .978
Billie Hays      82           .345     CF        .989
Tank Derron      73           .302     LF        .982
```

join	Joins Lines from Two Files	
Name	**Options**	**Arguments**
join	[-t, -j]	*file1 file2*

Description:	The join command combines matching lines from *file1* with lines from *file2*. The lines should be sorted in ascending ASCII order. Each line is divided into fields by a separator character. By default, blanks and tabs are separators. Each line has a join field, which is the first field by default. Lines match if the join fields match. In that case, the join field is printed, then the remaining fields from *file1*, and then the remaining fields from *file2*. Lines without matching join fields are not permitted. Advanced users may wish to check a manual for additional options.
Options:	-t*c* Use the character *c* as the join field.
	-j*nm* Use field *m* of file *n* as the join field.
Examples:	join spring fall
	This command joins lines using the default behavior.
	join -t: -j1 3 parts1 parts2
	This command uses the colon for the field separator and uses the third field of parts1 as the join field.

The Tab and Space Characters

Many keyboards have a Tab key. Sometimes it is labeled "Tab"; sometimes it features an arrow: →. Pressing the Tab key causes the cursor to move to the right, typically eight spaces at a time. A tab produces *absolute* moves; that is, it moves to predefined locations on the screen. Thus, whether the cursor is in column one or six, a tab moves the cursor to column nine. (A *relative* move would move the cursor, say, eight spaces from the current cursor position.)

A tab is part of the ASCII character set; it is character 9. The space also is a character—character 32. Each, for instance, takes up the same amount of storage space as *B* or any other alphabetic character. One consequence of this is that text containing tabs may look like text containing spaces but nonetheless be different. Suppose, for example, that the tabs are spaced by eight and that you type

```
sam<Tab>adams
```

It would appear like this on the screen:

```
sam     adams
```

Typing

```
sam<Space><Space><Space><Space><Space>adams
```

also produces that appearance:

```
sam     adams
```

But the first takes up just 9 memory slots (8 letters, 1 tab), while the second uses 13 memory slots (8 letters, 5 spaces).

The unexpected presence of tabs may produce surprises when you do editing. In vi, for instance, you may try to remove one space and find that eight disappear, for you really were removing a tab.

The chief values of tabs are saving storage space and producing nicely aligned columns of data. This second point means that tabs often occur in the sort of text used with join.

Checking Your Spelling: *spell*

You have just completed an important letter, but you are worried about your spelling. You could sit down and check each word with a dictionary, or you can let UNIX do that for you. Suppose your letter is in the file sendcash. You can give the command

```
spell sendcash
```

and UNIX will then compare each word in your file with words in a spelling list it maintains. If one of your words is not on the list or is not derivable from some standard rules (adding an *s* or an *ing*, for example), that word is displayed on the terminal. (If you make lots of spelling errors, you may need to use redirection to save all your errors in a file.)

Suppose sendcash looks like this:

```
Dear Ruggles,

I'm at a real nice place. It's the sub-basement of Mildew
Hall at Forkney College; have you ever been their? If you
have, you will knoe that I need mony bad! Please, please
send some soon! The autochthons here are spooky. I'm
looking forward to recieving your next letter.
                                        Love,
                                        Buffy
```

The output of the spell command would look like this:

```
autochthons
Buffy
Forkney
knoe
mony
recieving
Ruggles
```

This example points out some of the pitfalls of spell. First, it may not recognize some proper names. Second, although it caught the words knoe, mony, and recieving, it did not catch the fact that their should have been spelled there. The spell command can check to see if a word is on its list, but it cannot tell whether you used it correctly. Third, spell does not tell you the correct spelling. Finally, you may know some words, such as autochthons and certain four-letter words, that are not on spell's list. Nonetheless, spell is a big help, especially with long files. Now let's see about editing files.

The *sed* Stream Editor

The sed command does wholesale editing work. It has many of the capabilities of ed or ex, but it is used differently. Instead of letting you interactively modify a file, it just takes a file as input, reads and modifies it one line at a time, and sends its output to the screen. You can think of the contents of the input file as streaming through the editor, modified as it flows through, hence the name *stream editor* (see Figure 13.2). (The sed editor was developed from ed, not ex, which is why it is not the sex editor. However, ex duplicates many ed commands.) This design makes sed efficient for large files. Perhaps more important, it allows sed to be used with pipes and redirection and this makes sed into a handy tool for many tasks. In particular, it often is used in shell scripts.

Figure 13.2. *sed* is a stream editor.

sed Basics

Give sed an input file and minimal instructions, and it will print the contents of the file line by line:

```
$ sed '' tale.start
        Once upon a time a delightful princess named Delita lived in
the Kingdom of Homania.   One day, as Princess Delita walked
amidst the fragrant flowers and artful bowers of the West Garden,
she spotted a glistening stone.   Picking it up, Delita discovered
that the stone looked wet but was dry to the touch.   Suddenly the
$
```

Note: sed's first argument consists of its instructions, and it usually is enclosed in single quotes. For your example, you used single quotes containing nothing.

Here, sed reveals the contents of the file tale.start just as the cat command would. The difference, of course, is that sed will accept further instructions. For instance, look at this:

```
$ sed  's/Delita/Melari/'  tale.start
        Once upon a time a delightful princess named Melari lived in
the Kingdom of Homania.   One day, as Princess Melari walked
amidst the fragrant flowers and artful bowers of the West Garden,
she spotted a glistening stone.   Picking it up, Melari discovered
that the stone looked wet but was dry to the touch.   Suddenly the
$
```

Here we have added an *ed* substitution command to the command line. The command pattern is

```
sed    'ed-command'    filename
```

The sed command looks at each line in turn, applies the command if applicable, and prints the result. In our example, the first, second, and fourth lines contained the word Delita, so those lines were printed with the substitution of Melari for Delita. The other lines were printed unchanged.

Note that the original file tale.start is left unchanged by sed. If you want to save your changes, you have to use redirection. For example, you could have typed

```
sed    's/Delita/Melari/'    tale.start > tale.1
```

This command would have placed sed's output in the file tale.1 instead of on the screen.

Note, too, that sed is best used for wholesale changes to the whole file. It is great if you want to replace every Delita with Melari. If you want to change just one or two occurrences of a word and leave other occurrences of that word unaltered, you are better off using one of the regular editors.

You have just seen that sed can be used to make substitutions. What other abilities does it have at its disposal? Let's take a look.

sed Editing Instructions

A typical instruction has two parts: an *address specification* telling which lines are affected, and a *command* telling what to do to the affected lines. If there is no address given, then all lines are affected. The address can be specified numerically or by pattern matching, much as in ed. The commands, too, largely stem from ed and, hence, ex. The most common commands are listed in Table 13.1. They work much as they do in ed, and we will bring out details in the examples to come. The sed command's normal method, as we have said, is to print the modified line if a change has taken place and to print the original line if no change was made. This norm is overridden by the -n option, which causes only those lines affected by a p command to be printed. We will give an example soon, but first let's see how to specify an address.

Specifying Lines

The sed command uses two methods. The first is to specify an address with a number. You can use a single number to indicate a particular line. For instance, to delete the third line of your sample file, try

```
$ sed '3d' tale.start
     Once upon a time a delightful princess named Delita lived in
the Kingdom of Homania.  One day, as Princess Delita walked
she spotted a glistening stone.  Picking it up, Delita discovered
that the stone looked wet but was dry to the touch.  Suddenly the
$
```

Or you can use two numbers separated by a comma to indicate a range of lines:

```
$ sed '2,4 s/e/#/' tale.start
     Once upon a time a delightful princess named Delita lived in
th# Kingdom of Homania.  One day, as Princess Delita walked
admidst th# fragrant flowers and artful bowers of the West Garden,
sh# spotted a glistening stone. Picking it up, Delita discovered
that the stone looked wet but was dry to the touch. Suddenly the
$
```

Here the substitution command affected just the second through fourth lines. (Recall that a simple substitution command affects only the first occurrence of a pattern on a line. Thus, only the first e on each affected line is replaced by a #.)

Table 13.1.   Common *sed* commands.

Command	Action
a \	Appends following line(s) to affected lines
c \	Changes affected lines to following line(s)
d	Deletes affected lines
g	Makes substitutions affect every matching pattern on a line instead of just the first
i \	Inserts following line(s) above affected lines
p	Prints line, even under the -n option
q	Quits when specified line is reached
r *filename*	Reads *filename* ; appends contents to output
s/old/new/	Substitutes new for old
w *filename*	Copies line to *filename*
=	Prints line number
! *command*	Applies *command* if line is *not* selected

The second approach to identifying lines is to specify a pattern; the pattern is contained between slashes. The next example prints only those lines containing `Kingdom`. It uses the `-n` option, which suppresses printing of those lines not affected by a `p` command.

```
$ sed -n '/Kingdom/p' tale.start
the Kingdom of Homania. One day, as Princess Delita walked
$
```

What if we omitted the `-n`? Then the `Kingdom` line would be printed twice, and the rest once.

The patterns can be literal, as in the last example, or they can involve certain metacharacters. This next example deletes lines containing `princess` or `Princess`:

```
$ sed    '/[Pp]rincess/d'   tale.start
amidst the fragrant flowers and artful bowers of the West Garden,
she spotted a glistening stone.  Picking it up, Delita discovered
that the stone looked wet but was dry to the touch. Suddenly the
$
```

We will take up `sed`'s pattern-matching scheme after we finish with more basic matters.

One of the more basic matters is that these two modes (numerical, pattern) of specifying lines can be combined. For instance, to delete all lines from line 1 through the first line containing `fragrant`, do this:

```
$ sed    '1,/fragrant/d'   tale.start
she spotted a glistening stone. Picking it up, Delita discovered
that the stone looked wet but was dry to the touch. Suddenly the
$
```

Now let's look a bit further at some of the commands.

sed Command Highlights

The last few examples show how to use the `d` and `p` commands. These work much as in `ed`, but `ed`'s `a`, `c`, and `i` commands have become `a\`, `c\`, and `i\`. We will use the append command (`a\`) to show the proper form for using these three commands. (*Note*: `csh` shell users need to use a double backslash (`\\`) at the end of a continuation line instead of the single backslash shown in the following examples.)

```
$ sed    'a\
> Hey la la! Doo de dah!'   tale.start
    Once upon a time a delightful princess named Delita lived in
Hey la la! Dooh de dah!
the Kingdom of Homania. One day, as Princess Delita walked
```

```
Hey la la! Dooh de dah!
amidst the fragrant flowers and artful bowers of the West Garden,
Hey la la! Dooh de dah!
she spotted a glistening stone. Picking it up, Delita discovered
Hey la la! Dooh de dah!
that the stone looked wet but was dry to the touch. Suddenly the
Hey la la! Dooh de dah!
$
```

Since we did not give any sort of line identification, our addition was added after every line of the original. (Adding a blank line instead of our choice would have double-spaced the original.) Note, too, how the append command is used. First comes the a, then the backslash (\), which indicates that the shell should look at the next line. The > prompt shows that shell *is* looking at the next line. This next line contains the text to be added, and the closing quote mark indicates the end of the command. You could add more than one line by using more backslashes:

```
$ sed 'a\
> doobie doobie\
> do' dumbsong
```

The insert command (i\) works much the same, except it places the new line(s) before each of the original lines. The change line command (c\) has the same form, too:

```
$ sed 'c\
> Oh marvelous delight! Sing to me!' tale.start
Oh marvelous delight! Sing to me!
Oh marvelous delight! Sing to me!
Oh marvelous delight! Sing to me!
Oh marvelous delight! Sing to me!
Oh marvelous delight! Sing to me!
$
```

Each of the original five lines were changed to the new text. Of course, you usually would attach some sort of address specifier to a change command so that it would affect just some lines.

The q command causes the editor to quit after it reaches the specified line:

```
$ sed '2q' tale.start
    Once upon a time a delightful princess named Delita lived in
the Kingdom of Homania. One day, as Princess Delita walked
$
```

As we mentioned in Chapter 12, this form is useful for looking at the beginnings of files.

The next command we wish to highlight is the substitution command. You have already seen that the form of this command is

```
s/oldpattern/newpattern/
```

where *newpattern* replaces *oldpattern*. In this form, the command affects only the first occurrence of *oldpattern* in a line. Adding the g command (for global) to the end of the instruction makes every occurrence in the line affected. Compare these two examples:

```
$ sed '1s/e/#/' tale.start
    Onc# upon a time a delightful princess named Delita lived in
$ sed '1s/e/#/g' tale.start
    Onc# upon a tim# a d#lightful princ#ss nam#d D#lita liv#d in
```

One very important feature of the s command is that it can use sed's pattern-matching abilities for *oldpattern*. Let's see how that works.

Pattern-Matching in *sed*

The sed command uses patterns to specify lines in its substitution command. These patterns can be literal, or they can use metacharacters to specify more general patterns. The scheme is similar to the shell's filename expansion scheme (*, ?, and all that) but is not quite the same. Table 13.2 shows the metacharacters used by sed. (You can use these same metacharacters in ex, ed, and vi.) Look over the table and then look at our examples.

Table 13.2. Common *sed* metacharacters for pattern-matching.

Metacharacter	Action
\	Turns off the special meaning of the following character
^	Matches the beginning of a line
$	Matches the end of a line
.	Matches any single character
[ ]	Matches any *one* of the enclosed characters; characters can be listed ([aqg4]) or be given as a range ([c-h])
[^ ...]	Matches any character *not* in the ... list
pat*	Matches zero or more occurrences of *pat*, where *pat* is a single character or a [ ] pattern
&	Used in the *newpattern* part of an s command to represent reproducing the *oldpattern* part

Quick Examples

Here we will show you some brief examples illustrating the use of the metacharacters of Table 13.2.

Command	Result
/Second/	Matches any line containing Second
/^Second/	Matches any line *beginning* with Second
/^$/	Matches an empty line, that is, one with nothing between the beginning and end of the line. Note that this does not match a line of blank spaces, since a space itself is a character.
/c.t/	Matches lines containing cat, cot, and so on. Note that this pattern can be part of a word. For instance, apricot and acute would be matched.
/./	Matches lines containing at least one character
/\./	Matches lines containing a period. The backslash negates the special meaning of the period.
/s[oa]p/	Matches sop or sap but not sip or sup or soap; only one letter is permitted between the s and the p
/[s^oa]p/	Matches sip or sup but not sop or sap
s/cow/s&s/	Replaces cow with scows
/co*t/	Matches ct or cot or coot or cooot, and so on. That is, it matches a c and a t that are separated by any number (including zero) of o's. Note that use of the * is different from the shell's use.

Now let's see how these metcharacters can be used and combined in the context of sed commands.

Simple *sed* Solutions

Let's try some examples that are typical of the problems sed can solve. Suppose you want to remove all the blank lines from a file called rawtext. You could do this:

```
sed '/^$/d' rawtext
```

However, as we pointed out previously, this locates empty lines only. The text might contain lines that are not empty but that have only blanks. The next command gets those lines, too:

```
sed '/^ *$/d' rawtext
```

Note that the * follows a blank, so the search pattern says to find lines that contain only zero or more blanks between the beginning and the end of the line (see Figure 13.3).

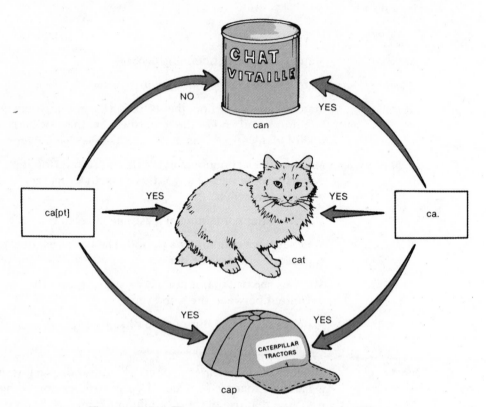

Figure 13.3.   The *sed* command can match patterns.

Suppose that you want to add a blank line to each line. One solution was suggested earlier:

```
$ sed 'a\
> ' rawtext
```

Here we have appended a line consisting of one blank space to each line. Another approach is

```
$ sed 's/$/\
> /' rawtext
```

This time you substituted a carriage return for the end of the line. The carriage return is an invisible character, and you made the substitution by typing a backslash and then Return.

Next, suppose that you want to print all lines containing the word *hopefully*:

```
sed -n '/[Hh]opefully/p' rawtext
```

The -n option suppresses the printing of other lines, and [Hh] catches both capitalized and uncapitalized occurrences.

Now suppose that you want to remove all the comments from a FORTRAN program. FORTRAN comments have a C in the first column, so this would work:

```
sed '/^C/d' prog.f
```

If your system allows both lowercase and uppercase, use

```
sed '/^[cC]/d' prog.f
```

Note that the ^ indicates that the C (or c) must be at the beginning of a line.

Assume that you wish to print a letter and that you would like to shift the left margin five spaces to the right:

```
sed 's/^/     /' letter
```

Just substitute five spaces for the beginning of each line.

Now suppose that you have a file in which you want to change the name *Bob* to *Robert* and *Pat* to *Patricia*. Oops! How do you enter more than one command? Read on.

Multiple Commands

Sometimes you may need more than one editing command. Just add in each command, one command to a line. (Be sure to enclose the entire command list in single quotes.)

```
$ sed 's/Bob/Robert/g
>      s/Pat/Patricia/g' actii
```

Each time a new input line is accepted, it is subjected to each command in the order given. For example,

```
$ sed 's/cat/dog/g
>      s/dog/pigs/g ' petreport
```

would first convert all cats to dogs and then all dogs (including former cats) to pigs.

There is one problem with our first example. A line like

```
Patience is needed, Pat.
```

will become

```
Patriciaience is needed, Patricia.
```

because a sed search does not distinguish between patterns that are complete words and those that are just part of a word. The pattern /Pat / (with a space) will pass up Patience, but it also would miss Pat followed by a period. You have to anticipate ways in which Pat might not be followed by a space:

```
$ sed 's/Bob/Robert/g
>      s/Pat[ \.,;:\!?\'\"\]]/Patricia/g' actii
```

Have we thought of all the possibilities? Perhaps not. And did we put backslashes in the right place? Let's try another approach:

```
$ sed 's/Bob/Robert/g
>      s/Pat[^a-z]/Patricia/g' actii
```

Instead of thinking of all the possible ways Pat might be used, you simply eliminate the possibility you do not want, namely, that Pat is the beginning of a word. (Recall that [^a-z] means any character other than those from *a* through *z*.)

Tags

However, this pattern still has a fault. When something like Pat! is found, the whole string, including the !, is replaced by Patricia, and the ! is lost. You need a way to replace the Pat while keeping the !. You can do this with *tags*. To "tag" part of a pattern, enclose it with a \(to the left and a \) to the right. Then, in the *newpattern* part of the command, you can refer to the first such enclosed pattern as \1, the second as \2, and so on. Using this method gives this command:

```
sed 's/\(Pat\)\([^a-z]\)/\1ricia\2/g' actii
```

Here, the \1 stands for Pat, and the \2 stands for [^a-z]. You simply squeeze ricia in between these two patterns. Just as & gives you a means to refer to an entire expression, the \(...\) and \1 notation lets you refer to a part of an expression.

Shell Scripts and *sed*

If you find yourself using a particular sed concoction often, you may wish to put it into a shell script. For instance, our double-space example could be rendered

```
sed 'a\
' $*
```

and placed in the file twospace. Once that file is made executable, you can type

```
twospace jane.letter ¦ pr ¦ lp
```

to format the letter and print it. Or you could make the printing part of the script:

```
sed 'a\
' $* ¦ pr ¦ lp
```

This last example points out how sed lends itself to UNIX programming and to shell scripts. Since it produces an output instead of modifying the original file, it can be made part of a piping process linking various UNIX utilities. This convenience is, of course, one of the chief justifications of the filter approach to designing programs.

Here is one more example. Suppose you want a program that sorts one or more files alphabetically and prints the first ten lines. You can use the following script:

```
sort $* ¦ sed 10q
```

Once you start making use of UNIX tools in this fashion, you are on the road to being a true UNIXer. Well, enough said about sed—it is time to inspect nroff.

Text Formatting with *nroff* and *troff*

A *text formatter* handles such tasks as setting up margins, line-spacing, paragraph formats, and so on. The UNIX text formatters are nroff and troff. The nroff (*new runoff*) command formats material for a line printer, while troff formats material for a typesetter. The troff command is the more versatile of the two, because it can select different types of styles and sizes and draw boxes. Aside from a few matters like that, the two accept the same instructions. We will use nroff as an example, but what we say applies equally to troff.

You have three levels of simplicity and power on which to use nroff. The simplest and least powerful level is to use nroff unadorned upon an ordinary file. The next level, which brings a great leap in power, is to use an nroff *macro*. This involves placing a few nroff commands into a file of text. The third and most powerful level, which brings a great increase in complexity, involves putting many nroff commands into a file. You will start with the first level, then look a bit at the second level, and touch upon the third.

Level 1: *nroff*

First, get a file with some text. Here are the contents of the speachify file:

```
Eighty-seven years before the present time,
a group of men
who could be termed,
with some degree of appropriateness, the ancestors of us here
today and of this distinguished nation, assembled
```

```
themselves with the intention, a great intention, we might
add, and one that proved successful,
of modifying for the purpose of improvement our already noble and
notable nation.
```

Now feed this file to `nroff`:

```
nroff speachify
```

Oops! The output runs off the screen! Like `pr`, `nroff` formats the text to a printed page of 66 lines, so enough blank lines are added to your input to bring the total to 66. You can use `sed` to look at the beginning:

```
$ nroff speachify ¦ sed 10
Eighty-seven years before the present time, a group  of  men  who
could  be termed, with some degree of appropriateness, the ances-
tors of us here today and of this distinguished nation, assembled
themselves  with  the intention, a great intention, we might add,
and one that proved successful, of modifying for the  purpose  of
improvement our already noble and notable nation.
```

Now you can see what `nroff` hath wrought. First, it has *filled* each line. That means it tries to use enough words in each line to make it as close as possible to the maximum line length without exceeding it. For `nroff` this maximum length is 65 characters by default, including spaces. Second, it has *right-justified* or "adjusted" the text. This means spacing the text so that the right margin is even. Third, it has hyphenated a word to get a better fit. That is about all this simple usage does, so let's move on to the next level.

Level 1.5: Messing Around

We did not mention this level in our introduction because it is not really a level of *using* `nroff`. Rather, it is a level of experimenting with `nroff`—seeing how `nroff` commands (or "requests") are made and finding out what they do.

First, what does a typical `nroff` command look like? Here are a few:

```
.ce                          ← center next line
.sp 3                        ← insert 3 blank lines
.ti 8                        ← indent next line 8 spaces
```

That is the typical appearance: a period followed by two lowercase letters followed (possibly) by an argument.

Next, how are they used? They are placed in the text file. Each command is placed on a line of its own and at the beginning of the line (see Figure 13.4). When `nroff` reads the file, it assumes that any line beginning with a period is an `nroff` request. If it does not recognize what follows, it ignores that text. Otherwise, it implements the request when it outputs the following text. For example, let's add .ce to our text and see what happens. First, here is the new text:

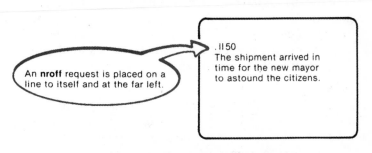

An **nroff** request is placed on a line to itself and at the far left.

```
.ll 50
The shipment arrived in
time for the new mayor
to astound the citizens.
```

Figure 13.4. Positioning an *nroff* request.

```
.ce
Eighty-seven years before the present time,
a group of men
who could be termed,
with some degree of appropriateness, the ancestors of us here
today and of this distinguished nation, assembled
themselves with the intention, a great intention, we might
add, and one that proved successful,
of modifying for the purpose of improvement our already noble and
notable nation.
```

Submit it to nroff:

```
nroff speachify ¦ sed 10q
```

You get this output:

```
         Eighty-seven years before the present time,
a group  of  men  who  could  be  termed,  with  some  degree  of
appropriateness,  the  ancestors  of  us  here  today and of this
distinguished nation, assembled themselves with the intention,  a
great intention, we might add, and one that proved successful, of
modifying for the purpose of improvement our  already  noble  and
notable nation.
```

The result is that the line following the request was centered. Perhaps that is why .ce is labeled the centering request.

Of course, you can read in the manual what these *embedded* commands do, but actually using them makes it clearer. To save you the time of constantly reediting a file to insert new requests, here is a shell script that lets you test one request at a time:

```
# nrtest -- a shell script for testing nroff
sed '1i\
'$2 $1 ¦ nroff ¦ sed 20q
```

This script inserts its second argument at the beginning of the file named by the first argument. The output is filtered through `sed` so that you get just the first 20 lines, about a screenful.

Let's put the script in a file called `nrtest` and use it to see the effect of adding an argument to the `.ce` request:

```
$ nrtest speachify .ce4
              Eighty-seven years before the present time,
                        a group of men
                      who could be termed,
    with some degree of appropriateness, the ancestors of us here
  today and of this distinguished nation, assembled themselves with
  the intention,  a  great   intention,  we might add, and one that
  proved successful, of modifying  for the purpose  of  improvement
  our already noble and notable nation.
$
```

Now four lines are centered! (The `nroff` command will accept either `.ce4` or `.ce 4`; use the first form so that your shell script will take the whole request as $2.)

Here is another example:

```
$ nrtest speachify .ll30
Eighty-seven years  before the
present  time,  a group of men
who could be termed, with some
degree of appropriateness, the
ancestors of us here today and
of  this distinguished nation,
assembled themselves with  the
intention,  a great intention,
we might  add,  and  one  that
proved      successful,     of
modifying for the  purpose  of
improvement  our already noble
and notable nation.
```

This time we used a `.ll` (line length) request to produce a line 30 characters long.

Not all `nroff` requests produce discernible results when inserted at the front of a file, but Table 13.3 consists of some that do. We have included a brief description, but it is fun to try them out yourself. Try, for instance, a `.tra#e\$o%` request.

Table 13.3. Some *nroff* requests.

Request	Action
.ce *n*	Center Next *n* lines
.in *n*	Indent text *n* spaces
.hy *n*	Turn on auto-hyphenation for $n >= 1$, off for $n = 0$.
.ll *n*	Set line length to *n* characters
.ls *n*	Set line spacing to *n* (2 = double-spaced, and so on)
.na	Do not justify right margin ("no adjust")
.nf	Do not fill text
.sp *n*	Put in *n* blank lines
.ti *n*	Temporarily (next line) indent *n* spaces
.tr *abcd*..	Replace *a* with *b*, *c* with *d*, and so on. The space between request and argument can be omitted.

Level 2: *mm* Macros

The term *macro* signifies a command or instruction that is constructed from several more basic units. The nroff command lets you construct your own macros from the basic instructions. The chief tool is the .de request that lets you define a single symbolism to represent several requests. For example,

```
.de PG
.sp
.ti5
..
```

defines .PG to mean space one line and temporarily indent five spaces. The .. marks the definition's end.

You could study nroff assiduously and create your own set of macros, but most users use a *macro package*. This is just a set of predefined macros designed to handle common situations, such as creating paragraphs and making footnotes. System V features the mm (for *m*emorandum *m*acros) package.

Macros are used the same way ordinary requests are. Here, for example, you will insert the mm macro for an indented paragraph (.P 1):

```
.ce
A Stirring Speech by Senator Phineas Phogblower
```

```
.sp
.P 1
Eighty-seven years before the present time,
a group of men
who could be termed,
with some degree of appropriateness, the ancestors of us here
today and of this distinguished nation, assembled
themselves with the intention, a great intention, we might
add, and one that proved successful,
of modifying for the purpose of improvement our already noble and
notable nation.
```

Now that you have the instructions in place, how do you get them noticed? This way:

```
nroff -mm speachify
```

or

```
nroff -cm speachify
```

The second version uses a precompacted version of the macros that runs faster and is the one that usually should be used. In fact, this second option is used often enough that System V allows us simply to type

```
mm speachify
```

to produce the same effect.

If you use troff for typesetting, the corresponding commands are these:

```
troff -mm speachify
troff -cm speachify
mmt speachify
```

With either evocation of nroff, you get this output:

```
                    - 1 -


        A Stirring Speech by Senator Phineas Phogblower

            Eighty-seven years before the present time, a group of
        men who could be termed, with some degree of
        appropriateness, the ancestors of us here today and of this
        distinguished nation, assembled themselves with the
        intention, a great intention, we might add, and one that
        proved successful, of modifying for the purpose of
        improvement our already noble and notable nation.
```

Here we have suppressed several blank lines following the text.

As you can see, the .P 1 macro produced a paragraph with the first line indented five spaces. Notice that the right margin is not justified. This is the default choice for `nroff -mm`. The `troff -mm` command uses justified margins as a default. Finally, note a page number was placed at the top.

There you have the essence of mm — embed appropriate macros in the text. The next step would be to learn all of mm's 87 macros. That is a bit more than we care to cover here. Instead, we will concentrate on some of the more common examples. If you need to learn more, see *The Documenter's Workbench* from AT&T, or similar documentation. Meanwhile, you can find some typical mm macros in Table 13.4. We will give examples using most of them.

Table 13.4. Some *mm* macros.

Macro	Meaning and Typical Usage
.AF	Define company name for memos—place company name in double quotes on same line. (*Bell Laboratories* is the default.)
.AL	Start an automatically numbered list—used with .LI and .LE
.AU	Author's name—place on same line and enclose in quotes
.DL	Start a list marked with dashes—used with .LI and .LE
.FC	Formal close—ends a letter with *Yours very truly,*
.FE	Marks the end of a footnote
.FS c	Marks the start of a footnote, with c being the footnote marker
.I	Italics (underlined in `nroff`)
.LE	List end—marks the end of a list (see .AL, .DL)
.LI	List item—text starting next line is the next item in a list (see .AL, .DL)
.MT n	Specifies memo type. n = 0 gives memo form. n values of 1, 2 and 3 add various labels. n = 4 yields a released-paper form, and n = 5 results in a letter style.
.ND	New date—place desired date on same line in quotes
.P n	Start paragraph. n = 0 is a block paragraph, n = 1 is an indented paragraph (five spaces by default).
.R	Roman font.
.SG	Adds a signature line, using the name from .AU
.TL	Uses the next line for a title.

Making a Report

Let's use some macros to put a simple report together. Here is the original text:

```
.AU    "Bart Bargletoot"
.MT    5
.P     0
Dear Flossie,
.sp
.P     1
Well here I am in the Big City!
Cousin Bert tells me they have upward of 40,000 folks here at
Great Forks, and that's not counting those outside the city
limits!
The hustle and bustle is quite amazing, but I'm adjusting to it.
Though it does seem strange to walk by people without either
giving a "howdy."
.P     1
I'm missing you, of course. You would have loved the eating
place Bert and Bette (that's Bert's fiancee) took me to last
night.
It was all-you-can eat ribs'n'chicken with three hotnesses
of barbecue sauce to choose from.
I was the only one there with enough sense to use one of their
big trays for piling up the vittles.
The others put food on little dishes, then put the dishes on the
tray--seems kinda dainty to me.
.P     1
Well, give my love to Geezer, Flopnose, and TS.
I'll see you
soon.
.FC
.SG
```

We show the output in Figure 13.5. As you look at the input and output versions, note these points. First, unlike most nroff commands, the .AU command has its associated text on the same line. One reason for this is that the author's name does not necessarily appear in the output text in the same position it does in the input text. In this case, for example, the name does not appear until the end of the letter, as requested by the .SG signature macro. Second, the letter wound up dated. That is one effect of the .MT 5 macro. Since UNIX systems keep track of the date, you do not have to supply that information. Third, note that you can mix in regular nroff requests like .sp with the mm macros. Mixing requests with macros can create disaster, but some requests (including all our examples aside from .in, .hy, and .na) are safe to use. Fourth, note how we started each sentence on a new line. It is not necessary to do this, but makes it simpler to add or remove sentences later, particularly if you use a line editor such as ed or ex.

```
                                          December 22, 1991

Dear Flossie,

     Well here I am in the Big City! Cousin Bert tells me
they have upward of 40,000 folks here at Great Forks, and
that's not counting those outside the city limits! The
hustle and bustle is quite amazing, but I'm adjusting to it.
Though it does seem strange to walk by people without either
giving a "howdy."

     I'm missing you, of course, You would have loved the
eating place Bert and Bette (that's Bert's fiancee) took me
to last night. It was all-you-can eat ribs'n'chicken with
three hotnesses of barbecue sauce to choose from. I was the
only one there with enough sense to use one of their big
trays for piling up the vittles. The others put food on
little dishes, then put the dishes on the tray—seems kinda
dainty to me.

     Well, give my love to Geezer, Flopnose, and TS. I'll
see you soon.

                                   Yours very truly,

                                   Bart Bargletoot
```

Figure 13.5.   Output of letter.

It is not too difficult to produce a letter if you are happy with the form these mm macros produce. We should point out that we have just used default values for many things. These can be overridden. If, for example, you want to use a different date, a different closing, a different indentation, a different line spacing, you can. But that takes us deeper into mm than we care to go at this time. Instead, let's look at another common task, creating a memo.

A Simple Memo

There are several macros specifically designed to go at the beginning of a memo. The ones you will use are .TL, .AF, .AU, and .MT. An important point is that, if present, these macros must be used in this order. (Thus, in your letter, you put .AU before .MT). You will use .FS and .FE to create a footnote. Also you will use .DL, .LI, and .LE to create a dashed list. First, you create the input text.

```
.ND    "May 19, 2832"
.TL
Calashian Hats
.AF "Galactic Express Travel"
.AU "Gauis Cho McLeod"
.MT 0
.P 0
Tourists are choosing to visit the planet Calash*
.FS *
System 2301.234.08 of the Canopus Sector
.FE
in rapidly increasing numbers, drawn, no doubt, by the colorful
and exotic civilization that the Calashian settlers have created.
Some visitors, unfortunately, have experienced difficulties
because of their ignorance of local customs.
Please advise our clients
.I
not to wear hats
.R
while visiting Calash.
This may seem odd in view of the fact that Calash is reknown for
the variety of hats worn by the inhabitants.
Bear in mind, however, that the Calashians have evolved an
elaborate hat code; to wear a hat is to make a statement about
oneself.
Here are some examples:
.DL
.LI
An orange billed cap with a yellow plume indicates the wearer to
be in a snappish mood and seeking like company.
.LI
A dark blue conical hat with mauve braiding indicates a wearer
willing to debate philosophical matters with anyone who will
provide him wine.
.LI
```

```
A purple sombrero with green trim indicates a wearer of vast
wealth looking for an evening of amiable frivolity.
.LE
.P 0
The point here is that by wearing a hat, a tourist unknowingly
creates unforeseeable attitudes towards himself.
One recent visitor, for instance, was soundly slapped with a
yellow fish by several young ladies before getting rid of his
hat.
.P 0
Please impress upon all our Calash-bound clients the importance
of this matter.
.SG
```

The .MT 0 request causes our text to be arranged in memo format. See Figure 13.6 for the result.

Note how the memo layout is set up for you. Note, too, how the list procedure works. First you declare the type of list (.DL). Then you precede each list item with .LI. And you mark the end of the list with .LE. If you were to change the .DL to .AL, then the items would be labeled with the numbers 1, 2, and 3 instead of dashes. Several other list varieties and variations are available.

In creating a footnote, you use .FS and .FE to mark the bounds of the footnote. You follow the .FS with the footnote symbol used in the main text, and this symbol is then used to mark the beginning of the footnote.

The company name comes out in boldface, and the italicized portion (after the .I) comes out underlined. This assumes your printer is equipped to do so.

Once you have tried your hand at a few examples, you may wish to burrow into the manual yourself and find out what else you can do. Other features include macros for numbered and unnumbered topic headings and subheadings and macros for abstracts.

Level 3: Naked *nroff*

On this level you are free to use the basic nroff requests as you desire. Probably, the most profitable way would be to create your own set of macro definitions. However, please note that the mm macro package is able to deal with most situations. Most typically, the basic nroff requests are used to supplement the macro commands.

We have not reached the end of the text formatter story yet. UNIX has two more utilities designed to work with nroff and troff. We will take a brief look at them now.

```
                      Galactic Express Travel


subject: Calashian Hats          date: May 19, 2832

                             from: Gauis Cho McLeod


Tourists are choosing to visit the planet Calash* in rapidly
increasing numbers, drawn, no doubt, by the colorful and exotic
civilization that the Calashian settlers have created. Some
visitors, unfortunately, have experienced difficulties because of
their ignorance of local customs. Please advise our clients not
to wear hats while visiting Calash. This may seem odd in view of
the fact that Calash is reknown for the variety of hats worn by
the inhabitants. Bear in mind, however, that the Calashians have
evolved an elaborate hat code; to wear a hat is to make a
statement about oneself. Here are some examples:

—An orange billed cap with a yellow plume indicates the
  wearer to be in a snappish mood and seeking like
  company.

—A dark blue conical hat with mauve braiding indicates a
  wearer willing to debate philosophical matters with
  anyone who will provide him wine.

—A purple sombrero with green trim indicates a wearer of
  vast wealth looking for an evening of amiable
  frivolity.

The point here is that by wearing a hat, a tourist unknowingly
creates unforeseeable attitudes towards himself. One recent
visitor, for instance, was soundly slapped with a yellow fish by
several young ladies before getting rid of his hat.

Please impress upon all our Calash-bound clients the importance
of this matter.
                             Gaius Cho McLeod
   _____

   * System 2301.234.08 of the Canopus Sector
```

Figure 13.6.   Text arranged in memo format.

Formatting Helpmates: *tbl* and *eqn*

Document preparation often involves putting together tables of data, and technical documents often make use of equations. The `tbl` and `eqn` programs use their own instruction set to convert descriptions of tables and equations into `nroff` and `troff` requests. We will outline how to use them without going into details. Suppose, for example, you are creating a table. You would include the material for the table between the `.TS` (table start) and `.TE` (table end) macros. The enclosed material would include the `tbl` instructions and the data to be used. Before and after this material would be the normal text of the document. Since `tbl` should act on the table before `nroff` reaches it, you could use a command like this, assuming the document in the file `Report`:

```
tbl Report ¦ nroff -mm
```

Or you can use the `-t` option of `mm`:

```
mm -t Report
```

The `eqn` program is used similarly.

Conclusion

This chapter has taken you further into the world of text processing and of filters. You have seen how cut, paste, sed, and nroff all stake out their own territory in the business of modifying and shaping text. Because these programs can be linked to each other and to other programs using pipes, they become tools that can be combined in a multitude of ways to accomplish a multitude of tasks. Suppose, for instance, you want to paste together two files of names and that you want the names to be separated by three spaces. The paste command will not do that, because it only places one character between joined lines. But you can pipe cut's output to sed and have sed replace that one tab with three spaces, and the job is done.

So when you have a job to do, first ask yourself if there is a UNIX command that will do it. If the answer is no, then ask if there is a combination of UNIX commands that will do the task. The more you learn about UNIX, the more likely it is that your answer will be yes.

Review Questions

1. Devise commands to do the following in the file firdata:

   a. Print columns 4 and 22.

   b. Print columns 4 through 22.

   c. Set the field delimiter to an asterisk and print fields 2 through 4 and 6 through 8.

2. Devise a sed command to do each of the following tasks to the file essay:

   a. Replace every instance of Edgar with Elgar.

   b. Print lines 10 through 15 of the file.

   c. Put every occurrence of San Francisco Treat in double quotes.

   d. Delete lines containing the sequences ude or aked.

Answers

1. a. cut -c4,22 firdata; b. cut -c4-22 firdata; c. cut -d"*" -f2-4,6-8 firdata
2. a. sed 's/Edgar/Elgar/g' essay; b. sed -n '10,15p' essay; c. sed 's/San Francisco Treat/"&"/g' essay; d. sed '/ude/d; /aked/d ' essay

Exercises at the Terminal

Copy our memo text (or make up your own) and find the effect of changing `.MT 0` to `.MT 1`, `.MT 2`, and so on.

14

Information Processing: *grep*, *find*, *sort*, *awk*, and *Shell* Scripts

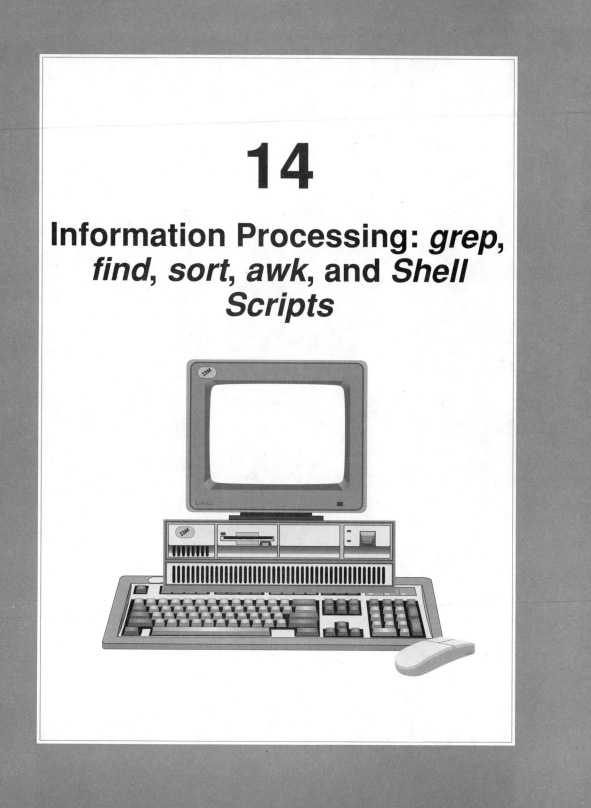

Chapter 14

Information Processing: *grep*, *find*, *sort*, *awk*, and *Shell Scripts*

In the cool confines of the Programming Division of Dray Conglomerate, Delia Delphond doffed her softball cap and shook her auburn curls loose. She had just finished updating the statistical files for her softball team, the Byte Boomers. Now she copied the files for the other teams in the company league; it was her turn to prepare the league stats. First, she used sort to put together a league master file of batting statistics arranged alphabetically by player. Then, using the field-specification option of sort, she created a file listing the players in descending order of batting averages. Next, again using the field-specification sort option and piping it through head -10, she created files giving the top ten players for each of several categories: home runs, RBIs, hits, runs, triples, doubles, walks, stolen bases, and strikeouts. Curious about how her team was doing, she used grep to find Byte Boomers on the top ten lists. Good, they were making a fine showing. The name *D. Delphond*, in particular, appeared in several lists. Smiling, she turned her attention to the team statistics. Using awk, she had UNIX sum up the "at bats," the hits, and so forth, for each team and calculate the team averages. Then she went on to handle the pitching stats.

Delia enjoyed going through the statistics, but she did not care much for her next task, preparing a press summary for the company paper, *Draybits*. She would much rather bat than write. However, with the help of a UNIX editor, she put together a blurb of rather irregular line length. She ran the file through `spell` and corrected the errors that had shown up—words such as "avarage" and "notewordy." Next she invoked a shell script of hers that first sent the file through `nroff` to tidy it up and then forwarded the result through `mail` to the *Draybit's* newspaper editor.

She leaned back in her chair and relaxed for a few moments. Not for too long, however, because she had her regular work to do, too. Besides being a nifty shortstop, Delia was a prolific C programmer. She had scattered her program files through several subdirectories, and now she decided to gather them in one place. She created a directory for that purpose and then set up a `find` command that would locate all her files with names ending in `.c` and move them to the new directory.

Delia checked the time (using `date`, of course). It was time for her next project, the long-awaited salary raise! She put her cap on at a jaunty angle, picked up the analysis she had prepared using the UNIX system, and set off for the president's office; Dray would not have a chance . . . .

As you can tell from the preceding scenario, UNIX can be an important tool for information processing. So far, we have concentrated on the more basic operations for information processing. Now we will turn to a few UNIX commands and utilities that take you beyond the basics. Many of them are really useful only when you deal with large numbers of files and directories. (Both commands and utilities are programs run by UNIX. We use the word *utility* to indicate a program more elaborate than a command.) We will describe some of the simpler examples, such as `grep`, in detail. Others, such as the powerful `awk`, are rather extensive in scope and rules, and we will give them just a brief introduction.

Finding Stuff: *grep* and *find*

The `grep` and `find` commands are useful when you have to look through several files or directories to find a particular file entry or file. The `grep` command lets you find which files contain a particular word, name, phrase, and so forth. The `find` command lets you find files that satisfy some criterion of yours (a certain name, a certain suffix, not used for two months, and so on) and then lets you do something to those files (print the names, move them to another directory, remove them, and so on). We introduced `grep` in Chapter 9. Now let's take a more complete look.

File Searching: *grep*

Sometimes, through necessity or curiosity, you may want to search one or more files for some form of information. For example, you may want to know which letter files contain references to the Wapoo Fruit Company. Or you may have a set of files constituting a large C program and you want to know which ones use a certain function. Let's look at a simpler example using just one file. On most systems, there is a file called /etc/passwd that contains information about the system users. (See the following box.) Suppose you want to find out more about someone using the login name of physh and your system does not have the finger command. Then you can have the /etc/passwd file searched for the word physh, and the line(s) containing that word will be printed. To do this, give the command

```
grep physh /etc/passwd
```

The response might look like this:

```
physh:x:201:10:Jon Foreman:/home/physh:/bin/csh
```

This line from the /etc/passwd file is interpreted in the following box; the important point is that the pattern of the command was

```
grep pattern filename
```

The */etc/passwd* File

The UNIX system has to keep track of who is allowed to use the system. It must also keep track of login names, group memberships, passwords, and user identification numbers. UNIX may want to know your phone number and, on multiple shell systems, which shell you use. All this information is kept in the /etc/passwd file. Let's look at the sample line we used in the previous grep example and see how such a file can be set up.

```
physh:x:201:10:Jon Foreman:/home/physh:/bin/csh
```

The line is divided into seven *fields*, with each field separated from the adjoining fields by a colon (:). (We will discuss fields again when we revisit sort.)

1. The first field contains the user's login name (physh).

2. In prior UNIX versions, the second field held the user's encrypted password. To increase system security, Release 4 now stores the encrypted password in the /etc/shadow file, which regular users cannot read. The x in the /etc/passwd file just acts as a place holder.

3. The third field contains the user identification number (201).

4. Next comes the user's group number (10).

5. Then is the personal information (Jon Foreman).

6. The sixth field contains the user's home directory (/home/physh).

7. The final field indicates the user's login shell; if this field is blank, the system uses the sh shell.

As you can see, the basics of using `grep` are pretty simple. On the other hand, the following explanation will be a little lengthy. That's because we will describe some additional features of `grep` that you may want to use.

More generally, `grep` is used this way:

```
grep option(s) pattern filename(s)
```

Let's look at each part of this form, starting with `filename(s)` and working backward.

Filenames

You can give one filename or several for `grep` to search. When you use more than one filename, `grep` will tag each line that it finds with the name of the file that the line was located in. For example, if you type

```
grep dentistry boyd carson douglass ernst
```

the response might look like this:

```
boyd:without which the undoubted charms of dentistry would be
boyd:unless, of course, you are speaking of dentistry.
boyd: I would rather suffer the agonies of amateur dentistry
douglass:in dentistry. Aside from that, he was in no way
```

Here, three lines containing `dentistry` were found in the `boyd` file, and one was found in the `douglass` file. None were found in the remaining files.

You can use wild card substitution for filenames when using `grep`. Consider the commands

```
grep reverse *.c
```

and

```
grep Renaldo /home/phoebe/*
```

The first would search for `reverse` in all files ending in `.c` (that is, files written in C) in your current working directory. The second would search all the files in the `/home/phoebe` directory for `Renaldo`.

If you do not specify any filename with `grep`, it will look to the standard input.

Patterns

So far, you have used single words for the pattern. In general, the pattern can be a string or a limited form of a regular expression. A *string* is just a sequence of ordinary characters. All the examples that we have used so far for `grep` patterns are strings. A *regular expression*, on the other hand, may include characters with special meanings. For example, `grep` recognizes the pattern `b.g` as representing any three-character string beginning in b and ending in g. The pattern b.g is a regular expression, and the . in it is a special character playing much the same role that a ? does when used in a shell command. Like the shell, grep recognizes certain regular expressions for patterns, but the rules it uses are not the ones used by the shell.

Strings merit a closer look, since most of the time that you use grep you probably will use strings. If the string is only a single word, you can use it just as in the previous examples. But, what if you want to find something like *Los Angeles*? The command

```
grep Los Angeles cityfile
```

will not work, for grep will think that the pattern you sought was Los and that Angeles was the name of the first file to be searched. To avoid this confusion, you can place the pattern in single quotes; that is, use

```
grep 'Los Angeles' cityfile
```

and all will be well.

When grep looks for a string, it does not care whether it finds the string by itself or embedded in a larger string. For example, the command

```
grep man moon
```

will not only find the word man in the moon file but also find such words as *woman*, *mantra*, and *command*, because they all contain the string man within them. The BSD UNIX implementation of grep has a -w option (whole words only) that picks up only lines that contain the pattern as an isolated word. If your system lacks that option, you might try putting spaces in the pattern, as in ' man ', but that will fail to pick up lines in which man is the first or last word. It will also fail to pick up constructions such as man. or man, because these all lack one of the specified spaces. (Remember, a space is a character too.)

You may run into problems if the *pattern string* you use contains some of the special characters used by UNIX (for example, * or ?) or by grep regular expressions (for example, . or [ ).

Sometimes, it is sufficient to enclose the pattern in single quotes. For instance, the command:

```
grep * froggy
```

will confuse UNIX, but the command

```
grep '*' froggy
```

will cause the system to search the froggy file for lines containing *.

You also can use the backslash (\) to turn off the special meaning of a character, as we described in Chapter 11:

```
grep \? dinnerreview
```

Forms of Regular Expressions

Now we can take a look at the forms of regular expressions recognized by grep. Basically, these forms (with some omissions) are the same as those used by ed and ex. Here's a rundown of the most important rules:

1. A period (.) in a pattern stands for any one character. It plays the same role in grep patterns as the ? does in UNIX shell wild card substitution.

    Thus, the command:

    ```
    grep 'c.n' horply
    ```

    will find such strings as *can* and *con*, but not *coin*, since *coin* has two characters, not one, between the *c* and the *n*.

2. A string in brackets (that is, enclosed in [ ]) matches any one character in the string. (This is the same as the UNIX shell's use of brackets.) Thus, the pattern:

    ```
    [wW]easel
    ```

    will match *weasel* or *Weasel* but not *wWeasel*. You can use a hyphen to indicate a range of characters. For example,

    ```
    [m-t]ap
    ```

    would match the strings *map*, *nap*, and so forth, up to *tap*.

3. Preceding a string in brackets with a caret (^) causes grep to make matches using the characters *not* in the list. For instance,

    ```
    [^m-t]ap
    ```

    would match strings like *cap* and *zap* but not strings like *map* and *tap*.

4. A regular expression preceded by a ^ will match only those lines that begin with the expression. Thus, the command

    ```
    grep '^James' slist
    ```

    would find the first of the following lines and would skip the second:

    ```
    James Watt
    Henry James
    ```

5. Similarly, a regular expression followed by a $ will match only those lines with the expression at the end. Therefore,

    ```
    grep 'James$' slist
    ```

    would find *Henry James* but not *James Watt* in the preceding example.

You can use both the ^ and the $ if you want to find only lines that match the pattern in their entirety. For example, the command

```
grep '^The King of Red Gulch$' oddfile
```

would find the line *The King of Red Gulch* and skip over the line *The King of Red Gulch sauntered over to Doc Buzzard's table.*

6. A backslash (\) followed by any character other than a digit or parenthesis matches that character, turning off any special meaning that character might have. For instance, suppose you want to search a file for mentions of FORTRAN files, which have names ending in .f. You can type

```
grep '\.f' forttext
```

If you omitted the \, grep would interpret the period as described in rule 1.

Options

The options for grep are indicated in the usual way by using flags. Here is a sample command and the response:

1. The -n option precedes each found line with its line number in the file. Here is a sample command and the response:

```
grep -n FORTRAN Johnletter

237: wanted to search a file for mentions of FORTRAN files,
```

2. The -v option causes grep to print those lines that *don't* match.

3. The -c option prints a count of the number of lines that match, but does not print the lines themselves. If you are searching several files, it prints the name of each file followed by the number of matching lines in that file.

grep **Searches a File for a Pattern**		
Name	**Options**	**Arguments**
grep	[-n, -c, -v, -w]	*pattern* [*filename(s)*]
Description:	The grep command searches the named files for lines containing the given pattern and then prints the matching lines. If more than one file is searched, the name of the file containing each line is printed too. If no filename is given, grep looks to the standard input; thus,	

grep can be used with pipes. The pattern can be a single string, or it can be a limited form of regular expression as described in the text. A pattern containing spaces or special characters such as * should be set off by single quotes. Normally, grep will match any string containing the pattern; for example, hose matches whose.

Options:

-n Precedes each matching line with its line number.

-c Prints only a count of matching lines.

-v All lines but those matching are printed.

-i Ignore differences between uppercase and lower-case letters.

Example:

```
grep -n hop peter bugs
```

This command searches the files peter and bugs for occurrences of the string hop. It prints the matching lines along with line numbers.

Finding Files: *find*

The find command searches for files that meet some criterion. You can search for files that have a certain name or are a certain size or files not accessed for a certain number of days or files having a certain number of links—and this is just a partial list. Once the files are found, you can have the pathnames printed, and you can have the files themselves printed or removed or otherwise acted upon. The search will begin at the directory you specify and will then descend through all its subdirectories and all their subdirectories, and so forth, leaving no nook or cranny unexplored (except, of course, for forbidden nooks and crannies). A branching search such as this is termed *recursive*.

It would be difficult to fit the capabilities of the find command into the usual format for commands, so find has its own unique structure. The basic sequence goes like this:

```
find directory pathname     search criterion     action
```

The directory pathname is the pathname of the directory that will be recursively searched (all subdirectories, and so on) for the desired files. The search criterion identifies the files that are sought. The action tells what to do with the files once they are found. The criterion and the action are identified with special flags, which we will discuss soon.

Here is an example of a `find` command:

```
find /home -name calendar -print
```

The directory pathname is /home, so the search starts here and proceeds recursively through all directories branching off this directory. The search criterion is -name calendar. This means that UNIX will search for files bearing the name calendar. Finally, the action is -print, meaning that each time a file is found that meets the search criterion, its pathname is displayed. The output might look like this:

```
/home/flossie/calendar
/home/nerkie/calendar
/home/sluggo/calendar
```

This output would tell us which users were using UNIX's calendar feature.

Naming the directory is straightforward, but the search criteria and action sections need further discussion.

Search Criteria

The `find` command recognizes several search criteria. They take the form of an identifying flag word (a hyphen joined to a word, for example -name) followed by a space and a word or number. Here are the more common ones:

1. *Finding a file by name.* Use the -name flag followed by the desired name. The name can be a simple word as in the preceding example, or it can use the shell wild card substitutions: [ ], ?, and *. If you use these special symbols, place the name in single quotes. Here are some examples of acceptable uses.

Criterion	Files Sought
-name nail	Files named nail.
-name '*.c'	All files whose names end in .c.
-name '*.?'	All files for which the next to last character is a period

2. *Finding a file by last access.* Use the -atime flag followed by the number of days since the file was last accessed. Plus and minus signs may be used to indicate greater than or less than.

Criterion	Files Sought
-atime 7	Files last accessed exactly 7 days ago
-atime -14	Files accessed more recently than 14 days ago

3. *Finding a file by last modification.* Use the -mtime flag followed by the number of days since the file was last modified. Plus and minus signs may be used to indicate greater than or less than.

Criterion	Files Sought
-mtime 20	Files last modified 20 days ago
-mtime +45	Files modified more than 45 days ago

4. *Finding files modified more recently than a given file.* Use the -newer flag followed by the name of a file.

Criterion	Files Sought
-newer slopware	Files modified more recently than slopware was

Actions

For the action section of the command, you can choose from three flag options: -print, -exec, and -ok.

1. *The* -print *option.* This option prints the pathname for every file found that matches the criterion.

2. *The* -exec *option.* This option lets you give a command to be applied to the found files. The command should follow the flag and should be terminated with a space, a backslash, and then a semicolon. A set of braces { } can be used to represent the name of the files found. For example,

```
find . -atime +100 -exec rm {} \;
```

would find and remove all files in your current directory (and its offshoots) that have not been used in over 100 days.

3. *The* ok *option.* This option is just like the -exec option except that it asks for your "ok" for each file found before it executes the command. For instance, if you gave the command

```
find . -atime +100 -ok rm {} \;
```

and the system found a file called first.prog that satisfied the criterion, the system would then query you:

```
<rm... ./first.prog> ?
```

If you reply with the letter y, the command is executed; otherwise it is not. A command along the lines of this example is a handy aid in cleaning up your file systems.

For Advanced Users: More Complex Forms of *find*

You can expand each of the basic sections of the `find` command to pinpoint more exactly what you want done.

The Directory Pathname

You actually can give a list of directories to be searched. For instance,

```
find /home/lester /home/festus . -name '*.p' -print
```

would search `lester`'s home directory, `festus`'s home directory, and your current directory for files whose names end in `.p` and would then print the pathnames of those files.

Primaries

The search criteria we have given are called *primaries*. You can combine them or act upon them in the following three basic ways:

1. The `!` operator negates a primary. It should precede the primary and should be isolated by spaces on either side.

Criterion	Meaning
`-newer fops`	Files revised more recently than `fops`.
`! -newer fops`	Files not revised more recently than `fops`.
`! -name '*.f'`	Files whose names do not end in `.f`.

2. Listing two or more criteria in a row causes `find` to seek those files that simultaneously satisfy all criteria.

Criteria	Meaning
`-name calendar -size +2`	Files named `calendar` having a size greater than two blocks.
`-size +2 -size -6`	Files whose size is greater than two blocks and less than six blocks.

3. Separating two criteria with a `-o` flag (a space on either side) causes `find` to search for files that satisfy one or the other criterion.

Criteria	Meaning
-name turk -o -name terk	Files named turk or terk.
-atime +7 -o -mtime +14	Files that have not been accessed within 7 days or modified within 14 days

find Searches Designated Files and Acts upon Them

Name	Options	Arguments
find	None	directory pathname(s) search criteria action(s)

Description: The find command searches the named directories recursively for files matching the specified criteria. It then performs the specified actions on the files.

Search Criteria: In the following, *n* represents a decimal integer. It can be given with or without a sign. With no sign, it means *n* exactly; +*n* means greater than *n*; -*n* means less than *n*.

-name filename	Files named filename.
-size n	Files of size *n* blocks (one block is 512 bytes).
-links n	Files with *n* links.
-atime n	Files accessed *n* days ago.
-mtime n	Files modified *n* days ago.
-newer filename	Files modified more recently than the file filename.

Actions:

-print Print the pathnames of the found files.

-exec command \;	Executes the given command upon finding a file. The symbol { } represents the found file.
-ok command \;	Same as -exec, except your approval is requested before each execution. Reply with a y to have the command executed.

> Note: There is a procedure for combining criteria. An ! (iso-
> lated by spaces) before a criterion negates it. Giving two
> or more criteria means that all must be satisfied by the
> file. Separating two criteria by an -o (isolated by spaces)
> means one *or* the other. Escaped parentheses, / (and \),
> can be used to clarify groupings.
>
> Examples:
>
> ```
> find . -name boobtube -print
> ```
>
> This command searches through the current directory
> and all its offshoots for a file named boobtube.
>
> ```
> find . -atime +30 -atime -60 -exec mv {} ./old\;
> ```
>
> This command finds all files in the current working
> directory (and its offshoots, and their offshoots, and so
> on) that have been used within 60 days but not within
> 30 days. These files then are moved to the directory
> ./old.

Revisiting *sort*: Using Fields

In Chapter 11, you saw that sort sorted files on the basis of the beginning of each
line. This is useful, for example, if you have a mailing list in which people are listed
last name first. But you might want to sort that same list on the basis of city or state.
You *can* do that, providing you have set up your file accordingly. The key is to break
each line into *fields*. As you will see, you can instruct sort to look only at certain fields
when sorting. Thus, you can set up the file so that last names are in the first field and
states in, say, the sixth field. Having the file sorted by the sixth field would then sort
the file by state.

Fields and Field Separators

What makes up a field? That is a matter of definition. If you do not specify differently,
fields are nonempty, nonblank strings separated by blanks. (A *blank* is a space or a
tab.) For example, in Figure 14.1 the first field in the line is "McHaggis," the fifth field
is "Drive," and the last field is "94889." For some types of files, the blank is a fine field
separator, but not for a mailing list. The reason is that a metropolis such as
"Hogback" uses one field, but a town like "San Luis Obispo" uses three fields, and
this would throw off the numbering of the field containing the state.

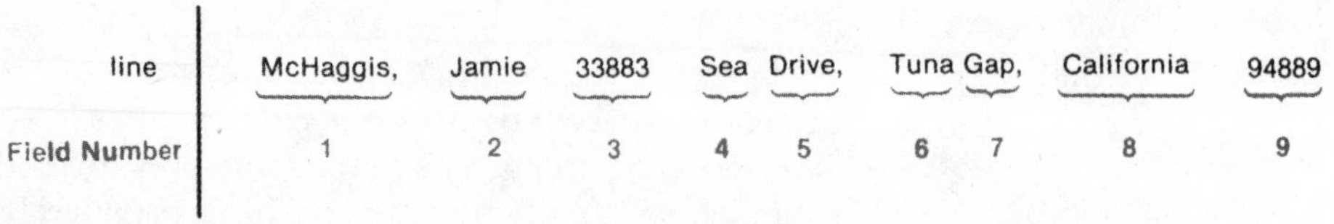

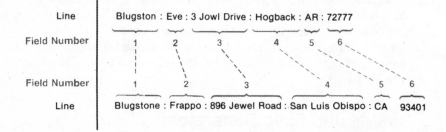

Figure 14.1.   Fields in a line.

To get around this sort of problem, you can choose your own field separator (see Figure 14.2). A common choice is the colon (see Figure 14.3). You could make a file entry look like this:

```
McHaggis:Jamie::33883 Sea Drive:Tuna Gap:California:94888
```

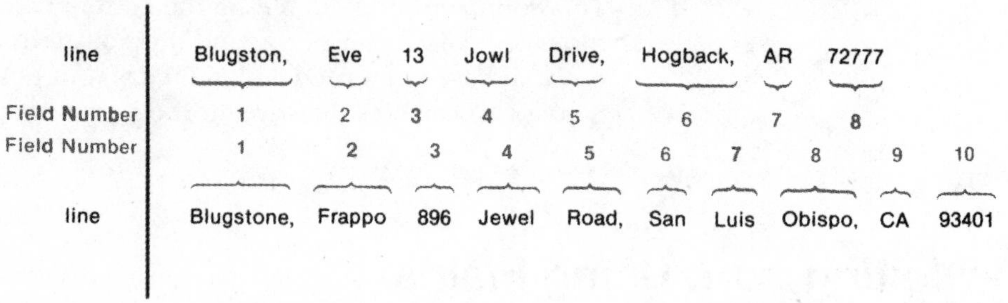

Figure 14.2.   The problem that occurs when a blank is used as a field separator.

Figure 14.3.   Using a colon as a field separator.

In this case, the first field is the last name, the second field is the first name, the third field (empty) is the middle name or initial, the fourth field is the street address, the fifth field is the city, and so on. Note that a field now can have spaces within it, as the fourth field does, or it can be empty, as is the third field. The value of the empty field is that it is a placeholder; even though a middle name is missing in this case, the address is still in the fourth field. Also notice that we have not left any spaces at the beginnings or ends of the fields. This, as you may remember, is because a space itself is a character. Therefore, : Wickley : is a field containing nine characters (the first and last being the space character), and it would be sorted differently from the seven-character field :Wickley:. The -b option of sort would ignore leading blanks but not the trailing blanks in a field, so it is simpler to just leave out extra blanks in the first place. Of course, there is another possibility: you also could carefully use the exact same number of blanks for each entry.

Using Fields with *sort*

But how does sort know to use a colon instead of a blank as a field separator? You have to use the -t option to tell it so. When you use this option, you follow the -t with the symbol that is to be the field separator. The symbol follows the t directly with no spaces. Thus, to use the colon as a separator, you would use -t: as the flag.

Next, how do you tell sort which fields to use? You include a flag consisting of a plus sign followed by a number. This tells sort how many fields to *skip*. For example, the command

```
sort -t: +4 maillist
```

tells sort to recognize colons as a field separator and to skip four fields before comparing lines in the maillist file. The comparison thus will start with the fifth field, which, in the preceding address example, corresponds to the city, and will proceed to the end of the line.

When you run the previous command, suppose that two lines are identical from the fifth field onward to the end of the line. How does sort decide to arrange these two lines? It looks at the complete line and sorts the lines on that basis. A definite example will help clarify this and later points, so let's suppose that maillist contains these entries:

```
Morgan:Joe::315 Second Street:Riesenstadt:Ca:94707
Vegetable:Joe:Fritz:1002 Market Pl.:Riesenstadt:CA:94707
Morgan:Joe::315 Second Street:Redville:OH:40817
Morgan:Joe::315 Second Street:Hot'n'wet:TX:72727
Antibody:Aristotle:Asis:26 Furtz Way:Redville:OH:40822
Zircon:Bilbo:Nagy:1313 Ratgut Blvd.:Hot'n'wet:TX:72702
```

Then the result of sort -t +4 maillist is

```
Zircon:Bilbo:Nagy:1313 Ratgut Blvd.:Hot'n'wet:TX:72702
Morgan:Joe::315 Second Street:Hot'n'wet:TX:72727
Morgan:Joe::315 Second Street:Redville:OH:40817
Antibody:Aristotle:Asis:26 Furtz Way:Redville:OH:40822
Morgan:Joe::315 Second Street:Riesenstadt:CA:94707
Vegetable:Joe:Fritz:1002 Market Pl.:Riesenstadt:CA:94707
```

The last two lines in the sorted list have the same city, state, and ZIP code, so the tie was decided by looking at the rest of the line and, alphabetically, `Morgan` precedes `Vegetable`.

You also can tell `sort` where to stop the comparison by using a flag consisting of a minus sign followed by a number. This tells `sort` to stop at the end of the numbered field. Thus,

```
sort -t: +4 -6 maillist
```

would mean to sort the file on the basis of the fifth and sixth fields. If two or more lines have identical fifth and sixth fields, they are then sorted further on the basis of the whole line as before.

Multiple Fields

With `sort`, you can create your own sorting scheme by using multiple fields. The `sort` command will first sort the file using the first field pattern you give it. Then, within a block of lines that are identical for those fields, it will sort further using the next field pattern you give. For example, consider the command

```
sort -t: +0 -1 +5 maillist
```

The first field pattern is `+0 -1`, which is simply the first field; in this case, the last name. So, first, the file is sorted by last name. The second field pattern is `+5`, which means field six to the end of the line. (Whenever a plus (+) field option is given without a minus (-) field option, the pattern comparison goes to the end of the line.) In this case, the second pattern corresponds to state and ZIP code. Thus, all those address lines containing the same last name are further sorted on the basis of state and ZIP code. This command would yield

```
Antibody:Aristotle:Asis:26 Furtz Way:Redville:OH:40822
Morgan:Joe::315 Second Street:Riesenstadt:CA:94707
Morgan:Joe::315 Second Street:Redville:OH:40817
Morgan:Joe::315 Second Street:Hot'n'wet:TX:72727
Vegetable:Joe:Fritz:1002 Market Pl.:Riesenstadt:CA:94707
Zircon:Bilbo:Nagy:1313 Ratgut Blvd.:Hot'n'wet:TX:72702
```

Note how the various Morgans are arranged in order of state, not city.

On the other hand, the command

```
sort -t: +5 -6 +1 maillist
```

would sort the file first by state. Then those with the same state would be sorted by field two (first name) to the end.

To repeat the main point of this section, when you give a series of field ranges by which to sort, the initial sorting is done according to the first range. Then any ties are resolved by the next range, and so on. Any remaining ties are resolved by looking at the whole line; sort always has a reason for putting lines where it does.

Subdividing a Field

You can refine the sorting process even further. Within each field, you can have sort skip a certain number of characters. This is done by adding a decimal point to the field number and following it with the number of characters to be skipped. For instance,

```
sort +2.3 inventory
```

would skip the first two fields and three characters when sorting the file inventory; that is, it would start at the fourth character of the third field.

Flag Options and Fields

Several of the sort options we discussed in Chapter 9 can be applied globally or just for certain fields. The choice is controlled by the placement of the option letter. Consider the following two commands:

```
sort -r +4 -5 somefile
sort +4r -5 somefile
```

In the first command, the r (reverse) option is invoked universally. Lines will be in reverse order on the basis of field five, and ties will be resolved by applying reverse order to the whole line. In the second command, the r option applies only to the initial ordering using field five; ties are resolved by applying normal order to the whole line. If a field locator option has any additional options appended, then all global options are overridden for that field. That is, if the instruction is

```
sort -n +4 -5 +6r somefile
```

then the -n option will apply to field five but not to field seven. (Remember, the +6 means skip six fields, so the -r option will begin with field seven.)

Of the sort options discussed in Chapter 9, the following options can be used but they are limited to a field: b, d, f, n, and r. The method is (as in the preceding discussion) to append the letter to the field number.

The sort command is so flexible and has so many options that you should be able to tackle almost any sorting problem except, perhaps, multiple-line records (where the information for each entry is spread over more than one line) and your laundry.

sort **Sorts Files**		
Name	**Options**	**Arguments**
sort	`[-tc, +n.m, -n.m]`	`[filename(s)]`

Description:	The sort command, used with its options, enables you to sort files on the basis of chosen fields within a line.
Options:	`-tc` Sets the field separator to be the the character *c*.
	`+n.m` Skips *n* fields and then *m* characters before beginning comparisons. A *+n* is the same as *+n.0*.
	`+ and -n.m` Stops comparison after skipping *n* fields from the beginning plus *m* characters. A *-n* is the same as *-n.0*.
Notes:	The b, d, f, n, and r options can be appended to the field locator flags. This causes the option to apply to just that field. Options appearing before the field locators apply globally except that all global flags are turned off for fields with a local flag.
	If multiple fields are specified, sorting is first done by the first field given. Lines having that field identical are then sorted by the second specified field, and so forth. Remaining ties are resolved by looking at the whole line.
Example:	`sort -t: -r +2 -3 +5n sauerbrot`
	The field separator is declared to be a colon. The file sauerbrot is sorted in reverse order by field three. Lines having the same field three are further sorted numerically by the sixth field to the end of the line. The numerical sorting is not in reverse order. Lines identical to this point are then sorted on the basis of the whole line, again using reverse order.

A Quick Peek at *awk*

Suppose you have a file in which the first column is the name of an item, the second column is its price, and the third column is the number sold. You want to add a fourth column giving the money value of the sales, but you don't want to make the calculation yourself. (Why get a computer if you have to do the work yourself?) Can you get UNIX to help? You have a file of names, debts, and last payment dates. You want to create a file containing information about everyone who owes more than $50.00 and has not paid in two months. Can UNIX help you? The answer to both questions (surprise!) is yes, providing you know how to use awk.

The awk program was created by Alfred Aho, Brian Kernighan, and Peter Weinberger of Bell Labs. Some suspect an awkward connection between the name of the utility and the names of the authors. In any case, awk is one of the most interesting of the UNIX utilities, and although we do not have space here to explain it completely, we wanted to give you an idea of what it can do and how it works.

In UNIX-speak, awk is a *pattern scanning and processing language*. By pattern scanning, we mean that awk can look through a file for certain patterns. In this, it is like grep, except that awk is both more general (the patterns can be rather sophisticated) and more specific (the patterns can be limited to particular fields within a line). Processing means that once awk finds an appropriate line, it can do something with it, for example, print it, change it, or sum numbers in it.

One important use of awk is as a file processor. Given a file consisting of three columns of numbers, for example, awk can produce a new file consisting of the original three columns plus a fourth that is the arithmetic product of, say, the first two columns. Indeed, awk can do many of the same things that a spreadsheet program can. The awk command works with text as well as numbers. For example, a simple awk program can scan an address list and print those people who live on a certain street. (The grep command could do something similar, but grep would be fooled by entries containing people with the same name as the desired street.)

There are two methods of using awk. One method is to type something in the form

```
awk program filename
```

where *program* consists of the instructions and *filename* is the name of the file awk is to act upon. The second method is to type

```
awk -f file filename
```

where *file* is the name of the file containing the program instructions. This second method is, perhaps, a bit more difficult, but it is much less likely to produce syntax error messages when you use symbols in the program that also have special meaning to the shell. We will confine our examples to the second method.

A program consists of one or more program lines. A program line consists in general of two parts, a pattern and an action; the action is enclosed in braces. Here's one possible line:

```
/rotate/ { print }
```

The pattern is `rotate` (simple string patterns are enclosed in slashes) and the action is `print`. Using this, the `awk` program finds lines containing the string `rotate` and prints them; it is equivalent to using `grep rotate` *filename*.

Learning to use `awk` consists of learning the many possibilities for defining patterns and learning the possible actions. (Actually, the `print` action is not needed here, since a line that matches a pattern is printed automatically if you omit giving any action. Also, if you give an action without a pattern, that action is performed on all lines.)

We will not go into the many pattern-defining options, but we will let you in on the secret of using fields. Fields are defined as they are for `sort`; that is, fields are strings separated by blanks. Again, as in `sort`, you can choose some other character to be a field separator, but the method of doing so is different. (One way is to use the `-F` option followed immediately—no spaces—by the chosen character.)

The `awk` program has a labeling system for fields: `$1` is the first field, `$2` is the second field, and so forth. The label `$0` has a special meaning; it stands for the entire line. These field labels can be used in patterns and actions both. Here are some examples:

Pattern	Meaning
`/fish/`	Any line containing the string `fish`
`$1 ~ /fish/`	Any line whose first field contains the string `fish`

Pattern	Meaning
`$3 ~ /fish/`	Any line whose third field contains the string `fish`
`$1! ~ /fish/`	Any line whose first field does not contain the string `fish`

Action	Meaning
`{print $2}`	Print only the second field
`{print $4, $2}`	Print the contents of the fourth field and then of the second field
`{print $2, $2+$4}`	Print the second field and then the sum of the second and fourth fields
`{s=$2+$4;print s}`	Add the second and fourth fields, and print the sum

Note the use of ~ and ! in the patterns. The tilde (~) means that the pattern to the right is contained in the field to the left. The !~ combination means that the pattern to the right is not contained in the field to the left. Also note that the `print` instruction can be used with individual fields and with combinations of fields.

You can do arithmetic in the action parts: + is addition, − is subtraction, * is multiplication, and / is division. You can include more than one action by separating them by a semicolon, as in the preceding example.

Let's take a look at a simple example using some of these ideas. The file `sales` contains six columns of information. The first column is the name of an item, the second column is the selling price of the item, and the next four columns are quarterly sales figures for the item. (This is such a simple example that the prices remain constant for a year.) The file looks like this:

```
carts     29.99 45 13 55  22
corks      0.02 30 20 25  93
doors     49.99 40 15 20  25
geese     15.00  2  8  1 128
nighties  50.00 11 23 15  82
```

We would like to add two more columns: total items sold and total cash sales. We create a file called, say, `addup` that looks like this:

```
{total=$3+$4+$5+$6; print $0, total, total*$2}
```

This action contains two parts separated by a semicolon. The first part sums the sales and cleverly calls the total `total`. The second part prints the original line (`$0`), followed by the total, and then the `total*$2`, which means "total" times the second column.

The command

```
awk -f addup sales
```

produces this output:

```
carts     29.99 45 13 55   22 135 4048.65
corks      0.02 30 20 25   93 168 3.36
doors     49.99 40 15 20   25 100 4999
geese     15.00  2  8  1 128 139 2085
nighties  50.00 11 23 15   82 131 6550
```

You could save the output in a file called sumsales by using redirection:

```
awk -f addup sales > sumsales
```

This introduction just scratches the surface of awk. The on-line manual has a concise summary of awk, but the Bell Labs publication *Awk—a pattern scanning and processing language* (also published in the *Support Tools Guide*), by A. V. Aho, B. W. Kernighan, and P. J. Weinberger, is easier to read and is much more informative. It also is much longer.

nawk and *oawk*

Release 4 of UNIX System V finds awk in a stage of transition as it expands its abilities and features to become nawk (for *new awk*). Meanwhile, the old awk continues under the name oawk. As far as the simple examples we have discussed, oawk and nawk behave the same—the differences become important only in more advanced uses. If you simply ask for awk, instead of oawk or nawk, Release 4 will use oawk. In future releases, however, oawk will be phased out, and nawk will be called awk.

More on Shell Scripts

Shell scripts can do much more than what we have shown so far. Indeed, a full description is quite beyond the scope of this book. But we would like to add three more shell script skills to your repertoire. The first skill is making a shell script interactive, letting it and the user indulge in a dialogue. The second skill is creating a loop, letting the same script cycle through several times so that it can process several items. The third skill is creating a script that chooses between different alternatives. We will discuss only sh scripts, but, as you may recall, you can run sh shell scripts under the ksh and csh shells, too. You may wish to review the sections in Chapter 11 on shell scripts and shell variables before continuing.

Interactive Shell Scripts: *read*

An interactive program allows two-way communication between the program and the user. We already have a way to have a script speak to the user: just use the echo command. The `read` command gives the user the means to talk back. For example, let's put the following shell script in the file `hello`:

```
echo Hello! What\'s your name\?
read NAME
echo Golly, $NAME, it\'s a privilege to meet you.
```

(We've used the backslash to turn off the special meanings of the shell metacharacters in the messages.) When the user types a response to the first `echo`, the `read` command assigns that response to the shell variable `NAME`. Then the next `echo` prints out that value again.

```
$ sh hello
What's your name?
Rembrandt da Vinci
Golly, Rembrandt da Vinci, it's a privilege to meet you.
$
```

The `read` statement takes in one line of input. You can use more than one variable after a `read`. In that case, the first variable gets the first word, the second variable the second word, and so on. Any leftover words get assigned to the last variable. Any leftover variables get assigned nothing. In our example, there was just one variable, so all the words were assigned to it. Here is a revised `hello` using more than one variable.

```
echo Hello! What\'s your name\?
read NAME1 NAME2
echo Golly, $NAME1, it\'s a privilege to meet you.
echo Are you any relation to Vicky $NAME2?
```

And here is a sample run:

```
$ sh hello
Hello! What's your name?
Alexander the Great
Golly, Alexander, it's a privilege to meet you
Are you any relation to Vicky the Great?
$
```

As advertised, the first word was assigned to `NAME1` and the rest of the input line was assigned to `NAME2`.

Now that you know how to make an interactive script, let's move on to one way of making loops.

The *for* Loop

The simplest way to set up repetition in a shell script is to use what is known as a `for` loop. Here is a simple example. (For heuristic reasons, we have shortened the noble epic song contained therein.)

```
for i in horse duck cow chicken
do
    echo Old Macdonald had a $i
    echo Eeii eeii ooo
done
```

Before explaining this script, lets see what it does. (Assume it is in the file McFarm.)

```
$ sh McFarm
Old Macdonald had a horse
Eeii eeii ooo
Old Macdonald had a duck
Eeii eeii ooo
Old Macdonald had a cow
Eeii eeii ooo
Old Macdonald had a chicken
Eeii eeii ooo
$
```

Now the intent should be clear. The i is a shell variable. The list of animals are values the variable assumes in succession. The instructions between do and done are executed with i set to the first value (horse) from the list. Then i is set to the next value (duck), and the instructions between do and done are executed again. This continues until all the variables have been used.

You can use any name you like for the variable. You could replace i with beast and $i with $beast, and the program would work the same. However, i is the name most often used. The general form is

```
for variable-name in value1 value2 . . .
do
    commands
done
```

The indentation is not necessary, but it makes it easier to see where loops start and stop.

A for loop also can get variable values from outside the shell. Here is a modified McFarm:

```
for i in $*
do
    echo Old Macdonald had a $i
    echo Eeii eeii ooo
done
```

Recall that $* stands for all the arguments of a script. Thus, our new version works like this:

```
$ sh McFarm snake moose muskrat
Old Macdonald had a snake
Eeii eeii ooo
Old Macdonald had a moose
Eeii eeii ooo
Old Macdonald had a muskrat
Eeii eeii ooo
$
```

Now the variable i took on each of the three arguments in turn for a value. The combination

```
for i in $*
```

occurs so frequently that UNIX accepts the abbreviation

```
for i
```

as having the same meaning. This means you could rewrite the last version of McFarm as

```
for i
do
  echo Old Macdonald had a $i
  echo Eeii eeii ooo
done
```

This version would work the same, cycling through each argument given to the script.

There are many ways to get values to a for loop variable. Here are some of them:

1. List the values explicitly, as in

```
for name in kathleen kate tana georgiana anita
```

2. Take the values from shell script arguments, as in

```
for i in $*
```

or the equivalent

```
for i
```

3. Take filenames from a directory as values. The shell expands combinations (other than $*) involving * and ? into filenames. Thus

```
for file in *
do
  cat $file
done
```

would cat in succession each file in the current working directory, and

```
for file in FORT/*.f
do
   mv $file old$file
done
```

adds the prefix old to all the FORTRAN files in the FORT directory.

4. Take values from a shell variable. Here is yet another revision of hello:

```
echo Hello! What\'s your name\?
read NAME
for N in $NAME
do
   echo $N
done
echo is quite a name.
```

Running it, you get

```
$ sh hello
Hello! What's your name?
Willie Joe Frogflapper
Willie
Joe
Frogflapper
is quite a name.
$
```

The read command gave the value *Willie Joe Frogflapper* to NAME. Then N was assigned each name from this list, one at a time. Thus, each cycle through the loop printed just one name. Notice that a for loop can have other commands before and after it.

5. Take values from the output of a command. Recall that the backquotes allows you to obtain the output of a command. Using this, you can rework McFarm to take names from a file called animals:

```
for i in 'cat animals'
do
   echo Old Macdonald had a $i
   echo Eeii eeii ooo
done
```

Then the words in the file animals are used as successive values for i. The for loop is invaluable when you want to process several files in some manner. Many commands, of course, already can handle several files. For example, to do a word count on several files, you can just type

```
wc phys chem biol astr
```

The wc command already has a loop mechanism built in, so you do not have to make a loop to use it. But some commands do not work that way. For instance, we used a loop earlier with the mv command in order to change the names of several files. Or if you wanted to sort a bunch of files, returning each sorted output to the corresponding original file, you could use a loop:

```
for file in $*
do
  sort -o $file $file
done
```

Similarly, you often need a loop to apply two or more processes in turn on a set of files:

```
for file in $*
do
    spell $file > sp.$file
done
```

Here each file in turn is checked for spelling, with the misspelled words redirected to an appropriately named new file. A for loop can be typed as a direct command rather than run as a shell script. The sh and ksh shells recognize the keyword for and will display a secondary prompt (>) until you complete the loop by typing done. Here is an example:

```
$ for file in report summary text news
> do
>     mv $file $file.old
> done
$
```

The other control commands we mention also can be used in this fashion. Now that we have seen the basics of looping, let's try choice-making.

Choosing Actions: The *case* Statement

Many software packages are *menu-driven*; that is, they offer you a *menu* of choices and ask what you want. The case statement makes it easy to set up shell script menus. Here is a simple example showing how a case statement works:

```
echo Please enter the number of the program you wish to run:
echo '1 date              2 who'
echo '3 ls'
read choice
case $choice in
```

```
1) date ;;
2) who ;;
3) ls ;;
*) echo That wasn\'t one of the choices ! Bye. ;;
esac
```

You used quotes in `echo` to preserve the spacing; otherwise, `echo` ignores what it conceives of as surplus spaces. Now let's see what the script does. Assume the script is in the file `askme`. Here are two sample runs:

```
$ sh askme
Please enter the number of the program you wish to run:
1  date            2  who
3  ls
1
Mon May 18 14:23:52 PDT 1992
$ sh askme
Please enter the number of the program you wish to run:
1  date            2  who
3  ls
why
That wasn't one of the choices! Bye.
$
```

When you enter a *1*, then the case statement causes the command with the 1) label to be run. The command labeled *) executes when something other than *1*, *2*, or *3* is entered. The double semicolon (;;) marks the end of each choice, and the `esac` (case spelled backwards) marks the end of the `case` statement.

There is nothing magical about using numbers to label the cases. You could just as easily use letters. Just remember to follow each choice with a) when using it as a label:

```
echo Please enter the letter of the program you wish to run:
echo  'a date
echo  'c  ls'
read choice
case $choice in
a) date ;;
b) who ;;
c) ls ;;
*) echo That wasn\'t one of the choices! Bye. ;;
esac
```

The general form of the `case` statement is

```
case value in
choice1)  commands ;;
```

```
choice2)   commands ;;
. . .
esac
```

The list of choices is scanned to find the first one that matches the value. The choice labeled `*)` matches any value, so it often is used as the last choice to act as a catchall. (Making it the first choice would cause the first choice to match any value, and the `case` would not be searched any further. So do not do that.) If no choices match and if there is no `*)` choice, then nothing is done, and the program moves on to whatever comes after the `case` statement.

Let's look at a few more examples.

```
echo which of these words means a short, obese lump of a person?
echo dotterel drotchel fadge fustilugs
read answer
case $answer in
fadge) echo Correct you are! ;;
dotterel ¦ drotchel ¦ fustilugs) echo Nope, $answer is wrong. ;;
*) echo Very wrong: $answer is not even a choice! ;;
esac
```

Aha! Something new! The ¦ here is *not* a pipe. Rather, it serves as an "or." It lets us attach more than one label to the same response. Let's put this in a file, `quiz`, and see if it works.

```
$ sh quiz
Which of these words means a short, obese lump of a person?
dotterel drotchel fadge fustilugs
drotchel
Nope, drotchel is wrong.
$
```

So far our examples have used a shell variable for the value-part of a `case` statement. As the next example shows, you can also use shell script arguments:

```
case $1 in
dog) echo Man\'s best friend ;;
[aeiouAEIOU]*) Echo word beginning with a vowel ;;
??) echo a two-letter word ;;
*) echo I don\'t know ;;
esac
```

Notice, too, that you can use the shell's pattern-matching skills in formulating the choices. Put the script in the file `whatisa` and run it a few times:

```
$ sh watisa owl
word beggining with a vowel
$ sh watisa dog
```

```
Man's best friend
$ sh whatisa cat
I don't know
$ sh whatisa oo
word beginning with a vowel
$
```

The last example (oo) illustrates our earlier claim that a case stops after the first match. That is, oo matches the ?? pattern, but since it also matches the preceding pattern for vowels, the case does not check any further than the first match.

The case value portion can be a shell variable or a shell script argument or anything else that produces a value. For example,

```
case 'pwd' in
```

would be a valid beginning of a case statement. The backquotes cause the output of pwd, namely the current working directory, to be the value against which the choices are compared.

What if you want more than one command to be executed for a given choice? Then just use the standard conventions of the command line. That is, you can separate commands on one line by a semicolon, and you can use a backslash to extend a command to the next line. See Chapter 11 for more details.

In summary, the case statement is a powerful and flexible tool. The value portion of the statement can come from shell variables, shell-script arguments, or command outputs. The patterns that are matched to this value can use shell metacharacters such as *, ?, and [ ]. The patterns can also use the metacharacter ¦ to mean "or," so that more than one pattern can correspond to a given command. The commands themselves can use pipes and redirection, and more than one command can be attached to a given choice. Beyond all that, you can use case statements in for loops and vice versa. And still we have left much unsaid!

What Else?

If you wish to learn more on shell scripts, you can find a substantial discussion in the System V Documentation. The discussion includes more commands often used in shell scripts, such as test, eval, and shift. It also covers more control structures, such as an if statement and a while loop.

Review Questions

A. Using *grep* to Match Patterns

For each `grep` pattern on the left, indicate which pattern(s) following it would be matched.

1. `'to'`   a. hot   b. to   c. toad   d. stool   e. Top

2. `'t.n'`   a. tin   b. stun   c. nation   d. stony   e. tnuch

3. `'a[o-t].'`   a. art   b. act   c. task   d. tort   e. at

B. Using *find*

Describe what each of the following `find` commands would do.

1. `find $HOME -name '*.c' -exec mv { } $HOME/cdirect \;`

2. `find . -name '*.c' -size +3 -ok rm { }\;`

3. `find /home \(-size + 10 -atime + 20 \) -o -size + 30 -print`

C. Questions

The following questions all refer to a file named `maillist` whose contents are

```
Morgan:Joe::315 Second Street:Riesenstadt:CA:94707
Vegetable:Joe:Fritz:1002 Market Pl.:Riesenstadt:CA:94707
Morgan:Joe::315 Second Street:Redville:OH:40817
Morgan:Joe::315 Second Street: Hot'n'wet:TX:72727
Antibody:Aristotle:Asis:26 Furtz Way:Redville:OH:40822
Zircon:Bilbo:Nagy:1313 Ratgut Blvd.:Hot'n'wet:TX:72702
```

1. What order would each of the following commands produce?

    a. `sort -t: +3n -4 +6n maillist`

    b. `sort -t: +3n -4 +6nr maillist`

    c. `sort -t: +6.3n maillist`

2. What instruction will sort `maillist` by state, and then by city within state, and then by name within city?

Answers

A. 1. b,c,d; 2. a,b,d; 3. a,c.

B. 1. Search your home directory recursively for files whose names end in .c and move them to the directory $HOME/cdirect. 2. Search your current working directory recursively for files whose names end in .c and have a size in excess of three blocks. Then for each found file, ask user if it should be removed. 3. Seach the /home directory recursively for all files that either are bigger than 10 blocks and have not been used in over 20 days or else are bigger than 30 blocks. Print the pathname of these files.

C. 1.a.

```
Antibody:Aristotle:Asis:26 Furtz Way:Redville:OH:40822
Morgan:Joe::315 Second Street:Redville:OH:40817
Morgan:Joe::315 Second Street:Hot'n'wet:TX:72727
Morgan:Joe::315 Second Street:Riesenstadt:CA:94707
Vegetable:Joe:Fritz:1002 Market Pl.:Riesenstadt:CA:94707
Zircon:Bilbo:Nagy:1313 Ratgut Blvd.:Hot'n'wet:TX:72702
```

C. 1.b.

```
Antibody:Aristotle:Asis:26 Furtz Way:Redville:OH:40822
Morgan:Joe::315 Second Street:Riesenstadt:CA:94707
Morgan:Joe::315 Second Street:Hot'n'wet:TX:72727
Morgan:Joe::315 Second Street:Redville:OH:40817
Vegetable:Joe:Fritz:1002 Market Pl.:Riesenstadt:CA:94707
Zircon:Bilbo:Nagy:1313 Ratgut Blvd.:Hot'n'wet:TX:72702
```

C. 1.c.

```
Zircon:Bilbo:Nagy:1313 Ratgut Blvd.:Hot'n'wet:TX:72702
Morgan:Joe::315 Second Street:Riesenstadt:CA:94707
Vegetable:Joe:Fritz:1002 Market Pl.:Riesenstadt:CA:94707
Morgan:Joe::315 Second Street:Redville:OH:40817
Antibody:Aristotle:Asis:26 Furtz Way:Redville:OH:40822
Morgan:Joe::315 Second Street:Hot'n'wet:TX:72727
```

2. sort -t: +5 -6 +4 -5 +0 maillist

Exercises at the Terminal

1. Duplicate as many features as you can of those described in the introductory story.

2. Devise an interactive version of the cp command. Have it query the user for the name of the file to be copied and for the name to be given the copy.

3. Devise an interactive program that will copy, link, or change the name of a file, as the user selects. If you like, you can have this shell procedure call upon the shell procedure of Exercise 2.

15

UNIX Networking

Chapter 15

UNIX Networking

One modern trend is for computers to become faster, more powerful, and easier to use. Equally important is the trend to link computers together into networks. Networking can be tightly knit—several computers on the same site sharing each other's resources (files, printers, and so on). The user need not be aware that several computers are linked together. Networking also can be fairly loose—only occasional interchanges of information between computers. In this chapter, we will look at three aspects of networking:

- Logging onto remote computers
- Exchanging files between systems
- Using the worldwide UNIX news network

Varieties of Networking

First, let's look at some of the different forms networking can take. At one extreme, two or more computers can be networked so intimately that they appear as a single computer to the user. In this case, you usually do not have to worry about networking matters. Next, two computers can have their separate identities but maintain a permanent communication link. With this setup, you can use the `rlogin` command to log onto one computer system from another computer system, assuming you have accounts on both systems. You can use the `rcp` command to copy files from one system to another. Another configuration consists of two or more computers that are not permanently connected, but which can establish direct contact through a modem or other link. In this case, you can use the `cu` command to call up one UNIX system from another system, login to the called system (if you have an account on it), and transfer files. The most widespread form of UNIX networking consists of systems that periodically make contact with each other and transfer information. In this case, you may not be able to login directly on the other systems. Indeed, you may not even have accounts on them. But you still can use the `uucp` family of commands to transfer files between systems. Beyond that, you can tap into the network news and share in a worldwide discussion of facts and fancy.

In this chapter, we will cover these topics, beginning with `.rlogin`.

Remote Logins Via *rlogin*

When two or more computer systems maintain continuous network connections, you can login to one system from the other providing you have accounts on both systems. The system you start from is called the *host* or *local* system, and the system you wish to login to is called the *remote* system. The `rlogin` (for *remote login*) command provides the means for you to log in to a remote system from a host. To use it, type the command and follow it with the network name of the UNIX system that you wish to connect to. For instance, here's a sample remote login from the `unicom` system to the `sparker` system:

```
$ rlogin sparker
Password:
Last login: Thu Jan 16 11:59:07 from unicom
SunOS Release 4.0.3c (SPARKER) #2: Sat Jan 18 16:09:40 PST 1992
Hello, You are now on Sparkie turf !!!
$
```

Note that this example asked for the user's password but not for the login name. That's because `rlogin` assumes that you have the same login name on both systems, therefore it automatically supplies the remote system with your login name from the local, or host, system. Suppose, however, you have different login names on each system. Then you can use the `-l` option with `rlogin` to provide the login name you use on the remote system. For instance, if your remote login name is `titan`, you would log in this way:

```
$ rlogin -l titan sparker
```

If you like, you can set things up so that you do not have to enter your password when you make a remote login. The idea is to create a file called `.rhosts` (for *remote hosts*) in your home directory on the remote system. Next, add a separate line to `.rhosts` consisting of the name of the host system and your host system login name. Be sure to leave a space between the two names. For example, if you (`charon`) want to login to the sparker system from the unicom system, you would place the following line in the .rhosts file in your home directory on the sparker system:

```
unicom charon
```

When you login from the unicom system, the sparker system checks charon's .rhosts file. If the computer name and user name match the computer name and login name typed in from unicom, then sparker lets you log in without asking for a password.

To quit from a remote login, you go through the usual logout procedure:

```
$ <Ctrl-d>
Connection closed.
$
```

The Connection closed message indicates that you have been returned to your host computer.

rlogin Login to a Remote System		
Name	**Options**	**Arguments**
rlogin	**[-l]**	*systemname*
Description:	The rlogin command enables you to login from one UNIX system to another, as long as they are connected. The *systemname* argument represents the name of the remote system. Typically, the /etc/hosts file lists possible remote login systems. A password is not required if you place your local system name and login name in the .rhosts file in your home directory on the remote system.	
Option:	-l *username*	Specifies the desired login name on the remote system. If you omit this option, rlogin assumes your login name on the remote system is the same as on the local system.
Examples:	rlogin bebop	
	This command enables you to login to the computer system named bebop.	
	rlogin -l dizzie bebop	
	This command enables you to login to the computer system named bebop with user name dizzie.	

File Transfer Via *rcp*

Suppose you want to copy a file from your account on the sparker system to the unicom system. Again, we are assuming that these two systems maintain an on-going communication link. Also, we assume that you are only logged into the unicom system. You can use the rcp (for *remote copy*) command to copy a file between both systems. This command works much like cp except that you have to identify the remote system. You do this by preceding the file pathname with the name of the remote system and a colon. For instance, suppose charon wants to copy the vole file from her home directory on the remote sparker system to her current directory on the host unicom system. She engages in the following exchange with UNIX:

```
$ rcp sparker:/home/charon/vole .
$
```

Here sparker: indicates the remote system to use and the period (.) denotes the current directory. As with cp, rcp does not output any text to the screen unless something goes wrong. Also, as with cp, the final name in the command line can be a file name or a directory name. For instance, the command

```
rcp shoppinglist sparker:/home/charon/newlist
```

copies the shoppinglist file in the current directory to charon's home directory on the sparker system and renames the file newlist.

Suppose the unifoo system is part of the same network. Then you can copy a file from your account on unifoo to your account on sparker while you are logged in to unicom. Just use a system identifier for both the source and the destination. For instance, the command

```
rcp unifoo:/home/charon/*.data sparker:/home/charon/Fish
```

copies all the files with names ending in .data from charon's home directory on the unifoo system to the Fish subdirectory in the sparker home directory.

If you omit the full pathname for a remote destination, rcp assumes the path is relative to your home directory on that system. For instance, the last example could be reexpressed as follows:

```
rcp unifoo:*.data sparker:Fish
```

If you have a different login name on the remote system than on the host system, you can prefix the remote system name with your login name on that system and an @ symbol. For instance, if your login name on the remote system is titan, you could copy a file as follows:

```
rcp frappage titan@sparker:Works
```

This would copy the frappage file to the Works subdirectory of your home directory on the sparker system.

rcp Copy Files Between Remote Systems		
Name	**Options**	**Arguments**
`rcp`	**None**	`filename1 filename2` `filename(s) directory`

Description:	The `rcp` command enables you to copy files from one UNIX system to another, as long as they are connected. In general, each file name has the following format: `systemname:pathname` Here `systemname` represents the name of the remote system. Typically, the `/etc/hosts` file lists those systems for which `rcp` is possible. You can omit the `systemname` and colon for files or directories in the system you are currently logged in to. Like `cp`, `rcp` can copy one file to another or copy a group of files to an indicated directory. If the pathname for the remote system is a relative path, it is interpreted relative to your home directory on that system.
Example:	`rcp charts bebop:/home/dizzie/newcharts` . This command copies the file `charts` from your current directory to the `/home/dizzie/newcharts` file on the `bebop` system.

Communicating with *cu*

Perhaps you have an account on another UNIX system that cannot be accessed via `rlogin` from your current system. If there is a direct phone or modem link to the other system, you can use the `cu` command to call the other system. Once connected, you follow normal procedures for logging in. Your current terminal then becomes a remote terminal for the called system. In addition, the `cu` command allows you to transfer files between your system and the called system.

Logging Onto Another System

Suppose you are logged in to one UNIX system and want to connect to another system using `cu`. One way is to use the telephone number as an argument. For instance,

`cu 5551212`

will cause your system to dial the 5551212 number. Of course, both your system and the remote system must have the proper hardware installed to make this possible. The telephone number can include an = sign to indicate "wait for a dial tone." That is, if you have to dial 9 to get an outside line, use 9=5551212.

If the destination computer has a name your system recognizes, you can use the system name instead of the phone number. For instance, the command

```
cu unifog
```

will establish a connection with the unifog system. Your system should list recognized systems in the /etc/uucp/Systems file. The uuname command lists the recognized systems.

Once the cu command connects you to the other system, your terminal will be acting as a remote login terminal for the other system. You will have to login as usual, so you will need an account on the system:

```
$ cu unifog
Connected
login: feebu
password:
Welcome to unifog
$
```

Working with *cu*

When you log in to the remote system, you will be logged in simultaneously to your original host system and to the remote system. To handle this dual environment, the cu command runs two separate processes. A *transmit* process reads lines from the standard input (the keyboard, by default) and transmits them to the called system. However, lines beginning with a tilde (~) are processed as instructions to the calling system rather than transmitted. Similarly, a *receive* process takes data from the remote system and echoes it on the standard output (your terminal by default). Again, lines beginning with a tilde are exceptions.

Let's look at some examples of commands that use a tilde. Suppose you originally logged in to the unixette system, then used cu to login to the unifog system. If you type the who command:

```
who                          ← who is on the remote system
```

the transmit process sends this command to the unifog system, which displays a list of the users on that system. But suppose you want to know who is logged in to your local system, unixette. The ~! prefix causes the transmit process to send the following command to your home system instead of to the remote system:

```
~!who                        ← who is on the local system
```

Next, suppose you want to copy a file from the remote system to the local system. The cu program has a ~%take command for this purpose. For instance, suppose you want to copy the toby file from the remote system to your local system, renaming the copy ornottoby. You can give this command:

```
~%take toby ornottoby
```

This causes the transmit process to tell the remote system to send back the contents of the toby file, and the receive process to direct those contents to the local ornottoby file instead of to your terminal. If you omit the second file name, cu will give the copy the same name as the original file.

The ~%put command works much like ~%take, except that it copies a file from your local system to the remote system. For instance, the command

```
~%put ruffles
```

copies the ruffles file from your local system to the remote system and names the copy ruffles.

To terminate a cu session, first logoff the remote system. Then terminate the cu connection using the ~. command:

```
$ <Ctrl-d>          ← logoff the remote system
NO CARRIER          ← remote session terminated
> ~.                ← terminate cu program
$                   ← back on local system
```

The cu program recognizes several such tilde commands, called *escape sequences*. Table 15.1 summarizes many of the escape sequences, while the Summary describes the command in general.

Table 15.1. *cu* tilde escape sequences.

Escape Sequence	Effect
~.	Terminate the connection.
~!	Escape to the local interactive command interpreter (normally the sh shell).
~!cmd	Run the command cmd on the local system.
~$cmd	Run the command cmd on the local system and send its output to the remote system as a command to be run on the remote system.
~%cd	Change the directory on the local system. (New with Release 2.)

continues

Table 15.1.   continued

Escape Sequence	Effect
~%take *original* [*copy*]	Copy the file *original* from the remote system to the file *copy* on the local system. If *copy* is omitted, use the original name for the copy, too. The ~%take command uses echo and cat on the remote system. If tabs are to be copied on the remote system without being expanded to spaces, the stty command should be used to set tabs mode there.
~%put *original* [*copy*]	Copy the file *original* from the local system to the file *copy* on the remote system. If *copy* is omitted, use the original name for the copy, too. The ~%put command uses stty and cat on the remote system. It also requires that both systems use the same current erase characters and the same current kill characters.
~~*line*	Transmit the line ~*line* to the remote system. This is used when you call system B from system A, then call system C from system B. A ~ can be used to execute commands on system A, and ~~ can be used to execute commands on system B.
~%break	Transmit a BREAK to the remote system. Can be abbreviated to ~%b. (A regular BREAK would be interpreted by the local system.)

cu Call Up Another System

Name	Options	Arguments
cu	[-s]	*telnumber*
		systemname

Description:	The cu command connects a local UNIX system to a remote UNIX system. The first form identifies the system by a telephone number. The second identifies the called system by its uucp *systemname*, as shown in the /etc/uucp/Systems file. Once the connection is made, the local terminal acts as a remote terminal to the called system. While in cu, you can give various tilde escape sequence commands as described in Table 15.1.

Option:	-s *speed*	Specify the transmission speed baud rate. By default, the speed is "*any*," meaning the system will use whatever speed the next available communication device has, as listed in the device file. If a speed is given, cu uses the first available device having the specified speed. Not used in the *systemname* mode.
Examples:	cu 5551000	

This command calls a computer that has the 5551000 telephone number. The computer will use the first available device and baud rate.

cu -s 2400 5551000

This command calls a computer known to have a 2400 baud modem. The local computer will use the first available device supporting that speed.

cu flox

This command calls a computer having a *systemname* flox.

File Transfer with the *uucp* Family

The cu command can connect you to another UNIX system, but you still need to login to that system. Normally you use cu to call systems on which you have an account. The uucp (*UNIX-to-UNIX copy*) command, on the other hand, allows you to transfer files to or from a system on which you do not have an account. Essentially, you tell the uucp command which file you want transferred to which system, and it takes care of the transfer. Unlike the case for rcp and cu, the file transfer does not take place immediately. Instead, uucp keeps a record of what it is supposed to do, then attends to its obligations the next time your system is connected to the other system. Depending on how your system is set up, it may attempt to establish a connection right away, it may connect at some preestablished time, or it may wait until it is called (polled) by the other system.

The related uuto and uupick commands provide a somewhat different interface for the same basic services.

Using *uucp*

The basic form for uucp is:

```
uucp source destination
```

Here, as you have probably surmised, *source* represents the file you wish to transmit, and *destination* represents the copy. As with cp, *destination* can be a file name, in which case it is used as the name for the copy, or it can be a directory name, in which case the copy has the same name as the original. In general, both *source* and *destination* consist of two parts—a system name and a pathname, separated by an exclamation point. (Users of the csh shell should use \!.) You can drop the system name for files on the local system. The uuname command lists the system names your system recognizes.

Let's see how this works. Suppose that you (frikacee) wish to copy the file spot from your home directory on the unifog system to the /home/jug directory on the unifoo system. Then you can give this instruction:

```
uucp unifog!/home/frikacee/spot unifoo!/home/jug
```

This will create a copy of the spot file, also called spot in the /home/jug directory on the unifoo system. If you are already in the frikacee directory, you can omit the rest of the pathname. If your are logged in to the unifog system, you can omit the system name. Thus, you could abbreviate the last command:

```
uucp spot unifoo!/home/jug
```

There is a potential problem with this example. As far as unifoo is concerned, uucp is just another user which, in general, won't be able to create files in your directories. To get around these problems, you can use a special public directory in which you and uucp can create files. Under System V, Release 4, this directory is named /var/spool/uucppublic—older systems use /usr/spool/uucppublic. By default, this public directory is the *only* directory in which uucp can write, although the system administrator can modify that restriction. The uucp command can create subdirectories in the public directory. Also, many systems restrict uucp to copying only from the public directory. In that case, to send a file, you first would have to copy it to your local public directory, then send that copy.

The usual UNIX practice is to place a file in a subdirectory named after the intended recipient. For example, to send a file to Banshee:

```
uucp newsong unifoo!/var/spool/uucppublic/Banshee/newsong
```

This causes uucp to create a subdirectory called Banshee in the remote system's public directory. There are a couple of shortcuts you can take in giving this command. First, uucp translates ~/, when following a site name, to /var/spool/uucppublic/. Using ~/ is a good idea—not only is it easier to type, but it would still work if a system used a different name, such as /usr/spool/uucppublic, for its public directory. Second, you can use a trailing / to peg a name as being a directory rather than a file. That is, you can replace the previous command with the following:

```
uucp newsong unifoo!~/Banshee/
```

This also copies the newsong file into the Banshee subdirectory of the remote system's public directory. Because the command does not specify a name for the destination file, uucp uses the original name, newsong. Incidentally, if you omit the final / in this example, the command would interpret Banshee as a file name, thus making it the name of the copy file, and uucp would not create a subdirectory by that name.

How does the recipient know you have sent him or her a file? You can send a message via electronic mail. Or you can use the -n option and have uucp automatially send a mail message notifying the recipient. And you can use the -m option to have uucp report to you via mail when the file transfer has been completed. The -n option requires you follow the n with the recipient's login name. Thus, the following command notifies both the sender and the recipient when the file has been sent:

```
uucp -m -nBanshee newsong unifoo!~/Banshee/
```

More on System Names

Suppose you want to send a file to the fluxion system, however fluxion is not on your system's system list. But you happen to know that fluxion is on unifoo's system list, and your system knows about unifoo. You can have uucp send a file to unifoo and have the file relayed from unifoo to fluxion. Just use the exclamation point to concatenate the names:

```
uucp jumbo unifoo!fluxion!~/Ellie/
```

If you use csh, keep in mind that the csh shell regards the exclamation point as a metacharacter for history commands. To use the exclamation point as part of a system address, you must escape it by preceding it with a backslash or by enclosing it in single quotes or double quotes:

```
uucp newsong unifoo\!~/Banshee/
uucp jumbo 'unifoo!fluxion!'~/Ellie/
```

uucp Transfer Files Between Systems

Name	Options	Arguments
uucp	[-n, -m]	*sourcefile destination*

Description:	The uucp command enables you to transfer files from one UNIX system to another. In general, *sourcefile* and *destination* have this form:

systemname!pathname

The uuname command lists those *systemnames* that uucp recognizes. By default, the only destination directory open to uucp is /var/spool/uucppublic, which can be abbreviated as ~/. You can indicate the local system by omitting the system name and exclamation point.

Options:	-n *username*	Notify *username* that a file has been received via uucp.
	-m	Notify sender upon successful delivery of file.
Examples:	uucp newsong unifoo!~/Banshee/	

This command sends the newsong file to the Banshee subdirectory of the /var/spool/uucppublic directory on the unifoo system. (The Banshee subdirectory is created if it does not already exist.)

uucp unifog!/home/buzz/figs ~/mine/

This command retrieves a file from the unifog system, placing it in the mine subdirectory of the local /var/spool/uucppublic directory.

The *uuto* and *uupick* Commands

The uuto command simplifies sending a file to the public directory, and the uupick command simplifies retrieving files. The uuto command assumes you want to send files to the public directory, so you do not have to specify a destination directory. Instead, you specify the destination system and the recipient's login name, separated by an exclamation point. For instance, to send the newsong file from the unifog system to the user Banshee on the unifoo system, give the following command:

```
uuto newsong unifoo!Banshee
```

This command not only transmits the file, it notifies the recipient automatically of the file's arrival. As with uucp, you can use a -m option to have notification sent to you, too.

To collect files sent to you via uuto, use uupick. The uuto command establishes a subdirectory with your login name, and the uupick command scans this subdirectory for files sent to you. Actually, the subdirectory is further subdivided into subdirectories that organize files sent to you by the system that sent them. Thus, the example above would have placed a newsong file in the unifog subdirectory of the Banshee subdirectory. Also, all the uuto user subdirectories would be placed in the receive subdirectory of the public directory. Anyway, if Banshee ran the uupick command, Banshee would see something like the following:

```
$ uupick
from system unifog: file newsong ?
```

To move the file from the public directory to your current directory, respond to the ? prompt with the m command, for *m*ove. Optionally, you can provide a directory name indicating where to move the file. Once the file has been moved, uupick will show the name of the next file, if any, awaiting you. Type the q command to quit uupick. Table 15.2 lists the most common responses to the uupick ? prompt.

Table 15.2.   *uupick* responses.

Command	Effect
<Enter>	Go to the next entry.
d	Delete the entry .
m [*directory*]	Move the entry to the named directory. The current directory is the default if none is given.
p	Display the file contents on the standard output (the terminal, by default). If a directory is named, list its contents.
q	Quit.

uuto Send a File to Another System		
Name	**Options**	**Arguments**
uuto	[-m]	*filename system!user*
Description:	The uuto command transmits the file given by *filename* to the user on the system having the login name of *user* and notifies the user via mail that the file has arrived. The uuname command will list acceptable system names.	

447

The file is placed in the public `uucp` spool directory on the destination system.

Option: `-m`   Notify the sender upon successful delivery of the file.

Example: `uuto bugs kauai!gecko`

This command sends the `bugs` file to user `gecko` on the `kauai` system.

---

uupick **Retrieve a File Sent via *uuto***

Name	Options	Arguments
uupick	**[-s]**	***systemname***

Description: The `uupick` command retrieves files sent via the `uuto` command. When running, `uupick` provides a ? prompt. Respond to the ? with the commands listed in Table 15.2.

Option: `-s systemname`   Search only for files arriving from system `systemname`.

Example: `uupick`

This command checks for files sent by `uuto`.

The USENET Network and Netnews

The USENET communication network is an exciting glimpse into the future of computing. It is a loose network among the world's UNIX sites created for the public sharing of information and ideas. It is a kind of public bulletin board on which you can post a query or comment and then check later for responses. Or you simply can follow the publicly-posted interchanges of others. USENET has a broad scope. You can find articles (*news*) about programming languages, philosophy, jobs, computer games, physics, particular computers, such as IBM PCs and Macintoshes, politics, and sports—just to name a few topics. Over 1,000,000 users at approximately 40,000 UNIX sites use USENET. Thousands of new items are posted daily. To help manage this flow of information, contributions are organized by topic into over 500 separate *newsgroups*, so you can concentrate just on those areas that interest you. *Netnews* is the collection of programs that manages the flow of information through the USENET network.

USENET Organization

From this brief description, it may seem as if USENET would require a large centralized agency to manage the system. It doesn't. Instead, USENET is run on a cooperative, voluntary basis by the UNIX sites that use it. We can group sites into three categories: *leaf* sites, *intermediate* sites, and *backbone* sites. A leaf site communicates directly with just one other site, receiving news from that site and sending news to that site. An intermediate site communicates with several nearby sites, including a backbone site. A backbone site plays a more important role. Not only does it feed news to and collect news from other nearby intermediate and leaf sites, it also communicates with two or more other backbone sites to provide long-distance networking. See Figure 15.1.

Suppose, then, you post a news item at a leaf site. At some prescheduled time, your system will get in touch with another USENET member, probably an intermediate site. Typically, systems will use modems and phone lines to handle the actual transfer. News readers at the intermediate site then get to see your article. Meanwhile that site will communicate your item to other local leaf sites and intermediate sites, and readers at those sites will see your contribution. The intermediate site also will forward your news to a backbone site, which sends it on to other backbone sites. These sites will distribute your news item among local intermediate sites and on to other backbone sites. Thus, your news item gradually spreads though the network, eventually reaching leaf sites thousands of miles away.

The economic cost of USENET is low for leaf and intermediate sites, usually just the cost of the local phone calls used to transfer information. As a public service, the backbone sites (often universities and corporations) support the more costly long-distance communications as well the person-power to administer aspects of the news.

USENET and You

Unlike commercial bulletin boards such as Compuserve, Genie, and Prodigy, USENET does not enroll individuals. Instead, it enrolls entire UNIX sites. (However, if you happen to run UNIX or XENIX on your own personal computer, you can qualify as a UNIX site.) To join USENET, a UNIX site only needs to ask an existing USENET user to provide the free Netnews software package and to exchange news. Once that's done, every user at the new USENET site has access to the Netnews services.

The administrator for your site does control which news groups are forwarded to your system and for how long articles stay on file. After all, you don't want old news to fill all your system's available storage space.

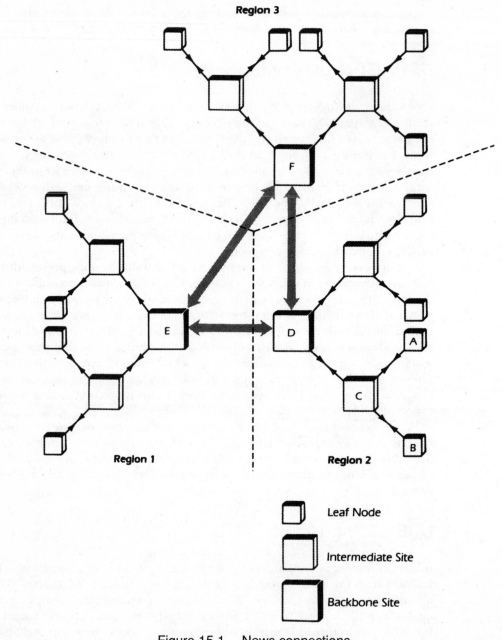

Figure 15.1.   News connections.

To access the USENET network, you use one or more of the programs that come with the Netnews software package. Typically, this package will include most or all of the programs from the following list:

- readnews   a basic program for reading news and replying

- rn   a more advanced program for reading news and replying

- nn   an advanced, menu-driven program for reading news and replying

- vnews   a screen-oriented program for reading news and replying

- postnews   a program for posting new articles

The various news-reading programs differ in their features and levels of sophistication, much as the various UNIX editors differ from each other. These programs are not an intrinsic part of UNIX. Instead, they have been developed by several UNIX users for their own use and as a public service. You won't find the Netnews software described in the standard UNIX documentation; that's one reason we'll describe some of them here. Also, if your UNIX system has installed Netnews, it most likely has added program descriptions to the UNIX on-line documentation. If that's the case, you can use the man command to study these programs.

We will concentrate on readnews, rn, and postnews. Before looking at how these programs work, let's examine how the newsgroups are organized.

Newsgroup Organization

To make the amount of information carried over USENET manageable, news articles are organized into various newsgroups. This process has produced over 500 newsgroups, so the newsgroups themselves have to grouped. USENET follows the UNIX-like approach of hierarchical organization, with broad interest areas subdivided into narrower subgroups, and these groups may be subdivided further. A newsgroup's name indicates its place in the USENET hierarchy, with periods in a name indicating group subdivisions. For instance, sci.math is the general math newsgroup, which is a subdivision of the science group. There also is a sci.math.stat group for those particularly interested in statistics. Table 15.3 shows the main topic areas for groups. None of these is a newsgroup itself, but each has numerous divisions and subdivisions that are newsgroups.

Table 15.3.   Topic areas.

Group Prefix	Topic
comp.	Computers
misc.	Miscellaneous
news.	USENET
rec.	Recreation, arts, and leisure
sci.	Science and technology
soc.	Society and social issues
talk.	Discussions, dissertations, and debates

Other prefixes may refer to geographical regions or to organizations. For example, the ca. prefix refers to California, so the ca.politics newsgroup would discuss California politics.

Table 15.4 lists a few representative newsgroups to give you a feeling of what's available.

Table 15.4.   Representative newsgroups.

Newsgroup	Topic
comp.ai	Artificial intelligence
comp.binaries.amiga	Binary-coded programs for the Amiga computer
comp.emacs	EMACS editors
comp.fonts	Font design, conversion, and use
comp.lang.c	The C programming language
comp.laser-printers	Laser printers, hardware and software
comp.society	The impact of technology on society
comp.society.women	Women's roles and problems in computing
comp.sources.games	Postings of recreational software
comp.sys.ibm.pc	IBM personal computers
comp.sys.mac.hardware	Macintosh hardware discussions
comp.unix	UNIX features and bugs

Newsgroup	Topic
comp.unix.questions	Group for UNIX newcomers
comp.unix.wizards	Advanced UNIX newsgroup
misc.consumers	Consumer interests and product reviews
misc.kids	Children
misc.wanted	Want ads
news.announce.important	General announcements
news.announce.newusers	Information for new users of Netnews
rec.arts.books	Books of all kinds
rec.arts.movies.reviews	Movie reviews
rec.audio	High-fidelity
rec.music.folk	Folk music
rec.sport.cricket	Discussion of the sport of cricket
sci.astro	Astronomy
sci.space	Space and space programs
soc.culture.french	French culture and history
soc.history	History
talk.philosophy.misc	General philosophical discussions
talk.rumors	Electronic backyard fence

News-Reading Programs and *.newsrc*

The various programs for reading the news share some common features. They let you browse through the news articles delivered to your site. They keep track of which items you have read so that when you start up a news-reading program, you are just exposed to new articles. They let you skip over articles and even entire newsgroups. They let you *unsubscribe* to individual newsgroups. When you unsubscribe to a group, a news-reading program will skip over that group automatically in the future. And they let you reply to articles you have read.

The news-reading programs use the .newsrc file as a tool for managing the news. The first time you run a news-reading program, it creates this file, which initially consists of a list of all the news groups delivered to your site. Each line looks something like this:

```
comp.ai: 1-124
```

Here, `comp.ai` is the newsgroup name, and the numbers represent the number of the articles you have not yet read. The Netnews software numbers each article for each newsgroup in the order in which they have arrived at your site, so the numbering at one site won't be the same as the numbering at the other site. This particular example indicates that you haven't read articles 1 through 124 in the artificial intelligence newsgroup. When you read news and when additional news arrives, the news-reading program updates the `.newsrc` file. So if you read some of the artificial intelligence items and some new contribution arrives overnight, the `.newsrc` entry might look like this:

```
comp.ai: 10-50,60-93,125-132
```

What happens if you unsubscribe to a newsgroup? It still remains listed in the `.newsrc` file, but with an exclamation point appended to the name. For instance, if you unsubscribed to the artificial intelligence newsgroup, the listing would look like this:

```
comp.ai! 10-50,60-93,125-132
```

The news-reading programs go through the newsgroups in the same order as which they are listed in `.newsrc`. You probably won't have to deal with the `.newsrc` file directly, but knowing about it will reassure you that the news-reading programs accomplish their tasks honestly, not by magic.

Now let's look at some of the news-reading programs.

The *readnews* Program

The `readnews` program is the most primitive and the most widely available news-reading program. To run the program, just type its name at the UNIX prompt:

```
$ readnews
```

If this is the first time you have used the program, it will take a while to construct your personal `.newsrc` file, which, by default, will be placed in your home directory. (Remember, to list a file name that begins with a period, you use the `ls` command with the `-a` option.) Eventually, the program will announce the first newsgroup and print a *header* describing the first item of net news to be offered to you:

```
$ readnews
- - - - - - - - - - - - - - - - - - - - - - - - - - - - - -
Newsgroup comp.sys.mac.hardware
- - - - - - - - - - - - - - - - - - - - - - - - - - - - - -
```

```
Article 128 of 154, Thu 14:28.
Subject: removal of honey from keyboard
From: pooh@unibear (Rudyard Pooh @ University of Bearkly)
(8 lines) More? [ynq]
```

readnews Basics

The part between the parallel lines of hyphens tells you that you are reading the `comp.sys.mac.hardware` newsgroup. The first article offered for your pleasure is number 128 of 154. (The previous 127 articles have either been read by you previously or have already been purged from the system.) A `Subject` line, much as in `mail`, summarizes the topic for this particular article. The `From` line identifies the sender by login name and UNIX site network name as well as by the sender's regular name and site name. The next line informs you that this article consists of 8 lines and asks what you want to do. A `y` response means, yes, you want to read the item. An `n` response means no, you do not want to read the item but you want to see the next header. And a `q` response means you want to quit the `readnews` program.

Suppose you respond by typing `y` and pressing the return key. Then the program displays the contents of the article on screen:

```
------------------------------
Newsgroup comp.sys.mac.hardware
------------------------------

Article 128 of 154, Thu 14:28.
Subject: removal of honey from keyboard
From: pooh@unibear (Rudyard Pooh @ University of Bearkly)
(8 lines) More? [ynq]y


   Someone I work with (not me!)spilled some honey into a Mac Plus
keyboard,which has stopped working. He tried cleaning it with
vinegar, but that did not work. Can anyone suggest a better
method or solvent?
   --

Rudyard Pooh   University of Bearkly Geological Survey
pooh@unibear.isgs.edu

Article 129 of 154, Thu 14:29.
Subject: Sounds, System 7, Mac IIfx
From: blegh@arts.uchicane.edu (Cecily Blegh @ University of
Chicane)
```

```
Newsgroups: comp.sys.mac.hardware,comp.sys.mac.system
(33 lines) More? [ynq]
```

If the article is too long to fit on the screen, the program will display the beginning of the article followed by the prompt

```
--More--
```

at the bottom of the screen. In this case, just press the Space Bar to continue with the article.

When readnews finishes displaying an article, it displays the header for the next article. The example above shows an optional Newsgroups line that appears for articles posted in more than one news group. This article, for example, relates both to the Macintosh hardware and the Macintosh operating system, so the author posted it to both comp.sys.mac.hardware and comp.sys.mac.system.

At this point, readnews once again offers you the [ynq] choice. Again, you would enter y to read the article, n to skip to the next article, or q to quit readnews. However, these are not your only options. For instance, you can enter N (uppercase *n*) to skip to the next newsgroup instead of to the next article in the current newsgroup. (Entering n after the last article of a newsgroup also takes you to the next newsgroup.) Let's try the N response:

```
Article 129 of 154, Thu 14:29.
Subject: Sounds, System 7, Mac IIfx
From: blehg@arts.uchicane.edu (Cecily Blegh @ University of
Chicane)
Newsgroups: comp.sys.mac.hardware,comp.sys.mac.system
(33 lines) More? [ynq]N
-----------------------------
Newsgroup comp.sys.mac.announce
-----------------------------

Article 61 of 67, Jun  1 00:33.
Subject: About Macintosh Usenet Groups
Summary: General Introduction.  Last 'real' change October 1.
From: geoff@pmafire.inel.gov (Geoff Allen @ WINCO)
(253 lines) More? [ynq]
```

This displays the banner for the next newsgroup and the heading for the first article in the group. Thus, responding with y or n lets you step through the news, article by article, either reading or skipping each article. Responding with N lets you step through the news, newsgroup by newsgroup. If you want to terminate reading a long article, type Ctrl-C, and if you want to terminate readmail, type q when the [ynq] prompt appears.

More *readnews* Commands

If you find you have no interest in a particular newsgroup (and with hundreds of newsgroups to choose from, you can be selective), you can use the *unsubscribe* feature to cause readnews to skip over that newsgroup automatically in the future. Simply type U in response to the [ynq] prompt when in that newsgroup. If, at some later time, you decide to resubscribe, use a UNIX editor to find the corresponding line in the .newsrc file and replace the exclamation point with a colon. That, is to resubscribe to the artificial intelligence newsgroup, find the line

```
comp.ai! 10-50,60-93,125-132
```

and change to:

```
comp.ai: 10-50,60-93,125-132
```

Suppose you want to reread an article. Can you back up? Yes. just type p at the [ynq] prompt to go back to the previous article. An uppercase P will take you back to the previous newsgroup.

To see a list of unread articles, enter an l at the [ynq] prompt. Entering an L lists all articles, including ones you have read. If you decide you are interested in article number 786, type 786, and readnews takes you to the corresponding article. If, upon reading the list, you decide you are not interested in them, you can enter a K. This marks the rest of the articles in the current news group as having been read. That means they won't be served up to you the next time you read the news.

If you think you have made a mistake, such as realizing you have just entered K when there really is an article you wanted to read, you can exit readnews with an x command instead of the q command. The x command terminates the news without updating the .newsrc file, meaning you can now restart readnews without having removed articles from your reading list.

Using *readnews* to Save an Article

If you find an article you would like to save, enter s at the [ynq] prompt. This saves the article whose heading appears above the prompt. If you have just read an article, you will be looking at the heading for the *next* article, so make sure you save the article you really want. You can first type p to take you back to the heading for the article you just read. More simply, you can enter s-, which means "save the preceding article." For instance, the following example saves Article 128, but entering s instead of s- would have saved Article 129.

```
- - - - - - - - - - - - - - - - - - - - - - - - - - - - - -
Newsgroup comp.sys.mac.hardware
- - - - - - - - - - - - - - - - - - - - - - - - - - - - - -


Article 128 of 154, Thu 14:28.
Subject: removal of honey from keyboard
From: pooh@unibear (Rudyard Pooh @ University of Bearkly)
(8 lines) More? [ynq]y


   Someone I work with (not me!)spilled some honey into a Mac Plus
keyboard,which has stopped working. He tried cleaning it with
vinegar, but that did not work. Can anyone suggest a better
method or solvent?
- -


Rudyard Pooh    University of Bearkly Geological Survey
pooh@unibear.isgs.edu

Article 129 of 154, Thu 14:29.
Subject: Sounds, System 7, Mac IIfx
From: blehg@arts.uchicane.edu (Cecily Blegh @ University of
Chicane)
Newsgroups: comp.sys.mac.hardware,comp.sys.mac.system
(33 lines) More? [ynq]s-                   ← Saves Article 128
```

Where does the saved article go? It goes into a file called `Articles` in your home
directory. Other files you save will be appended to the `Articles` file. Incidentally, the
articles are saved in a mailbox format so that you can use the `mail` program to peruse
them. Just use the `-f` option to cause `mail` to use `Articles` instead of your regular
mailbox:

```
mail -f Articles
```

Then `mail` will use the article headings just like mail headings so you can scan
through the subject headings and select which items to read.

If you prefer, you can supply your own choice of file name for saving articles.
The following example, for instance, saves Article 128 in a file called `honey`.

```
- - - - - - - - - - - - - - - - - - - - - - - - - - - - - -
Newsgroup comp.sys.mac.hardware
- - - - - - - - - - - - - - - - - - - - - - - - - - - - - -


Article 128 of 154, Thu 14:28.
Subject: removal of honey from keyboard
From: pooh@unibear (Rudyard Pooh @ University of Bearkly)
(8 lines) More? [ynq]s honey
```

Using *readnews* to Reply Via USENET

At some point you may wish to reply to something you have read. The `readnews` program gives you the opportunity to reply via public news or via private `email`. To reply via public news, use the `f` (for *follow-up*) command. For example, suppose you have ideas about cleaning honey from a keyboard. You would enter `f` at the prompt for that article (or `f·` at the prompt for the following article:

```
Article 128 of 154, Thu 14:28.
Subject: removal of honey from keyboard
From: pooh@unibear (Rudyard Pooh @ University of Bearkly)
(8 lines) More? [ynq]f
```

The `readnews` program prompts you to enter a short summary of what you will be saying:

```
Please enter a short summary of your contribution to the
discussion
Just one or two lines ...   (end with a blank line)
>        boiling water
>
```

Most often, readers enter a blank line immediately to skip the summary.

Then the program will ask if you want to include a copy of the original article in your reply. Often, it's a good idea in order to provide the context for your answer, because many readers may see your answer without having seen the original article. However, you should edit down the quoted material so you do not waste space. To help you do that, `readnews` starts up one of the UNIX editors (which editor it uses depends on your implementation) with the copied text included. The copied lines are prefixed with a > symbol for identification. Here's an example that uses the `vi` editor:

```
Do you want to include a copy of the article? y
OK, but please edit it to suppress unnecessary verbiage,
signatures, etc.
"/tmp/post020688" 31/1849
Subject: Re: removal of honey from keyboard
Newsgroups: comp.sys.mac
Summary: ignore if sent by mistake
References: <72830@unibear.UUCP>

In article <72830@unibear.UUCP>, pooh@unibear (Rudyard Pooh @
University of Bearkly)) writes:
> Someone I work with (not me!)spilled some honey into a Mac
>Plus keyboard, which has stopped working. He tried cleaning
>it with vinegar, but that did not work. Can anyone suggest a
```

```
>better method or solvent?
--

>Rudyard Pooh    University of Bearkly Geological Survey
>pooh@unibear.isgs.edu
```

Note that `readnews` establishes a new `Subject` line for your response by adding a `Re:` prefix to the original. Then it adds a summary line consisting of the optional summary you just typed. Also, if you quote the original article, `readnews` adds a little introduction explaining that fact. At this point, you can use the editor to edit the quoted text and to add your own thoughts. When you are done, exit the editor in the normal fashion:

```
Boiling water works wonders with honey, but I'm not sure
about its effect upon keyboards.
:wq
```

Next, `readnews` prompts you for your next action. To send the article, enter `s`:

```
What now?  [send, edit, list, quit, write, append] s
Posting article...
Article posted successfully.
(8 lines) More? [ynq]
```

You are placed back in the normal `readnews` mode, ready to move on to the next article. Meanwhile, your article has been posted under your login name. The next time your site communicates with another USENET site, your message will be sent on its way.

Net Etiquette

Before replying to other articles or posting your own, you should learn about net etiquette, sometimes termed *netiquette*. This concerns matters such as when you should publicly post answers and when you should use email, what is considered abuse of the system, how to indicate you are saying something with a smile on your face, and so on. The most accessible resource for netiquette is the `news.announce.newusers` newsgroup, which contains a couple of articles on the topic along with other useful articles for new users.

Using *readnews* to Reply Via Electronic Mail

To reply by private `email` instead of by public news, respond to the `[ynq]` prompt with `r` (for *r*eply) instead of with `f`. The `r` command puts you in an editor and creates a heading for you:

```
----------------
Newsgroup forsale
----------------


Article 2 of 2, Thu 19:31.
Subject: Giants Tickets For Sale
From: michael@unicom.UUCP (Michael Lindbeck @ Science Computer
Center, College )
Newsgroups: ba.sports,ba.market,forsale
(61 lines) More? [ynq] r
"/tmp/fol026138" 5/126
To: pacbell!ucbvax!unicom.UUCP!michael
Subject: Re: Giants Tickets For Sale
News-Path: michael
References: <286@unicom.UUCP>
```

The poster's From address becomes your To address. You then type your reply and exit the editor. When you do, readnews sends your response and brings you back to its usual mode:

```
I'd like the tickets for July 23.
:wq
Sending reply.
Article 2 of 2, Thu 19:31.
Subject: Giants Tickets For Sale
From: michael@unicom.UUCP (Michael Lindbeck @ Science Computer
Center, College )
Newsgroups: ba.sports,ba.market,forsale
(61 lines) More? [ynq]
```

Learning More About *readnews*

Because USENET is not part of standard UNIX, you won't find it discussed in the usual printed documentation. However, if readnews has been installed on your system, you most likely can read about readnews in the on-line documentation. Just type the following at the UNIX prompt:

```
$ man readnews
```

For a short, concise summary of readnews commands, you can type ? at the readnews prompt.

Table 15.5 summarizes the commands we have discussed.

Table 15.5. **Summary of common *readnews* commands.**

Command	Meaning
y	Yes. (Or just press Return.) Display this article and go on to next article.
n	No. Go on to next article without displaying the current one.
q	Quit. Update .newsrc.
U	Unsubscribe. You won't be shown this newsgroup anymore.
r	Reply. Reply to article's author via mail.
f [*title*]	Submit a follow up article.
N [*newsgroup*]	Go to next newsgroup or named newsgroup.
s [*file*]	Save. Article is appended to file (default is Articles).
-	Go back to last article.
p	Back up to the previous article.
P	Back up to the previous newsgroup.
K	Mark the rest of the articles in current group as read.
x	Exit. Do not update .newsrc.
l	List unread articles in newsgroup.
L	List all articles in newsgroup.
num	Go to article number *num* (*num* is an integer).
f-, r-, and s-	Refer to the previous article.

The *rn* Command

The readnews program served well when the volume of news was smaller, but the burgeoning flow of news made a more powerful program like rn desirable. The rn program adds the following capabilities to readnews:

- Presents news in a more hierarchical fashion—news level, article level, and pager level (moving within an article).

- Makes it easier to follow the discussion of a particular topic (a *thread*) through the news.

- Allows you to use grep-like regular expression patterns to search through news for particular topics.

Actually, rn provides many features beyond these, but we will just cover basic usage.

Starting Out with *rn*—the Newsgroup Level

Let's look at a sample run. To start the rn program, enter rn at the UNIX prompt. If you do not have a .newsrc file, rn will begin by setting up one for you in your home directory and then offering you some helpful advice:

```
$ rn
Trying to set up a .newsrc file--running newsetup...

Creating .newsrc in /home/brainful to be used by news programs.
Done.

If you have never used the news system before, you may find the
articles
in mod.announce.newuser to be helpful. There is also a manual
entry for rn.

To get rid of newsgroups you aren't interested in, use the 'u'
command.
Type h for help at any time while running rn.
```

Next, it lists the names of the first few newsgroups, indicates the number of articles in each group, and asks you what you wish to do about the first group in the list:

```
Unread news in comp110              12 articles
Unread news in forsale               4 articles
Unread news in general              16 articles
Unread news in jobs                  1 article
Unread news in localnews            24 articles
etc.

********    1 unread article  in comp110--read now? [ynq]
```

At this point, you are in the newsgroup level of rn. If you reply to the prompt with n, rn then inquires about your intentions for the next group. Thus, by repeatedly pressing n, you can step through groups without examining the articles in them. One thing you will notice immediately is that the program responds as soon as you type a y, n, or q. Unlike the case for readnews, you do not have to press the Return key to send the command.

Before going on to reading articles, let's mention a few more commands you can type at the newsgroup level. The q command will terminate rn, returning you to the UNIX shell. The p command will take you to the nearest preceding newsgroup with unread news, and the P command will take you to the preceding newsgroup, even if it has been read. The u command will unsubscribe you from the current newsgroup. To subscribe or resubscribe to a newsgroup, use the g command followed by the newsgroup name. For instance, to subscribe to the ba.test newsgroup, give this command:

```
g ba.test
```

This takes you to the indicated newsgroup and, if you are not already subscribed to the group, gives you the option to join:

```
Newsgroup ba.test is currently unsubscribed to--resubscribe? [yn]
```

If you reply by pressing y, rn resubscribes you to the group and modifies your .newsrc file to reflect ba.test's new status.

Starting Out with *rn*—the Article Level

To read articles in a newsgroup, respond to the newsgroup-level prompt with y, and rn will take you to the first available article in that newgroup:

```
*******   1 unread article  in comp.sys.mac--read now? [ynq]y
Article 39667 (236 more) in comp.sys.mac:
From: storm@unix.cis.pag.edu (Roger Richards)
Newsgroups: comp.sys.mac.misc,comp.sys.mac
Subject: system7:Let's get this straight
Keywords: system 7, 7.0
Message-ID: <133928@unix.cis.pitt.edu>
Date: 30 May 91 18:22:19 GMT
Organization: Univ. of Pagfoot, Computing & Information Services
Lines: 21 `


--MORE--(24%)
```

Now that you have the article heading before you, you can read it or skip to the next article. To read it, press the y key or the Space Bar. To skip the article, press n.

```
System 7 is newer than System 6 or 5. The relevant clue is that 7
comes after 5 and 6 numerically. Also, refer to the
famous paper on this subject by...

Rog.
End of article 39667 (of 39673)--what next? [npq]
```

At this point, rn suggests three choices. The n choice means go to the next article, the p choice means return to the previous article (the one you just read), and q means to quit the article level and return to the newsgroup level. By pressing n repeatedly, you will step through all the articles in the newsgroup. Each time a new header is displayed, you can choose to read the article (press y) or move on to the next article (press n). Each time you finish reading an article, you can go on to the next (n), return to the preceding article (p), or return to the newsgroup level (p). Actually, you have several other choices, but those are the ones that rn prompts you.

Starting Out with *rn*—the Pager Level

If an article is a long one, rn uses a subprogram called a *pager* to step through the article a screenful at a time. The pager works much like more (Chapter 4), meaning that pressing the Space Bar advances a screen page at a time, while pressing Return advances a line at a time. Also, you can use the g command to search forward and backward through an article for key phrases. And you can use b or Ctrl-b to back up a screenful. When the pager is working, it displays the

```
--MORE--(24%)
```

prompt at the bottom of the page—the percent indicates the fraction of the article that has been read.

Listing Articles

One very handy command, which works at any of the three levels, is the = command, which lists articles in the current newsgroup:

```
*******  20 unread articles in news.announce.newusers--read now?
[ynq] =
  402 Introduction to news.announce
  403 Rules for posting to Usenet
  404 A Primer on How to Work With the Usenet Community
  405 Answers to Frequently Asked Questions
  406 Emily Postnews Answers Your Questions on Netiquette
  407 What is Usenet?
  408 Hints on writing style for Usenet
  409 USENET Software: History and Sources
  410 List of Active Newsgroups
  411 Alternative Newsgroup Hierarchies
  412 Regional Newsgroup Hierarchies
  413 Publicly Accessible Mailing Lists, Part I
  414 List of Moderators
```

```
What next? [npq]
```

If you want to read article 405, type 405. (When typing numbers, you have to press the Return key.) Incidentally, if you are new to the USENET, you should read, and perhaps save, the articles in the news.announce.newusers group.

Saving Articles

To save an article, you can type s followed by a file name at the pager level or article level. Then rn saves the article in a file by that name. Unlike readnews, which, by default, places articles in your home directory, rn places articles in a News subdirectory—rn automatically creates this subdirectory in your home directory. (If you do not provide a file name, rn creates a file named after the current newsgroup.)

Suppose, for example, you decide to read article 405. First, you respond to the prompt with that article number:

```
What next? [npq] 405


Article 405 (19 more) in news.announce.newusers (moderated):
From: spaf@cs.purdue.EDU (Gene Spafford)
Subject: Answers to Frequently Asked Questions
Message-ID: <14694@ector.cs.purdue.edu>
Date: 21 May 91 04:49:12 GMT
Organization: Dept. of Computer Sciences, Purdue Univ.
Lines: 659
Supersedes:
/home/spool/news/news/announce/newusers/702:<13122@medusa.cs.purd
ue.edu>


--MORE--(1%)
```

It's a long article, and when you finish, you think you want to save it. So you type s and a filename:

```
End of article 405 (of 421)--what next? [npq] s newsquestions

File /home/nero/News/newsquestions doesn't exist--
        use mailbox format? [ynq] y
Saved to mailbox /home/nero/News/newsquestions
End of article 405 (of 421)--what next? [npq]
```

Here rn asks if you want to use the mailbox format. This format let's you use the mail program to read the file, so it's convenient to reply with a y, as in the example. Note that the new file is placed in the News subdirectory. When rn finishes with that task, it asks you what to do next. Again, you can continue reading articles or return to the newsgroup level.

Suppose you list the articles in a newsgroup, read a few, and want to dispose of the rest of the articles without reading them. Then you can type the c command. This marks the rest of the articles in the newsgroup as having been read so you won't be exposed to them again. You can give the c command at the pager level, article level, or newsgroup level. The rn program then will ask you to verify your decision, which you can do by typing a y.

The Space Bar

The Space Bar is a handy key. Pressing it in the pager level advances you to the next page. Pressing it when you have a prompt such as

```
what next? [npq]
```

means take the first choice listed in the brackets. These choices change depending upon the level, and, as you will soon see, past history. Usually the first choice is the one most commonly selected, so you will often find that pressing the Space Bar is the quickest way to the next action you want.

Following a Thread

Now let's look at how to follow a thread, that is, a series of articles on a particular subject. The key to doing this is the Ctrl-n key. This causes rn to search through the current newsgroup for the next article having the same topic as the current one. The rn program uses the Subject line to tell if the topic is the same. For instance, suppose you use = to list the articles in a particular group and notice a running discussion on a topic that interests you. Start by noting the number of the first article on the topic and type in that number:

```
What next? [npq] 7884
```

```
Article 7824 (58 more) in talk.icecream:
From: doveman@esvax.hamavnet.com
Newsgroups: talk.icecream
Subject: Is ice cream fattening?
Message-ID: <1991Jun14.172004.55@itvax.eggnet.com>
Date: 15 Jun 91 00:20:04 GMT
Organization: Eggnet Computer - ICE Group; Culver City, CA
Lines: 5

Hello,
         Some one told me that ice cream is fattening. Could this
possibly be true?
-- Elmer
End of article 7824 (of 7903)--what next? [npq]
```

To follow responses to this article, press Ctrl-n and rn **will then seek the next** Subject **line with the same topic:**

```
End of article 7884 (of 7903)--what next? [npq]<Ctrl-n>
Searching...

Article 7891 (57 more) in talk.icecream:
From: jan@uyumi.ir.uyumi.edu
(SAME) Subject: Re: Is ice cream fattening?
Message-ID: <1991Jun15.195908.10647@uyumi.ir.uyumi.edu>
Date: 15 Jun 91 23:59:08 GMT
References: <1991Jun14.172004.55@itvax.eggnet.com>
Organization: Univ of Yumi
Lines: 13

In article <1991Jun14.172004.55@itvax.eggnet.com>,
doveman@itvax.eggnet.com
 writes:
>Hello,
>        Some one told me that ice cream is fattening. Could
>this possibly be true?
>-- Elmer
A cup of ice cream might contain 250-350 Calories, much of them
coming from fat. However, I believe ice cream is fattening ONLY
if you eat it.

Janice Kriem
End of article 7891 (of 7903)--what next? [^Nnpq]
```

Note that rn noticed that we were following a thread, so it altered the prompt to make Ctrl-n (^N) the first choice. That means you can continue following a thread simply by pressing the Space Bar, because it always selects the first choice:

```
End of article 7900 (of 7903)--what next? [^Nnpq]<Space Bar>

Searching...

Article 7901 (56 more) in talk.icecream:
From: anne@cs.adelaine.ice (Anne Kneck-Dotal)
(SAME) Subject: Re: Is ice cream fattening?
Message-ID: <3674@cs.adelaine.ice>
Date: 16 Jun 91 16:34:31 GMT
References: <1991Jun14.172004.55@itvax.eggnet.com>
Organization: The University of Adelaine Consortium
Lines: 13

In article <1991Jun14.172004.55@itvax.eggnet.com>
doveman@itvax.eggnet.com
writes:

>       Some one told me that ice cream is fattening. Could
>this possibly be true?

I have an uncle who is 92, who has eaten at least a pint of ice
cream every day of his adult life, and he's not fat.
Hope this helps,

    Anne.
End of article 7901 (of 7903)--what next? [^Nnpq]
```

Once again, all you have to do to pursue the thread is to press the Space Bar. If there are no more articles in that thread, rn takes you to the earliest unread article in the news group.

You may have noticed what appears to be an inconsistency, namely that the last article purports to be 7901 of 7903, yet rn states that there are 56 more articles. That's because this example, in selecting articles about a particular topic, has skipped over other articles in the newsgroup, and the total of 56 includes all the unread articles.

Marking Articles as Read and Unread

When you read an article, rn marks it as read. This means that when you quit rn, it updates your .newsrc file so that the marked article no longer shows up when you read the mail. Even before rn quits, once you read an article, it no longer will show up in an article list when you enter the = command.

Suppose you are part of the way through an article and decide you have read enough of it. As noted earlier, you can type the n command to skip the rest of the article and go to the next one. This act automatically marks the article as read, even though you have only read part of it. But if you want to leave it on the reading list for a later time, you can enter m instead of n. This marks the current article as unread.

Suppose you have scanned through a list of 120 articles and read the 18 that interest you. How can you mark the rest as read? The slow way is to use n to skip through the rest of the article headings one by one. The fast way is to use c to mark all the articles in the current newsgroup as having been read. When you do so, rn will ask you to verify your intent:

```
Do you really want to mark everything as read? [yn]
```

Press y or the Space Bar to confirm your choice.

Searching in *rn*

You can search on three levels in rn. On the newsgroup level, you can search newsgroups for names matching a given pattern. On the article level, you can search for Subject lines containing a given pattern. And on the pager level, you can search for particular patterns in an article. For the first two levels, you press the / key to initiate a forward search and you press the ? key to initiate a backwards search. You use the g key to initiate a search at the pager level.

Let's start at the newsgroup level. Suppose you want to jump ahead to a newsgroup that discusses games. Then, at the newsgroup level prompt, you can respond with /games. This means search forward for the first subscribed newsgroup containing games in its name:

```
*******   5 unread articles in comp.sys.mac--read now? [ynq]
/games
Searching...
*******   12 unread articles in comp.sys.mac.games--read now?
[ynq]
```

Typing ?games instead of /games would have caused rn to search through previous groups containing games in the newsgroup name.

Now let's consider the article level. Suppose you recall from a recent = command that there is an article about cheese but that you forgot to jot down the article number. You can use the /cheese command to search for the next unread article containing cheese in the Subject line:

```
End of article 2864 (of 2916)--what next? [npq] /cheese
Searching...
```

```
...2900
Article 2903 (20 more) in misc.consumers:
From: fawg6844@uxa.csu(Fanny Waginski)
Subject: Best cheeses for fondu
Message-ID: <1991Jun14.235258.29126@uxa.csu>
Date: 14 Jun 91 23:52:58 GMT
Organization: Universal Xenophilic Auxiliaries
Lines: 21
--More--
```

You can use the Ctrl-n key to follow the thread, if any.

Similarly, you can use ?cheese to search through unread articles preceding the current one.

Within an article, you can use g *pattern* to search ahead within the article for a particular pattern.

More generally, with all levels the search word can be a grep-style pattern. For example, if you don't recall if the word you wish is cheese or Cheese, you can use /[cC]heese or /.heese or /*heese. As with grep, the /.heese pattern matches any six-letter pattern ending with heese, such as pheese and sheese, while *heese matches any pattern ending in heese, include sucheese and plain heese. You can read more about such patterns, called regular expressions, in the discussion of grep in Chapter 14.

Replying to an Article

As does readnews, rn lets you respond to an article either by email to the author or by a follow-up article on the netnews. To reply by mail, use the r command at the article or pager level. To post a response by news, use the f command at the article or pager level. Either method places you in an editor to compose your response. The f command gives you the option of including the original article. When you finish, each command gives you the option of sending or aborting your response.

Summary of Common *rn* Commands

The rn program has many more capabilities than those described here, but the ones we have described provide the basic tools you need. Table 15.6 summarizes some of the more common rn commands. Note that some commands behave the same on all levels but that others do not.

Table 15.6. Common *rn* commands.

COMMAND	Newsgroup Level	Article Level	Pager Level
n	go to next newsgroup	display to next article	go to next article
y	go to first article in newsgroup	N. A.	go to next page
q	quit rn	go to Newsgroup level	go to end of article
=	list unread articles in the current group		
p	go to previous newsgroup with unread news	go to previous unread article	
P	go to previous newsgroup whether or not it contains unread news	go to previous article, unread or not	
num	go to article number *num* in the current newsgroup		
u	unsubscribe to the current newsgroup		
g *groupname* g *pattern*	go to newsgroup *groupname* with the option of resubscribing		search forward for the next line containing *pattern* in it
c	mark all articles in the current newsgroup as read		
s *filename*		save the current article to the *filename* file in the *News* subdirectory of your home directory	
[spacebar]	choose the first selection in a list of choices provided in a prompt		go forward one screen page
^N		proceed to the next article on the same subject	
m	move newsgroup (not discussed)	mark the current article as unread	
/*pattern*	search forward for the next subscribed newsgroup containing *pattern* in its name	search forward for the next unread article containing *pattern* in its *Subject* line	

?pattern	search backwards for the next subscribed newsgroup containing *pattern* in its name	search backwards for the next unread article containing *pattern* in its *Subject* line	
r		reply to an article by email	
f		reply to an article by posting an article	

Posting News with *postnews*

As you have seen, you can use the various news-reading programs to post replies to articles. The postnews program lets you originate articles. Since you probably don't want to appear as a fool to hundreds of thousands of USENET readers, you should practice using this program by posting mail to a test newsgroup specifically created for letting users practice their netnews skills.

To post an article, first enter postnews after the UNIX prompt. The program begins by asking if you are responding to another message. Type n to indicate no— this implies that you intend to create a new article:

```
$ postnews
Is this message in response to some other message? n
```

Next, the program asks you to complete a Subject line and an optional Keywords line for the article header:

```
Subject: Testing the postnews program
Keywords: Test
```

Then postnews asks you to list the newsgroup or groups that you wish to post:

```
Newsgroups (enter one at a time, end with a blank line):

The most relevant newsgroup should be the first, you should
add others only if your article really MUST be read by people
who choose not to read the appropriate group for your article.
But DO use multiple newsgroups rather than posting many times.

For a list of newsgroups, type ?> ba.test
>
```

For testing, you should choose a test group with local scope. For example, the ba.test group restricts distribution of its articles to the San Francisco Bay Area. Note that postnews enables you to post an article to more than one newsgroup. This is called *cross-posting*. As the postnews directions suggest, you should apply restraint when using this feature. The articles in the news.announce.newusers give advice on this topic.

After you finish listing the newsgroups, postnews starts up whichever editor your system uses (vi for the following example) and places a header at the beginning. Then you can enter your article:

```
"/tmp/post005777" 5/84
Subject: Testing the postnews program
Newsgroups: ba.test
Keywords: Test


This is a test. If this were an emergency, this article
would contain something of stupendous brilliance.
~
~
~
~
~
~
~
:wq
```

After you exit the editor, postnews gives you several options:

```
What now? [send, edit, list, quit, write, append] s
2 >>
```

The send choice posts your article to the netnews, the edit choice puts you back in the editor, the list choice displays your article for your inspection, the quit choice aborts your message and exits postnews, the write selection lets you save your article in a file, and the append choice lets you append your article to a file. These last two choices let you keep a record of what you have posted.

Summary

As you can see, UNIX networking is a rich field. With rlogin and rcp you can log onto a connected remote system and transfer files between it and your local sysem. With cu, you can call up a remote system, log onto it, and transfer files between it and your local system. With uucp, uuto, and uupick, you can transfer files between your system and other systems without logging on to the other systems and without even having accounts on them. And the Netnews software connects you to a worldwide network of computer users.

Review Questions

1. Suppose a user has login name jill on the unifox system and the login name hill on the well system. If these two systems were connected, how would she log onto her well account from her unifox account? How can she transfer the foibles file from her well account to her unifox account?

2. Suppose user jill on the unifox system has an account under the login name jill on the unifoo system, which has a phone number of 555-5555. Assuming both systems have modems, how can she log onto the unifoo system? How can she transfer the fables file from her unifoo account to her unifox account?

3. Suppose jill's unifox system can access the unicom system via uucp. How can she transfer the feeble file from her home directory to the jack sub-directory of the unicom public uucp directory?

4. What happens the first time you run a news-reading program such as readnews or rn?

5. What is a newsgroup?

6. How do you move from one news group to the next in readnews and in rn?

7. How do you move from one article within a particular newsgroup to the next article in readnews and in rn?

8. What does it mean to unsubscribe to a newsgroup and how do you do so in readnews and in rn?

9. What are the three levels of rn?

10. How do you save a news item in readnews and in rn?

11. How do you reply to a news article via email in readnews and in rn?

12. How do you reply to a news article via the news in readnews and in rn?

Answers

1. She could use `rlogin` as follows:

```
$ rlogin -l hill well
Welcome to the Well!
$
```

This assumes that her home directory on the `well` system has a `.rhosts` file containing the following line:

```
unifox jill
```

Otherwise, she would be asked for her password.

To transfer a file, she does not need to login to the `well`. She can use the `rcp` command:

```
$ rcp hill@well:foible .
```

Here the period is the usual UNIX abbreviation for the current working directory. If her login name on both systems were the same, she could omit the `hill@` part.

2. She could use the `cu` command as follows:

```
$ cu unifoo
Connected
login: jill
password:
Welcome to unifoo
$
```

While logged in, she could use the `cu ~%take` escape sequence to copy the file:

```
$ ~%take fable
```

3. She can do the following:

```
$ uucp feeble unicom!~/jack/
```

4. It sets up the `.newsrc` file, which keeps track of the articles you've read and of the news groups to which you've subscribed.

5. The various articles transmitted over the net news are organized into newsgroups. Each newsgroup is devoted to a particular subject matter indicated by the group name. For instance, `sci.astro` would be devoted to topics related to astronomy.

6. In readnews you type N to go to the next news group. In rn, you go to the newsgroup level, then type n.

7. In readnews you type n to go to the next news group. In rn, you go to the article level, then type n.

8. If you unsubscribe to a newsgroup, the news-reading programs won't list that group when you read the news. In readnews, type U to unsubscribe, and in rn type u.

9. The first level is the newsgroup level. Here commands typically move you from one group to another. The second level is the article level. Here commands typically move you from one article to another in the same group. The third level is the pager level. Here commands typically move you from one location within an article to another location in the same article.

10. Use the s command. If, in readnews, you've already moved on to the next article, use s- to save the previous article. Normally, for both rn and readnews, you should follow the s command with the filename you wish to use for the saved material.

11. With either program, enter r to reply via email. In rn you should be at the pager level or article level.

12. With either program, enter f to reply via the news. In rn you should be at the pager level or article level.

Exercises at the Terminal

1. Check your system's /etc/rhosts file to see what systems, if any, are open to the rlogin command.

2. If you are in a position to do so, try the rlogin command.

3. If you are in a position to do so, try the cu command.

4. Give the uuname command to see what systems, if any, your system has uucp relations with.

5. Use readnews to read the network news.

6. Delete the .newsrc file created by readnews, then try rn for reading the news.

7. Once you've decided which newsreader you prefer, unsubscribe from those newsgroups that don't interest you; this will make news reading much more manageable.

A

A Quick Index to Commands

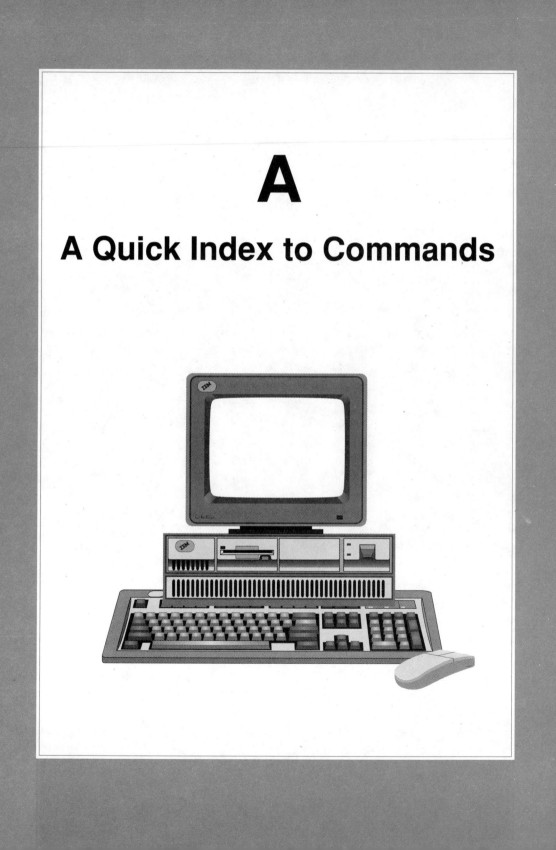

Appendix A

A Quick Index to Commands

Command		Page

B

ASCII Table

Appendix B

ASCII Table

Numerical Conversion

Decimal-Hexadecimal-Octal-Binary-ASCII Numerical Conversions

DEX X_{10}	HEX X_{16}	OCT X_8	Binary P X_2	ASCII	Key
0	00	00	0 000 0000	NUL	CTRL/1
1	01	01	1 000 0001	SOH	CTRL/A
2	02	02	1 000 0010	STX	CTRL/B
3	03	03	0 000 0011	ETX	CTRL/C
4	04	04	1 000 0100	EOT	CTRL/D
5	05	05	0 000 0101	ENQ	CTRL/E
6	06	06	0 000 0110	ACK	CTRL/F
7	07	07	1 000 0111	BEL	CTRL/G
8	08	10	1 000 1000	BS	CTRL/H, BACKSPACE
9	09	11	0 000 1001	HT	CTRL/I, TAB
10	0A	12	0 000 1010	LF	CTRL/J, LINE FEED
11	0B	13	1 000 1011	VT	CTRL/K
12	0C	14	0 000 1100	FF	CTRL/L
13	0D	15	1 000 1101	CR	CTRL/M, RETURN
14	0E	16	1 000 1110	SO	CTRL/N

DEX X_{10}	HEX X_{16}	OCT X_8	Binary P X_2	ASCII	Key
15	0F	17	0 000 1111	SI	CTRL/O
16	10	20	1 001 0000	DLE	CTRL/P
17	11	21	0 001 0001	DC1	CTRL/Q
18	12	22	0 001 0010	DC2	CTRL/R
19	13	23	1 001 0011	DC3	CTRL/S
20	14	24	0 001 0100	DC4	CTRL/T
21	15	25	1 001 0101	NAK	CTRL/U
22	16	26	1 001 0110	SYN	CTRL/V
23	17	27	0 001 0111	ETB	CTRL/W
24	18	30	0 001 1000	CAN	CTRL/X
25	19	31	1 001 1001	EM	CTRL/Y
26	1A	32	1 001 1010	SUB	CTRL/Z
27	1B	33	0 001 1011	ESC	ESC, ESCAPE
28	1C	34	1 001 1100	FS	CTRL<
29	1D	35	0 001 1101	GS	CTRL/
30	1E	36	0 001 1110	RS	CTRL/=
31	1F	37	1 001 1111	US	CTRL/-
32	20	40	1 010 0000	SP	SPACEBAR
33	21	41	0 010 0001	!	!
34	22	42	0 010 0010	''	''
35	23	43	1 010 0011	#	#
36	24	44	0 010 0100	$	$
37	25	45	1 010 0101	½	½
38	26	46	1 010 0110	&	&
39	27	47	0 010 0111	'	'
40	28	50	0 010 1000	(	(
41	29	51	1 010 1001	)	)
42	2A	52	1 010 1010	*	*
43	2B	53	0 010 1011	+	+
44	2C	54	1 010 1100	'	'
45	2D	55	0 010 1101	-	-
46	2E	56	0 010 1110	.	.
47	2F	57	1 010 1111	/	/
48	30	60	0 011 0000	0	0
49	31	61	1 011 0001	1	1
50	32	62	1 011 0010	2	2

DEX X_{10}	HEX X_{16}	OCT X_8	Binary P X_2	ASCII	Key
51	33	63	0 011 0011	3	3
52	34	64	1 011 0100	4	4
53	35	65	0 011 0101	5	5
54	36	66	0 011 0110	6	6
55	37	67	1 011 0111	7	7
56	38	70	1 011 1000	8	8
57	39	71	0 011 1001	9	9
58	3A	72	0 011 1010	:	:
59	3B	73	1 011 1011	;	;
60	3C	74	0 011 1100	<	<
61	3D	75	1 011 1101	=	=
62	3E	76	1 011 1110	>	>
63	3F	77	0 011 1111	?	?
64	40	100	1 100 0000	@	@
65	41	101	0 100 0001	A	A
66	42	102	0 100 0010	B	B
67	43	103	1 100 0011	C	C
68	44	104	0 100 0100	D	D
69	45	105	1 100 0101	E	E
70	46	106	1 100 0110	F	F
71	47	107	0 100 0111	G	G
72	48	110	0 100 1000	H	H
73	49	111	1 100 1001	I	I
74	4A	112	1 100 1010	J	J
75	4B	113	0 100 1011	K	K
76	4C	114	1 100 1100	L	L
77	4D	115	0 100 1101	M	M
78	4E	116	0 100 1110	N	N
79	4F	117	1 100 1111	O	O
80	50	120	0 101 0000	P	P
81	51	121	1 101 0001	Q	Q
82	52	122	1 101 0010	R	R
83	53	123	0 101 0011	S	S
84	54	124	1 101 0100	T	T
85	55	125	0 101 0101	U	U
86	56	126	0 101 0110	V	V

DEX X_{10}	HEX X_{16}	OCT X_8	Binary P X_2	ASCII	Key
87	57	127	1 101 0111	W	W
88	58	130	1 101 1000	X	X
89	59	131	0 101 1001	Y	Y
90	5A	132	0 101 1010	Z	Z
91	5B	133	1 101 1011	[	[
92	5C	134	0 101 1100	\	\
93	5D	135	1 101 1101	]	]
94	5E	136	1 101 1110	∧	∧
95	5F	137	0 101 1111	—	—
96	60	140	0 110 0000	'	'
97	61	141	1 110 0001	a	a
98	62	142	1 110 0010	b	b
99	63	143	0 110 0011	c	c
100	64	144	1 110 0100	d	d
101	65	145	0 110 0101	e	e
102	66	146	0 110 0110	f	f
103	67	147	1 110 0111	g	g
104	68	150	1 110 1000	h	h
105	69	151	0 110 1001	i	i
106	6A	152	0 110 1010	j	j
107	6B	153	1 110 1011	k	k
108	6C	154	0 110 1100	l	l
109	6D	155	1 110 1101	m	m
110	6E	156	1 110 1110	n	n
111	6F	157	0 110 1111	o	o
112	70	160	1 111 0000	p	p
113	71	161	0 111 0001	q	q
114	72	162	0 111 0010	r	r
115	73	163	1 111 0011	s	s
116	74	164	0 111 0100	t	t
117	75	165	1 111 0101	u	u
118	76	166	1 111 0110	v	v
119	77	167	0 111 0111	w	w
120	78	170	0 111 1000	x	x
121	79	171	1 111 1001	y	y
122	7A	172	1 111 1010	z	z

DEX X_{10}	HEX X_{16}	OCT X_8	Binary P X_2	ASCII	Key
123	7B	173	0 111 1011	R	R
124	7C	174	1 111 1100	¦	¦
125	7D	175	0 111 1101	T	T
126	7E	176	0 111 1110	~	~
127	7F	177	1 111 1111	DEL	DEL, RUBOUT

P=Parity bit; "1" for odd number of 1s, "0" for even number of 1s

C

Glossary

Appendix C

Glossary

argument—An item of information following a command. It may, for example, modify the command or identify a file to be affected.

assembly language—A mnemonic code representing the basic instructions understood by a particular computer.

background—Running the system so that the terminal is left free for other uses.

backup—A file copy set aside as insurance in case something happens to the original.

baud rate—The rate at which information is transmitted between devices, for example, between a terminal and the computer. One baud is one unit of information (a bit) per second. A hundred baud is about 9 characters a second, or 110 words a minute.

Berkeley Software Distribution—UNIX versions developed at the University of California, Berkeley. They bear names such as BSD 4.4.

bit—The smallest unit of information or memory for a computer. A bit can have the value 0 or the value 1, and it forms the basis of the binary coding used internally by computers.

block—A standard chunk of memory used as a unit by the computer; a block typically consists of 512 bytes.

Bourne shell—The UNIX shell used by the standard Bell Labs UNIX.

buffer—A temporary work area or storage area set up within the system memory. Buffers are often used by programs, such as editors, that access and alter text or data frequently.

bug—A design error in the hardware or software of a computer system.

byte—A unit of information or memory consisting of 8 bits. A byte of memory will hold 1 character.

C shell—The standard shell provided with Berkeley standard versions of UNIX.

call—To summon a program into action.

change mode—To alter a set of parameters that describes a file, telling who can use the file and how it can be used. The chmod command is used to do this.

character—A letter, numeral, punctuation mark, control character, blank, or other such symbol.

character string—A series of characters, for example, gofats and hot&#$&23.

chip—A small chunk of silicon bearing the equivalent of a large number of electrical components; an integrated circuit.

clobber—To wipe out a file.

command—An instruction to the computer. A command typically is a character string that is typed at a keyboard and is interpreted by the computer as a demand for a particular action.

command interpreter—A program that accepts commands from the keyboard and causes the commands to be executed. The shell is the UNIX command interpreter.

command line—A line consisting of one or more commands, each followed by its arguments, if any.

compiler—A master program that converts a high-level computer language (such as FORTRAN) into *machine language*.

concatenate—To string together two or more sequences, such as files, into one longer sequence. The cat command, for example, concatenates files.

control characters—Characters that are typed by pressing a key while the Ctrl key is depressed. For instance, a Ctrl-h is typed by pressing the *h* key while the Ctrl key is depressed.

CPU—Abbreviation for *central processing unit*. This is the part of the computer in which calculations and manipulations take place.

cursor—A marker on the screen, which is usually a rectangle of light or an underline mark.

directory—A file containing a list of associated files and subdirectories.

directory pathname—The complete name by which the directory is known. The pathname gives the sequence of directories by which the directory is linked to the root directory.

echo—To repeat a stream of characters. For example, the commands you type to the computer are echoed on the screen.

editor—A program to assist you in writing material to be stored in files. Editors allow you to modify existing files and create new ones.

EOF—Abbreviation for *end of file*. Files are terminated with a particular end-of-file character, usually a Ctrl-d, that tells the system it has reached the end of the file.

escape—To divest a special character of its special meaning by preceding it with a backslash character. For example, the UNIX *shell* interprets a ? to represent any single character, but a \? (an "escaped" question mark) is interpreted as just a question-mark character.

event—A previous line of input from the terminal, usually either a command line or an attempted command line. The *history* function maintains a numbered list of the last several events that you have entered.

event identifier—A shorthand code used by you to identify earlier events on the *history* list.

execute—To run a command or program. (Not to be confused with kill.)

field—A subsection of a line. Programs such as sort and awk can look at individual fields within a line.

field separator—The character used to separate one field from the next. A string of one or more spaces is the usual field separator.

file—A sequence of bytes constituting a unit of text, data, or a *program*. A file can be stored in the system memory or on an external medium such as tape or disk.

filename expansion—The process by which UNIX matches filenames with *metacharacters* to actual filenames; for example, matching ?oo? to foot and loop.

filling—Adjusting the line lengths in text so that all lines have about the same length.

flag—An argument to a command signifying a particular *option* or modification. UNIX flags usually are indicated by a leading hyphen.

foreground—Running under direct control of the terminal. The terminal cannot be used for anything else until a foreground job finishes or is halted.

formatting—Arranging text or data into a suitable visual form.

global—Having extended or general scope. For example, a global substitution of one word for another in a file affects all occurrences of the word.

hardware—The mechanical and electrical components of a computer system.

history—A UNIX facility that maintains a numbered list of previous commands and provides a shorthand notation letting you repeat or modify previous commands.

home directory—The directory assigned to you by the system manager, usually the same as your *login directory*. Additional directories that you create would stem from your home directory.

housekeeping—Keeping track of which files are where, of who is doing what, and the like.

input—Information fed to a command, a program, a terminal, a person, and so on.

interactive—Allowing the computer and the user to carry on a dialogue.

interpreter—A master program that translates a high-level computer language (such as BASIC) into *machine language*, a line at a time. Interactive languages use interpreters instead of *compilers*.

interrupt—To break off a command or other process and thus terminate it; also, a signal that accomplishes this.

job number—An identification number assigned to a job by the C shell. Unlike the *process ID*, this number is local to the terminal.

kill—To terminate a process before it reaches its natural conclusion.

learn—A computer-aided instruction program provided with UNIX.

line editor—An editor that works on a line as the basic unit. In general, the user identifies the line to be changed and then indicates the change desired.

link—An entry in a directory file that links a user-assigned name for a file to the systems identification number for that file; a name you give to a file.

loading—Putting the machine-language instructions of a program into memory.

local—Having limited scope; the opposite of global.

login—The process of gaining access to the computer system to begin a session.

login directory—The directory you are placed in when you log in, usually your *home directory*.

login name—The name by which the computer system knows you.

logout—The process of signing off the system.

machine-collating sequence—An extended alphabetical sequence that encompasses uppercase letters, lowercase letters, numerals, punctuation marks, and the various other characters recognized by the system.

machine language—The basic set of instructions understood by a given computer. These instructions are represented internally by means of a binary code.

macro—A compound instruction put together from simpler instructions.

mail—A computer system facility that allows the sending and holding of messages via the computer.

map—To assign a new interpretation to a terminal key. For example, in vi you can map, say, the key to represent the sequence [o] [Esc] [j].

metacharacter—A character having a special meaning to UNIX. For example, the UNIX shell interprets the ? character to stand for any single character.

microprocessor—The essential electronics of a computer miniaturized to a single chip.

modem—Short for *mo*dulator-*dem*odulator; a device for connecting a terminal or printer to a computer via a telephone line.

multitasking—Allowing more than one user to access the same program at the same time.

multiuser—Permitting more than one user to use the system at the same time.

network—The linking of several computers.

null character—An invisible character that has an internal code of 0 and that occupies no space if printed; not to be confused with a blank, which is invisible but occupies a space.

object file—A file containing machine-language code.

on-line—Connected to the system and in operation.

operating system—A master program that handles the varied tasks involved in running a computer system, including the user-computer interface.

option—A variation on, or modification to, a command, usually requested by use of a *flag*.

optional argument—An *argument* accepted but not required by a command.

output—Information produced by a command, program, and so on, and sent elsewhere, for example, to the terminal, to a file, or to a line printer.

overwrite—To write on an existing file, eliminating what previously was there.

owner—The person who created a file.

page—To advance text on the screen by one screen (or page) at a time.

password—A secret word, chosen by you, with which you reassure the computer system that you are who you claim to be.

pathname—A name for a file or directory specifying the location of the file or directory in the directory system.

peripheral input-output—Input and output devices attached to a computer, for example, terminals, printers, and tape drives.

permission—The yes-or-no specification of what can be done to a file. A file has read permission, write permission, and execute permission.

pipe—To make the output of one command or program into the input of another. Also, the UNIX operator (¦) that accomplishes this.

pipeline—The program linkage established by performing one or more pipes.

process—A particular computer activity or job.

process ID—A unique, system-wide identification number assigned to a process.

process status—The current state of the process: running, stopped, waiting, and so on.

program—A sequence of instructions telling a computer how to perform a task. A program can be in machine language, or it can be in a higher-lever language that is then translated into machine language.

prompt—A character or character string sent from a computer system to a terminal to indicate to the user that the system is ready to accept input. Typical prompts are % and $.

protection—Safeguarding a file from accidental erasure or from the unwanted inspection of others. Protection can be accomplished, for example, by using chmod to deny others the right to read a file.

recursive—In reference to a directory system, the application to a directory, to all its offshoots, to all their offshoots, etc. In reference to a computer program, the describing of a program that calls itself.

redirection—The channeling of output to a file or device instead of to the standard output. The channeling of input from a file or device instead of from the standard input.

regular expression—A pattern representing a class of character strings. The grep command, for example, recognizes the regular expression h.t to mean any three-character string beginning with h and ending with t.

root directory—The base directory from which all other directories stem, directly or indirectly.

scope—The range over which an action or definition applies.

scroll—To shift text up or down one or more lines on the screen.

search and replace—In editing, an operation that finds one or more occurrences of a word or pattern and replaces it with another.

shell—A UNIX program that handles the interaction between user and system.

shell script—A file containing a sequence of shell commands. It can be used as input to the shell or can be declared an executable file.

smart terminal—A terminal possessing some computing power of its own.

software—The programs used on a computing system.

special character—A character with special meaning beyond its literal one; a *metacharacter*.

standard input—Short for *standard input device*. The device from which a program or system normally takes its input, usually a terminal.

standard output—Short for *standard output device*. The device to which a program or system normally sends its output, usually a terminal.

stopped job—A job that has been halted temporarily by the user and that can be resumed at his command.

string—A sequence of characters.

subdirectory—A *directory* branching off from another directory.

time-sharing—The allocation of computer resources among several users.

tools—Compact, well-designed programs designed to do a specific task well. Several tools can be linked together to perform more complex tasks.

user—A person using the computer system.

visual editor—An *editor* that shows one screen of text at a time and allows the user to move a cursor to any part of the screen and effect changes there.

wild card—A *metacharacter* used to represent a range of ordinary characters. Examples include the shell's use of * and ?.

word processing—The use of editors and other computer programs to prepare, alter, check, and format text.

working directory—The *directory* in which your commands take place, given that no other directory is specified.

write—To place text in a file.

D

Summary of UNIX Abbreviations

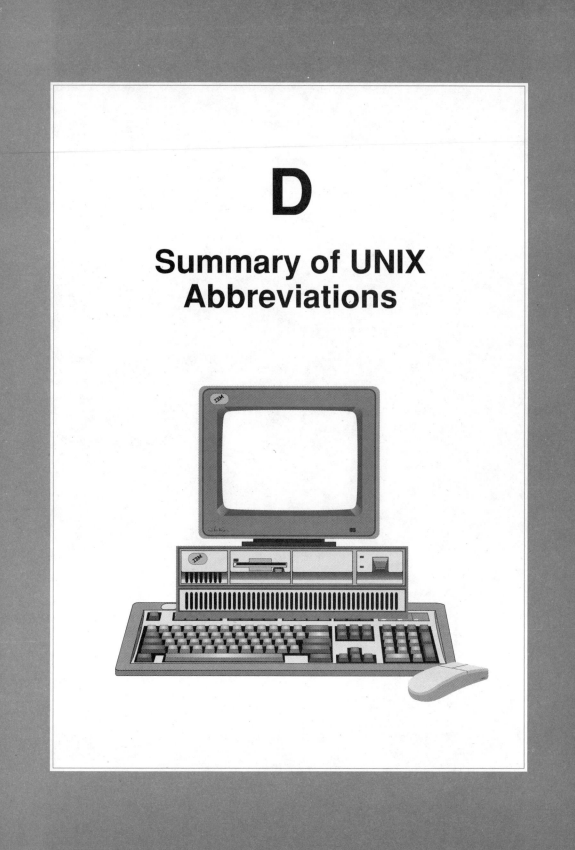

Appendix D

Summary of UNIX Abbreviations

Shell Abbreviations for Files and Directories

The following abbreviations can be used to represent the names of files and directories:

?   Represents (or *matches*) any single character.

*   Matches any number of characters (including none).

[ ]   Matches any *one* character from the list included between the brackets; a hyphen (-) can be used to indicate a range

Examples:

Abbreviation	Some Matches	No Match
l?t	lit lot lst	lt lout
l*t	lot lout latent lt	bots abbot
l[aou]t	lat lot	bout
l[3-6]	13 15	12 133
l[3-5][7-9]?	138q 1472	127n 138

The following can be used in identifying directories:

.   Your current working directory.

..   Parent directory to your current working directory.

Examples:

Abbreviation	Meaning
cp ../recipe .	Copy the file recipe from your parent directory into your current directory.
cd ..	Change directories to the parent directory of your current working directory.

Abbreviations Used by *grep*, *ed*, *edit*, and *ex*

The following abbreviations are used in search patterns:

.   Matches any single character (works the same as the shell abbreviation ?).

[]   Matches any *one* character found in the list between the brackets; a hyphen (-) can be used to indicate a range of characters.

^   Matches beginning of line, for example, the following pattern must begin the line.

$ Matches end of line, for example, the preceding pattern must end the line.

Examples:

Abbreviation	Matching Line	Nonmatching Line
car.o	a carton of milk	carts of fish eyes
car[gt]	a cargo of gold	a tub of carp
^car[gt]	cartoon of frog	a fine cartoon
car.o$	a fresh cargo	fresh cargos

Shell Script Abbreviations

`$0`	The name of the shell script
`$n`	The *n*th argument of the shell script
`$*`	The complete argument list of the shell script

Suppose the following command has been given, where `freem` is a shell script:

```
freem click clack clock
```

Then, within the script,

`$0`	represents `freem`
`$2`	represents `clack`
`$*`	represents `click clack clock`

awk Abbreviations

Here are some abbreviations used by the `awk` utility.

`$n`	The *n*th field of a record (by default, a record is a line).
`$0`	The entire record.
`NF`	The number of fields in the current record.
`NR`	The ordinal number of the current record.
`FILENAME`	The name of the current input file.

Examples:

`{print $3}`	Print the third field.
`{print $3/NR >> FILENAME`	Divide the contents of the third field by the current line number and write the result at the end of the current file.

E

UNIX Command Reference

Appendix E

UNIX Command Reference

How to Use This Reference

This reference is best used for commands with which you are already somewhat familiar. If you are using a command for the first time, read the discussion of the command in the text or refer to your on-line manual.

- Type the commands (shown in a computer typeface) exactly as you see them.

- When a word or letter is printed in the italic version of the computer typeface, you should substitute an actual value, filename, range of numbers, or other appropriate parameter for the italicized word.

- Substitute your filenames for *file*, *file1*, and so on.

- Repeatable arguments are followed by ellipses (...).

- Arguments in brackets [ ] are optional. Do not type the brackets.

- The number in parentheses ( ) following the entry refers to the page number in the text where this command is discussed.

Starting Up

login—sign on. (482)

passwd— change login password. (482)

Manipulating Files and Directories

cat—concatenates and prints. (71)

```
cat filename
```

Example:

```
cat file2 displays file2 on terminal.
```

---

cd—changes directory. (213)

```
cd
cd directoryname
```

Example:

cd /home/reggie/foods/carbo places you in the home/reggie/foods/
carbo directory.

---

chmod—change modes or permissions on files. (344)

```
chmod ugo, + -, rwx file... or directory...
```

Who:

u   Login owner (user).

g   Group.

o   Other users.

Op-codes:

+   Add permission.

-    Remove permission.

Permissions:

r   Read.

w   Write.

x   Execute.

Example:

> chmod o-rwx private removes read, write, and execute permissions for others from the file called private.

---

compress— compress file for storage (puts .Z after filename) (353)

compress *filename*

Example:

> compress flowers

---

cp—make copy of files. (218)

cp *file1 file2*
cp *file... directory*

Example:

> cp flim flam makes a copy of the file flim and calls it flam.

---

ln—make file links. (222)

ln *file... file...* or ln *file... directoryname*

Example:

> ln hist /usr/francie links the file hist to the /usr/francie directory.

---

lp, cancel, and **lpstat**—use the line printer. (482)

lp [-d] *file*
cancel *ID number*
lpstat [-p] *file ...*

Options:

-d   Selects printer.

-p   Reports printer status.

Example:

> lp some stuff sends the files some and stuff to the printer.

---

ls—list contents of directory. (71)

ls [-a, -c, -l, -m, -r, -s, + *others*] *directory...*

Options:

-a List all entries.

-c List by time of file creation.

-l List in long format.

-p Marks directories with a /.

-r Reverse the order of the listing.

-s Give the size in blocks.

Example:

ls -c will list contents of current directory in order of the time of creation.

---

mkdir—make a new directory. (213)

mkdir *directoryname*

Example:

mkdir Chapter4 creates a new subdirectory called Chapter4 in the present directory.

---

more—view long files one screenful at a time. (82)

more *file*...

Options:

See on-line manual for many options.

---

mv—move or rename files. (220)

mv *filename1 filename2* or *filename1 directoryname*

Example:

mv gappy happy changes the name of the file gappy to happy.

---

rm—remove files. (217)

rm [-i, -r] *file*...

Options:

-i Protect existing files.

-r Delete a directory and every file or directory in it. (Be careful!)

Example:

rm rodgers removes the file rodgers.

rmdir—remove directories. (216)

```
rmdir directory...
```

Example:

> rmdir budget65 removes directory budget65 if it does not contain any files.

Redirection Operators—<, >, >> (483)

Example:

> cat listA listB >> listC appends the files listA and listB to the file listC.

Pipes ¦ (483)

Example:

> cat listA listB ¦ lpr joins two files and *pipes* the result to the line printer.

---

uncompress—expand compressed file (354)

```
uncompress filename.Z
```

Example:

> uncompress flowers.Z

---

zcat—display compressed file in an uncompressed format (483)

```
zcat filename.Z
```

Example:

> zcat flowers.Z

Communication

cu—call another system (436)

```
cu [-s] telnumber
cu systemname
```

Option:

> -s   speed in baud

Example:

```
cu -s 2400 5551212
```

finger—provide information about users. (41)

```
finger [-m, -l, -s] name
```

Options:

-m	Search only login names.
-l	Display long form.
-s	Display short form.

Example:

`finger -s john` finds all users with login name of `john`.

mail—receives mail. (516)

`mail` or `mailx`

Commands:

`<Return>`	Read next message, exit `mail` after last message.
-	Go back to previous message.
p	Print the first message.
s `filename`	Append message to `filename` (default is `mbox`).
d	Delete message.
q	Quit mail.
*	Provide a summary of `mail` commands.
?	Provide a summary of `mailx` commands.
`<Ctrl-d>`	Same as q.

Plus other commands. Differences may exist from system to system.

mail—sends mail. (54)

`mail` *loginname(s)* or `mailx` *loginname(s)*

Example:

`mail dick bob` or `mailx dick bob`

(text of message here)

`<Ctrl-d>`

use ? to display a summary of `mailx` commands.

mesg—permit or deny message from talk. (347)

mesg [-y,-n]

Example:

mesg n prevents people from using write to interrupt you.

---

postnews—send messages to Netnews. (483)

postnews prompts you for the necessary information to send or post items on Netnews.

---

rcp—Remotely copy files between systems. (435)

rcp *filename1 filename2*

Example:

rcp charts bebop:/home/dizzie/newcharts

---

readnews—read the news from Netnews. (457)

See the summary in Chapter 15 or type h at any prompt inside rn or try man readnews for a list of readnews commands.

---

rlogin—remote login. (436)

rlogin *systemname*

Option:

-1   Login under a different user name

Example:

rlogin sparker

---

rn—read the news from Netnews. (462)

See the summary in Chapter 15 or try man rn for a list of readnews commands.

---

uucp—transfer files between systems. (443)

uucp [-m, -n] *sourcefile destination*

Options:

-m   Notify sender that file was delivered.

-n *username*   Notify username that a file was sent.

Example:

```
uucp newsong unicom!~/Banshee/
```

uupick—retrieve a file sent via uuto. (446)

```
uupick [-s]
```

Option:

-s *systemname*   Search for files from *systemname* only.

Example:

```
uupick
```

uuto—send a file to another system. (446)

```
uuto [-m] filename system!user
```

Option:

-m   Notify sender after delivery.

Example:

```
uuto bugs unicom!gecko
```

Housekeeping Utilities

cal—provide a calendar. (39)

```
cal [month] year
```

Example:

cal 05 1942 will provide the calendar for May 1942.

calendar—a reminder service. (351)

You create a file in your home directory called calendar. UNIX sends you reminders by mail.

Example:

Your calendar file might look like:

```
Buy goose March 19
call gus mar.20 at 3 pm
3/23 Report due
```

date—give date and time. (481)

pwd—print working directory. (216)

who—who is on the system. (40)
```
who [am i]
```
Example:
who tells who is on the system.

On-Line Help

help—ask for help. (63)

man—find manual information by keywords. (63)
```
man section
```
Example:
man cat displays the on-line manual explanation of cat.

Text Processing and Formatting

cut—cut out selected fields of a file. (362)
```
cut [-c, -d, -f] file ...
```
Options:

-c list	Pass on the columns in the list.
-f list	Pass on the fields in the list.
-dk	Change delimiter character to k.

Example:
cut -f3, 6 -d: address prints fields 3 and 6 of the file address. Fields are separated by a colon.

ex—line-oriented text editor. (482)

```
ex file
```

---

emacs— display editor. (482)

```
emacs file
```

---

join—join lines from two files. (366)

```
join file1 file2
```

Options:

-tc	Use character *c* as a separator.
-j*n m*	Use field *m* of file *n* as the join field.

Example:

> `join names addresses` joins lines common to both files. Note that files should be sorted first.

---

nroff—advanced typesetting. (381)
See Chapter 13 for details.

---

pr—print partially formatted file. (483)

```
pr [-d,-l,-p,-t,-w] file...
```

Options:

-d	Double-space lines.
-l*k*	Set page length to *k* lines.
-p	Pause until a Return.
-t	Suppresses heading on each page.
-w*k*	Set line width to *k* positions.

Example:

> `pr -pl20 myths` prints file `myths` on the terminal 20 lines at a time.

---

vi—the screen-oriented text editor. (483)

```
vi file
```

Information Handling

awk—pattern scanning and processing language. (417)
See Chapter 14 and the awk manual.

---

cmp—compares two files. (336)

cmp *filename1 filename2*

Example:

cmp Janice Susan finds and prints, by byte and line number, the first difference between the two files.

---

comm—finds lines common to two sorted files. (336)

comm [-1,-2,-3] *file1 file2*

Options:

-1 Do not print the first column.

-2 Do not print the second column.

-3 Do not print the third column.

Example:

comm listA listB prints three columns. First, lines only in listA, secondly, lines only in file listB, and thirdly, lines in both files.

---

diff—finds the difference between two files or directories. (336)

diff [-b, -e, -r] *file1 file2* or *directory1 directory2*

Options:

-b Ignores trailing blanks.

-e Output in the form of ed commands.

Example:

diff giftlist1 giftlist2 shows how to make giftlist1 like giftlist2.

---

echo—echoes argument. (306)

echo [*any string of characters*]

Example:

echo You have just won $1,000,000.!!

You have just won $1,000,000.!!

---

find—find designated files and act on them. (400)

    `find` *pathname searchcriteria action(s)*

Search Criteria:

`-name` *filename*	Files named *filename*.
`-size` *n*	Files of size *n* blocks.
`-links` *n*	Files with *n* links.
`-atime` *n*	Files accessed *n* days ago.
`-ntime` *n*	Files modified *n* days ago.
`-newer` *filename*	Files modified more recently than the file *filename*.

+ others

(Note: *n* without a sign means exactly *n*, +*n* means greater than *n*, -*n* means less than *n*.)

Actions:

`-print`	Print the pathname of the found files.
`-exe` *command* `\;`	Execute the given command upon finding a file; { } represents the found file.
`-ok` *command* `\;`	Same as `-exec`, except your approval is requested before each execution; reply with a y.

Example:

    `find /home/bob -ntime -10 -print` finds all files in `home/bob` directory that have been modified within 10 days and prints pathnames.

---

grep—search a file for a pattern. (228)

    `grep [-n, -c, -v]` *pattern file*...

Options:

`-n`	Precede each matching line with its line number.
`-c`	Print only a count of matching lines.
`-v`	Print all lines that do not match.

Example:

    `grep -iw hop bugs` searches the file `bugs` for the words hop, hop, "Hop," and so on.

---

head—look at the head of a file. (331)

    head [-n] *file*

Option:

-n	Print *n* lines.

Example:

> head -15 hunter **prints the first 15 lines of the file** hunter.

---

sort—sort and merge files. (275)

    sort [-b, -d, -f, -n, -o, -r] *file*...

Options:

-b	Ignore initial blanks.
-d	"Dictionary" order.
-f	Ignore upper- and lowercase letters.
-n	Sort numbers by value.
-o *filename*	Output to file called *filename*.
-r	Sort in reverse order.

Example:

> sort -fr -o sortbag grabbag **sorts the file** grabbag **in reverse order, ignoring upper- and lowercase letters. The results are stored in** sortbag.

---

spell—find spelling errors. (369)

    spell *file*...

---

tail—give the last part of a file. (331)

    tail [-*n*] *file*

Option:

-n	Start *n* lines from the end.

Example:

> tail -20 gate **prints the last 20 lines of the file** gate.

---

uniq—remove duplicated lines from file. (340)

```
uniq [-u, -d, -c] inputfile [outputfile]
```

Options:

-u	Print only lines with no duplicates.
-d	Print one copy of lines with duplicates.
-c	Print number of times the line is repeated.

Example:

uniq -d ioulist urgent scans the file ioulist for lines that appear more than once. One copy of each line is placed in the file urgent.

---

wc—word count. (329)

```
wc [-l, -w, -c, -p] file...
```

Options:

-l	Counts lines.
-w	Counts words.
-c	Counts characters.
-p	Counts pages (66 lines).

Example:

wc -w essay counts the number of words in file essay.

Running Jobs and Programs

at—schedules commands at a later time. (280)

```
at [-r, -l] time [day] job ...
```

Options:

-r job	Remove jobs previously scheduled.
-l [job]	List all jobs scheduled.

Example:

at 18 who > wholist runs the commands who > wholist at 18 hours (6:00 pm).

---

cc—compile C programs. (481)
```
cc [-c, -o] file...
```
Options:

    -c   Create object file that suppresses loading.

    -o *filename*   Use *filename* for file a.out.

Example:

    cc payroll.c compiles payroll.c file, with the executable program placed in a.out file.

---

csh—start up a C shell, end with Ctrl-d. (481)
The C shell creates a new environment with many commands.

---

f77—compile FORTRAN programs. (482)
```
f77 [-c, -o] file...
```
Options:

    -c   Create object code file that suppresses loading.

    -o *filename*   Use *filename* for a.out.

Example:

    f77 payroll.f compiles payroll.f file, with the executable code placed in a.out file.

---

kill—terminate jobs. (277)
```
kill [-9] job number or process ID
```
Option:

    -9   This is a sure kill.

---

ksh—start up a Korn shell, end with Ctrl-d. (482)
The Korn shell creates a new environment with many commands.

---

pc—compile Pascal programs. (482)
```
pc [-c, -o] file...
```
Options:

    -c   Create an object code file that suppresses loading.

    -o *filename*   Use *filename* for a.out.

Example:

    `pc payroll.p` compiles `payroll.p` file, with the executable code placed in `a.out` file.

---

ps—the Process Status Report. (278)

    `ps [-a]`

Option:

    `-a`   Displays `ps` information for all terminals.

---

shl—shell layer manager. Commands available include. (282)

    `create [name]`   Create a layer called name.

    `block name [name ...]`

    `delete name [name ...]`

    `help`

    `layers [-1] [name ...]`

    `resume [name ...]`

    `toggle`

    `unblock name [name ...]`

    `quit`

See Chapter 11 for more information.

---

tee—split output. (272)

    `tee [-i, -a] file`

Options:

    `-i`   Ignores interrupts.

    `-a`   Sends output to the end of named file.

Example:

    `ls -l /usr ¦ tee -a clutter` produces the long listing of the `/usr` directory on the terminal and also appends it to the end of the file `clutter`.

---

time—time a command. (351)
    time *commandname*

Example:

    time cc woo.c runs the command cc woo.c and prints the execution time when finished.

F

The *ex/vi* Command Reference

The *ex/vi* Command Reference

The *ex* Line Editor—a Quick Summary

The command for editing the file *filename* is

    ex *filename*

If no such file exists yet, it will be created when this command is given.

Modes

Command Mode: Lets you use any commands described below.

To enter: You are placed in the Command Mode when you invoke ex. To enter Command Mode from Text Mode, begin a new line with a period (.) and press the Return key. The Command Mode prompt is a colon (:).

Text Mode:	Lets you use the keyboard to enter text.
To enter:	Use an a, i, or c command.
Open/Visual Mode:	Starts up the vi editor.
To enter:	Type o or vi.
	To return to ex, type Q.

Commands

In general, commands consist of an address and an instruction. The address identifies the lines to be affected.

Addresses

n	The nth line.
n,k	Lines n through k.
.	The current line.
$	The last (final) line.
$+n$	n lines after the current line.
$-n$	n lines before the current line.
$-n,$	The last n +1 lines.
/pat	Search forward for the pattern pat.

Instructions

For clarity, we will include simple forms of addresses with the instructions. Instructions shown with an address range will also accept a single address. Instructions operate on the current line if no other address is given.

n,kp	Print lines n through k.
na	Append (text is added after line n).
ni	Insert (text is inserted before line n).
n,kd	Delete lines n through k.
n,kc	Change lines n through k to new text.

`n,kmj`	Move lines *n* through *k* to after line *j*.
`n,kcoj`	Place a copy of lines *n* through *k* after line *j*.
`s/pat1/pat2/`	Replace the first occurrence of *pat2* with *pat1* on the current line.
`nr filename`	Read and insert `filename` at line *n*.

Searches

`/pattern`	Causes ex to search for the next line containing a pattern.
	A search pattern can be used in place of an address in a command, for example:
`/slop/d`	Delete the next line that contains `slop`.
`/dog/s/dog/hog/`	Find the next line containing `dog` and replace the first occurrence of `dog` on that line with `hog`.
`/dog/s//hog/`	Short form of the preceding command.

The Global Parameter *g*

The g parameter, when following an s command, makes the substitution affect all occurrences of *pat1* in a line. When preceding an s command, it makes the command affect all lines. Both uses can be made in the same command:

`g/house/s//home/g`	Substitutes `home` for `house` everywhere in the file.

The Undo Command *u*

A friendly command that lets you undo the last change made to the buffer.

Saving Text and Quitting the Editor

Editing work is done in a temporary buffer and must be "written" into a file to save it.

`w`	Writes the current text into a permanent file.
`q`	Quits the editor if no changes since previous `w`.

wq	Write and quit.
q!	Emphatic form of quit. No changes recorded.
n,kw file2	Writes lines *n* through *k* into *file2*.
n,kw >>file3	Appends lines *n* through *k* to *file3*.

The *vi* Screen Editor—a Quick Summary

The command for editing the file *filename* is

    vi *filename*

If no such file exists yet, it will be created when this command is given.

Modes

<u>Command Mode:</u>	<u>Lets you use any commands described below.</u>
To enter:	You are placed in the Command Mode when you invoke vi. To enter Command Mode from Text Mode, press the Escape key.
<u>Text Mode:</u>	<u>Lets you use the keyboard to enter text.</u>
To enter:	Any of the following commands will put you in the Text Mode: a, i, o, O, R, and c.

Using *ex* Commands

While in Command Mode, type a colon and follow it with the desired ex command, for example:

    :g/dog/s//mango/g

or

    :14,42w newfile

End all ex commands with a Return. You are returned to the regular Command Mode of vi after the ex command is executed.

Cursor Movement Commands

The vi commands take place at the cursor location. These commands help you to place the cursor where you want it to be in the text. The cursor will not move beyond the bounds of the existing text.

j	Moves the cursor down one line.
k	Moves the cursor up one line.
h	Moves the cursor left one space.
l	Moves the cursor right one space.
Ctrl-d	Moves the screen down a half page.
Ctrl-u	Moves the screen up a half page.
Ctrl-w	Moves the screen up a full page.
Ctrl-f	Moves the screen forward a full page.
nG	Moves the cursor to the nth line of file.

Text Entering Commands

a	Appends text after cursor position.
i	Inserts text before cursor position.
o	Opens a new line below cursor position.
O	Opens a new line above cursor position.

Text Deletion Commands

x	Deletes character under cursor.
dw	Deletes from cursor to beginning of next word.
dd	Deletes line containing cursor.
d)	Deletes rest of sentence.
d}	Deletes rest of paragraph.

These commands can be preceded by an integer to indicate the number of characters, words, and so on, to be affected.

Text Alteration Commands

The R, cw, and c) commands need to be terminated with an Esc.

r	Replace character under cursor with next character typed.
R	Write over old text, beginning at cursor position.
cw	Change word (beginning at cursor) to new text.
c)	Change sentence (starting at cursor) to new text.
J	Join next line down to line with cursor.
u	Undo last command.
U	Undo all changes to line with cursor.

Search Commands

/pattern	Search for next occurrence of pattern.
?pattern	Search for preceding occurrence of pattern.
n	Repeat the last search command given.

The Last Command

u	Undo the last command.
.	Repeat the last command.
U	Undo all changes on the current line.

Text Moving Commands

yy	Yank a copy of a line; place it in a buffer.
p	Put after the cursor the last item yanked or deleted.
P	Put before the cursor the last item yanked or deleted.
"cY	Yank a copy of a line, place it in buffer c, where c is any letter from a to z.
"cP	Put after the cursor the contents of buffer c.

Note: Also see the text deletion commands.

Saving Text and Quitting the Editor

Editing work takes place in a temporary work area and must be saved by *writing* it into a permanent file.

Esc :w	Write the current text into the permanent file.
Esc :q	Quit if no changes since last w.
Esc :q!	Emphatic form of quit; no changes written.
Esc :wq	Write and quit.
Esc ZZ	Write and quit.
Esc :n,kw *file2*	Write lines *n* through *k* into another file.
Esc :n,kw >> *file2*	Append lines *n* through *k* to another file.

Note: All ex commands that start with a colon must end with a Return.

Screen Enhancement Options

Esc :set nu	Show line numbers.
Esc :set wm=*k*	Wrap margin at *k* characters from right.
Esc :set redraw	Keep screen display current.
Plus others	

G

Entering and Exiting the UNIX Shell

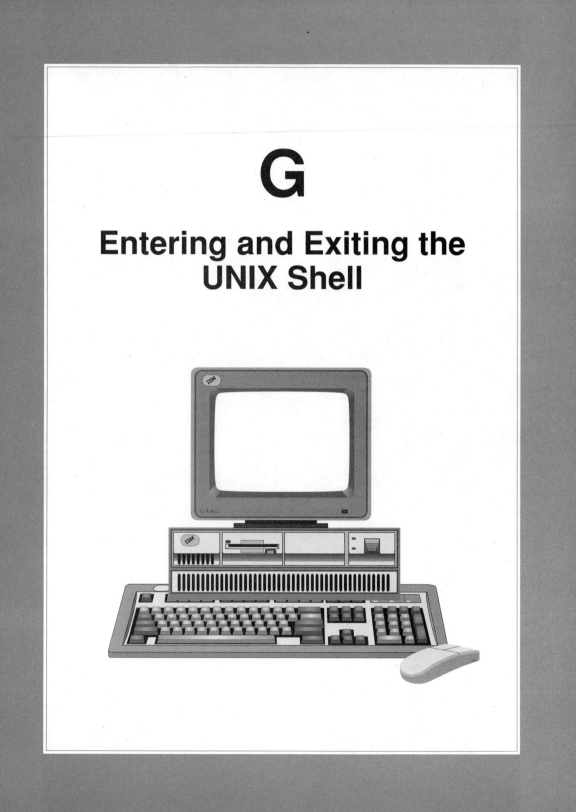

Entering and Exiting the UNIX Shell

One of the major problems facing beginning UNIX users is how to go from the shell to various utilities and then return to the shell. Here are some commonly used commands for going back and forth:

In	Utility	Out
ex *filename*	EX EDITOR	wq or q
mail	MAIL—RECEIVE	\<Return\>
mail *username*	MAIL—SEND	. (lone period)
man *command*	ON-LINE MANUAL	interrupt key
Ctrl-z	TO SUSPEND A JOB	fg
Ctrl-s	SCREEN OUTPUT	any key
login	UNIX SHELL	EOF
vi *filename*	VI EDITOR	\<Esc\>:wq or ZZ or :q!

The following keys send commands to UNIX:

Interrupt key   The *interrupt* signal stops most processes. On most systems, the signal is sent by typing Ctrl-c. Other common choices are the Del or Rub keys.

EOF   The *End-Of-File* character is usually transmitted by typing Ctrl-d.

To see which characters are used to control your terminal input and output, type the UNIX command:

```
stty
```

You should be given a list of characters currently used to

1. Erase character.

2. Erase line.

3. End of file.

4. Control terminal output.

5. Other things.

These control characters can be changed as described in Chapter 12.

INDEX

Symbols

! (exclamation point), 419
$ scope, 117
& symbol (running jobs in background), 275
(scope, 117
) scope, 117
%% percent signs, 188
' (single quotation mark), 403
-- hyphens, 188
(.) dot character, 138
: colon, 163
* wild card, 230-232
** asterisks, 188
. (period) directory abbreviation, 234
.. (two periods) directory abbreviation, 234
;; (semicolon, double), 426
< redirection operator, 270
= command, 465-466
> redirection operator, 86-89, 267-269
  in electronic mail, 89-90
> > redirection operator, 269
? question mark, 170, 230-231
@ symbol, 108
\\ (double backslash), 374
/ (search) operator, 164, 170
^ caret character, 294

` (backquotes), 428
{ scope, 117
¦ (pipeline) operator, 271-272
} scope, 117
~ (tilde) directory abbreviation, 234, 419
~% put command, 441
~? key combination, 54
0 scope, 117

A

a (append) ex editor command, 142-143
A Portable FORTRAN 77 Compiler, 252
a.out command, 481
abbreviations, 164-165
  directories, 234-235
actions, commands, 408
addresses, 136
  lines, 138-139
  specification, instructions, 372
advanced typesetting, 520
alias command, 58
aliases, 301
aligning fields, 367
American Standard Code for Information Interchange, *see* ASCII
apl interpreter command, 258
APL language, 258

N

O

X-Z

Dear Reader:

Thank you for considering the purchase of our book. Readers have come to know products from The Waite Group for the care and quality we put into them. Let me tell you a little about our group and how we make our books.

It started in 1976 when I could not find a computer book that really taught me anything. The books that were available talked down to people, lacked illustrations and examples, were poorly laid out, and were written as if you already understood all the terminology. So I set out to write a good book about microcomputers. This was to be a special book, very graphic, with a friendly and casual style, and filled with examples. The result was an instant best-seller. Today the Waite Group has over 70 computer books on the market, and many more are published each year. And no matter what your level of computer interest and expertise, we think The Waite Group has a title you'll like. Our books cover the DOS and Unix operating systems, as well and the C, C++, BASIC, and 80x86 assembler languages. Our titles cover the most popular compilers including those from Microsoft and Borland.

THE
WAITE
GROUP

We have honed the reader levels of our books into a number of best-selling approaches: our *Primer Plus*® and *Programming Primers* guide beginners from the introductory concepts through to a working knowledge of writing professional programs. Our *Bibles* have evolved into comprehensive reference books that appeal to intermediate and advanced programmers and power users. They include standard formats that make looking up any command or function quick and easy, provide clear examples, compatibility information, understandable syntax statements, jump tables and concise tutorials. Power users and programmers should check out our *Tricks of the Masters* books. These titles provide hints, tips, examples, and in-depth discussions that go far beyond the basic principles and facts found elsewhere. You'll discover obscure nuggets of information, work-arounds, and compelling discussions by experts that will hone your programming skills.

We're sure that you'll get to know the signature of "The Waite Group" on a book title as a stamp of a first quality book. A catalog of our titles can be obtained by filling out our reader response card, found in this book.

Thanks again for considering the purchase of this title. If you care to tell me anything you like (or don't like) about the book, please use our reader response card.

Sincerely,

Mitchell Waite
President

Primer Plus is a registered trademark of The Waite Group, Inc.

100 Shoreline Highway   Suite A-285   Mill Valley,   California   94941   415-331-0575   Fax 415-331-1075

Waite Group Reader Feedback Card
Help Us Make A Better Book

To better serve our readers, we would like your opinion on the contents and quality of this book. Please fill out this card and return it to *The Waite Group*, 100 Shoreline Hwy., Suite A-285, Mill Valley, CA, 94941 (415) 331-0575.

Name _____

Company _____

Address _____

City _____

State _____ ZIP _____ Phone _____

1. How would you rate the content of this book?

- ☐ Excellent
- ☐ Very Good
- ☐ Good
- ☐ Fair
- ☐ Below Average
- ☐ Poor

2. What were the things you liked *most* about this book?

- ☐ Pace
- ☐ Content
- ☐ Writing Style
- ☐ Accuracy
- ☐ Examples
- ☐ Listings
- ☐ Appendixes
- ☐ Design
- ☐ Cover
- ☐ Index
- ☐ Quizzes
- ☐ Size
- ☐ Price
- ☐ Illustrations
- ☐ Construction

3. Please explain the one thing you liked *most* about this book. _____

_____

_____

4. What were the things you liked *least* about this book?

- ☐ Pace
- ☐ Content
- ☐ Writing Style
- ☐ Accuracy
- ☐ Examples
- ☐ Listings
- ☐ Appendixes
- ☐ Design
- ☐ Cover
- ☐ Index
- ☐ Quizzes
- ☐ Size
- ☐ Price
- ☐ Illustrations
- ☐ Construction

5. Please explain the one thing you liked *least* about this book. _____

_____

_____

6. How do you use this book? For work, recreation, look-up, self-training, classroom, etc?

_____

_____

_____

_____

7. What would be a useful follow-up book to *C Programming Using Turbo C++* for you?

_____

_____

8. Where did you purchase this particular book?

- ☐ Book Chain
- ☐ Small Book Store
- ☐ Computer Store
- ☐ Other: _____
- ☐ Direct Mail
- ☐ Book Club
- ☐ School Book Store

_____

9. Can you name another similar book you like better than this one, or one that is as good, and tell us why?

_____

_____

10. How many Waite Group books do you own? _____

11. What are your favorite Waite Group books?

_____

12. What topics or specific titles would you like to see The Waite Group develop?

_____

_____

_____

_____

13. What programming languages do you know?

_____

14. Do you own an earlier edition of this book?

_____

15. Any other comments you have about this book or other Waite Group titles?

_____

_____

_____

_____

16. ☐ Check here to receive a free Waite Group catalog.

30194